The 2015 Solo and Small Firm Legal Technology Guide

CRITICAL DECISIONS MADE SIMPLE

Sharon D. Nelson, Esq., John W. Simek and Michael C. Maschke

INTRODUCTION BY JAMES A. CALLOWAY, ESQ.

Library of Congress Cataloging-in-Publication Data
The 2015 Solo and Small Firm Legal Technology Guide: Critical Decisions Made Simple. Sharon Nelson, John Simek, and Michael Maschke: Library of Congress Cataloging-in-Publication Data is on file.

ISBN: 978-1-63425-074-0

Dedication

SHARON NELSON AND John Simek dedicate this book to their children, Kelly, Sara, Kim, JJ, Jason, and Jamie, and to their grandchildren, Samantha, Lilly, Tyler, Evan, Jordan, Cash, and Parker—here's to many more vacations together on the Outer Banks!

Michael Maschke dedicates this book to his beautiful wife, Summer, and their expanding family, especially to Lily and baby Sutton! I couldn't be more blessed than with you three in my life.

Contents at a Glance

About the Authors   xvii
Acknowledgments   xxi
Preface to the Eighth Edition   xxiii
Introduction   xxvii

Chapter 1: Computers   1
Chapter 2: Computer Operating Systems   15
Chapter 3: Monitors   21
Chapter 4: Computer Peripherals   23
Chapter 5: Printers   33
Chapter 6: Scanners   41
Chapter 7: Servers   45
Chapter 8: Server Operating Systems   57
Chapter 9: Networking Hardware   67
Chapter 10: Miscellaneous Hardware   79
Chapter 11: Smartphones   85
Chapter 12: Productivity Software   93
Chapter 13: Security Software   105
Chapter 14: Case Management   111
Chapter 15: Time and Billing Software   125
Chapter 16: Litigation Programs   139
Chapter 17: Document Management   141
Chapter 18: Document Assembly   149
Chapter 19: Cloud Computing   153
Chapter 20: Collaboration   161
Chapter 21: Remote Access   171
Chapter 22: Mobile Security   179
Chapter 23: More from Apple   187
Chapter 24: iWin: iPad for Litigators   201

Chapter 25: Unified Messaging and Telecommunications   243
Chapter 26: Utilities   251
Chapter 27: Social Media for Law Firms—An Overview   275
Chapter 28: Taking Your Firm Paperless   301
Chapter 29: Tomorrow in Legal Tech   325

Glossary   339
Index   357

Contents

About the Authors   xvii
Acknowledgments   xxi
Preface to the Eighth Edition   xxiii
Introduction   xxvii

Chapter 1: Computers   1

Desktop Computers   1
  Personal Computers (PCs)   1
  Apple Computers (Macs)   5
Laptops   8
  Personal Computers (PCs)   8
  Apple Computers (Macs)   11
Netbooks/Ultrabooks   12
Tablets   13

Chapter 2: Computer Operating Systems   15

Microsoft Windows XP Operating System   15
Microsoft Windows Vista Operating System   15
Microsoft Windows 7   16
Microsoft Windows 8   18
Mac OS X Version 10.7 (Lion) Operating System   18
Mac OS X Version 10.8 (Mountain Lion) Operating System   19
Mac OS X Version 10.9 (Mavericks) Operating System   19
Mac OS X Version 10.10 (Yosement) Operating System   20

Chapter 3: Monitors   21

Chapter 4: Computer Peripherals   **23**

Mouse   23
Keyboards   25
Wireless Keyboard Desktops   25
External Storage Devices   26
    External Hard Drives   27
    Flash Drives   28
Speakers and Headphones   30

Chapter 5: Printers   **33**

Stand-Alone Printers   33
Networked Printers   35
    Low-Volume Network Printers   35
    High-Volume Network Printers   36
    Color Network Printers   37
Multifunctional Printers/Copiers   38

Chapter 6: Scanners   **41**

    Low-Volume Scanner   42
    High-Volume Scanner   43

Chapter 7: Servers   **45**

    Solo—File and Printer Sharing   45
    Small Firm—File and Printer Sharing/Hosting Services   47
    Small Firm—Database/Applications Server   49
    Virtual Servers   50
    Peer-to-Peer   54

Chapter 8: Server Operating Systems   **57**

    Microsoft Windows Server 2003—Any Edition   57
    Microsoft Windows Server 2008 R2   57
    Microsoft Windows Small Business Server 2008 Standard and
        Premium Editions   59
    Windows Server 2008 Standard Edition   60
    Windows Server 2008 Enterprise Edition   60
    Microsoft Small Business Server 2011 Standard and Essentials   60
    Microsoft Windows Server 2012   61
    Microsoft Server 2012 R2   62
    X64 Operating Systems   62
    Mac OS X Server 10.7 (Lion)   63

Mac OS X Server 10.8 (Mountain Lion)   63
Mac OS X Server 10.9 (Mavericks)   64
Mac OS X Server 10.10 (Yosemite)   64
Linux-Based Operating Systems   65

Chapter 9: Networking Hardware   **67**

Switches   67
Entry-Level and Intermediate-Level Routers   69
Firewalls/IDS/IPS Devices   71
Racks   73
Cabling   74
Wireless Networking Devices   75

Chapter 10: Miscellaneous Hardware   **79**

Fire Safe   79
Battery Backup Devices   80
Fax Machines   82
Backup Solutions   83

Chapter 11: Smartphones   **85**

Chapter 12: Productivity Software   **93**

Microsoft Office   93
Corel Suite   95
OpenOffice.org   97
Adobe Acrobat   98
Power PDF   100
OCR Software   101
Voice Recognition Software   102

Chapter 13: Security Software   **105**

Stand-Alone   105
Enterprise Versions   106
    Integrated Security Solutions   107
    Antispam Protection   109

Chapter 14: Case Management   **111**

Amicus Attorney   113
Time Matters   114
PracticeMaster   116

Clio   118
Rocket Matter   119
Firm Manager   121
MyCase   121
HoudiniEsq   122
Others   123

Chapter 15: Time and Billing Software   **125**

Manual Generation   126
Accounting Software—QuickBooks   126
Billing Specific—Timeslips   129
Billing for a Mac   131
  Bill4Time   131
  EasyTime   132
Billings Pro   132
Integrated Packages   133
PCLaw   133
Tabs3   134
Amicus Premium Billing   135
Final Thoughts   136

Chapter 16: Litigation Programs   **139**

Chapter 17: Document Management   **141**

DocuShare   142
WorkSite   142
Worldox   142
Matter Center   144
Acrobat   146
Web-Based   146
NetDocuments   146
Plain Folders   147
Searching   147

Chapter 18: Document Assembly   **149**

HotDocs   149
ProDoc   151
ProLaw   151
Final Words   152

Chapter 19: Cloud Computing   **153**

Contract Considerations   157
Hybrid Solution   158

Chapter 20: Collaboration   **161**

Google Drive   162
Acrobat   165
Microsoft Word   166
SharePoint   166
Office 365   167
Skype   168
Dropbox   169
Desktop Sharing   169

Chapter 21: Remote Access   **171**

Virtual Private Networking   171
GoToMyPC   172
LogMeIn   173
TeamViewer   174
Mobility Tips   174

Chapter 22: Mobile Security   **179**

Software   179
Encryption   180
Wireless   181
AirCard   182
Public Computer Usage   183
Smartphones   184
Final Words   186

Chapter 23: More from Apple   **187**

Hardware   188
    Apple iPad   188
    Apple Watch   191
    Touchfire Keyboard   192
    AirPort Extreme   192
    AirPort Express   193
    AirPort Time Capsule   193
    Apple Thunderbolt Display   194

Apple Wireless Keyboard 194
Apple Magic Mouse 194
Apple iPod 195
Software 196
Microsoft Office 2011 for Mac Home & Business 196
Toast 12 Titanium by Roxio 196
Norton Internet Security for Mac 197
Kaspersky Internet Security for Mac 197
Intuit Quicken 2015 for Mac 198
QuickBooks 2014 for Macs 198
Symantec Drive Encryption for Mac OS X 199
Apple iTunes 199

**Chapter 24: iWin: iPad for Litigators
by Tom Mighell, Esq., and Paul Unger, Esq. 201**

Introduction and Tour of iPad 201
Why Use an iPad in Your Practice? 202
Overview 203
Why Use an iPad in the Courtroom? 204
iPad Apps for Lawyers 205
Deadline Calculators 205
Lawyer's Professional Assistant 206
Depositions 208
The Deponent 208
TranscriptPad 208
Jury Selection/Tracking 210
iJuror 210
Honorable Mentions 211
Evidence Presentation 212
TrialPad 212
Honorable Mentions 214
Legal Research 215
Courtroom Chatting 216
BT Chat HD 216
Other Must-Have iPad Apps 216
1. Dropbox 217
2. Dictate + Connect 219
3. GoodReader 220
4. Microsoft Office for iPad 221
Honorable Mention: Documents To Go Premium 223

    5. Notability   223
    6. Noteshelf   224
    7. Keynote for iOS   225
    8. Scanning Apps   226
    9. PDF Expert   227
   10. LogMeIn/LogMeIn   229
   11. Find My iPhone (for the iPad)   230
Library of Other Favorite Apps   231
  Browsers—Alternatives to the iPad's Safari Browser   231
  Entertainment   231
  File Management   231
  Finance   231
  Food   231
  Games   232
  Legal-Specific   232
  Meetings and Calendars   232
  News   232
  Photos   233
  Productivity   233
  Reading   234
  Social Networking and Communications   234
  Travel   235
  Utilities   235
Navigation Tips & Settings   235
Passcode Lock   239
Resources   240
About the Authors   241

Chapter 25: Unified Messaging and Telecommunications   **243**
Unified Messaging   243
Google Voice   246
Voice over Internet Protocol (VoIP)   247
High-Speed Internet   249

Chapter 26: Utilities   **251**
X1   251
dtSearch   252
Credenza   254
Outlook Send Assistant   255
GreenPrint   255

Winscribe for the Legal Profession   256
Eyejot   257
Hightail (formerly YouSendIt)   257
Copy2Contact   258
TwInbox   259
TweetDeck   259
TinyURL   260
IrfanView   260
DBAN   261
SimplyFile   262
Shred 2   262
File Shredder   263
SnagIt   263
FavBackup 2.1.3   264
QuickView Plus   264
Sam Spade   265
Metadata Assistant   265
Litera Metadact and Metadact-e   266
Livescribe Echo Smartpen   268
YouMail   268
SmartDraw Business   269
CaseSoft TimeMap 5   269
Evernote   270
WinRAR/7-ZIP   271
Chrometa   271
eWallet   272
LastPass   272
WordRake for Microsoft Word   271

**Chapter 27: Social Media for Law Firms—An Overview
            by Jennifer Ellis   275**

Specific Sites and Applications   276
Marketing and Networking   277
    Advertising   277
    Networking   277
    Content   277
    Specific Sites   278
    Content of Posts   278
    Additional Ethical Issues   284
Discovery of Social Media   286
    Privacy Settings Are Important   286
    The Client's Social Media   287

Opposing Party and Witnesses   288
Trouble for Failure to Preserve   289
Ethical Pitfalls in Research, Discovery, and Communications   289
How to Obtain Access   292
Other Issues: Judges and Juries   297
Judges   297
Jurors   299
Conclusion   300

Chapter 28: Taking Your Firm Paperless
            by David J. Bilinsky, BSc, LLB, MBA   **301**

Introduction   301
Transitioning to Paperless:
  It Isn't (All) about the Technology (Really!)   302
Assessing Your Office Procedures and People:
  How Suited Are They to Going Paperless?   305
  Document Naming and Filing   305
  Converting Paper Documents to PDF   306
  Document Retention   306
  Backups and Archives   307
  File Retention and Destruction   307
  Knowledge Management   308
Begin with the End in Mind: Defining the Goals   308
A Bit about the Hardware That You Will Need   310
  Hardware   310
  Servers   311
  Hard Drive Storage   313
  Scanners   313
  Backup Systems   314
  Monitors   315
A Bit about the Software That You Will Need   316
  Document Management Considerations   316
  Think about the Role of Cloud-Based Services   319
  Think about Mobile Computing, Remote Access, and Apps   319
Setting New Business Processes to Align with Your Goals   320
How Will You Transition to Paperless?   320
Getting Buy-In from Your Team Members: Leading the Change   321
  Awareness about the Nature of Change   321
  The Three Levels of Change   321
  Management of Change   322
  Focus on Who Matters Most   322
  Celebrate the Successes   322

Learning from Your Experience and Continuing to
  Improve Your Systems   322
Conclusion   323

Chapter 29: Tomorrow in Legal Tech   **325**

Introduction   325
Legal Technology Audits (LTAs)   326
Giving CLE Credit to Law Practice Topics   327
Disruptive Innovation   328
Passwords—Not Dead Yet   330
Wearable Tech   331
Cybersecurity   332
Information Governance   333
Tablets Becoming True Laptop Replacements   334
Office 365   334
Stats Tell Us Where Legal Tech is Heading   335
Cloud Computing: Lawyers are Still Resistant   337
Windows 8 and 9   337
Final thoughts   338

Glossary   **339**
Index   **357**

About the Authors

Sharon D. Nelson, Esq.

 Sharon D. Nelson is the president of Sensei Enterprises, Inc. Ms. Nelson graduated from Georgetown University Law Center in 1978 and has been in private practice ever since. She now focuses exclusively on electronic evidence law.

Ms. Nelson, Mr. Simek, and Mr. Maschke are the co-authors of the eight most recent editions of this book (2008–2015). Ms. Nelson and Mr. Simek are also co-authors of *Locked Down: Information Security for Lawyers* (American Bar Association, 2012). Additionally, Ms. Nelson and Mr. Simek are co-authors of *The Electronic Evidence and Discovery Handbook: Forms, Checklists, and Guidelines* (ABA, 2006). Ms. Nelson is a co-author of *How Good Lawyers Survive Bad Times* (ABA, 2009). Ms. Nelson and Mr. Simek's articles have appeared in numerous national publications, and they frequently lecture throughout the country on digital forensics and legal technology subjects.

Ms. Nelson is a co-host of Legal Talk Network's *The Digital Edge: Lawyers and Technology* and *Digital Detectives* podcasts. Ms. Nelson and Mr. Simek have a regular legal tech column called "Hot Buttons" in the ABA Law Practice Division magazine *Law Practice*. Ms. Nelson is a member of the American Bar Association's Cybersecurity Task Force, its Standing Committee on Technology and Information Systems, and a member of the Editorial Board of *Law Technology News*.

Ms. Nelson is currently the Immediate Past President of the Virginia State Bar. She is past president of the Fairfax Bar Association, the current President of the Fairfax Law Foundation, past chair of the ABA's TECHSHOW Board, and past chair of the ABA's Law Practice Management Publishing Board. She currently serves as the Vice Chair of its Education Board. She is a member of the Sedona Conference. She is a graduate of Leadership Fairfax and serves on the Governing Council of the Virginia State Bar as well as on its Executive Committee. She is the former chair of the Virginia State Bar's Unauthorized Practice of Law Committee and serves on both its Technology Committee and its Standing Committee on Finance. She also serves on the Virginia Supreme Court's Advisory Committee on Statewide E-filing. She is a member of the ABA, the Virginia Bar, the Virginia Bar Association, the Virginia Trial Lawyers Association, the Virginia Women Lawyers Association, and the Fairfax Bar Association.

Ms. Nelson has served as a Court Appointed Special Advocate (CASA) for Abused and Neglected Children for the past four years.

John W. Simek

John W. Simek is the vice president of Sensei Enterprises, Inc. He is a Certified Information Systems Security Professional (CISSP) and a nationally known testifying expert in the area of digital forensics.

Mr. Simek holds a degree in engineering from the United States Merchant Marine Academy and an MBA in finance from Saint Joseph's University. After forming Sensei, he ended his more than twenty-year affiliation with Mobil Oil Corporation, where he served as a senior technologist, troubleshooting and designing Mobil's networks throughout the Western Hemisphere.

In addition to his CISSP designation, Mr. Simek is an EnCase Certified Examiner (EnCE), Certified Handheld Examiner, a Certified Novell Engineer, Microsoft Certified Professional + Internet, Microsoft Certified Systems Engineer, NT Certified Independent Professional, and a Certified Internetwork Professional. He is also a member of the High Tech Crime Network, the Fairfax Bar Association and the American Bar Association. In addition to co-authoring the books cited in Ms. Nelson's biography, he also serves on the Education and Publishing Boards of the ABA's Law Practice Division and on its governing Council. He currently provides information technology support to more than 250 area law firms, legal entities, and corporations. He lectures on legal technology and digital forensics subjects throughout the world.

He is a co-host of Legal Talk Network's *Digital Detectives* podcast.

Mr. Simek also serves as a Court Appointed Special Advocate (CASA) for Abused and Neglected Children.

Michael C. Maschke

 Michael Maschke is the Chief Executive Officer and a digital forensics examiner at Sensei Enterprises, Inc. He is a Certified Computer Examiner (CCE), an EnCase Certified forensic technologist (EnCE), and a Certified Information Systems Security Professional (CISSP).

Mr. Maschke holds a degree in telecommunications from James Madison University. He has significant experience with network troubleshooting, design and implementation, systems integration, and computer engineering. Prior to becoming the Chief Information Officer, Mr. Maschke oversaw Sensei's information technology department, which provided support to hundreds of area law firms and corporations.

He has spoken at the American Bar Association's TECHSHOW conference on information security and is a co-author of *Information Security for Lawyers and Law Firms* as well as the last seven editions of this book, all published by the American Bar Association.

Acknowledgments

ONCE AGAIN, WE WELCOME our good friend Jim Calloway as the author of the introduction to this book. Jim is the director of the Oklahoma Bar Association's Management Assistance Program. He frequently writes and speaks on legal technology issues, Internet research, law office management and organization, and legal ethics. He is often on the faculty with us at ABA TECHSHOW and is Sharon's co-host on the Legal Talk Network's *Digital Edge: Lawyers and Technology* podcast.

We are very happy that our friend and colleague Jennifer Ellis is a contributing author once again. She has updated her marvelous Social Media chapter for this edition of our book. Jennifer is a social media maven par excellence. You couldn't possibly get better advice.

Thanks go to good friends Tom Mighell and Paul Unger, who generously updated their excellent "iWin: iPad for Litigators" materials, this year as a chapter in the book—iPad aficionados will find a wealth of information in that chapter.

A brand new contributor this year is our long-time friend Dave Bilinsky. Dave is a Practice Management Consultant and lawyer for the Law Society of British Columbia. For several years, we had the honor of having Ross Kodner write an annual chapter on taking your firm paperless. With his untimely death (we miss you Ross!), Dave has gallantly stepped forward to author a new and wonderful version of this chapter, and we are deeply grateful.

We are thrilled to have Denise Constantine as our Manager of Book Publishing at the Law Practice Division. She has been a model of efficiency and is no doubt amazed (again) that we pretty much always finish our manuscript on schedule.

The entire publishing staff has been amazing to work with—it is always a pleasure. And we know a lot of authors who can't say that about their publishers!

We are very grateful to our good friend Dave Ries, an extraordinary litigator in Pittsburgh and a terrific self-taught technologist, who served as project manager for this book. His suggestions and thoughts enriched the final product immeasurably.

Finally, we again thank our colleagues here at Sensei, who carried the load while we were writing and were never too busy to deliberate over recommendations and to offer insightful comments. We don't come to work every day; we come to play, and we really like the folks we play with. Thanks, one and all!

Mike Maschke, Sharon Nelson, John Simek

Preface to the Eighth Edition

WHAT WE HOPE TO do with this book is simple: We want to help solo and small firm lawyers find the "sweet spot" of legal technology—the best value for the dollars. You don't need a yacht, and you won't be well-served by a rowboat. But there is a happy medium—professional-grade hardware and software that doesn't cost an arm and a leg.

This guide is an annual one, so you can't go too far wrong with our advice. Some chapters will remain almost absolutely current. At worst, we'll only be several months behind the curve. Still, if you can't afford your own legal technology consultant and you are concerned about those who are selling snake oil, at least this book should provide you with a neutral view of legal technology products.

As always, the parts of this book that age quickly are the hardware specifications. We are happy to give you our latest specs—just drop us a quick line at **sensei@senseient.com**. We've given out hundreds of updated specs over the years, so don't hesitate to write!

We do our absolute best to be vendor-neutral. Readers of previous editions will be keenly aware that our advice has changed from year to year as some products excel and others . . . well . . . decline—and sometimes precipitously. We have some exciting new products to talk about this year—nothing moves as fast as technology!

This is the only book we're aware of that deals with legal technology on a collective, annual basis. We are now in our eighth edition, so we must be doing something right. We seem to have a growing, loyal readership looking for independent advice on legal technology and finding a yearly dose of that advice compelling. In this book, we provide information on and recommendations for computers, servers, networking equipment, legal software, utilities, cool gadgets for lawyers, and more. We take an in-depth look at the technologies that will be around in 2015 and provide information on how these technologies will shape the way solo and small firm decision makers think about their technology decisions.

Our recommendations are what we would do in a solo or small practice ourselves: Invest in quality technology that will have a good shelf life and serve you well—that means buying business-grade (not consumer-grade) technology. And don't expect more than the machines can give. A server can be expected to last four to five years; a workstation or laptop, three to four. That's it folks. As the software also evolves, it demands ever more resources, and the hardware ages both physically and in its ability to handle the new software. Remember the Rule of Three in upgrading: You should be upgrading one-third of your technology each year. Sometimes you can stretch it to four, but if you try to limp along patching things with spit and promises, you are likely going to be in for a "big bang" upgrade, which is acutely painful to the average solo or small law firm. Leasing may help lessen this financial burden (at least on an annual basis), but you lose the option to change course quickly without paying penalty fees.

Be mindful of the fact that this book is written exclusively for solos and small law firms. There is no attempt to include big-firm products or solutions, though many big firm lawyers have enjoyed portions of this book. In addition, we want to stress that we have included our recommendations only, not all available products. If you don't see a product here, it is because that product is not among our usual recommendations. This is a best-of-breed selection to keep you from being confused by the veritable cornucopia of choices that exist. No one has time to wade through all the choices, so we've tried to give you limited, but tested, options that work.

We used to say that generally we couldn't serve as your legal technology consultant unless you were in the D.C. area, but we are now providing remote backup and disaster recovery service to law firms anywhere in the country. Today, we are moving folks to the cloud, using a data center in northern Virginia. This means we can now provide IT (information technology) support nationwide and use remote access to connect to any part of your network that is not housed in the data center. Call us if this is an option you want to explore. With all the law firm data breaches that have been reported in the last several years, our Information Security Department has been hopping, investigating data breaches and assessing and securing law firm networks. More information about our services may be found on our website, **www.senseient.com**, or you can call us at 703-359-0700 for further information. Security assessments should be an annual (at least) exercise for all law firms—and they cost less than you might think.

We are serious about our commitment to the legal profession and proud of our professional giveback through the ABA. If you have a question, we'll do our best to help. Just e-mail us at **sensei@senseient.com**. We appreciate all your comments and suggestions, as they help make each subsequent edition of this book better than the one before. Thanks, in advance, for your continuing help!

Introduction

by James A. Calloway, Esq.

"Any sufficiently advanced technology is indistinguishable from magic."
—Arthur C. Clarke, science fiction author

"One man's magic is another man's engineering."
—Arthur Robert A. Heinlein, science fiction author

"Modern cell phones are not just another technological convenience. With all they contain and all they may reveal, they hold for many Americans 'the privacies of life,'"

—Supreme Court Chief Justice John G. Roberts, Jr.,
writing for the majority in *Riley v California*, 573 U.S. ___ (2014)

Technology is increasingly intertwined with virtually all of our professional and personal lives. In *Riley v California*, the United States Supreme Court issued a landmark opinion holding that police officers must obtain a warrant before searching an individual's mobile phone. A generation or two ago, mobile phones did not exist, and, for most Americans, the idea of the privacy of personal data stored on a telephone would have been difficult to appreciate and comprehend.

Today's lawyers could not practice effectively without the use of computers, legal specific software and access to the Internet. The tools of law practice have evolved from books on shelves, 3" × 5" note cards, and file cabinets stuffed full of folders and paper, to computers, tablets, smartphones, and online searchable databases of legal information.

But the legal profession today finds itself in a paradox.

Legal work is about the management, analysis, and processing of information. Lawyers read and write. They prepare many documents. They research, often being forced to delve into difficult and challenging matters. Lawyers save and manage large amounts of data, even if most of them are not used to referring to their client files and other information by that label. It is simply inconceivable that worldwide changes in information technology and information management will not impact the legal profession. We experience the changes every day. There can be no doubt that law firms will continue to experience changes in the way they handle information and in the evolution of information technology tools.

But lawyers are also focused on the importance of precedent. There is safety in following established paths, and there are risks inherent in trying something new and untested. Lawyers are trained to be cautious and risk averse when they operate on behalf of their clients. The refrain "We have always done it this way and there have been no problems" resonates strongly with lawyers. This is compounded by lawyers' perception that they are too busy to learn something new.

So many in the legal profession find themselves caught between the rapidly evolving changes of today's technology tools and the professional resistance to experimentation and unnecessary risk-taking. They also find themselves without proper time to investigate or train on emerging technology tools. Precedent is of little value when innovations like the Internet, online social media, mobile technology and big data are unprecedented.

Small firm lawyers generally have more administrative responsibilities than their counterparts in larger law firms. In many situations, a small law firm will not have the budget for a full-time IT director and these duties will be split between an outside consultant and a lawyer or staff person with the aptitude or interest in law office technology.

The 2015 Solo and Small Firm Legal Technology Guide will not replace a law firm having a full-time IT director, but annually it provides the bedrock information for a small firm lawyer who is the firm IT director, like it or not. It also serves as an indispensable guide for a local consultant who has the ability to manage a law firm's technology infrastructure, but is not aware of all of the legal-specific technology products that are available today. Some of this book will be read and reread, while other portions will be skimmed or skipped depending on the immediate technology needs of the firm. But a law firm of any size cannot avoid dealing with technology issues today. Many lawyers who do not consider their law firms to be small will still greatly benefit from this guide. Many predict there will be many more individual practitioners, virtual practice groups, and virtual law firms in the future. The demarcation between large law firm technology and technology for small law firms may become increasingly irrelevant.

This is the third edition of the *Guide* released since the ABA has revised its Model Rules of Professional Conduct to reference the need for a lawyer to be competent with the technology tools the lawyer uses and have an awareness of cybersecurity and data protection issues.

The official comment to Rule 1.1 on Competence was amended to add the italicized language below:

> "To maintain the requisite knowledge and skill, a lawyer should keep abreast of changes in the law and its practice, *including the benefits and risks associated with relevant technology*, engage in continuing study and education and comply with all continuing legal education requirements to which the lawyer is subject."

No doubt this is threatening to some of our fellow lawyers. Some jurisdictions may not include this provision in their version of the Rules of Professional Conduct. But interaction with technology is unavoidable for today's lawyers. The lawyers need not be experts in all aspects of information technology. But some appreciation of a law office's technology infrastructure and reasonable skill in using the day-to-day technology tools is clearly important for good professional business operations.

The Internet abounds with information. But too often, Internet searches lead to biased information or promotional information placed online on behalf of a particular vendor or product. This guidebook can serve as a law firm's trusted source of basic information as well as in-depth information. It is a quick reference guide to understanding where a new product or software release fits into a law firm's overall strategy. There is a myriad of technology tools available today. A trusted consultant is of great value to modern law firms as he or she deals with a law office's technology. The authors of this guide bring their long experience working with the legal profession to the pages of this volume. It is certainly the most cost-effective technology review that any budget-conscious law firm could hope to obtain.

The legal profession is experiencing significant changes and it appears likely that even more changes are ahead. Many of these changes are directly related to the emergence of new technology tools that allow one lawyer or paralegal to do what would have required several individuals a decade or so ago. But there are other pressures for change, including a change in attitudes of clients, both corporate and individual.

Professor Richard Susskind has outlined many challenges for lawyers in his books *The End of Lawyers?* and *Tomorrow's Lawyers*. But one of his predictions that seems undeniable at this point is that in the future clients will want more for less in terms of their legal services. Most business clients find themselves in the same posture as law firms, with the need to constantly look to improve efficiency, utilize technology more efficiently, lower production costs, and provide a better value to consumers.

Business leaders faced with the challenge of constantly improving their operations and efficiency will require similar improvements from the law firms serving them in the same way they require their suppliers, employees, and associates to continue to innovate and improve.

The need to innovate and improve is simply a function of the times in which we live. People's lives are more intertwined with technology—as a glance around any public gathering will verify. There was a relatively short time, historically speaking, between the release of the mobile phone and the ubiquity of the mobile phone. To many, a mobile phone has now become a necessity. The constant flow of information and digital interaction can be addictive. Today, a family lawyer must understand social media and know how to retrieve and preserve relevant evidence contained in social media websites. The lawyer advising businesses cannot excuse himself or herself from the discussion when a business challenge involves Internet security or online violation of intellectual property rights. A lawyer may generally rely on an assistant to do e-filing, but the lawyer must have the training, ability, and confidence to personally e-file an important pleading should the need arise.

Lawyers produce documents as the evidence and result of their work. While many members of the public may not appreciate the value of legal documents and deride "paper pushers," lawyers will always understand the value of a well-drafted contract or settlement proposal presented to opposing counsel. But even the basic tools that a lawyer would use to prepare documents are changing as the use of the many "hidden" advanced features of word processors becomes commonplace and document assembly tools improve in affordability and ease of use. Lawyers whose keyboarding skills are less than adequate now rely on speech recognition software. Siri and other mobile speech recognition tools allow one the ability to dictate directly to digital text anywhere. All of these changes would have been hard to imagine a decade ago.

The 2015 Solo and Small Firm Legal Technology Guide can help you purchase new tools to replace those that have become outdated or broken. But the highest and best use of this guide is to use it to create change and set your law firm on a path to success by using the tools profiled and information provided in this book to build your own unique law office of the future.

CHAPTER ONE

Computers

Desktop Computers

Personal Computers (PCs)

The Dell OptiPlex line of computers continues to offer the perfect combination of performance and business-grade hardware at just the right price. All Dell computers can be purchased with a three-, four-, or five-year warranty and offer a large selection of available options for protecting your investment. They offer both hardware and software warranty protection of varying levels, along with same-day or next-business-day response for the replacement of failed computer hardware or software. We strongly recommend the purchase of a three-year warranty—the average life span of a business computer system—with any new computer. Purchasing software technical support, in our judgment, is generally not worth the additional cost, especially when most firms have an IT provider who is familiar with their software and setup and can assist when help is needed, rather than having to rely on Dell for assistance.

Dell also offers accidental damage protection for its computer systems, which covers damage caused by spilled liquids, drops, falls, and electrical surges for a period of three to five years, at an additional cost ranging from $34 to $55. This cost is much lower than in previous editions of this book.

Another option from Dell worth noting is its Keep Your Hard Drive program. Typically, if a hard drive crashes while under warranty, Dell will take the failed hard drive and replace it with a new or refurbished one. Citing privacy concerns—with all the recent data breaches in the news—Dell now offers its users the ability to keep their hard drives, even in the event a replacement is needed, but at an additional cost. The cost for this option ranges from $12 to $20, depending on the length of the warranty, and it is a small price to pay to maintain total control over and responsibility for the sensitive and confidential data on the hard drive. For recommendations on how to securely remove data from a hard drive before disposal, check out the Utilities chapter.

Below, we provide you with our recommendations for a Dell OptiPlex business-grade computer system with all of the hardware components included.

Windows-Based Desktop Computer

Hardware Component	Recommendation
Computer Model:	Dell OptiPlex 9020 Mini Tower
Operating System:	Microsoft Windows 7 Professional 64-Bit (Includes Windows 8.1 Pro license)
Processor:	4th Gen Intel Core i7-4770 Processor (Quad Core, 3.4 GHz Turbo, 8 MB, w/HD4600 Graphics)
Memory:	8 GB DDR3 Non-ECC SDRAM 1600 MHz
Video Card:	AMD RADEON HD 8570
Hard Drive:	1 TB 3.5-Inch SATA Hard Drive
Optical Drive:	16X DVD+/−RW
Network:	Intel Gigabit LAN 10/100/1000 Ethernet
Warranty:	3-Year Basic Hardware Service with 3-Year Next Business Day Onsite Service After Remote Diagnosis
Other Notes:	No mouse and keyboard required; no out-of-band systems management; USB 3.0 ports included

The fourth-generation Intel Core i7-4770 Quad Core 3.4 GHz processor will provide more than enough power to support both current and future versions of business-grade software, including the next version of the Windows Operating System, throughout the life cycle of the machine. The Intel Core i7 has replaced the Intel Core 2 Duo processor and has become the standard for business-grade systems. The Intel Core i7 Quad Core processor is offered with varying levels of clock speeds, with the 3.4 GHz version currently in the upper range of processor clock speeds offered by Dell for this model of computer system. The faster the processor, the higher the premium you will pay for having cutting-edge technology. The amount of memory included in this system is enough to support your business applications, handling even "memory hungry" applications with ease. Eight gigabytes (GB) of memory has become the recommended standard for the minimum amount of memory in business-grade computers, given the low cost and high gain in performance for the upgrade. This upgrade is a must-have option when purchasing a 64-bit system, which can actually take advantage of the additional resources.

The video card included in this system provides dual-link digital visual interface (DVI) outputs. By providing dual interfaces, this graphics adapter allows you to have dual monitors, an option we will never go without when purchasing a new computer system. In fact, John is considering a third! He calls his current setup 2-¾ monitors since there are two 20" wide screen monitors and the 15-½" display on the laptop. (Monitors, keyboards, and other peripherals are discussed in subsequent chapters.) A hard drive plays an important role in the configuration of your computer system because it is the hardware component where your information (files) is actually stored. In short, the better the hard drive, the faster your computer can read and write your data. This system comes with a 1 TB Serial ATA (SATA) hard drive, which will provide enough storage space for the average lawyer user. The 6 GBps SATA interface allows for more throughput and higher cache than the previous revisions of the SATA specification. In fact, Dell no longer offers earlier versions of SATA hard drives as an option when configuring an OptiPlex desktop or smaller capacity drives. We wouldn't be surprised if, in the near future, the usage of 3.5-inch hard drives is discontinued due to the large power requirements to operate them and their propensity to fail, especially as the cost of solid-state hard drives continues to fall. In fact, Dell now offers many choices for notebook-sized (2.5-inch) drives and solid-state drives for the OptiPlex model line.

When configuring an optical drive for the system, choosing the 16X DVD+/-RW drive will allow you to burn and read data from both CDs and DVDs. We used to recommend that you purchase your computer with a FireWire 400 or 800 Mbps (megabits per second) adapter, but that is no longer the case. Newer interfaces have come out within the past few years, such as USB 3.0 and Thunderbolt, a serial data interface primarily found on Apple computer systems, and are now beginning to be offered on a small number of Windows-based computers. Now that these technologies have been out for a few years, especially USB 3.0, it might be the time to jump on board—especially if you transfer a lot of data to external hard drives. In actuality, it's becoming harder to find USB 2.0 external hard drives, so you might as well take advantage of the increased speed. The Dell OptiPlex 9020 Mini Tower now includes four USB 3.0 ports (two on front, two on back) and six USB 2.0 ports.

Dell currently offers its computers preinstalled with the Windows 7 or Windows 8 operating systems. Even for die-hard techies like us, it would be a reach to think about using Windows 8 at this time in a business environment, especially without a touch screen monitor—remember the problems with Windows Vista and hardware drivers? Windows 8 hasn't caught fire with businesses as many industry analysts predicted it would, and given the current lack of implementation, it is considered by many to be another Microsoft failure, just like Microsoft Vista. It remains to be seen, but at this time we have no plans to upgrade our systems from Windows 7 to Windows 8 and may wait for the next release. The exception would be for touch devices like tablets or all-in-one computer systems, where Windows 8 would be a better alternative.

The three-year, next-business-day onsite parts and labor warranty will cover hardware defects and failures of the computer system for three years at a relatively small cost. The cost of this warranty is built into the cost of the recommended system and should be considered a requirement when purchasing a new computer for your business or firm. Dell provides the consumer with a toll-free phone number to call for technical support, and if any hardware needs to be replaced, Dell will send a support technician to your location to replace the defective part by the next business day. The hardware replacement and labor cost is covered by the warranty, so there should be no additional out-of-pocket costs.

There are some additional pointers to consider when configuring this desktop system. First, most users already have their own wireless keyboard and mouse and don't need another basic USB keyboard and mouse taking up space in the desk drawer. This can be avoided by removing them from the default configuration of this system, and you'll save about $10. For those of you who don't have a wireless keyboard and mouse—you should be looking at upgrading immediately. Our recommendations for a wireless desktop suite can be found in the Computer Peripherals chapter.

Another tip: Dell also includes by default an out-of-band management device, which shouldn't be necessary. Again, just removing this piece of hardware can save you approximately $30. If you consider yourself to be technically challenged, you may want to leave the management device for remote diagnostics by the support personnel.

For those users who are looking to purchase a new monitor or two, Dell does offer the ability to bundle monitors when configuring your new computer system. If you need a new monitor or two, it may be a good idea to save a few bucks and bundle them with the purchase of your new computer system. Based on a price comparison, it appears that you save about $50 or more per monitor when selecting them at the time of your computer purchase, and we're always looking for ways to save you money! As of this writing, one of the options for monitors is $100 less than Dell's online retail price when bundled—talk about hidden savings!

Keep in mind that, on average, the expected life cycle of a new business computer system is around three years, which is covered by the three-year warranty you purchased. The recommended Dell OptiPlex 9020 Mini Tower desktop computer can be configured and purchased from Dell's website starting at around $1,000.

Remember that the "sweet spot" in buying computers changes regularly. Our specs will get you close, but they will shift slightly during the lifespan of this publication. You can receive a courtesy copy of our current specs (for workstations, laptops, and servers—PC or Mac) by e-mailing **sensei@senseient.com** and simply making a request. We are generally able to get our current specs to you within twenty-four hours during the workweek. We are happy to report that many, many readers are taking advantage of this offer, so don't be shy. We are always pleased to help.

Apple Computers (Macs)

In the past, Apple computers (Macs) were used primarily by businesses with a need for multimedia functions, such as video editing and graphic design—both areas in which Apple systems have always excelled. Usually, Apple's appearance in an office environment was the result of someone having a personal preference for the Macintosh operating system over the Windows-based system.

Macs are still not as widely used in law offices as Windows-based computers are, but Apple's shift to using Intel-based processors in all of its systems, and the continued popularity of the iPad make them chosen more frequently now by solo and small firm lawyers. As a result of the change in processors, Macs can now run both the Mac OS X and Windows operating systems on the same computer. In a way, it's like having two systems in one.

A Mac computer can be easily configured to connect to and function on a Windows-based network, including communicating with and authenticating a Windows domain controller.

For those concerned with computer security, Mac systems are perceived to be more secure than their Windows-based counterparts since they are not targeted as often by malware, due to the overall smaller number of Mac users. Many Mac users would scoff at the suggestion that their computer should be running some kind of security software for protection. However, they would be wrong; Macs absolutely need security software—Apple itself now says so. Remember, the bad guys who write browser exploits (pieces of malware that take advantage of vulnerabilities in Internet browsers such as Firefox) don't care what operating system the computer is running. In fact, security companies consistently warn that malware writers who attack browsers are increasingly becoming the real threat, as vulnerabilities in operating systems are less frequently targeted.

The Flashback virus that affected over 700,000 Macs early in 2012 has been the largest attack on Mac OS X to date. In an unprecedented move, Apple released two security updates/fixes addressing just this vulnerability.

In early 2013, a new Trojan virus was discovered targeting computers running Mac OS X, creating an encrypted reverse-shell connection providing attackers with potentially unfettered access to infected machines. It was dubbed "Pintsized" for the very small, yet efficient, threat.

In 2014 alone, Mac users have battled viruses and Trojans that have been used in a number of targeted attacks against governments ("Appetite Trojan"); malware that spreads via spam messages—posing as an undelivered parcel notification from FedEx that steals documents from the local computer system ("LaoShu Trojan"); and finally the CoinThief Trojan, malware designed to steal login credentials related to various Bitcoin-related exchanges using malicious browser add-ons. To further illustrate the vulnerability of Apple products, Apple just released patches for 144 security flaws across seven of its products, including OS X Yosemite, Mavericks and iTunes.

So Apple users, please don't be naive—you, too, need virus and malware protection. In 2012, Apple removed from its website the language suggesting that you didn't need this type of protection and it now actively encourages the use of security software.

Apple's continuing release of security patches, even for the latest version of its operating system, is a clear sign of just how targeted this software and its applications are by the developers of malware. For years, we have recommended that security protection suites be installed on all computers, regardless of the operating system.

While they are still not commonplace, we are beginning to see Apple computers make their way into smaller law offices, especially in the solo, stand-alone environment. Now that Apple computers use Intel chipsets, users are taking advantage of the opportunity to better integrate their systems with the Windows world. Some users run Windows on their Mac computers as the primary operating system. Others use Boot Camp, a free utility provided by Apple at no charge with each system, to dual-boot between Windows and Mac OS. With Boot Camp, you can install a Microsoft Windows XP operating system or newer right alongside Apple's OS X on any Intel-based Macintosh computer. To run the

Windows 7 or newer operating system, you must upgrade your version of Boot Camp to version 4.0 or newer. The most current release of Boot Camp is version 5.1.

For those users who purchased Mac OS X Mountain Lion, this updated version of Boot Camp was included. Boot Camp guides users through the processes of creating a new partition of the local hard drive on which to install the Windows operating system and also provides all of the necessary Windows drivers required for hardware functionality. As an alternative to dual-booting with Boot Camp, some users have even purchased third-party products like Parallels Workstation or downloaded Oracle's VM VirtualBox, which allows them to run Windows, Linux, and other operating systems within the Mac OS itself. Virtual Machine (VM) software is described in more detail in a later section of this book.

The iMac desktop systems combine performance and ergonomics by putting the hardware components that make up the system in the same casing as the monitor, eliminating the need for separate components like a tower unit sitting underneath your desk. As a result, the space-saving design allows you to free up both desk and floor space without giving up performance. Below, we provide our recommendation for an iMac business-grade desktop system with all of the hardware components outlined.

Macintosh-Based Desktop Computer

Hardware Component	Recommendation
Computer Model:	21.5-inch iMac
Operating System:	Mac OS v10.10 Yosemite
Processor:	Intel Core i5 Quad Core 2.7 GHz (Turbo Boost up to 3.2 GHz)
Memory:	8 GB 1600 MHz DDR3 SDRAM
Video Card:	Intel Iris Pro Graphics
Hard Drive:	1 TB (5400-rpm) Hard Drive
CD/DVD-ROM:	8X SuperDrive (DVD+R DL/DVD±RW/CD-RW)
Network:	10/100/1000 Base-T Gigabit Ethernet Port, AirPort Extreme Wi-Fi (802.11a/b/g/n), Bluetooth 4.0
Warranty:	3-year AppleCare Protection Plan for iMacs
Other:	FaceTime HD Camera, Built-in 21.5-inch Monitor and Stereo Speakers, Dual Microphones, two Thunderbolt Ports, four USB 3 Ports, Mini Display-Port, Apple Wireless Keyboard and Magic Mouse, SDXC Card Slot, and Kensington Lock Slot

The 21.5-inch iMac comes with an Intel Core i5 Quad Core 2.7 GHz processor, 8 GB of memory, and the Mac OS v10.10 Yosemite operating system. This system can be configured for up to 16 GB of memory, which may be overkill for basic business usage. The 1 TB 5400 RPM SATA hard drive comes standard and will provide more than enough storage space and hard drive performance for the average lawyer. However, if you feel that you need additional storage space or performance speed, the hard drive can be configured with 256 GB or 512 GB of flash storage, or Apple's 1 TB Fusion Drive—a combination flash storage and regular hard drive. The flash storage media will contain the files necessary to boot and load the operating system, dramatically increasing the speed with which the computer system starts up. The hard drive can be upgraded to 3 TB in size, but this option is only available for the 27-inch version of the iMac.

The standard Ethernet adapter and AirPort wireless adapter will allow your computer to connect to the business network, whether over a wired network or wireless, even if it's Windows-based. The AirPort wireless adapter is compatible with 802.11a/b/g/n wireless networks.

The other standard hardware included with the iMac is the built-in Face-Time HD camera, stereo speakers, 21.5-inch LED-backlit display with IPS technology, four USB 3.0 ports, two Thunderbolt ports, and one SDXC memory card slot. This system also includes one Mini DisplayPort, which allows users to add a second external monitor to their computer system if needed, and the standard Apple wireless keyboard and Magic Mouse. The 21.5-inch iMac computer weighs 12.5 pounds and has a depth of about 7 inches, so finding room on your desk for one of these systems is very easy.

Apple's standard warranty with a new iMac provides you with ninety days of telephone support and one year of service coverage. We recommend that you upgrade the warranty to the extended AppleCare Protection Plan for iMac, which provides you with telephone and service support for three years. The cost to extend the warranty plan is $169 and is well worth it. The 21.5-inch iMac computer can be purchased from Apple's webstore starting at $1,099 and the pricing of the 27-inch iMac starts at $1,799.

Laptops

Personal Computers (PCs)
The Dell Latitude line of laptop computers continues to combine performance and mobility in a laptop system that remains at the top of its

class. These business-grade laptops are thin and extremely light, weighing less than four-and-a-half pounds. They are a perfect fit for the mobile lawyer and provide an ideal mobile computing solution. Below, we provide you with our recommendations for a Dell Latitude business-grade laptop with all of the hardware components included.

Windows-Based Laptop Computer

Hardware Component	Recommendation
Computer Model:	Dell Latitude E6440
Processor:	4th Gen Intel Core i7-4610M 3.0 GHz 4M Cache
Operating System:	Microsoft Windows 7 Professional 64-Bit
Memory:	8 GB DDR3 1600 MHz SDRAM
Video Card:	AMD Radeon HD 8690M
Hard Drive:	2.5-inch 500 GB Solid State-Hybrid Drive
CD/DVD-ROM:	8X DVD+/–RW drive
Network:	10/100/1000 Mbps Ethernet adapter, Intel Centrino Advanced-N 6235 802.11AGN Dual Band Wi-Fi Half-Mini Card
Warranty:	3-Year Basic Hardware Service with 3-Year Next-Business-Day Limited Onsite Service after Remote Diagnosis
Other:	14-Inch Wide HD+ LED screen, 90W AC power adapter, 9-cell/97 WHr primary battery, weighs 4.68 lbs., four USB 3.0 ports, VGA, HDMI, Memory Card Reader, Noise-Cancelling Digital Array Microphone and Light Sensitive Webcam, Fingerprint reader, and contactless smartcard reader

The Dell Latitude E6440 comes with a fourth-generation Intel Core i7-4610M 3.0 GHz processor and 8 GB of memory, which should be sufficient to run all of the business applications of a mobile lawyer. The system also comes preinstalled with Microsoft Windows 7 Professional 64-bit.

The system's fingerprint reader provides the level of security needed to protect your personal files and confidential data. When it's enabled, you can restrict user logon access to either the biometric access or to a user name and password. A fingerprint reader keeps data on the hard drive secure through encryption, with the hardware requiring successful authentication before the data contents can be decrypted. Enabling a start-up or hard drive password in the system's BIOS is a great way to add an extra layer of protection to your system and is highly recommended if you're storing sensitive client data on your laptop.

The AMD Radeon HD 8690M graphics card supplies crisp, clear graphics to the 14-inch wide LED display. The 500 GB hard drive will provide more than enough storage space for the mobile user, with a hard drive speed that will supply faster drive performance. The DVD+/–RW drive will allow you to burn and read both CDs and DVDs without the need to attach an external burner. The Ethernet adapter will allow you to connect your laptop to your network when you're in the office, and the wireless network adapter will allow you to stay connected when on the move. The Intel wireless adapter provides connectivity to 802.11a/b/g/n wireless networks, supporting dual-band operation (2.4 and 5 GHz) with data rates up to 300 megabits per second (Mbps). The 9-cell battery is an upgrade that will supply the laptop with power longer than the standard 6-cell battery and should charge faster as well. This battery upgrade is a must-have if you plan to use the wireless network adapter when running the laptop off of the battery, although this will add some slight weight to the unit. The 9-cell battery will provide you with approximately three hours' more battery life than the standard 6-cell battery, which will save you from searching for electrical outlets wherever you go. Finally, the integrated HD video webcam and digital microphone is great for videoconferences or recording audio, such as podcasts.

For frequent travelers and those who truly want to always stay connected, the Dell Latitude E6430 has a configuration option to add an internal mobile broadband card (3G/4G) for the Verizon, Sprint, T-Mobile, AT&T, and a few additional networks for an extra $87.50.

The three-year, next-business-day onsite parts and labor warranty is the same warranty described in the Desktop Computers section. The Dell Latitude E6440 can be purchased from Dell's website starting at around $1,529.

If you are particularly clumsy or accident-prone, you may want to consider adding the CompleteCare Accidental Damage Protection Plan to your purchase. This plan covers any damage to the laptop, including such things as liquid spills (one client has used this plan multiple times to cover the unwelcome effects of spilling red wine), surges, and dropping the device. Obviously, it does not cover intentional damage, theft, or normal wear and tear. For the additional $78.48 to $114.48, depending on the length of the warranty (3- to 5-year options), you will have peace of mind when you set your coffee cup (or wineglass) on the keyboard.

Apple Computers (Macs)

The Apple MacBook Pro is perfect for the mobile lawyer who requires a powerful notebook in a compact and lightweight design. The MacBook Pro laptop comes standard with a wide-screen Retina display, built-in FaceTime HD camera, wireless network adapter, and much more. The MacBook Pro laptop is available with 13- or 15-inch screens. Apple no longer sells a 17-inch version of this model. In prior editions of this book, Apple offered the Retina display only in the upgraded 15-inch model of the MacBook Pro. This is no longer the case. Now, all versions of both the 13- and 15-inch MacBook Pros come standard with the Retina display. The MacBook Pro is available only in the aluminum case with glass LED display. The MacBook Pro can be fully integrated into any Windows-based network without too much overhead and configuration. Below, we provide our recommendations for an Apple MacBook Pro business-grade laptop with all of the hardware components included.

Macintosh-Based Laptop Computer

Hardware Component	Recommendation
Computer Model:	15-Inch MacBook Pro
Operating System:	Mac OS v10.10 Yosemite
Processor:	Intel Core i7 Quad Core 2.2 GHz
Memory:	16 GB 1600 MHz DDR3
Video Card:	Intel Iris Pro
Hard Drive:	256 GB Flash Storage
CD/DVD-ROM:	8X SuperDrive (DVD+R DL/DVD±RW/CD-RW)
Network:	10/100/1000 Base-T Gigabit Ethernet Port, AirPort Extreme Wi-Fi (802.11a/b/g/n), Bluetooth 4.0
Warranty:	3-year AppleCare Protection Plan
Other:	FaceTime HD Camera, Built-in 15.4-Inch LED-Back-lit Display with IPS Technology, Stereo Speakers, two USB 3 Ports, two Thunderbolt Ports, SDXC Card Slot, and HDMI

The base 15-inch MacBook Pro laptop comes with 16 GB of memory and the Mac OS v10.10 Yosemite operating system. The Intel Iris Pro video card provides perfect high resolution to the 15.4-inch-wide Retina LED display, with a maximum resolution of 2880 × 1800 pixels. The 256 GB flash storage hard drive provides enough space to store all of your documents, pictures, and music. The 8X SuperDrive will allow you to burn and play both CDs and DVDs. The built-in AirPort Extreme Wi-Fi adapter will keep you connected on the road, and it supports the 802.11n standard. The AirPort Extreme Wi-Fi adapter is also backward compatible with 802.11a/b/g wireless networks. The aluminum body MacBook is very light, weighing just 4.46 pounds.

If you need more processing power, this model can be upgraded to an i7 2.5 GHz quad-core processor—for a pretty penny!

The multi-touch scrolling trackpad gives you precise cursor control, supports two-finger scrolling, tap, double-tap, and drag capabilities. If you have been a lifelong Windows user, be forewarned: There is no right-click button on the trackpad. To right-click on a Mac, you must hold down the Control key while clicking. A tip for former Windows users: Don't want to hold down the Control key to initiate a right-click with the mouse? You can tap the trackpad with two fingers rather than holding down the Control key—you just have to enable the option within the Keyboard & Mouse settings.

Have you ever tripped over a power cord and had your laptop come flying off the desk? With the 85W MagSafe 2 power adapter, you no longer have to worry. The magnetic power connector will cleanly disengage from the side of the laptop and cause no damage to the computer or the power cord. This a great gift to those of us who are occasionally less than graceful.

The sleek and elegant design of the MacBook Pro is what sets it apart from the competition. The design and celebrated ease of use makes the MacBook Pro a smart choice when purchasing a laptop for yourself or your firm. The MacBook Pro configured above can be purchased from Apple's webstore for $1,999.

Netbooks/Ultrabooks

Netbooks and ultrabooks continue to be very popular among mobile users, including lawyers. Essentially, these devices are highly portable mini-laptops. They are much smaller, cheaper, and lighter than most traditional laptops. As with the other computer recommendations, it is impossible to mention all of the available manufacturers and models of ultrabooks and netbooks.

More recently, netbooks have taken a backseat to the class of laptops called ultrabooks. Ultrabooks, which are becoming increasingly popular, are paper-thin laptops (nearly weightless when compared to a traditional laptop). Ultrabooks have more robust hardware specifications than netbooks, but they also command a higher price.

Apple released the MacBook Air, an ultrabook considered the first of its class, long before PC manufacturers released the first competitor. Much as the iPad has dominated Android-based tablets, in part because it was first to the market, the MacBook Air continues to be an extremely popular alternative to the regular laptop for a mobile user, and starts at a cost of $900 or so.

The MacBook Air is offered in both 11- and 13-inch models, with configurable internal flash storage capacity available from 128 to 256 GB. The 1.4 GHz Dual Core Intel Core i5 processor is more than capable of handling web browsing and document editing, but not a lot more than that, which is perfect for the mobile lawyer. The standard 4 GB of DDR3 memory is more than sufficient for everyday usage and can be upgraded to 8 GB.

If you were to hold an 11-inch model, weighing just 2.38 pounds, you'd never go back to using a standard laptop. The MacBook Air is available for purchase on Apple's website starting at $900.

Tablets

Most users would expect to see the iPad recommended in this section, but keep in mind the iPad is much more of a personal device than it is a "true laptop replacement." You will find our recommendations and thoughts on the iPad later in this book, so please don't worry.

Business-grade tablets, those that can truly replace a laptop, are quickly becoming the next big thing in solo and small firm technology. Sharon and John are being bombarded with questions on this very topic at many of the presentations that they give throughout the country—is there a tablet that can actually replace my laptop, while maintaining all of the functionality?

The answer is, yes there is. You can now leave your 4.5-pound laptop and clunky travel bag at home when you need to hit the road.

The Microsoft Surface Pro 3 is truly considered a laptop replacement. The tablet boasts a 12" display with a resolution of 2160x1440. The fourth generation Intel Core processor (i3, i5, i7) is the same processor that you will find in your laptop computer system, and it provides this tablet with more than enough horsepower to run your business applications smoothly. The tablet comes preloaded with Microsoft Windows 8.1 Pro, which means that you can load and run any of your necessary business software—allowing you to get the same functionality out of this device as you can out of your laptop—at just a fraction of the weight!

The device can be configured with 4 or 8 GB of memory and anywhere from 64 to 512 GB of storage space. For network connectivity, this device comes with a wireless adapter supporting 802.11a/b/g/n and Bluetooth 4.0. It has both a front- and rear-facing camera, as well as a stereo microphone perfect for videoconferencing. We would recommend that you give serious consideration to the 8 GB memory, 256 GB storage, i7 unit.

The Microsoft Surface Pro 3 tablet can be purchased online from Microsoft's webstore (**www.microsoft.com**) or from your local electronics retailer starting at $799.

CHAPTER TWO

Computer Operating Systems

Microsoft Windows XP Operating System

At the time of this writing, the Microsoft Windows XP operating system is no longer supported by Microsoft, and its use should be discontinued immediately.

If you have a computer running Microsoft Windows XP, the time to upgrade is overdue. We would even opine (at least lawyer/author Nelson would) that the continued use of Windows XP violates the ethical duties of a lawyer, because the security of client data is endangered by using an unsupported operating system which receives no security updates.

Microsoft Windows Vista Operating System

Microsoft Windows Vista operating system was released in January 2007 and was made available in six editions, with two editions designed for the business community—Windows Vista Business Edition and Windows Vista Enterprise Edition. Windows Vista Business Edition included several new business features, such as file system encryption, a full version of Remote Desktop, system image backup and recovery, Windows Shadow-Copy, and the IIS web server.

When first released, it was believed that eventually Windows Vista Business Edition would replace Microsoft XP Professional Edition as the dominant player in the business desktop operating system market, but this certainly was not the case. Many companies were hesitant to upgrade their business systems because of Vista's continuing incompatibility problems with some third-party software, licensing restrictions and costs, digital rights managements, driver issues for some peripherals, and the hardware requirements necessary to run the operating system. Vista ultimately did itself in and never took off.

Microsoft Vista turned out to be a complete and utter failure for Microsoft. The operating system was rejected almost immediately by consumers and businesses and ultimately was rated as the number two all-time technology flop by *InfoWorld*. Wow. (Trivia question: What was number one? If you guessed "security," you'd be correct.)

Microsoft Windows 7

Windows 7 is the successor to Windows Vista and was made available to the general public on October 22, 2009. Microsoft was ready to move on from the epic failure that was Vista, and they finally got it right with the release of Windows 7. It is more "XP-like," emphasizing performance improvements and eliminating the compatibility issues that plagued Microsoft Vista. We have been running the various versions of Windows 7 since it was first released as a beta and absolutely love it—as do many of our clients.

Windows 7 is available in six editions, but only a few of those are worth mentioning to the solo and small firm market:

Starter Edition—is primarily for small notebooks, such as a netbook. The Starter Edition is 32-bit only, supports only a single processor, and does not support multiple monitors, such as dual displays. This edition was not designed for business use.

Home Premium Edition—comes bundled with Internet Explorer 10, allows for a connection to a home network, and is for home use only. The upgrade (from a previous operating system) retail cost for this edition is $149.99 per license, and the full retail cost for this edition is $199.99 per license.

Professional Edition—includes all the features of the Home Premium Edition, plus allows connection to a company network, such as a domain, and includes a backup-and-restore utility to protect your system. The upgrade retail cost for this edition is $199.99 per license, and the full retail cost for this edition is $299.99 per license.

Ultimate Edition—includes all the features of the Professional Edition, plus BitLocker encryption to help secure your data. The upgrade retail cost for this edition is $219.99 per license, and the full retail cost for this edition is $319.99 per license.

All of these editions are available for purchase and download from Microsoft's website, and for an additional $14.95, you can elect to have a physical disk shipped to you as a backup.

For your business, you will need to purchase either the Professional or Ultimate Edition to install on your computer systems. Obviously, upgrading is less expensive than purchasing a full license. If you have computer systems running Windows XP, now is the time to upgrade.

Users may also upgrade their computer systems to Windows 7 from both Windows XP and Windows Vista. However, for users upgrading from Windows XP, you must be careful when performing an upgrade. This upgrade path actually performs a "clean" installation, and the user must back up all programs and data because the upgrade will not retain any of the information. There isn't a prompt during the upgrade process to notify users to back up their data, so this step must be performed before beginning the upgrade process. In other words, there is no direct upgrade path from XP to Windows 7. It is probably best to do a clean install anyway to clean up any past "sins" and remove any leftover files from applications that didn't completely uninstall in the past. You can get some advice about your hardware and software compatibility by running the free Windows Upgrade Advisor (**http://www.microsoft.com/ en-us/download/details.aspx?id=20**). This utility will tell you if your hardware is compatible and what software may need to be upgraded.

If you are upgrading from Windows Vista, most of you will not have to worry about the process deleting all of your information. As was the case when upgrading from Windows XP to Windows Vista, you need only perform a clean install if you are going to a version that is lower on the food chain (e.g., Windows Vista Ultimate to Windows 7 Home Edition).

Regardless of the upgrade path you take, we always strongly recommend that you back up your system and data before upgrading.

The only other installation scenario with a clean installation is an upgrade from a 32-bit version to a 64-bit version operating system, regardless of the edition. Microsoft released the first Service Pack for this operating system (SP1) to the public in February of 2011, and at the time of its release, it was not a mandatory update. This Service Pack addressed a number of security issues and fixed a few bugs related to HDMI audio and the printing of XPS documents.

Please note that Windows 7 can no longer be purchased online at the Microsoft Store, but it is still available when configuring a new system from Dell and from other third-party retailers, both online and in brick-and-mortar locations.

Microsoft Windows 8

Windows 8 is the latest version of the Microsoft Windows operating system and is the successor to Windows 7. It became available to consumers in early fall of 2012.

The Windows 8 user interface is built based on the Metro design language, featuring a new start screen, Internet Explorer 10, support for USB 3.0, and a new Windows Defender. Windows 8 has also added support for UEFI SecureBoot, which is a feature used to prevent unauthorized firmware, operating systems, or drivers from running at boot time.

There has been much controversy over the new Metro look, replacing the all-too-familiar Windows Start button. The Metro UI environment is tile-based, similar to the Start screen seen on the Windows Phone operating system. The Start button had originally been removed from the taskbar, but was later reinstated with the update, Windows 8.1, released in October 2013.

Windows 8 is available in four editions, three of which are focused on business-grade computers: Windows 8, Windows 8 Pro, and Windows 8 Enterprise. The Windows RT edition is built to run solely on tablet hardware.

Windows 8 has been available for about a year as of this writing, and it appears very likely that it is headed toward a fate similar to Windows Vista. The adoption of this operating system by businesses has been very slow, and even that may be a generous description. We have no plans to upgrade our systems to Windows 8, and we will continue to purchase new computers for our clients with Windows 7 preinstalled—as long as it's offered as an option. The one exception is for a touchscreen device, like a tablet. The tile interface is really made for touch and is similar to the iPad. Several of our colleagues have rolled out Windows 8, but only on tablets. It is not very practical to be reaching across your desk to touch your monitor.

Mac OS X Version 10.7 (Lion) Operating System

Mac OS X version 10.7 was released to the public on July 20, 2011. This release was Apple's eighth major release of Mac OS X. This version, nicknamed Lion, contains many new and changed features, such as FaceTime, AirDrop, Mac App Store, Auto Save, and Versions. As we expected, iCloud support for Mac OS X Lion is here and is included in a recent software update, v. 10.7.2.

Mac OS X Lion includes enhanced security features such as full disk encryption and application sand-boxing, which restricts the way applications can interact with other parts of the operating system. Apple also increased the security of the operating system through "addition by subtraction." It no longer preinstalls Adobe Flash Player and the Java Runtime Environment on newly purchased systems.

Mac users looking to upgrade can still purchase the Lion operating system from the Mac App Store for $29.99; however, it makes more sense to upgrade to Yosemite, the latest operating system.

Apple originally didn't plan to distribute physical media for this operating system, offering the product as an exclusive download from the Mac App Store, but its stance has since softened. Since August 2011, Apple continues to provide in-store downloads to consumers who don't have broadband Internet access.

Unfortunately, when OS X Lion was first released, a significant security flaw relating to passwords was discovered. Apple had changed the way it stores password hashes. This change allowed unauthorized users access to view the password hashes and crack them with ease. Apple addressed this huge security issue in a recent software update, v. 10.7.2.

Mac OS X Version 10.8 (Mountain Lion) Operating System

Released to the public on July 25, 2012, Mac OS X 10.8 is the ninth major release of Apple's OS X operating system. Many of the features included in this version of the operating system were migrated from Apple's iOS software, including Notes, Reminders, and Messages. This version also includes the latest version of the Safari web browser, Safari 6.

Some of the additional features in Mountain Lion include the Game Center, Notification Center, AirPlay Mirroring, Dictation, and full Facebook and Twitter integration within the operating system.

While users can still download the Mountain Lion upgrade from the Mac App Store for $19.99, it makes more sense to upgrade to Yosemite, the latest operating system.

Mac OS X Version 10.9 (Mavericks) Operating System

Released to the public in late 2013, Mavericks is the tenth major release of the OS X operating system. Some of the new features include integration with iBooks, a new Maps application (Google Maps competitor), reworked Calendar application, updated version of Safari, the introduction of an iCloud Keychain, improved notifications, Finder Tabs, and improved battery and performance-boosting technologies.

The cost to upgrade to this version is the best part—it's free. Users can download this update from the Mac App Store; however, it makes more sense to upgrade to Yosemite, the latest operating system.

Mac OS X Version 10.10 (Yosemite) Operating System

Released to the public in October 2014, Yosemite is the newest (eleventh) major release of the OS X operating system. With Yosemite, Apple introduced a revision to the operating system's user interface, with all of the graphics inspired by iOS 7. While it still possesses the desktop appearance, the inclusion of new icons, light and color schemes, and even new default fonts, Apple has put a lot of effort into the upgrading of the look and feel of the software.

Some of the new features of this operating system include the Handoff functionality, which allows the operating system to integrate with iOS 8 devices over Bluetooth LE and WiFi. The Notification center has been revamped and includes new features, such as a "Today" view, and the Spotlight feature is now a more prominent part of the operating system.

This operating system is installed on newly purchased Macs by default. If you're using a Mac that is running an older version of the Mac OS X operating system and your system meets the technical requirements to upgrade, we recommend that you do so for the added features and security improvements. And on top of that—there's no cost to do so. Talk about a no-brainer!

CHAPTER THREE

Monitors

Now THAT YOU HAVE your brand new computer or shiny new laptop, you are ready for the task of picking out that brand new monitor—and you can have all the real estate your heart desires these days. The era of 14-inch monitors is long gone. You might even be able to reclaim some territory on your desk—and actually see some wood for a change—even if you choose to have two or three monitors. We have standardized on two monitors for clients and ourselves, although John has recently started asking for a full-sized third instead of the "partial size" laptop screen!

Choosing a monitor can be an overwhelming task because of all the options and bells and whistles to choose from. If you don't know what you're looking for, you can be inundated with all of the technical jargon that advertisers use to get you to purchase their monitors.

Previously, we had separate sections for all the different types of monitors, but with this edition, we've grouped them all into one—because there really is only one type of monitor you should be looking for. We will walk you through the process and explain how to weed through all of the technical jargon, providing you with a solid recommendation for purchasing a monitor.

First and foremost, the days of CRT monitors are over. Charities won't even take these monitors as donations anymore, so they can only be recycled at this point. The flat panel monitor has taken over.

Flat-panel, wide-screen monitors have a flat viewing surface that provides a better viewing angle than CRT monitors did. They are also less bulky, taking up only a fraction of the desktop space and weighing next to nothing when compared to the weight of the ancient CRT dinosaurs. Flat-panel monitors have come down significantly in price over the past few years and are very affordable.

Flat-panel monitors, like computers, come in all different sizes, resolutions, and performance. The flat-panel monitor that we recommend is the Dell P2214H 22-inch wide-screen (16:9) LED monitor. This monitor offers an optimal resolution of 1920 × 1080 at 60 Hz, which will provide you so much desktop real estate that you won't know what to do with it all. The higher resolution will enable you to view documents, images, and videos with stunning detail, vivid colors, and seamless motion. The display can be rotated and viewed horizontally or vertically, depending on your preference.

This monitor accepts video graphics array (VGA) and digital visual interface (DVI) inputs, and offers a contrast ratio of 1000:1 and maximum viewing angle of 178 degrees. It also includes four built-in USB 2.0 ports (three downstream ports, one upstream port) for connecting your peripheral devices, and it only weighs about 7 pounds. If needed, this device can be mounted on a wall using a standard VESA wall mount. The Dell P2214H 22-inch wide-screen monitor can be purchased online from Dell's website for $229 and comes with a standard three-year hardware warranty. If bundled with the purchase of a new computer from Dell, you may be able to get a much better deal on the price.

If you need a larger viewing area, you may want to consider using dual wide-screen monitors. Of course, your computer must have dual-monitor support, which most of the newer computers have by default. Usually, you will find that purchasing dual monitors, or in some cases three monitors, will be cheaper than purchasing a single large one. And anecdotally, we have found that folks who move to dual monitors never want to go back. Certainly, none of the authors would accept anything less than dual monitors—and we are all beginning to covet a third, although we would really need bigger desks, if not a special built-in shelf.

CHAPTER FOUR

Computer
Peripherals

IF YOU THOUGHT PURCHASING the right computer and monitor was tough, wait until you realize how many options there are when it comes to selecting computer peripherals. Having the right computer peripherals can make your computing experience faster, more comfortable, and a better overall experience. Wireless devices have brought peripherals into a new dimension, getting rid of that Gordian knot mess of wires that we all used to struggle to untangle. Below, we provide recommendations for mice, keyboards, wireless desktops, external storage devices, and speakers. As always, bear in mind that there is a universe of choices. These are our top picks.

Mouse

The optical mouse has condemned the classic "rollerball" mouse to extinction. Many users can remember the days when if your mouse acted up, you would simply need to clean the dirt and lint off the wheels. Optical technology allows you to navigate with better speed, precision, and reliability. An optical mouse uses light-emitting diode (LED) technology that bounces light off of a surface onto a sensor. It is important to note that the surface needs some texture to work properly. It won't work on glass, for instance, so you still may need to carry a mouse pad with you in the event you're caught working on an unusable surface. In a hotel, there's usually a magazine in your room that will suffice. The sensor inside the mouse analyzes the patterns in the images and compares them with previous captured images to determine how far the mouse has moved and relays the coordinates to the computer. Who knew this technology existed with a simple computer mouse? It is really quite a scientific marvel. An optical mouse contains no moving parts and therefore does not require the maintenance and cleaning that the legacy rollerball mouse did.

Our recommendation for a simple yet reliable optical mouse is the Microsoft Comfort Mouse 4500. This optical mouse provides advanced performance, ergonomic design, and five customizable buttons. As an example, one button can be programmed for "delete" and one can be defined as the "back" button for your browser. This mouse takes performance seriously, delivering extreme movement accuracy by using Microsoft's BlueTrack technology. The BlueTrack technology that measures the movement of the mouse uses a large blue beam and a high image sensor to track movement and speed. Microsoft even advertises that you can use this mouse on your carpeted floor, granite countertops in the kitchen, the armrest of a lobby chair, or even your pant leg. Wow.

The mouse connects to the computer using the USB port on your computer. It's a wired device requiring no batteries for trouble-free performance, and it can be used comfortably in either hand. The Microsoft Comfort Mouse 4500 device is compatible with both Windows and Mac computers, including the Windows 8.1 operating system. The Microsoft Comfort Mouse 4500 sells for $24.95 and can be purchased directly from Microsoft's website.

For portability, those users who travel with laptops and want a nifty little wireless travel mouse may also want to consider the excellent Microsoft Wireless Mobile Mouse 4000. This mouse uses Microsoft's BlueTrack technology to smoothly track the mouse movements on virtually any surface. This notebook mouse also includes the standard back button and scroll wheel, in an ergonomic design that we've all become accustomed to. If you are concerned about the current battery life, the mouse includes an indicator light that will glow red when the batteries need to be replaced—and it only requires a single AA battery. The batteries should last ten months or more before needing replacement. Of course, you do need to look at the light periodically so that you don't end up with a dead mouse and have to scramble for a new battery. This mouse is compatible with both Windows and Mac computers, including the Windows 8.1 operating system and can be purchased online from Microsoft's website for $34.95.

Keyboards

Finding the right keyboard for your computer can be a tedious task, as you sift through all of the different keyboards and features to find one that truly suits you—and there are a world of choices for personal preferences at all cost points. When selecting a keyboard, choose one that is ergonomically designed so that stress placed on your wrists is minimized. Second, you shouldn't have to give up comfort to gain enhanced features, such as the My Favorites buttons or buttons that will adjust the volume level of your speakers, including the Mute button. Also, you shouldn't have to break the bank to find a keyboard that will work for you.

The keyboard we recommend is the Natural Ergonomic Keyboard 4000 from Microsoft. This keyboard provides a great blend of ergonomic design with functionality. The reverse slope keyboard has a cushioned palm rest that allows you to rest your wrists and hands when typing and provides greater comfort, promoting a more natural hand, wrist, and forearm posture. The My Favorites keys are customizable to allow you to open your most frequently used software, pictures, videos, and music.

You can even browse the Internet with the push of a button. The Multimedia keys allow you to control your media player from your keyboard, along with the volume level of your speakers. The two buttons we use most on our keyboards are the Mute and Calculator buttons, which are must-haves for any keyboard selection.

This keyboard now includes an improved number pad, relocating the equal sign, parentheses, and backspace keys just above the numbers. The keyboard connects to your computer through the USB interface and comes with software to help you customize your keyboard's features. It can be used with either a Windows or Mac computer. The Natural Ergonomic Keyboard 4000 from Microsoft can be purchased for around $50 from your local electronics retailer.

Wireless Keyboard Desktops

With the introduction of wireless technology, wireless keyboard desktops have become extremely popular—so popular that it's becoming harder and harder to find a USB keyboard and mouse. A wireless keyboard desktop is a keyboard and mouse desktop combination that connects to your computer wirelessly using radio frequency (RF) technology. The keyboard and mouse are powered with standard or rechargeable batteries and transmit their signals to a desktop receiver that is connected to the computer. It requires very little setup to install and it eliminates the need for cables, which have plagued computer users since the first PC came into existence.

Our recommendation when purchasing a wireless keyboard desktop is the Logitech Wireless Wave Combo MK550. This wireless keyboard desktop comes with a wave key design that provides superior comfort with full-size and full-travel keys designed for quiet operation. The slight regular curve of the keyboard features consistently sized keys, which lets you type with confidence and ease. The keyboard uses the standard QWERTY layout, so you don't have to relearn how to type, as you do with some of the other curved keyboards. The height of the keyboard is adjustable, with three options for leg height, allowing you to choose the position that's most comfortable for you. The keyboard uses 128-bit AES encryption to secure data as it's transmitted from the keyboard to the receiver, and both the keyboard and mouse use the 2.4 GHz wireless spectrum to connect to the receiver. Logitech claims that the keyboard can operate up to three years before the batteries need to be replaced, and if true, the batteries should last the expected lifetime of the keyboard. The package includes four AA batteries, with both the keyboard and mouse requiring two each.

Logitech's wireless laser mouse M510, which is part of the MK550 combination, should operate for up to two years before the batteries will need to be replaced. The laser mouse uses a small infrared laser instead of an LED, which increases the resolution and sensitivity of the mouse. The laser mouse keeps your hands pain-free with the integration of contoured sides and soft rubber grips. The Logitech Wireless Wave Combo includes a three-year limited hardware warranty. This wireless desktop system is compatible with Windows 7 or Windows 8. The Logitech Wireless Wave Combo MK550 can be purchased for around $79.99 from your local electronics retailer or online at **www.logitech.com**.

External Storage Devices

External storage devices are pieces of hardware that connect to your computer using USB, FireWire, eSATA or some other type of interface and are used to store electronic data. These devices come in all sizes, shapes, colors, and volumes of storage space. They have all but replaced the CD-

ROM, DVD and backup tapes as the leading means to store electronic data because of their portability, low cost, and vast amount of storage space. Be sure to consider some type of secure authentication or encryption for external storage, especially if confidential client information is backed up or stored on these devices. Most products now come with some sort of built-in hardware or software encryption that can be enabled at no additional cost. Just be sure to remember your passphrase, because if you forget it, there's no way to recover your data.

External Hard Drives

External hard drives are great storage media to store videos, pictures, and music, and to back up the data from your internal hard drive. These devices are very easy to install and use. Most external hard drives are plug and play, which means you simply have to plug them in to your computer to use them—and nothing else! External hard drives are not as fast as internal hard drives, but they are relatively inexpensive. For the volume of information they can store, they are a very good, inexpensive backup solution. Also, lawyers who are otherwise technically challenged seem to do well with this form of backup, which can really be reduced to the push-of-a-button or an automated method that so many lawyers seem to prefer—set it and forget it.

The Seagate Backup Plus Desktop Drive is the external hard drive that we recommend for all lawyers and users. The Backup Plus Desktop Drive comes with available capacities of 2, 3, 4 and 5 TB of storage space. These capacities allow you to select the amount of storage space that best meets your requirements and may provide enough storage capacity to contain backups from more than one computer system. The Backup Plus Desktop Drive comes with backup software to automatically back up your data to the device, and it is Windows 8 compatible. You can now even use the Seagate Mobile Backup App to easily back up photos and videos on-the-go directly from your mobile device to the Backup Plus Desktop Drive.

All of the models should provide enough storage space to back up easily all of the data required by most lawyers. If you're looking to back up multiple computers and/or a server, then you probably will need to purchase the larger-sized drives—and make sure that you purchase more than one. We recommend that if you're using this external hard drive to back up your company data and files, then you should rotate drives on a weekly basis—keeping one onsite and the other one offsite. This will allow your firm to recover its information in the event of a disaster such as a fire in the office.

These devices connect to your computer through the USB 3.0 interface (backwards compatible with USB 2.0) and can be placed flat or on their side. The drive is whisper quiet and relatively small in size, so it can sit on your desk or on top of your computer without taking away valuable space. Compatible with both Windows and Mac computers, the drive includes an NTFS driver for Mac that will allow interoperability between systems without the need to reformat the drive. The Backup Plus Desktop Drive can be purchased online at **www.seagate.com** for between $99 and $219, depending on the storage capacity, and it comes with a two-year standard warranty.

Flash Drives

USB flash drives (thumb drives) are small, portable storage devices that use flash memory to store electronic data. Currently, they are offered with storage volume sizes ranging from 4 GB to 1 TB. For the most part, USB flash drives with capacities of 2 GB and smaller have been discontinued. USB flash drives offer many advantages over other portable storage devices, such as the floppy disk, CD-ROM, and DVD. In particular, they are smaller, more durable, faster, and can hold more data. Unfortunately, these devices can pose a great security risk for small businesses and law firms because their small size makes them absurdly easy to lose. This risk can be minimized, however, by purchasing the SanDisk Ultra USB 3.0 flash drive.

This model is available with 16, 32, 64 or 128 GB of storage space for your files and comes standard with 128-bit AES hardware encryption to keep your data secure. Using the SanDisk SecureAccess software, a user can protect access to private files with password protection and encryption. The software creates a file vault (protected folder) on the USB drive, creating a secure storage location for the user to place and keep all sensitive and confidential data. This flash drive is also fast, featuring read speeds up to 80 Mbps.

The SanDisk SecureAccess software is compatible with the Windows 8 and Mac OS X v.10.5+ operating systems, although Mac users will have to download the supporting software from the App Store.

The SanDisk Ultra USB flash drives can be purchased online at **www.sandisk.com** for between $35 and $110, depending on the storage capacity, and all come with a five-year limited warranty. Some of the other online retailers that Sandisk may refer you to to purchase its products may have lower retail pricing—so check carefully.

For those users who require top-of-the-line security, look no further than the 4 GB Personal S250 Secure Drive from IronKey, which also comes in 2, 8, 16, and 32 GB versions. The D250 model does come in a 64 GB version, but we prefer the more robust S250 model. A comparison of the two models is provided in Figure 4.1, from IronKey's website:

As outlined in Figure 4.1, the main difference between the two models is the speed with which data can be read or written to and from the device.

This USB device is designed for the needs of sensitive military, government, and enterprise networks and includes AES hardware encryption that has been validated to meet government Federal Information Processing Standard (FIPS) requirements, specifically FIPS 140-2 Level 3. The security features require no software or drivers to enforce, with all the security being handled by the device hardware, and the features are always on.

IRONKEY S250 VERSUS D250 HARDWARE COMPARISON

FEATURES	S250	D250
Capacity	2GB, 4GB, 8GB, 16GB, 32GB	2GB, 4GB, 8GB, 16GB, 32GB, 64GB
Speed	Up to 31MB/s read Up to 24MB/s write	Up to 29MB/s read Up to 13MB/s write
Dimensions	75mm X 19mm X 9mm	75mm X 19mm X 9mm
Weight	0.9 oz (25 grams)	.9 oz (25 grams)
Waterproof	MIL-STD-810F	MIL-STD-810F
Operating Temperature	0°C, +70°C	0°C, +70°C
Storage Temperature	-40°C, +85° C	-40°C, +85°C
Durability	Ruggedized	Ruggedized
Operating System Encryption Compatibility	Windows 7 Windows Vista Windows XP SP2+ Macintosh OS X 10.5+ Linux 2.6+	Windows 7 Windows Vista Windows XP SP2+ Macintosh OS X 10.5+ Linux 2.6+
Hardware Encryption	Data: AES Cipher-Block Chaining mode Encryption Keys: 256-bit Hardware DRNG PKI: 2048-bit RSA Hashing: 256-bit SHA FIPS Validations: 140-2 Level 3	Data: AES Cipher-Block Chaining mode Encryption Keys: 256-bit Hardware DRNG PKI: 2048-bit RSA Hashing: 256-bit SHA FIPS Validations: 140-2 Level 3
Hardware Interface	USB 2.0 high speed Section 508 Compliant	USB 2.0 high speed Section 508 Compliant

Figure 4.1 IronKey Secure Drive Comparison

The device requires that a user authenticate with a password before encryption keys are enabled and data can be accessed. This device is even waterproof! As they tend to be inadvertently placed in washing machines while in the pocket of your pants, this is an excellent feature, though we've not yet put it to the test.

This device has a self-destruct mechanism (think *Mission: Impossible*) that will wipe (i.e., permanenetly and irretrievably remove) the data contents if a user or thief tries to break into the IronKey and enters 10 incorrect passwords. The Password Manager and Password Generator applications are also included. The Password Generator application will generate very secure passwords of whatever length and complexity you desire. The Password Manager securely stores your passwords on the IronKey along with the associated web address. Merely insert your IronKey device in your computer and go to a website that requires a user ID and password. The IronKey will prompt you to save the credentials if it is the first time the IronKey has "seen" the website. If the logon credentials are already stored on the IronKey, a dialog box will be presented to confirm that the ID and password should be retrieved from the secure Password Manager application. Make sure you back up your password "vault" to the IronKey website in case your IronKey is lost or damaged. Unfortunately, the current version of the Identity Manager (password vault) does not work with the latest versions of Firefox or Internet Explorer. An update is being worked on, but was not available as we went to publication.

The password information is backed up to IronKey in a secure encrypted fashion. If you ever lose your IronKey device, just retrieve your password information from the IronKey website. The device even comes preloaded with a portable version of Firefox, which, when launched and used with the provided Secure Sessions Service, encrypts and keeps all of your Internet traffic private and secure. The IronKey Personal S250 Secure Drive can be purchased online from IronKey's website (**www.ironkey.com**) for from $93 to $510, depending on the storage capacity.

Speakers and Headphones

Lawyers (and their staff) often tell us that the most important peripheral device they need for their computer is a pair of speakers. They like to be able to listen to music while they work and are adamant about fidelity. Without breaking the bank, reasonable-quality desktop speakers can be purchased to provide the user with a clear, true sound. Logitech, a leading provider of speaker systems for computers, makes the LS21 speakers. They offer 2.1 stereo sound with a subwoofer, providing enhanced bass, and the speakers come in a slim, stylish profile. These speakers offer quality audio at a reasonable price. The speakers have a stereo headphone jack, an auxiliary input where you can connect your iPod or MP3 player and integrated controls located on a wired remote. They even include a cable-management system to help reduce the clutter of wires. The Logitech LS21 speakers can be purchased online for around $30 from **www.logitech.com**.

If you purchase one of the recommended Dell flat-panel monitors, consider adding a sound bar. The sound bar clips onto the bottom edge of the Dell flat panel and gets its power from the monitor itself. It provides a clean installation and doesn't take up any additional desk space. The model of the sound bar will vary depending on the Dell monitor that you wish to attach the speakers to, so be sure to check out Dell's website to ensure that you select the appropriate model.

Be careful of speaker "wars" in the office as people battle for the loudest music. Consider headphones to provide a quieter office environment.

If you use a laptop, desktop computer system, or a smartphone that supports Bluetooth and wish to keep your music to yourself, a number of wireless headphone options are available. Jabra makes the Revo Wireless headphones, solidly built with a lightweight aluminum frame and shatterproof headband. The headphones are very comfortable with a padded headband and memory foam ear cups. The device includes a rechargeable battery that lasts up to twelve hours on a single charge, provides up to 240 hours of standby time, and weighs only 8.47 ounces. This device only takes three or fewer hours to fully charge. The wireless device supports Bluetooth 3.0, including Audio/Video Remote Control Profile (AVRCP), which allows you to control your music from this device when it's streaming from your phone. This headset can be purchased online or from your local electronics retailer starting at $199.

CHAPTER FIVE

Printers

EVEN IN THE ERA of the "paperless" office, most law firms still print a lot of documents on a daily basis, probably more than any other type of business. To say that the practice of law tends to be less than green is a massive understatement—at least most firms have implemented a recycling program. Nonetheless, it is certainly critical to have a good, reliable printer to ensure that your firm is printing quality documents in the shortest amount of time. Below, we discuss and recommend printers for stand-alone systems, network systems, and multifunctional printers/copiers.

Stand-Alone Printers

The most basic type of printer is the stand-alone printer. This type of printer connects directly to a computer and is not placed on the network. It only has to be capable of handling a single user's print jobs. Even in environments where networked printers are used and recommended, there can be valid reasons to have stand-alone printers—perhaps so the bookkeeper can keep financial records from inadvertently being picked up by someone else. Senior partners may feel their information is so confidential that they want a printer in their office (though their staff often mutters that they are just too lazy to walk down the hall). Many makes and models of stand-alone printers are available to choose from, and each has different performance specifications, features, and available fonts.

The question about whether to use an ink-jet printer is dead. No more ink-jet. We highly recommend going with a laser printer. Ink-jet printers typically result in a higher cost of ownership over the long haul, with ink cartridges printing at a higher cost per page than the average laser printer. There are even studies that show a cost of $3,000–$5,000 per gallon for name-brand ink cartridges. Human blood is cheaper. Laser is better quality and more economical—case closed.

A stand-alone printer can be shared through enabling File and Print Sharing on your local computer, but we strongly counsel against this practice. It creates a host of security vulnerabilities that could compromise not only your system, but your entire network, and it causes a lot of management and configuration headaches for the IT administrator.

When discussing printers with our clients, we are frequently asked, "Should I purchase a color or a black-and-white laser printer?" You will pay a slight premium for a color laser printer, and in most instances it is not worth the cost when purchasing a stand-alone printer. It is usually more cost-effective to purchase a color laser printer to be placed on the local computer network and shared so that more than one user can print to it.

The Hewlett Packard (HP) LaserJet Pro P1606dn black-and-white laser printer is the perfect solution for the stand-alone or network (up to five users) printer. The printer has a built-in Ethernet connection for network connectivity and prints in duplex (two-sided) mode by default. This printer prints as many as 26 pages per minute, comes standard with a paper input capacity of 250 sheets, and has a recommended monthly volume of up to 2,000 pages but can support a monthly duty cycle of up to 8,000 pages if needed. The printer has a first-page-out speed of 7 seconds and supports all the common page types, such as letter, legal, executive, and envelopes. This printer comes standard with 32 MB of memory and connects to your computer using the USB interface. It should be noted that the printer doesn't come with a USB cable, which will have to be purchased separately. For mobile users, this printer is compatible with Apple's AirPrint service, which allows users to print to the device from their iPad, iPhone, or iPod touch.

This black-and-white printer was designed for quick business printing and offers a cost-effective solution for personal printing. The printer is both Mac and Windows compatible, including Windows 7 and Windows 8. It also comes standard with a one-year limited warranty. The HP LaserJet Pro P1606dn printer can be purchased online for around $209.99 (before discounts) from **www.hp.com**. At the time of writing, this printer was discounted to a cost of $149.99 on HP's webstore.

If you're looking for tips on how to reduce the frequency with which you have to purchase replacement laser cartridges, there are a few things you can do. First, look into software that automatically removes wasted pages from printing jobs, especially common when printing out content from websites using your Internet browser. This printer comes with software called HP Smart Web Printing that you can install on your local computer, which reduces the wasted pages and space when printing from websites.

Another great tip is to change the print quality to "Draft" if the document is just going to be discarded shortly after printing and not something official that you're going to submit to court. This alone can save you lots of toner.

Networked Printers

Networked printers are used to provide a printing resource to multiple users. Networked printers are generally installed in a central location and then shared throughout the local network. The administration and security of these printers can be integrated into your network's security infrastructure, such as through Windows Active Directory for a Windows-based network, and networking a printer is much more secure than sharing it through the File and Print Sharing service. Installation in a central location simplifies the management, administration, and security of these devices. Network printers can be shared with the various computers and users that make up your network with very little overhead and effort. Many types of networked printers are available, and depending on your need—low volume, high volume, color—your options will vary. A popular request from many law offices is to have multiple trays for the printer. The capability to have multiple paper types loaded is usually available in the mid-range to higher-end printer models.

Low-Volume Network Printers

Low-volume network printers are designed for workgroups of users having a small to moderate print volume, as high as 5,000 pages per month. These printers are moderately priced and are primarily used to segment printing within offices based on user group or physical location. Network printers have more robust hardware than stand-alone printers to handle multiple jobs from different users at the same time.

The HP LaserJet Pro 400 Printer M401dw black-and-white network-based laser printer is great for a small law firm because it provides users with a highly reliable, cost-effective printer that is capable of handling the expected volume produced by an average small firm. The HP LaserJet Pro 400 Printer M401dw prints as many as 35 pages per minute and has a recommended monthly print volume of up to 3,000 pages. It comes standard with an input capacity of 300 sheets and 256 MB of memory, and it handles all paper sizes. This printer has a first-page-out speed of 8 seconds. As an added feature, the printer allows for automatic duplexing for printing double-sided documents. The printer has an embedded gigabit Ethernet network adapter to attach the printer to your local network and a built-in Wi-Fi 802.11 b/g/n adapter for wireless connectivity. This printer also supports Apple's AirPrint service, allowing users to print directly from their iPad, iPhone, or iPod Touch device. For additional security, this printer can prevent unauthorized access with management features including 802.1x authentication and password protection. Unlike some of the other HP printers, this model does come with a USB cable.

The memory of this printer can be upgraded if desired, and the printer's drivers are compatible with both Mac and Windows-based systems, including Windows 7 and Windows 8. The printer comes with a standard one-year warranty and includes a CD-ROM with the drivers and software necessary to configure the device. The HP LaserJet Pro 400 Printer M401dw black-and-white laser printer can be purchased online for around $400 (before any discounts) from **www.hp.com**. At the time of writing, this printer was discounted to a cost of $349.99 on HP's webstore.

High-Volume Network Printers
High-volume network printers are designed for businesses that need the capacity to print a large volume of pages on a monthly basis, and they are usually considered when your firm needs a printer that can produce more than 5,000 pages per month. These devices contain hardware that can handle the volume load and are built to print constantly.

The HP LaserJet Enterprise M4555h Multifunction Printer is ideal for firms that print large volumes of documents on a monthly basis. This printer has a recommended monthly printing volume of 5,000 to 20,000 pages and prints up to 55 pages per minute. The printer comes with a standard input capacity of 1,150 sheets, 3 paper trays, 1280 MB of memory, and an embedded gigabit Ethernet network adapter to attach the printer to your local network. This printer handles all paper sizes and can easily be upgraded with additional paper trays or envelope feeders for a maximum capacity of 2,100 sheets. The network connectivity can be upgraded to support wireless networks, a must-have option for those firms that use a wireless infrastructure for their local network. It should be noted that the printer doesn't come with a USB or network cable, which will have to be purchased separately if you want to connect the printer directly to a computer.

For future compatibility, this printer is IPv6-ready. For added security, this printer supports network authentication (LDAP, SMTP) that lets administrators control device access and secure print jobs through user authentication.

The printer comes with a one-year, next-business-day onsite warranty. It is compatible with both Mac and Windows-based networks, including Windows 8. A CD-ROM that contains both printer driver files and software necessary to manage and configure the device is included; in addition, the necessary software can be downloaded from HP's website. The HP LaserJet Enterprise M4555f Multifunction Printer can be purchased online for around $3,499.99 from one of HP's resellers, and it comes with a standard one-year warranty. At this cost, you may want to investigate using your digital copier as a printer, depending on your anticipated monthly print volume and cost per page.

Color Network Printers
Color network printers are essential for any law firm or small business that wants to print a significant volume of documents in color. If the color printer is networked, multiple users can have access to the shared resource, which is far more cost-effective than giving everyone a color printer. HP is still the leading manufacturer of color printers in terms of value, selection, overall reliability, and performance. Its color LaserJet printers are reasonably priced and produce high-quality color documents.

For a small business or law firm, the HP Color LaserJet CP4025dn printer is perfect for everyday color printing. This printer prints up to 35 pages per minute for both black-and-white and color and has a recommended monthly volume of 2,000 to 7,500 pages. Its first-page-out speed of less than 9.5 seconds means that the color print job starts almost as soon as it has been sent to the printer. The standard input capacity is 600 sheets, and the printer supports all paper sizes and can be upgraded with an envelope feeder.

The printer comes standard with 512 MB of memory and an embedded gigabit Ethernet network adapter that enables the printer to connect to your local network. If necessary, the memory can be upgraded to a maximum of 1 GB. The printer's drivers support both Mac and Windows-based systems, including Vista and Windows 7, and the printer can be networked for easy accessibility. Windows 8 and Windows 8.1 drivers are also available for download from the HP website. The printer comes with a one-year onsite limited warranty.

The HP Color LaserJet CP4025dn printer can be purchased online for around $1,300 (before discounts) from one of HP's resellers. It should be noted that the printer doesn't come with a USB or network cable, which will have to be purchased separately. That shouldn't be a problem since you will probably connect this printer to a network and not directly to a computer.

The largest operational cost for a color laser printer is the consumables. Color cartridges are not cheap, and color prints can be very expensive. One configuration point to make on all computers networked to your color printers: Change the default color setting to black. This will save on the printing and subsequent waste of color cartridges for unnecessary color copies.

Digital copier manufacturers are beginning to take over the task of color printing. Investigate using a color copier for your color print needs versus a stand-alone color printer, or if you have a large-scale color print job, you may want to consider the costs of outsourcing the project to your local copier store. You might be surprised at the amount of money you could save.

Typically, lawyers lease their copiers. As you work with your copier lessor, which normally provides your supplies, make sure you negotiate a low cost per color copy and only pay for the number of pages that you print. Don't pay for the consumables (e.g., toner cartridges) or maintenance, as these should be included as part of the per-page cost.

Multifunctional Printers/Copiers

Don't you wish there was a single device that you could install on your local network that could do everything your office needs—printing, faxing, scanning, and copying? Happily for lawyers, such devices are becoming a standard fixture today. Multifunctional printers (MFPs) offer the capability to print, scan, copy, and fax from the same device, combining the functions of multiple devices into just one and eliminating the need to purchase them separately. In the long run, purchasing or leasing an MFP can save you the time and money often expended to upgrade and service multiple devices.

MFPs are very expensive and are generally leased because of the high cost to purchase. When looking at whether to buy or lease MFPs, keep some functionality questions in mind:

- Do you want the ability to print in color and black-and-white?
- Do you need duplex printing?
- Do you want to scan documents to your hard drive, user box, or e-mail?
- Do you want incoming faxes to be sent to e-mail as an image file or just printed?
- Do you want to be able to link the use of the MFP to the firm's billing program?
- What printing capacity do you need?
- Do you need any finishing capabilities (e.g., stapling, folding, three-hole punch, etc.)?
- Do you need to implement any security on the unit, and if so, what?
- At the end of your lease, can the hard drive be securely wiped or erased?

The answers to these questions will give your vendors enough detail to provide you with the MFP device that best meets the firm's needs. Your digital copier may already have some of these features installed but not configured. Check with your vendor to see what capabilities your current copier has. In our office, we have a Konica Minolta Bizhub C224e MFP device. It allows us to print both in color and in black-and-white at speeds up to 22 pages per minute; scan to hard drive, user box, e-mail, or FTP; and to fax documents, although we do not use that feature. We are able to download our scanned documents from a built-in secure internal website as JPG, PDF, XPS, or TIFF files, as well as scan to an internal e-mail address—which we constantly use. This device has a 3,650 sheet max capacity with dual scanning speeds up to 160 pages per minute.

The Bizhub has advanced security features such as job erase, hard drive sanitizing and lock, user authentication and account tracking, IP address filtering, and secure print and scan encryption. Plus, there are options for biometric and HID proximity card authentication, should we ever need these advanced security features. Needless to say, the Bizhub provides us with a secure MFP option. We are huge fans—as this is our second model of one of these devices.

CHAPTER SIX

Scanners

ALMOST AS COMMON AS printers, scanners have become a necessary piece of equipment in most offices, as more paper documents are being scanned and stored electronically. The drive to a paperless office is still very much under way. The setup and operation of scanners has become simple to the point where even the most novice computer user can do it. Many of the tasks that once had to be performed manually are now automated, and in most cases the hookup entails connecting a single wire.

Not often do we have to insert a CD to install software anymore, now that preloaded drivers are prevalent. Network scanners, however, are a little more complex to set up and configuring them may require the assistance of your IT staff or your IT consultant.

Most desktop scanners communicate with the computer through the USB interface and come with a variety of software to assist in the scanning and file-conversion process. Some models come standard with optical character recognition (OCR) software that will read the scanned image and produce a document that is editable and searchable. Fujitsu is a manufacturer of home- and business-grade scanners that have been constantly rated the best models for businesses. In the following sections, we make recommendations for both low-volume and high-volume scanners from Fujitsu.

Some law firms may already have scanning capability in their digital copier. As we previously stated, check with your vendor to see if scanning with your copier is a more cost-effective solution than purchasing a stand-alone unit.

Low-Volume Scanner

The Fujitsu ScanSnap iX500 Desktop Scanner is a great value for a solid automatic document feeder (ADF) scanner. This desktop scanner scans up to 25 color pages per minute, has an ADF capacity of 50 sheets, and can handle both legal- and letter-sized paper. The scanner has a maximum scanning resolution of 600 × 600 dpi and connects to the computer via the USB 3.0 interface, which is responsible for the increase in scanning speed. This scanner also comes with a built-in wireless adapter allowing you to scan directly to a computer or mobile device. This scanner is compatible with Microsoft Windows 7 and Windows 8 (32-bit and 64-bit) and Mac OSX v.10.6 or newer. This scanner comes with bundled software that includes Adobe Acrobat X Standard Edition, ScanSnap Organizer v5.0, ABBYY FineReader Express Edition, ABBYY FineReader for ScanSnap 5.0 and CardMinder v5.0.

Adobe Acrobat X Standard software allows you to automatically convert scanned data into searchable PDF files. Some of the automatic features of this device include auto paper-size detection, auto de-skew, and auto blank-page removal. The auto blank-page removal eliminates the need to edit scanned documents because the scanner has the ability to recognize the deleted blank pages. The ABBYY FineReader software allows you to scan documents directly to applications such as Microsoft Word, Excel, and PowerPoint.

A new feature of this scanner is the ability to scan to the cloud. With the free ScanSnap Connect app, users can link their ScanSnap to their iPad, iPhone, or Android mobile device for viewing on the go. Users also have the ability to scan to Evernote, Google Docs, Salesforce, SugarSync, and Sharepoint. Again, as with all cloud services, please use caution and seek the advice of your IT staff when moving client data to the cloud to ensure that your documents are secure.

The scanner comes with a standard one-year limited warranty that can be upgraded to the Advanced Exchange Service program. The Fujitsu ScanSnap iX500 Desktop Scanner can be purchased online from Fujitsu's website (**www.fujitsu.com**) for $495 and comes with a one-year limited warranty. The inclusion of Acrobat Standard makes this a very worthwhile purchase.

High-Volume Scanner

The Fujitsu fi-5530C2 is perfect for legal professionals who need a high-speed scanner on a modest budget and are serious about scanning documents. The built-in automatic document feeder (ADF) holds 100 pages and scans up to 50 pages per minute (100 images) in 200 dpi in color, monochrome, and grayscale. This scanner comes standard with 64 MB of memory, and advanced software tools to allow administrators to centrally manage the scanner more productively and cost effectively.

Using the Fujitsu fi-5530C2 scanner, you can convert any document to Adobe PDF using Adobe Acrobat software, which at the time of the writing of this edition, is no longer included with the purchase of this scanner. Luckily, most lawyers already have access to this software. This scanner can handle a vigorous duty cycle of up to 4,000 documents per day and can handle documents ranging in size from a business card to a legal document without issue. The Ultra SCSI and USB 2.0 interface allows for simplified connectivity to your computer. The scanner is compatible with Microsoft Windows 7 and 8 computer systems. It should be noted that this scanner is not compatible with Macs. The Fujitsu fi-5530C2 scanner can be purchased online through one of Fujitsu's resellers for around $2,500 and comes with a three-month onsite limited warranty.

This amount of money is a lot for a solo or small firm operation to spend, especially on a scanner. We're sure that your digital copier could provide a less expensive solution for your scanning needs, especially if you have a newer unit that will provide a convenient ability to scan to e-mail—which none of these ScanSnap devices do. Consider that before you make a purchasing decision and you might be able to save yourself a lot of money.

CHAPTER SEVEN

Servers

ONE OF THE BIGGEST, most important and most expensive decisions
you will have to make regarding technology for your firm is which server
to purchase. A server is the mother ship of the network, so the purchase
decision should be made very carefully. It is absolutely not the time to be
penny wise and pound foolish. The choice of a server is a business decision—make no mistake about that—and if made with great consideration
and thought, it will allow your business to run efficiently and effectively
from a technology perspective.

Like workstations and laptops, servers come in every make, model, and
flavor. Unlike workstations, however, servers can be very expensive and
can consume a large chunk of your technology budget rather quickly.
Your firm will need to plan carefully when selecting a server—including
discussing future needs and goals—so that the desirable hardware and
software components can be identified. Plan carefully, because you don't
want to have to buy a new server every other year. Generally, the average
life span of a server is four to five years—so start planning (and budgeting)
well in advance!

Solo—File and Printer Sharing
The most simple and basic reason for getting a server is for file and printer
sharing. Centralizing electronic file storage and administration and installation of printers will save you time, money, and headaches when it comes
to maintaining and managing your network. Some servers are designed
specifically for the purpose of sharing files, documents, and printers. These
servers come with the most basic hardware and software and are relatively
inexpensive when compared to the mid-range to higher-end servers.

The Dell PowerEdge T320 server was designed for the small business to provide the most basic file- and printer-sharing capabilities. A listing of the server's hardware and software components, along with some technical specifications, is provided below.

File and Printer Sharing Server

<u>Hardware Component</u>	<u>Recommendation</u>
Model:	Dell PowerEdge T320
Chassis:	Tower
Operating System:	Windows Server 2012 R2, Standard Edition
Processors:	Intel Xeon E5-2430L, 2.00 GHz, 15 MB Cache
Memory:	16 GB RDIMM, 1600 MT/s, Low Volt, Dual Rank
Primary Controller Card:	PERC H310 Integrated RAID Controller
Hard Drive Configuration:	RAID-5
Hard Drives:	Three 600 GB 15K RPM SAS Hard Drives
Network Adapter:	Onboard Broadcom 5720 Dual Port 1 GB
Warranty:	3-Year ProSupport and Next Business Day Onsite Service
Other:	DVD+/-RW Drive

This Dell PowerEdge T320 was customized through Dell's website (**www.dell.com**) and contains an Intel Xeon 2.00 GHz processor with 16 GB of RAM. This server comes with the Windows Server 2012 R2 Standard Edition operating system. CALs (client access licences) are needed for each device or user that accesses the server.

The three SAS (serial-attached SCSI) 600 GB hard drives are configured in a RAID-5 (redundant array of independent disks) hard drive configuration for increased performance and fault tolerance. In a RAID-5 hard drive configuration, if one of the hard drives were to fail, the server would continue to operate until the failed hard drive could be replaced. In most other hard drive configurations, if a server's hard drive were to fail, the server would be inoperable until the disk was repaired or replaced. The RAID-5 configuration offers both fault tolerance with the parity hard drive and better performance than most other RAID or mirrored disk configurations. RAID-5 hard drive configurations are strongly recommended for all law firm servers.

In total, this server has about 1.2 TB of hard drive space available for the storage of electronic data, programs, and other applications. You used to be able to save a little bit of money by reducing the number of hard drives purchased and setting up a RAID-1 hard drive configuration, but since hard drives have come so far down in price, we no longer recommend this as an option. Also, RAID-5 is a more fault tolerant and flexible configuration.

The onboard dual gigabit network adapters will allow clients to connect to the server at gigabit speeds, assuming the rest of your network components (switches, cabling) are gigabit as well.

One of the most important features to consider when purchasing a server is the warranty. In most cases, you will not need both the hardware and software support. At a minimum, you must include a hardware warranty that will cover the hardware and labor cost to replace any of the components that may fail during the server's life cycle. This Dell PowerEdge server comes with a 3-year, next business day onsite parts and labor warranty at an included cost of about $400 when bundled with the server hardware. Having a hardware warranty for your server is critical to protecting your equipment, data, and business. This is no time to be miserly. This Dell PowerEdge T320 server was quoted on Dell's website for approximately $3,400 at the time of this writing.

Small Firm—File and Printer Sharing/Hosting Services

When purchasing a server for your network, you must decide what function the server will have in your day-to-day business operations. In addition to file and printer sharing, it's common for small firms to host their company's e-mail. Although you can also host a website, we recommend that you outsource that to a website hosting provider because of potential security, administration, and resource issues. The added hosting services (e-mail and/or web) will require a server with upgraded hardware to be able to provide the necessary resources for the services to operate reliably.

Previously, our server recommendations included those running Microsoft Small Business Server 2011, which, depending on the edition/add-on (Standard or Premium), included Microsoft Exchange Server and Microsoft SQL Server. As of July 1, 2013, in response to small business market trends and behavior, such as moving in the direction of cloud computing for applications and e-mail, Dell no longer offers this operating system as an option, and it has since been discontinued.

The Dell PowerEdge T620 was designed for small firms or businesses that are looking for a cost-effective solution to hosting their own e-mail or website. The server's hardware and software components, along with some technical specifications, are provided.

File and Printer Sharing/Hosting Services

Hardware Component	Recommendation
Model:	Dell PowerEdge T620
Chassis:	Tower
Operating System:	Windows Server 2012 R2, Standard Edition
Processors:	Dual Intel Xeon E5-2640 2.5 GHz, 15 M Cache, 7.2GT/s QPI
Memory:	32 GB RDIMM, 1600 MT/s, Low Volt, Dual Rank
Primary Controller Card:	PERC H710P Integrated RAID Controller
Hard Drive Configuration:	RAID-5
Hard Drives:	Three 3 TB 7.2K RPM Near-Line SAS 6 Gbps 3.5-Inch Hard Drives
Network Adapter:	Broadcom 5720 Dual Port 1 GB Network Interface Card
Warranty:	3-Year ProSupport and Mission Critical 4HR 7x24 Onsite
Other:	Redundant Power Supply, DVD+/-RW Drive

The Dell PowerEdge T620 listed here was customized through Dell's website. It contains Dual Intel Xeon 2.5 GHz processors with 32 GB of memory. The server specified above was customized in a tower chassis; however, the same model is available in a rack mount chassis at no additional cost. The rack mount chassis is for those firms and small businesses that maintain their servers and networking equipment in a rack. The processors will supply more than enough horsepower to configure the server as an e-mail or web server, and the 32 GB of memory will allow these services to run smoothly and will prevent the server from lagging or becoming bogged down.

The server comes with Windows Server 2012 R2 Standard Edition preinstalled. CALS will need to be purchased for each device and/or user that wishes to connect to the server. Dell offers a 5-pack of device or user CALS bundled with the server purchase for a price of $148.89.

The three 3 TB SAS hard drives are configured in a RAID-5 hard drive configuration and provide about 6 TB of storage space for your firm's applications and data. Again, this PowerEdge server comes with the 3-year ProSupport 4HR 7x24 onsite hardware warranty, which provides 3 years of 4-hour, same-day parts and labor warranty. The Dell PowerEdge T620 server was quoted on Dell's website for approximately $7,673 at the time of this writing.

Don't forget to consider backup software and any additional applications (e.g., antivirus, antispyware, antispam, etc.) when configuring the server, because you might get a better discount from the vendor if they are bundled and purchased with the server hardware.

Small Firm—Database/Applications Server

Your firm's software requirements, current and future, will play a big role in determining what hardware and software components your server will need to adequately support your firm in the coming years. So far, we have discussed the hardware and software specifications for a server used primarily for file and printer sharing and one capable of handling basic hosting services, such as e-mail and a website. When planning to use a server to host a database application, case management software, or e-discovery software, you must look at the minimum requirements for each piece of software and then go above and beyond the specifications that vendors provide. What vendors list should be regarded cautiously as a bare minimum. To run well and reliably, the software almost always requires more horsepower.

The recommended Dell PowerEdge T620 server is capable of handling most database and software applications as long as it's configured with advanced hardware to handle the powerful and robust database applications. The server's hardware and software components are provided below:

Database/Applications Server

Hardware Component	Recommendation
Model:	Dell PowerEdge T620
Chassis:	Tower
Operating System:	Windows Server 2012 R2, Standard Edition
Processors:	Dual Intel Xeon E5-2690 v2 3.0 GHz, 25 M Cache, 8.0GT/s QPI
Memory:	128 GB RDIMM, 1600 MT/s, Low Volt, Quad Rank
Primary Controller Card:	PERC H710P Integrated RAID Controller
Hard Drive Configuration:	RAID-5
Hard Drives:	Three 3 TB 7.2K RPM Near-Line SAS 6 Gbps 3.5-Inch Hard Drives
Network Adapter:	Broadcom 5720 Dual Port 1 GB Network Interface Card
Warranty:	3-Year ProSupport and Mission Critical 4Hr 7x24 Onsite
Other:	Dual, Hot-plug, Redundant Power Supply 1100W, DVD+/-RW Drive

The PowerEdge T620 server was customized through Dell's website and contains Dual Intel Xeon E5-2690 v2 3.0 GHz processors and 128 GB of memory. The processor is much faster than the processor included with the server discussed in the previous section.

This server comes with the Windows Server 2012 R2 Standard Edition operating system with Hyper-V capability for virtualized environments.

The three 3 TB hard drives are configured in a RAID-5 hard disk configuration and provide about 6 TB of storage space for applications and data. If more storage space is needed, this upgrade can be made when the server is configured to meet your needs, especially if you plan to use virtualization (explained in the following section).

The redundant power supply allows the server to stay powered on in the event that one of the power supplies fails. The server comes with dual embedded Broadcom Ethernet adapters, providing connectivity for up to two networks. The PowerEdge server comes with a 3-year ProSupport Mission Critical 4HR 7x24 onsite hardware warranty, which provides 3 years of a 4-hour, same-day parts and labor warranty. The Dell PowerEdge T620 server was quoted on Dell's website for approximately $11,846 at the time of this writing.

Virtual Servers

The large push within the IT industry continues to be toward virtualization bundled with cloud services. Microsoft continues to sell more licenses for virtual machines than it does for physical hardware. This is one trend that isn't going to reverse.

Simply put, virtualization means that a single piece of hardware contains and hosts multiple server or desktop images, otherwise known as machines. Virtualization enables the consolidation of data and applications onto a single physical hardware server. The reduction in hardware saves energy, management, and administration effort and reduces overall hardware and software costs, along with rack space, especially if your firm needs multiple servers.

Virtualization is used to separate hosting services and applications, creating independent machines, which allows for one virtual server to be down for maintenance without affecting the others. For example, if Windows Updates were downloaded onto a virtual server hosting file- and print-sharing services, this virtual server could be rebooted and have the updates applied without having to bring down or affect the entire host system, keeping other virtual servers online and available to users. It also means that you can quickly "spool up" a virtual machine for testing new applications or services without investing in additional hardware. Virtual servers are also very flexible and can be modified on the fly. Resources (e.g., RAM, disk space, processing power, etc.) can be modified while the virtual machine is running. Running short on disk space? No problem. Just go to the management console and add a few hundred giga-bytes to the virtual machine.

Previously, virtualization was implemented due to the costs, expertise, and the large budget required, and was not typically found in a small firm environment; however, this is no longer true. We are recommending that small firms consider virtualization technologies when making server hardware and software purchasing decisions, especially in scenarios where the client is hosting services such as e-mail internally.

Is server virtualization the best choice for your network environment? Probably, but you will need to answer a number of questions before making this determination.

First, what services and applications are running on your network? If your network is running Microsoft Exchange Server, SQL Server, and a case management application, most likely you will need multiple servers to host all of these services and software. Most case management applications now require a separate server to run on. By using virtualization, you can avoid purchase of another physical hardware server by installing the case management software on its own virtual server, as long as your virtual server meets, if not exceeds, the host specifications required by the vendor of the software.

When purchasing a host system (the server hosting the virtual servers), the most critical hardware options to consider are the amount of memory, number and type of processors, and amount of storage space. For each virtual server, 4 GB or more of memory must be allocated for the virtual server to operate. A larger amount of memory will be needed if the virtual server is hosting a database or other memory-hungry service. This does not account for the amount of memory that the host system will require. For example, if you have a host server running 3 virtual servers, you will need a minimum of 16 GB (better if you have 32 GB) of memory installed in the host server to supply the host and all of the virtual servers with enough memory resources to operate. To accommodate the necessary hardware, the host system must be running at least the Windows Server 2012 Standard Edition operating system.

When running virtual servers, you will need to ensure that the host system has enough processing capability to handle the processing load. At a minimum, you will want the system to contain Intel Xeon processors with a processing speed of 2.53 to 3.6 GHz. The optimum solution for stand-alone servers is to use Intel Xeon processors with the same speed range, and in virtualization solutions, you will need to have multiple processors with multiple cores. The Xeon processors that are in the servers recommended previously were designed by Intel for virtualization solutions, providing increased virtualization security, reduced storage and network latencies, and acceleration of fundamental virtualization processes throughout the system. The multicore processors combine two or more cores onto a single integrated circuit, providing multiprocessing capabilities to the chip. Multiprocessing allows the execution of multiple concurrent software processes in a system, which is vital in a virtualization solution.

The amount of storage space required to run all of the virtual servers and the host system will vary from solution to solution. When determining the amount of storage space the systems will require, you need to consider the services and applications that will be hosted. For example, a virtual server hosting Microsoft Exchange Server will require enough disk space to account for the current size and future growth of the Exchange Database stores along with the program files and operating system. If more space is needed at a later time, the amount of storage space allocated to each virtual server can be independently configured and modified in real-time. For ease of configuration and setup, bearing the cost of additional hard drive storage up front makes more sense than waiting to add more hard drives later. Plus, it's always recommended that the host system and virtual servers have available more than enough hard drive space, so problems with low disk space can be avoided. We have clients who have terabytes of disk space available just for their File and Printer Sharing virtual server. As an alternative to purchasing host-based storage, you may want to look into a Storage Area Network (SAN) device that would provide locally attached storage over a dedicated network, usually over Fibre Channel or iSCSI.

Microsoft offers free server virtualization solutions for Windows Server 2008, and Server 2012. For host systems running Windows Server 2008 or 2012, Microsoft has included the Hyper-V virtualization system with the base installation of the operating system, and this role is installed through the Server Roles interface. Hyper-V enables the consolidation of multiple server roles as separate virtual servers running on a single host system, allowing for different operating systems such as Linux,

Windows, and others to run in parallel. For more information regarding Microsoft's virtualization solutions, you can visit Microsoft's website at **http://www.microsoft.com/en-us/server-cloud/solutions/virtualization.aspx**.

Hyper-V was designed with enhanced security features in mind, providing an architecture that is less vulnerable to attack. This software includes a set of management and administration tools that can be used to manage the host and virtual systems' hardware from the same interface. It even allows administrators to migrate live systems from server to server. Windows Server 2012 has an updated version of Microsoft's Hyper-V, which includes such new features as network virtualization, multi-tenancy, storage resource pools, and cloud backup. The new version of Hyper-V also increases the amount of memory and storage and the number of virtual processors that each machine can be allocated. For more information regarding Microsoft's Hyper-V 2012 R2, you can visit Microsoft's TechNet website at **http://technet.microsoft.com/en-us/library/hh833684.aspx**.

Depending on the operating system of the host system, a few Microsoft-based software options are available for server virtualization, and they are fully supported. We have observed that the free Hyper-V implementations may have some issues sharing peripheral devices across the virtual machines. As an example, you may not be able to share the USB ports of the hardware with a virtual machine without some kind of workaround, which means that you can't copy files from a USB flash drive from the host system to the virtual system.

Software licensing will also play a role in determining your firm's ability to move to a virtualization environment. To say the licensing is easy to figure out when it comes to virtualization would be a flat out lie. Microsoft has muddied the waters when it comes to virtualization licensing, because it varies depending on the type of server operating system and the number of processors. Some operating system editions allow you to use the license key on the host and on up to two virtual machines. If you're running a host with Windows Server 2012 Datacenter Edition, you get a feature called Automated Virtual Machine Activation. With this feature, any virtual machine on this host running Windows Server 2012 R2 Datacenter/Standard/Essentials will automatically activate.

There are other alternatives to Microsoft's virtualization solutions, such as VMware's vSphere Hypervisor (ESXi). If you are investigating alternative virtualization solutions, you will need to work with your IT vendor to see what other options might be available. We currently recommend and use the VMware solution instead of Microsoft's Hyper-V solution. VMware has been in the virtualization game a lot longer than Microsoft, and you can share those USB ports with the virtual machines. VMware Tools also offers some other useful and time-saving administration capabilities. The stability of Hyper-V continues to be a concern among several of our clients, although it has improved with the 2012 R2 version of Hyper-V.

What we do know is this: the cost to purchase the hardware and software necessary to implement a virtualization environment for your network will be significantly less than the cost of purchasing multiple physical servers to fill the necessary roles your applications and services require.

Peer-to-Peer

Many small firms use the built-in peer-to-peer network capabilities of their computer systems as an alternative to purchasing a server. A peer-to-peer network, in its simplest form, is two or more computers that are able to communicate with one another to share files and folders, printers, and applications without using a server to accomplish these tasks. Peer-to-peer networks are commonly used in solo or small firm offices with only two or three computers. The computers, located on the same local network and belonging to the same Workgroup (Microsoft's name for a peer-to-peer network), can access shared resources in the Workgroups to which they are joined. Unless a computer is joined to a domain, it belongs to a Workgroup. By default, on Windows XP computers, the Workgroup name is MSHOME, and in older versions of Windows the default Workgroup is WORKGROUP. Just to complicate matters, Microsoft has changed the default Workgroup name in Windows 7 and 8 back to the original WORKGROUP.

Peer-to-peer networks may sound like a good solution for small firms that have only a few computers, but this type of network has some significant disadvantages compared to purchasing a server. First, when networking computers together, you are going to experience a slowdown and inconsistency in your system's performance. Workstations are not capable of handling concurrent access to their files by other computers. When this occurs, the system's resources are severely taxed, causing disruption to the users. Think of this as a tug-of-war for data. Your computer is trying to use data at the same time that someone else needs it. Because of the inconsistency and unreliability of the peer-to-peer network, corruption of shared files, such as case management and billing systems, occurs frequently. Since computers in a peer-to-peer network can be running different operating systems, software incompatibilities between the systems can occur. Management of user accounts, along with implementing the proper security controls to protect sensitive and confidential data, becomes a nightmare—and even more difficult should a breach occur that requires investigation.

The decentralization of critical firm data can lead to unnecessarily complex data backup scenarios, often resulting in important data not being backed up or protected. On top of all the issues above, the need to manage and administer multiple copies of the same software, such as antivirus protection on each individual computer, becomes needlessly tiresome. Software that is centrally managed is much more cost-effective to purchase and maintain, as opposed to managing each computer's software suites independently. Just figure in the added administration costs that your firm will pay its IT provider; this will more than cover the cost of a server—and then some!

There is an inaccurate perception that peer-to-peer networks save money and cost less than client/server networks. However, in the end, this is never the case. Yes, purchasing a server—even a lower-end unit—might seem expensive at first, but the costs of managing and maintaining a peer-to-peer network will always be higher than the costs you would have incurred if you had implemented a server/client network in the first place. The software licensing costs for peer-to-peer networks can be higher because you are purchasing single licenses. Software that is administered and maintained on independent computers will take more time than if it were centrally managed from a server. Technical support and consulting costs will be much higher in a peer-to-peer environment, a fact that is usually not considered when making the initial decision to purchase and use a peer-to-peer network. For most small network environments, even those involving as few as two computers, purchasing a server to centralize applications and data can save time and money—and the number of headaches you will have to endure—in the long run.

CHAPTER EIGHT

Server Operating Systems

CHOOSING THE HARDWARE COMPONENTS is just one step in selecting the right server for your business. The next step is determining what operating system and software will best meet the current and future needs of the firm. There are many variations of server operating systems currently available for both Windows and Mac servers, and they are described in detail below.

Microsoft Windows Server 2003—Any Edition

As of July 13, 2010, Microsoft Windows 2003 Server went into Extended Support and will continue to offer security updates until July 2015. This product is no longer available from Dell as an option when configuring a server on its website and shouldn't be considered when configuring a new system. We mention it here to point out the end-of-life date. If you are currently running this version of the server software, begin making plans to replace it before July 2015.

Microsoft Windows Server 2008 R2

Microsoft Windows Server 2008 R2 is the successor to Windows Server 2003. It was officially launched in late February 2008 and built from the same code base as Windows Vista, however, without all the problems that Vista had.

This operating system includes a lot of new features and enhancements, such as native support for IPv6, new security features such as BitLocker, and an improved Windows Firewall with a more secure default configuration. Also, the manner in which this operating system handles processors and memory is different from previous versions. Processors and memory are now treated as plug-and-play devices, meaning they are "hot-swap-pable." They can now be removed and replaced without shutting down the server, although sticking your hands into a hot, running server is probably not a very bright idea.

Windows Server 2008 includes expanded Active Directory functionality and a major upgrade to Terminal Services. Terminal Services now supports Remote Desktop Protocol 8.0, which provides the ability to share a single application over a Remote Desktop connection rather than the entire desktop, as was the case in previous versions. It also provides additional support for multiple monitors and stronger encryption algorithms for keeping data traffic secure.

In previous versions of the Windows operating system, if corruption or errors were found on a new technology file system (NTFS) volume, the volume would have to be dismounted and taken offline for the errors to be corrected. Windows Server 2008 supports a self-healing NTFS format that can detect and fix errors while online without having to bring down the entire system. Microsoft Windows Server 2008 is offered in both 32- and 64-bit versions.

Windows Server 2008, like previous versions, is offered in the following editions:

- Standard Edition
- Enterprise Edition
- Datacenter Edition
- HPC Server
- Web Server
- Storage Server
- Small Business Server
- Essential Business Server

Most of the editions listed above would not be considered when purchasing a server solution for a small business or law firm and will not be discussed in more detail in this book. However, the Standard, Enterprise, and Small Business Server editions are described below.

In February 2011, Microsoft released Service Pack 1 for Windows Server 2008 R2, which introduced two new features and addressed a number of security issues in this version of the operating system. The two new features, RemoteFX and Dynamic Memory, add support for 3-D graphics within a Hyper-V-based virtual machine, as well as dynamic memory allocation based on the resources the virtual machine requires at any given time. It is recommended that if you're running Windows Server 2008, you download and install the latest Service Pack from Windows Updates as soon as possible.

Microsoft Windows Small Business Server 2008 Standard and Premium Editions

Windows Small Business Server (SBS) 2008 is based on Windows Server 2008 and includes Microsoft Exchange Server 2007 Standard Edition, Windows SharePoint Services 3.0, and trial subscriptions for Microsoft's new security products, such as Forefront Security for Exchange.

The SBS 2008 operating system was officially launched on November 12, 2008. Like previous editions of SBS, the 2008 version is offered in both Standard and Premium editions. The Standard Edition is regarded as a single server solution for small businesses, your all-in-one operating system. In one server, you get file and printer sharing, e-mail, web hosting, and the ability to set up a domain for up to seventy-five users and/or devices. The Premium Edition contains all of the features and software that Standard Edition has, plus a license for the Microsoft SQL Server 2008 Standard Edition. The Premium Edition requires two separate servers, one for Windows Server 2008 with Exchange and the other solely for SQL Server. This requirement is going to be a problem for small firms on a tight budget, but it may be more affordable if used in a virtualized environment.

Windows SBS 2008 is offered only in a 64-bit version due to the requirements of Microsoft Exchange Server 2007, whose production version is 64-bit. This distinction is important when considering your hardware purchase. Make sure you have 64-bit hardware if you are considering using these new server operating systems.

On a more positive note, Microsoft has finally changed the way CALs are purchased for SBS. In earlier editions, CALs could be purchased only in groups of five, ten, or twenty licenses, but not anymore. CALs for SBS 2008 can now be purchased individually.

At the time of this writing, Dell has discontinued the option of configuring servers with the Microsoft Windows Small Business Server option, so we recommend using the Windows Server 2012 Standard Edition option at this time or purchasing the operating system from another supplier.

Windows Server 2008 Standard Edition

The Windows Server 2008 Standard Edition was designed to increase the reliability of your server infrastructure while simultaneously saving time and reducing costs when it comes to server maintenance.

Standard Edition comes with enhanced security features to help protect your data and network and includes powerful tools that give you greater network control. Windows Server 2008 Standard Edition comes with IIS 7.5, a powerful web hosting and services platform. The operating system also includes Windows Server Hyper-V—virtualization software designed to support machine virtualization—and an upgraded version of Terminal Services that supports Remote Desktop Protocol 8.0.

In terms of security, Standard Edition includes tools to improve auditing and secure startup, and it enables disk encryption using BitLocker. Standard Edition supports up to 32 GB of memory, 4 multicore processors, and up to 250 concurrent Terminal Service connections.

Windows Server 2008 Enterprise Edition

Microsoft Windows Server 2008 Enterprise Edition, like its predecessor, is an operating system that is aimed at medium to large-sized businesses looking for a server capable of handling enterprise-level services. Microsoft Server 2008 Enterprise Edition provides mission-critical applications through such features as failover clustering, fault-tolerant memory synchronization, and cross-file replication. This edition also features the latest advancements in security and is extremely scalable to support mission-critical applications.

This operating system is recommended for servers that will be hosting database applications, case management applications, or other software that requires more processing power and memory addressing than the Standard and SBS operating systems can support.

Microsoft Small Business Server 2011 Standard and Essentials

Microsoft Small Business Server 2011 (SBS 2011) is the successor to SBS 2008 and is offered in two versions: Standard and Essentials. A separate SBS Premium add-on is available for small firms that require SQL Server.

The Standard Edition is designed for small businesses and supports up to seventy-five users and/or devices. Like the previous SBS versions, this edition provides a single server solution for small businesses that includes e-mail, remote access, and file and printer sharing. This edition includes both Microsoft Exchange Server 2010 and SharePoint Foundation Server 2010.

The Essentials Edition is designed for small businesses and supports up to twenty-five users and/or devices. This edition is integrated with Microsoft's cloud services and doesn't require the end-user to purchase any CALs. This edition, unlike the Standard Edition, does not include Microsoft Exchange Server or SharePoint Foundation Server 2010.

For those small businesses that need to deploy additional servers on their network to run SQL Server 2008 R2 Standard, the Premium Add-on license is the component that they'll need to purchase. Additional server and SQL CALs are required with this component and will add cost to the purchase, depending on the number of users and computers that need to access this system.

At the time of this writing, Dell has discontinued the option of configuring servers with the Microsoft Windows Small Business Server option, so we recommend using the Windows Server 2012 Standard Edition option at this time or purchasing the operating system from another supplier.

Microsoft Windows Server 2012

In September 2012, Microsoft released this version of its operating system software, to coincide with the release of Windows 8. Server 2012 is offered in four editions, only three of which (Essentials, Standard, and Datacenter) would be considered when purchasing a server for a small business.

Server 2012 includes a number of new and enhanced features that IT administrators will love including:

- ♦ A newly redesigned user interface with a focus on easing server management tasks, including the administration of multiple servers from within the same window
- ♦ An updated version of Windows PowerShell with over 2,300 commands, compared to about 200 in Windows Server 2008
- ♦ A new version of Windows Task Manager
- ♦ IP Address Management (IPAM) role for discovering, monitoring, auditing, and managing IP address space used on the local network
- ♦ An updated version of Windows Active Directory, including simplified upgrading of the Domain Functional Level to Server 2012, a new graphical user interface (GUI), the ability to set multiple password policies within the same domain, and the ability to safely clone virtualized domain controllers
- ♦ An updated version of Hyper-V, which includes such new features as network virtualization, multi-tenancy, storage resource pools, cloud backup, support for an increased number of virtual processors, greater storage capacity, and more memory

- A new version of Internet Information Services (IIS) (version 8.0) used to host websites
- A new file system, Resilient File System (ReFS), that is intended for file servers and improves the features of NTFS

Microsoft Server 2012 R2

Windows Server 2012 R2 is the latest version of Windows Server, released in October 2013—it should be the operating system of choice when configuring a new server. This edition, like Windows Server 2012, was released in four editions: Foundation, Essentials, Standard, and Datacenter.

Some of the changes from Windows Server 2012 that were introduced in Windows Server 2012 R2 include:

- Automated tiering of frequently accessed files on the fastest physical media
- De-duplication for Virtual Hard Drives
- New version of Windows PowerShell (v4)
- Integrated Office 365 support
- Return of the Windows Start Button
- UEFI-based virtual machines
- Boot from SCSI device option
- Faster VM deployment (50 percent increase in speed reported)

We are currently running this operating system on some of our servers and include this operating system when configuring new servers for our clients. It has our stamp of approval at this time.

X64 Operating Systems

Until about seven years ago, 32-bit processors dominated the commercial marketplace, and 64-bit processors were found only in supercomputers or very high-end and expensive servers. Now, however, 64-bit processors are standard rather than an option when configuring a server or a desktop computer prior to purchase. The 64-bit operating systems have been developed to run on these processors and offer many advantages over their 32-bit counterparts. In fact, the newer versions of Microsoft's server operating systems are offered only in 64-bit versions.

First, these systems process more data per clock cycle, and second, they offer direct access to more virtual and physical memory than 32-bit systems. These advantages provide for more scalable, higher performing computing solutions, which is a requirement when running a virtualized environment. There are far fewer device driver issues with X64 operating systems now than when 64-bit systems first appeared on the market; however, it's always important to make sure everything is compatible before migrating from a 32-bit environment to a 64-bit environment.

The current versions of Windows desktop-based operating systems and server-based operating systems are all offered in 64-bit versions, and with most editions, that is the only option.

Mac OS X Server 10.7 (Lion)

Apple released Mac OS X Server 10.7, code-named Lion, in 2011.

This version of Mac OS X Server includes an application called the Server app, which is a simplified configuration process for setting up and administering the most critical functions of the server, including file sharing, e-mail, contacts, backups, and remote access, to name a few. The software also includes Apple's equivalent of Microsoft's Active Directory and a new feature that provides wireless file sharing for iPad devices that allows access to documents on the server.

Lion Server also includes updated versions of the iCal Server 3, Wiki Server 3, Mail Server 3, and Xsan software. This software requires a base purchase of OS X Lion from the Mac App Store and is actually purchased as an add-on or a bundled group of apps sold as Mac OS X Lion Server. While this edition can be purchased and downloaded from the Mac App Store, we recommend that if you upgrade, you upgrade to the latest operating system, Mac OS X Server 10.9.

Mac OS X Server 10.8 (Mountain Lion)

With the release of the Mountain Lion desktop software, Apple released its server counterpart. Mac OS X Server 10.8, nicknamed Mountain Lion, has several features that should appeal to small businesses and enterprises alike. This product, now an add-on from the Mac App Store, has new and enhanced features, including:

- Advanced administration through the Server app
- Profile Manager that provides one-stop administration of all Apple devices within an organization, including both Mac and iOS devices

- The ability for iOS users to self-enroll their devices for system management through an internal web portal
- Revamped wiki service, providing collaboration and document and project management capabilities
- Renaming of various services to match their Mountain Lion desktop equivalents, e.g., iChat Server is now Messages Server, iCal Server is Calendar Server
- iPad/iWork integration
- Push notifications
- Active Directory integration

While this edition can be purchased and downloaded from the Mac App Store, we recommend that if you upgrade, you upgrade to the latest operating system, Mac OS X Server 10.9.

Mac OS X Server 10.9 (Mavericks)

Mac OS X Server 10.9, nicknamed Mavericks, was released in the fall of 2013 as a downloadable package from the Mac App Store, just like Mountain Lion was. This Server app costs only $19.99 for the upgrade; however, you should upgrade to the latest Mac OS X server software, Yosemite, if your current hardware meets the necessary requirements.

One of the new features in the Mavericks operating system is a new XCode Server used in iOS development—Caching Server 2, which speeds up the download and delivery of software through the App Store, Mac App Store, and iTunes Store so that copies can be downloaded faster to computers and iOS devices from the local cached resource. Some of the additional new features include Profile Manager—simplifying the deployment and configuration of new Mac computers and iOS devices; File Sharing—using SMB2, sharing files and folders between Macs, PCs, or iPads is significantly faster and easier to set up; Time Machine Backups—the server can act as a designated Time Machine Backup location for all the Mac computers on the network.

Mac OS X Server 10.10 (Yosemite)

Mac OS X Server 10.10, nicknamed Yosemite, was released in October of 2014 as a downloadable package from the Mac App Store, just like the previous versions of the Server software have been. This Server app costs only $19.99 for the upgrade and should be the server operating system of choice at this point.

Some of the new features include an easier than ever ability to share data and folders between Mac, iPad and PCs, using the new superfast protocol for sharing files in OS X Server, SMB3. This new protocol helps protect against data tampering and eavesdropping by encrypting and signing data while in transmission, adding another layer of security protection to your server.

The new Profile Manager simplifies deploying, configuring and managing Mac computers and iOS devices, including user accounts, and allows Administrators the ability to perform push installs of OS X enterprise apps and iOS media assets including PDF, ePub and iBooks Author files.

The Caching Server automatically speeds up the downloads and delivery of software updates through the App Store, Mac App Store, iTunes Store, iTunes U and iBooks Store, to users on the network whose apps need updating.

Linux-Based Operating Systems

Linux-based operating systems are similar to Unix-based operating systems and are built on an open-source kernel packaged with system utilities, software, and libraries. The underlying source code of the operating system can be freely modified, used, and redistributed, and it is supported by a community of programmers and volunteers.

Linux is now packaged for different uses, primarily servers, which contain modified kernels along with a variety of software packages tailored to different requirements. Some of the commercially available distributions that are backed by corporations are Fedora (Red Hat), SUSE Linux (Novell), Ubuntu (Canonical Ltd.), and Mandriva Linux. Each of these distributions has versions specifically designed and programmed to run on server-based hardware to provide management, web and e-mail hosting services, and file and printer sharing, along with other services and functionality that are available in both Mac and Windows-based server operating systems. There are also desktop versions for each of these versions of Linux, which only hold a microscopic fraction of the desktop operating system market share.

Unless you're a serious technologist, you don't want to go anywhere near Linux-based operating systems.

CHAPTER NINE

Networking Hardware

NETWORKING HARDWARE TYPICALLY REFERS to equipment that allows network devices to communicate with one another, but not always. Other types of networking hardware include server racks, cabling, and other devices that help make up the computer network. Here we provide descriptions and recommendations for the most common types of networking hardware that you will require in a solo or small firm computer network.

Switches

A switch is a piece of networking hardware that connects network segments (discrete sections of the network), allowing multiple devices to communicate with one another. For example, if two or more computers are connected into the same switch and are located within the same defined network, the switch will allow these devices to communicate. Switches inspect data packets as they are received and, based on the source and destination hardware addresses, will forward the data packet appropriately. By delivering the packet of information only to the device it was intended for, network bandwidth is preserved, as well as confidentiality, and the information is delivered much more quickly. In comparison, network hubs send the traffic to all ports, irrespective of the destination device, and are rarely seen in a production environment anymore. Unlike network hubs, switches are "intelligent" devices and can operate on more than one layer of the Open Systems Interconnection (OSI) model, such as a multilayer switch. Switches allow traffic to pass through them at speeds of 10 Mbps, 100 Mbps, 1 Gbps, or 10 Gbps, depending on the speeds of the ports.

The International Organization for Standardization created the OSI model as a way of subdividing a communications system into seven layers: Physical, Data Link, Network, Transport, Session, Presentation, and Application. We could write a whole book on the OSI model, but others already have.

Most solo and small law firms will not need expensive high-end network switches for their computer infrastructure. In the majority of situations, a switch is needed only to connect computer workstations to the server and to the router for Internet access. NETGEAR offers reasonably priced switches in a variety of configurations to meet almost any solo or small firm need. The ProSAFE Fast Ethernet Unmanaged Switch series is a good choice for the solo or small law firm because of the low cost, ease of setup, and reliability. Setup of these devices requires no configuration—just plug in the power and network cables and you're ready to go.

When purchasing a switch for your firm, you will need to determine the number of connections or ports the switch will need. Next, you will have to determine the speeds of the ports that you will require. Will all of your computers need the ability to connect to the server at gigabyte speeds, or will just a handful of devices need that kind of speed? Remember, you certainly will pay more for a 48-port switch with 48 gigabit ports than if you buy a 48-port switch with only two gigabit ports and 46 10/100MB ports. Given the bandwidth of today's networks and applications, it's almost a requirement to purchase a switch with gigabit ports, and the added speed is worth the additional cost. The ProSAFE Fast Ethernet Unmanaged Switches from NETGEAR can be found on its website at **www.netgear.com**. These switches are also offered in a 1U rackmount solution that will fit standard 19-inch racks, and are backed by a NETGEAR ProSAFE lifetime hardware warranty.

For those law firms that require or desire tighter security controls over their computer systems and users, a managed switch may be the solution. A managed switch, unlike an unmanaged switch, is a device that can be administered or controlled. Advanced features include the ability to limit how computer systems can "talk" with one another at the physical level (private virtual LANs), advanced performance monitoring, Layer 3–based prioritization, and increased bandwidth control. These switches also support Quality of Service (QoS), which can be used to prioritize certain network traffic over other functions, such as VoIP phones. A good cost-effective managed switch for small to medium-sized law firms is the ProSafe Gigabit Smart Switch from NETGEAR. This managed switch can be found on NETGEAR's website (**www.netgear.com**) starting at around $200 and can be purchased with differing numbers of ports and connection speeds, depending on the requirements.

As an alternative, Dell manufactures some very cost-effective switches for network connectivity. They have managed and unmanaged versions as well as multi-gigabit port models.

Entry-Level and Intermediate-Level Routers

A router is a computer-networking device that connects two or more independent networks—e.g., your firm's local computer network and your Internet Service Provider's (ISP) network. A router's job is to determine the proper path for data to travel between the networks and to forward data packets to the next device along the path—basically to get your data from point A to point B. Routers come in all shapes and sizes and can have different features. For a solo or small firm, the most basic router will often be sufficient to connect the local network to the Internet, as well as protect computers and other hardware devices on the local network from outside attacks. A basic router will require some configuration from the default values to communicate with the ISP's network, as well as to strengthen the security and protection it provides to your information systems. Most basic routers are capable of handling only broadband Internet connections, such as cable or DSL, by using the Ethernet port coming from the cable or DSL modem. If your firm has a T-1 or any variant of this Internet connection, your ISP will probably provide you with a router.

The increasing number of data breaches has created a lot of discussion recently about which router a solo or small firm should use. Whichever router your firm chooses, it must have a built-in firewall and logging capabilities. There can be no exceptions. Previously, we recommended a Linksys router as a basic routing solution for solo and small firms. When configured correctly, this device could provide adequate protection for your firm's data and information systems. However, our recommendation has changed.

Today, the bad guys have gotten so good at breaking into law firms that it's becoming increasingly hard to keep them out. When they do get in, most law firms don't realize that they've been compromised for months. For this reason, there is no longer an entry-level routing solution that we can recommend with confidence. Your firm's data is just too valuable.

Given the types of data that your firm stores, such as Social Security numbers, credit card numbers, patient/medical records, and other sensitive client information, the only way to combat hackers and have a chance of keeping them out is through the implementation of a defense-in-depth security strategy. This type of information protection strategy provides security at all levels of your computer network, including the point at which your local network interfaces with the public Internet. For this reason, we recommend the Cisco Small Business RV Series line of routers, even for a solo lawyer.

The Cisco Small Business RV Series routers provide high-performance connectivity for small businesses and have built-in threat defense, including a proven stateful packet inspection firewall, intrusion detection system, and an optional content filtering subscription package to restrict a user's access to undesirable websites that may contain malware and phishing attacks. The Cisco RV130W router offers a wireless option for those firms that require it. The Cisco Small Business RV Series routers start at around $150.

A Cisco device is a little more complicated to configure from the command line, although a graphic user interface (GUI) is available to assist those less familiar with the Cisco configuration syntax. Unless you are comfortable with the syntax of Cisco's IOS (yes, Apple used the iOS term after Cisco), we recommend that you not attempt to configure the device. Seek out the expertise of your IT professional or another resource that "speaks" Cisco's IOS language.

It's becoming harder to find a router for a small- to medium-sized business that doesn't include wireless 802.11 capabilities. Be careful when purchasing these devices for your firm's computer network, as you may unintentionally open up your network to unwanted guests if your system is not configured properly. The majority of these devices come preconfigured with open, unsecured wireless networks—which may be OK for your guest network, but even most wireless devices now have an option to set up a separate guest network to keep your visitor's computer network separate from the firm's. You can never be too safe. Remember, you also have the ability to disable the wireless capability if you don't need it.

Make sure you consult with your IT vendor on best practices when implementing a wireless network for your law firm. And for heaven's sake, make sure all the default settings are changed. Even "script kiddies" know all the default settings.

Firewalls/IDS/IPS Devices

An intrusion detection system (IDS) is used to detect many types of malicious network traffic and computer usage that can't be detected by a conventional firewall or router. These malicious activities include network attacks against vulnerable services (web hosting, e-mail, databases, etc.); data-driven attacks on applications; host-based attacks, such as privilege escalation; unauthorized logins; and access to sensitive files. Privilege escalation is the act of exploiting a known vulnerability in an application to gain access to resources that would have otherwise been protected. When an IDS and an Intrusion Prevention System (IPS) are used in combination, they also can detect and prevent malware such as viruses, Trojan horses, and worms from entering the network.

An IDS/IPS device is commonly placed at the gateway of the computer network so that all incoming and outgoing network traffic passes through it. This allows the device to scan all incoming/outgoing traffic before it is passed on to the destination located on the local computer network, denying the entry of any malicious traffic and prohibiting the exit of any malicious traffic. A firewall has the ability to permit or deny data traffic based on port number, originating or receiving Internet Protocol (IP) address, and protocol type, to name just a few, and it is usually based on rules that are set up and configured by an administrator. An IP address is a unique address or identifier assigned to a networked device, such as a computer, that allows the device to communicate with other networked devices. Just think of an IP address as being the same as a home address, which is a unique way to identify your home's physical location.

A firewall device with these described capabilities is critical for the protection and security of your firm's computer equipment and information systems. For those users who have a broadband Internet connection at home, a router with firewall should also be used to protect your home-based computer network from outside attacks. This is especially important for those lawyers who work remotely, because you do not want your clients' data to become compromised while working offsite. According to the Internet Storm Center, which is part of the SANS Institute, it takes only twenty minutes or less for an unprotected and unpatched computer connected to the Internet to become compromised. Imagine that the computer is yours and it contains confidential client data. This is the stuff of which nightmares are made.

For this reason, we recommend the Cisco ASA 5500-X Series Adaptive-Security Appliance, which provides a good solution for solo and small firms looking to secure their local computer network from outside attacks. This appliance integrates a world-class firewall, unified communications (voice/video) security, SSL (Secure Sockets Layer) and IPSec (Internet protocol security) VPN, intrusion prevention, and content security services into a single piece of hardware. These devices offer advanced security features such as granular control of applications and micro-applications with behavior-based controls, highly secure remote access, and near-real-time protection against Internet threats. Combining all of the functionality into one piece of network hardware eliminates the need to purchase a single device for each function. Using a single piece of hardware saves time in setup and configuration, eliminates complexity, and tremendously reduces the cost to adequately secure your business computer network.

The Cisco ASA 5500-X Series provides intelligent threat defense and secure communications services that stop attacks before they affect your firm's business continuity. The firewall technology is built on the proven capabilities of the Cisco PIX family of security appliances, allowing valid traffic to flow into and out of the local network while keeping out unwelcome visitors. The URL- and content-filtering technologies implemented by the device protect the business as well as the employees from the theft of confidential and proprietary information and help the business comply with federal regulations, such as HIPAA and Gramm-Leach-Bliley. The application control capabilities can limit peer-to-peer and instant-messaging traffic, which often lead to security vulnerabilities and can introduce viruses and threats to the network. The implementation of a Cisco ASA 5000-X Series device will deliver comprehensive, multilayer security to your computer network and will help you to sleep better at night knowing your electronic data and equipment are protected. The Cisco ASA 5500-X Series Adaptive-Security Appliance can be purchased from Cisco Systems online at its website (**www.cisco.com**) or through a distributor.

The cost of the Cisco ASA 5500-X Series device can range in the thousands of dollars, depending on the number of licenses, features, warranty, and support purchased with the product. When purchasing this device, we absolutely recommend that you get SmartNet maintenance. SmartNet allows you access to the excellent technical support personnel of Cisco, hardware replacement for failures, and upgrades to the device operating system.

Make no mistake about it—this is an excellent high-end firewall well worth the investment to protect your network and confidential information.

Racks

A rack unit or enclosure is a piece of hardware that is used to store, organize, and secure your networking and computing equipment. Most often, rack units are used to hold rack-mount servers and network communication equipment such as firewalls and switches. Many types of computer and networking hardware are offered in rack-mount sizes, due to the need to place and secure equipment within a single physical location. Rack units can be portable units mounted on caster wheels, bolted to the floor, or, if small enough, mounted on the wall. The amount of space that is available for the servers and networking equipment will greatly affect which type of rack to purchase. The leading manufacturers of rack units and enclosures are American Power Conversion (APC) and Chatsworth.

APC NetShelter SX enclosures are rack enclosures with advanced cooling, power distribution, and cable management for server and networking devices. The 19-inch rack is vendor neutral and is guaranteed to be compatible with all EIA-310 compliant 19-inch equipment, which covers nearly all rack-mountable equipment. The 19 inches refers to the horizontal distance between the mounting screws for the equipment. These enclosures offer large cable access slots in the roof to provide overhead cable egress, which is useful when cable runs come down through the ceiling. The bottom design allows for unobstructed cable access through a raised panel floor, which is common in network data centers. The enclosures are well-ventilated with perforated front and rear doors to provide ample ventilation for servers and other networking hardware that require unobstructed air flow to keep systems cool. The front and rear doors can be arranged to open in either direction, depending on the layout of the room. For physical security protection, both of these doors can be locked.

The enclosure contains rear cable-management channels to assist in managing the plethora of cables that servers and network equipment require. The frame design of the NetShelter SX enclosures is made with heavy-gauge mounting rails and casters to provide support for up to 3,000 pounds of equipment. APC's NetShelter SX enclosures are offered in many different sizes (stand-alone, datacenter, colocation, etc.) and can be purchased with accessories, such as UPS battery backups, retractable keyboard, mouse pad, flip-down monitor, cable-management arms, additional fans, and power distribution centers. The APC NetShelter SX rack enclosures can be purchased online at APC's website (**www.apc.com**), and the basic enclosures start at around $1,500.

If you're hesitant to spend $1,500 on a piece of equipment just to hold your servers and networking devices, you may be able to find used racks from local businesses that are moving or have been closed, or through your local online classifieds, at only a fraction of the price.

Cabling

Now that you have all of your computer equipment selected and purchased, you will need to decide how to wire your data and voice network and what type of network patch cables to purchase to connect your computers to the network drops (cables from the wall outlet to the hub/switch location). These patch cables come in various lengths and are primarily offered in two different types.

First, you have the category 5e cable, which is not the same as the generically termed Cat5 specification. Second, you have the category 6 cable, more commonly referred to as Cat6, along with category 7 cables used for networks requiring data transfer speeds of up to 10 Gbps. Each type of cable has a different maximum throughput speed that it's capable of handling. As with computers, as time progresses, newer cable standards are developed that can handle greater data transfer speeds. There is even a category 8 cable that should be standardized shortly, promising a new copper speedway for data centers in the not-too-distant future, operating up to speeds of 40 Gbps.

The Cat6 standard cable is becoming increasingly popular as more and more networking and computer devices operate and communicate at gigabit speeds. Current data transfer rates and applications operating at speeds of 1 Gbps are starting to push the limits of category 5 cabling; although category 5e cable is rated for gigabit speeds, it should be used with caution. The trends of the past and predictions for the future indicate that data rates have been doubling every 18 months. The category 6 cables offer double the amount of bandwidth capacity of category 5 cables and a better transmission performance. The category 6 cable provides a higher signal-to-noise ratio, allowing for higher reliability for current applications and higher data rates for the future. Analysts have indicated that the majority of new wiring installations are using Cat6 cabling. This decision is fairly easy because all Cat6 cabling is backward compatible with Cat5e cabling.

Category 7 cabling is only commonly seen in data centers and is not yet widely used in local networks. If your firm is planning on wiring the office for data and voice, it makes all the sense in the world to wire with Cat6 cabling. Remember, once the dust has settled from the construction, it would be extremely costly to have any type of cabling pulled out and replaced. The approximately 10 percent premium that you currently will pay for Cat6 cabling over Cat5e cabling is worth the added cost. As time goes on, the premium is getting smaller and smaller.

Wireless Networking Devices

A wireless networking device allows for communication between devices without being physically connected by wires or network cables. In a solo or small firm, if the investment cost to wire an office space with data cables is too expensive, a wireless solution may be the answer. Plus, who wants networking cables all over the place? This is particularly true in older properties—and may be aesthetically desirable in historic buildings. A wireless network is extremely convenient for lawyers who use laptops, smartphones, or tablets because they can move from their office to the conference room with these devices and still stay connected to the local network and Internet. However, we do not recommend wireless connections while connecting to a database or database applications such as some case management systems. Wireless connections could cause database corruption, which would require a reload of backup data. The cost to purchase a wireless networking device is extremely low, and the benefits gained are worth the small investment. However, do not implement a wireless network without taking the proper security precautions. By default, most wireless routers and access points are preconfigured not to enable encryption. This means that by default, all communications between computers and the wireless device are unencrypted and therefore insecure. How many people have connected their laptop to an unencrypted wireless network so that they could check their e-mail or perform online banking? We see this all the time—even at legal technology conferences!

Wireless networks should be set up with the proper security. First and foremost, encryption should be enabled on the wireless device. Most wireless devices come preconfigured with either an unencrypted network or a network encrypted using the wired equivalent privacy (WEP) 64- or 128-bit algorithm. Ultimately, neither of these solutions is adequate. WEP is a weak encryption algorithm and can be cracked in a matter of minutes using free open-source software. Do not use WEP! Frankly, the Federal Trade Commission and the Canadian Privacy Commissioner have both found WEP encryption insufficient to secure credit card information, so we suggest it not be used at all. Some time ago, WPA using the TKIP (temporal key integrity protocol) algorithm was cracked by a group of Japanese scientists in about a minute. So avoid WPA as well. This means that you should be encrypting using WPA2 only.

If the wireless network is for the firm only, enable MAC (media access control) filtering on the wireless device. MAC filtering essentially limits the devices that may communicate with the wireless device. If the MAC address of a computer's wireless network card does not match an authorized MAC address, then the wireless device will not communicate with the unauthorized computer. Enabling MAC filtration will also stop employees from connecting their personal smartphones to the wireless cloud without authorization, even if they know the appropriate network name and passphrase. This is an added layer of security. Most commonly, wireless routers and access points ship with default network names such as Linksys or NETGEAR. While in operation, these devices will broadcast their names so that wireless clients can locate the wireless networks. It is strongly recommended, for security reasons, that the default name of the wireless network be changed (not to something identifying who you are—such as TheSmithLawFirm) and that SSID (service set identifier, which is essentially the network name) broadcasting be disabled.

If your router doesn't come equipped with built-in wireless support, there are other wireless solutions available for the solo and small firm that provide reliable and secure network connections.

Linksys continues to be a very popular manufacturer of wireless networking devices for residential users and small to medium-sized businesses. Its products have only gotten better since the company was purchased by Cisco a few years ago. Cisco sold the Linksys line to Belkin, but the products are still rock solid. The Linksys Smart Wi-Fi Router EA3500 is an all-in-one Internet sharing router with a four-port switch. Although this router can be used to connect your local computer network to the Internet, it should be implemented as a wireless access point only in coordination with another firewall/IDS/IPS device. The 802.11n wireless standard protocol is used by this device and offers data transmission speeds up to 300 Mbps. This standard is about six times as fast as the 802.11g standard, which offered data transmission speeds up to 54 Mbps. One of the benefits of the 802.11n standard is that it is backward compatible with all 802.11b/g devices. This router supports the latest wireless security encryption standards, such as WPA2, to keep your data communications secure.

The Linksys Smart Wi-Fi Router EA3500 can be purchased online from the Linksys website (**store.linksys.com**) or from your local electronics retailer for around $99.99.

Wireless device manufacturers continue their push to get consumers to purchase their 802.11n wireless products. The 802.11n standard has been approved for a few years, so it's fine to purchase 802.11n products. Wireless networks that use the 802.11n standard will see an improvement in connection speeds and range beyond previous 802.11 standard connections. To use the new standard, all wireless devices will have to be 802.11n compatible; otherwise, the wireless network will operate using only the same standard as the "oldest" wireless device on your network. Further, to get transmission speeds as fast as advertised, you'll have to be relatively close to the access point, and only a limited amount of devices can be connected and using the wireless network at the same time. You may also see devices that support the latest 802.11ac standard. The 802.11ac standard was ratified and approved in January 2014, but is not widely used at this time. You may see wireless routers that advertise and do, in fact, support the 802.11ac standard, but only 802.11n should be used at this time.

If you work out of a large office space, in a building with a lot of brick or mesh metal wiring embedded within the walls, or in a cubicle next to a microwave, you can purchase a piece of hardware to extend or improve the wireless signal strength in your office. These wireless range extenders cost around $100 and can be purchased online.

CHAPTER TEN

Miscellaneous Hardware

ASIDE FROM ALL OF the computer hardware, software, and networking equipment, many other types of hardware deserve to be discussed. These additional devices can provide mobility, security, or functionality that would benefit a solo or small firm.

Fire Safe

A fire safe is an important and often overlooked piece of hardware to have in your office to protect your backup media, software licenses, and other valuables from destruction during a fire or other natural disaster. And don't put the items in the safe and leave the door open; it is astonishing how often we see this. Let the safe serve its purpose and don't succumb to the temptation of convenience by leaving it open. Most come with a locking mechanism, so take advantage of the added security to protect your firm's information.

It is strongly recommended that you store backups, software licenses, copies of technical contracts with third parties, insurance policies, emergency contact lists and other important documents in a fire safe. Purchasing a fire safe is a relatively inexpensive investment; they can be purchased from your local office supply store for a couple of hundred dollars. There are many sizes and shapes of fire safes, so you shouldn't have a problem finding one that suits your needs. The key specification is the rated internal temperature. The safe may be rated to keep the contents from burning, but it also needs to avoid damaging the contents, such as by melting a tape casing, which is why the internal rated temperature is important. If you keep important business records offsite for redundancy, make sure that this information is stored in a fire safe as well. Your ability to recover from a disaster is only as good as the weakest point in the plan.

Battery Backup Devices

A battery backup device is an electronic device that supplies secondary power in the absence of main power, such as during a power outage. Battery backup devices can also protect electronic hardware from power spikes and dirty electricity. These devices come in all sizes and power capacities, and, depending on what devices you are looking to protect, this will affect the size and capacities you choose. APC is the leading manufacturer of battery backup devices used for protecting computers, servers, and other networking hardware and equipment.

It is strongly recommended that every computer within the local network be placed on a battery backup device, such as the APC Back-UPS 350. At our office, we have our computers, printers, routers, switches, phones, and voicemail system all on battery backup devices to protect our hardware investment. This battery backup device will supply your computer system with power for up to five minutes after an outage has occurred. During this time, the battery backup device will communicate with the APC software installed on the computer (bundled with the device) and will instruct the computer to shut down properly and safely. The Back-UPS 350 supports up to 210 watts and has 3 NEMA 5-15R battery backup outlets and 3 NEMA 5-15R surge protection outlets. You may elect to have a larger UPS for your computer system in order to achieve a longer run time.

Many computers and servers will experience software or hardware errors after a power outage because they did not have the opportunity to shut down properly—often referred to as a hard shutdown—which is a quick way to lose or corrupt your data. When computers and (horror of horrors) servers go down hard, the result is often not pretty—actually it's more of a catastrophe. There is a great chance for data loss or system failure in the event of an outage. By purchasing battery backup devices for your computers and other electronic equipment, you are protecting your hardware and software investment and avoiding possible IT costs to correct all the problems that might ensue from a hard shutdown. The APC Back-UPS 350 can be purchased from APC's website (**www.apc.com**) for $79.99.

We've discussed battery backup devices for workstations and laptops, but what about servers? Servers require much more power to operate than a desktop or laptop computer. Therefore, they will require more battery capacity to allow them to operate during a power outage and/or the time necessary to properly shut down. On top of that, they take much longer to shut down properly than a workstation due to the greater number of services and processes constantly running on a server. To properly shut down, the average server will take upward of 10 minutes or more if it is hosting multiple virtual machines, so supplying the server with enough power to accomplish this task is important. Certainly, you do not want your server to experience a hard shutdown, because the risk is great for data loss or hardware failure. Battery backup devices for servers can be purchased as a tower unit or rack mountable, depending on what your firm needs to support its server configuration.

The APC Smart-UPS 1500VA is an ideal battery backup solution to protect a single server from the power outages, power spikes, or dirty electricity that can damage the server's internal hardware components. The Smart-UPS 1500VA is offered in both tower and rack-mountable forms and can supply a server with enough power to allow the server to shut down properly. Note that this unit has only enough capacity to supply power to one server and its peripheral devices. If there is a need to purchase a battery backup device for multiple servers, there are models with greater capacities that will be able to handle the load.

As with all batteries, someday they will need to be replaced. Happily, the batteries in these devices are hot-swappable, which means they can be replaced without the need to shut down the battery backup device or the devices connected to the unit. It is important to replace batteries as soon as they fail so that the systems connected to the battery backup device continue to be protected in the event of a power failure, and—trust us— you'll know when the battery needs to be replaced, because the beeping alarm is really loud and annoying. Replacement batteries for these devices can be purchased online from APC's website. Because the batteries in these units are replaceable, this is one hardware investment that you will not be replacing every one to two years. In our experience, these devices will always outlast the life of the computers, servers, or equipment connected to them.

The APC Smart-UPS 1500VA comes bundled with software that can be installed on the server itself to enable the battery backup device to communicate with the server. This is necessary so that in the event of a power outage, the battery backup can alert the software installed on the server of the need to begin the shutdown process. The battery backup device connects to the server through a USB or serial cable. The APC Smart-UPS 1500VA can be purchased from APC's website for $579.

You can also purchase an optional network card for many of the larger UPS devices. The network card allows you to connect the communications over your data network and can support multiple servers. You configure the network card with an IP address, and the servers use the APC network shutdown software to "talk" to the UPS for status rather than communicating through the traditional USB or serial connection.

Fax Machines

Even though the need for fax machines has dwindled, they are still a staple in a law office and do get some use from time to time—we still receive a lot of faxes, and some clients and institutions insist that we receive information via the facsimile machine. Sometimes there just isn't enough time to scan a document and then e-mail it to a recipient, so instead the document will be faxed—or in some cases, although rare, the communicating party doesn't have access to an Internet connection. We still see plenty of solo and small firms where there is no interest in learning how to scan. The fax machine is the devil they know, and they don't want to change. So, even with all of the advancements in technology, the fax machine has a continued role. As previously stated, many digital copiers have fax transmission and receipt capabilities. Check with your vendor representative to see if using the copier is more cost-effective than purchasing a separate device.

If your firm is in the market for a fax machine, the device we recommend is the Brother IntelliFax-2940, which is a high-speed laser fax, phone, and copier. This model was designed for multiple users in a small business to easily share the benefits. Its design incorporates a high-capacity front-loading paper tray that makes replenishing the paper a task that doesn't require a degree in engineering to accomplish.

The IntelliFax-2940 is equipped with 16 MB of memory, allowing multiple faxes to be stored in memory for transmission when it senses the line is free. The 33.6 Kbps SuperG3 fax modem optimizes throughput, transmitting as fast as 2.5 seconds per page. The 250-sheet capacity paper tray is front loading for easy access, which means less time spent reloading paper. The paper tray can adjust to hold either letter- or legal-size paper.

This fax machine also comes with a 30-page auto document feeder. Access to incoming faxes can be protected through the use of a password, ensuring that only the appropriate parties see confidential faxes. Finally, if your needs exceed or grow beyond faxing and copying, this device comes with a USB interface and can serve as a laser printer capable of printing up to 24 pages per minute. This device comes with a standard one-year limited warranty. The Brother IntelliFax-2940 can be purchased online at Brother's website (**www.brother-usa.com**) for around $300.

Backup Solutions

As hard drive capacities get larger and the volume of electronic data created increases, media with greater capacities is required to store the daily, weekly, and monthly backup files. Luckily, the days of having to purchase expensive tape drives, autoloaders, and media have long passed. The options for media to store backups have increased while the cost continues to decline. Solo and small firms no longer need to purchase or implement an expensive backup system. Usually, a set of inexpensive external hard drives will do the trick. They offer more capacity than most tape media, are portable, have faster transfer rates, and are relatively inexpensive. And don't forget that you should keep at least one complete backup set offsite in the event that your entire office is lost—or inaccessible— during a disaster.

Depending on the backup solution that has been implemented, a lot of storage space may be necessary, especially if your firm has implemented a system where a full backup is run on a nightly basis. The Western Digital My Book adds secure high-capacity storage to your computer system and is compatible with both PCs and Mac computers. It comes pre-formatted with the NTFS file system, so if you're planning on using this device on an Apple-based network, you will have to format the external hard drive FAT32, depending on your requirements. The USB 3.0 (USB 2.0 backward compatible) interface allows the hard drive to deliver transfer rates up to 5 Gbps and can be connected to any computer or server that supports these types of connections. The Western Digital My Book comes with built-in hardware encryption, keeping your firm's data secure.

The Western Digital My Book is offered with storage capacities ranging from 2 to 6 TB in size, providing enough storage space for the average small to medium-sized firm backups. The unit also comes with a power adapter and cables to connect the device to a computer or server. If you have not yet purchased backup software, you can use the WD SmartWare Pro automatic backup software that comes bundled with the device. The software can be installed and used on both a computer and a server to back up your system and data files. The device comes with a three-year limited warranty. The Western Digital My Book can be purchased online or from your local electronics retailer starting at around $99 for the 2 TB version.

When evaluating backup solutions for your firm, be sure to enlist the recommendations of your IT staff. Cloud-based backup solutions are becoming more popular with small businesses and might have a place in your firm. When evaluating cloud backup providers, pay attention to where your data is physically stored (we would never use a provider that stores data outside of the United States—although the actions of the National Security Agency may cause us to rethink that statement), and be sure that the data is always stored in an encrypted format, regardless of whether it's in transit or at rest, and that you hold the only key.

Some folks think data is safer in Europe because of its tough data privacy laws, but that is not necessarily true. Besides the obvious headaches that accompany cross-border data issues, some European versions of The Patriot Act make U.S. law look namby-pamby by comparison. Who knows when those laws may be invoked?

CHAPTER ELEVEN

Smartphones

SMARTPHONES REMAIN THE NUMBER one tech accessory among lawyers. We all remember the time (it's getting more distant with each passing year) when a lawyer would carry two separate devices, a cell phone and a PDA (personal digital assistant). The cell phone was used to make phone calls, and the PDA was used to keep your notes and calendar. Some even allowed you to view your e-mail captured during the last synchronization with your work computer. Things have changed radically. Smartphones are like laptops—able to perform almost every function a laptop can, and in some instances, more—but at a fraction of the size. Because smartphones have so many capabilities, lawyers in firms of all sizes tend to view them as a necessity—a device they can no longer live without. Smartphones have become computers in and of themselves, with increasing functionality, and in some cases, they are more important to a lawyer than a computer system.

Among business users and especially lawyers, the smartphone debate has evolved into major warfare. Since its introduction and with its growing popularity, the Apple iPhone has grabbed the largest share of the lawyer market, and that is particularly true for solo and small firm lawyers.

According to the American Bar Association's 2014 Legal Technology Survey, the overall smartphone breakdown by platform among lawyers is as follows:

- Apple iPhone   66.8 percent
- Google Android   24.5 percent
- RIM BlackBerry   6.8 percent
- Windows Mobile   1.9 percent
- Don't Know   1.2 percent
- Other   3 percent

These numbers have resulted in some major changes over the past year:

♦ There are only two major players in the smart phone market (iPhone and Android).

♦ Both iPhone and Android devices saw their overall usage percentages increase from 2013.

♦ Blackberry usage continues to fall, down from 14 percent to just 6.8 percent in a year.

♦ Windows Mobile device usage continues to be almost non-existent among lawyers.

Both the Android and the iPhone continue to split the market share. We still expect to see the popularity of Androids increase. The BlackBerry is no longer a player and could become all but nonexistent in the United States a year or two from now, much like the Windows Mobile phone has become. BlackBerry (the name of the device and the company name) may have been lulled into inaction by its success, but the hot new technology clearly belongs to Androids and iPhones. Because BlackBerry is a Canadian company, Canada continues to keep it on life support.

A key functional requirement for any smartphone is the ability to synchronize data with your computer or server. E-mail synchronization is at the top of all lawyers' lists, followed closely by calendar synchronization. The Windows Phone 7 (previously known as Windows Mobile), Windows Phone 8 and 8.1, iPhone, and Android phones synchronize with Microsoft Exchange Servers via ActiveSync. This doesn't require any special hardware or software because the function is built into Exchange. However, there are some limitations, such as the inability to synchronize natively with Public Folders over the air. You may have to purchase third-party products to get all of the features you need for over-the-air synchronization of Public Folders, Personal Calendars or Contacts. Your mailbox will synchronize without any additional software. For those firms that don't host their own e-mail, users can set up their devices to retrieve e-mail directly from their e-mail service provider.

Our continuing recommendation for any lawyer (or anybody wanting to keep his or her data secure) is to not use an iPhone. The iPhone 6 security is better but there still are some problems. Apple released the next generation of iPhone 6 running iOS 8 in the fall of 2014. The new iPhone comes in two flavors, iPhone 6 and the iPhone 6 Plus. The iPhone 6 Plus is a whopping 5.5 inches long, which is huge for a smartphone. It's almost like you're holding an iPad Mini next to your head—too large if you ask us. Some of the improvements and features that come with the new version include two models varying in size (4.7 inches vs. 5.5 inches), thinner design, higher resolution Retina screen display, and new video recording features. The features of iOS 8 are discussed later on in the book in the "More From Apple" chapter.

Continuing on the finger print scanner that was introduced with the iPhone 5, the iPhone 6 allows uses to unlock their iPhone with a fingerprint, as well as approve purchases from iTunes, iBooks and the App Store without having to enter a password. Apple has released multiple fixes for various vulnerabilities as we go to press, but the fundamental insecurity of the fingerprint scanner cannot be fixed. However, it is unlikely that this will present a problem for most users, as there is some level of sophistication to the compromise. But if you are targeted by a professional, your data is not secure—after all, we leave our fingerprints everywhere we go.

The Government has made the same complaints about the release of the Android Lollipop operating system as they have about the encryption of the iPhone 6 models. The encryption of data on these mobile devices is preventing the National Security Agency from being able to access the encrypted contents of these devices, potentially hampering or slowing down their investigations. Anyone concerned with the privacy of an individual's data, should be happy that the Government has come out with these criticisms and should be thankful that we just may have a way to keep the data on our devices secure once and for all—whether from hackers or Big Brother!

Apple has made all kinds of marketing claims, yet there are many examples over the years demonstrating why an iPhone should not be trusted. On iPhones running certain older versions of the Apple iOS firmware, the PIN keylock code is easily replaced by a "blank" code. The iPhone also claims to store its data in encrypted form. That is true, but with some older versions of the iOS firmware you can place the phone in recovery mode and transfer the data to your computer. Apple conveniently decrypts the data as it sends it over the SSH connection, thereby negating the encryption scheme. You can remotely wipe the iPhone, but it needs to be connected to the cellular network to do it.

Not much has changed in the security model, or lack thereof, of Apple's iPhone devices. There still are security problems with the current generation of the devices. Within days of each new firmware version released, a new "jailbreak" method has been discovered. Although iOS 4 held up better than its predecessors, iOS 5, 6, 7 and 8 have all been jailbroken.

Since we know so many lawyers will (and do) ignore our advice, here's what we recommend:

(A) Only use the iPhone 6 or 6 Plus. If you're using the 3, 3G, or 4, upgrade immediately.

(B) Upgrade to the latest version of iOS 8.

(C) Enable a passphrase (not a four-digit PIN) on the device. Enable device wiping upon a set number of unsuccessful logon attempts.

As of this writing, the iPhone 6, iPhone 6 Plus, and iOS 8 have been released. Given the insecurity of the fingerprint scanner, make sure you configure a strong lock code and not the default four-digit PIN. There are tools available that can brute force the four-digit PIN on an iOS 4, 5, or 6 device in ten to forty minutes, even if the device is configured to wipe data after 10 invalid attempts. By the time this book is printed, we fully expect that the software will be updated to also brute force iOS 7 and 8 in a similar fashion. We are well aware that our advice is largely ignored here, as the glamour of the iPhone continues to mesmerize everyone, including lawyers. It is a very slick phone, but remember that the new ABA Model Rules adopted in 2012 require that you balance the risk of the technology you use against the security of client data!

With the introduction of iOS 5, Apple introduced the iCloud service. When enabled and configured, iOS devices use this service to backup information from your local device to the cloud. The iCloud service removes the necessity to connect your iOS device to your computer and either backup or update your device by using iTunes. All of this now takes place wirelessly, over your mobile data connection or your local Wi-Fi network. However, while convenient, there are some serious concerns with data privacy. First, consider that all information from your local device, whether the iPhone or iPad, is being sent to Apple for storage. The information may be encrypted by Apple, but it holds the decryption key and will turn the decrypted data over to law enforcement when the right paperwork is supplied. Recent news events have highlighted the insecurity and dangers of iCloud, especially if you want to store your nude selfies on Apple's service.

For any cloud storage provider, whether iCloud, Dropbox, or some other provider, we always recommend that you encrypt the data prior to using and initiating the service. By following this process, the user holds the decryption key—not the service provider.

For iOS devices, using an app like BoxCryptor encrypts the files on your local device before the information is synchronized with the cloud storage provider. BoxCryptor encrypts files on the local device using AES-256-bit and RSA encryption, providing the necessary security to keep your files and information secure. This also allows the user to hold and maintain possession of the decryption key, which is very important. This product used to be free, and still is for personal use, but costs $96 per year for a single-user business license.

During 2014, many vendors of Android smartphones continued to release phones designed for business use. They include enhanced security and enterprise management capabilities, like encryption, support for virtual private networks, support for more ActiveSync controls, and remote locking and wiping. Unveiled in June and made available to the public in November of 2014, Google announced the release of version 5.0 of Android, called Lollipop. The most notable feature of the latest version is that encryption is enabled by default. Previously, encryption was an option but had to be turned on by a user. This feature has even been mentioned by the Government, noting how unhappy it is that devices now come encrypted by default. It must be a sign that the encryption is pretty secure! The new operating system also uses Security Enhanced Linux (SELinux), an enhanced application level security model that was developed by the NSA that enforces application isolation on the device that malware cannot bypass.

Besides the security enhancements, Google also included a refreshed notification system that its users will be sure to love. Notifications can now be grouped by the application that produced them, and now can be displayed on the lock screen. As Android matures and continues to increase in popularity, it's very possible that it may become the smartphone of choice, even surpassing the iPhone among lawyers. Be sure to keep an eye out in the coming months for a notification on your Android device that Lollipop is now available to download and install on your device.

For die-hard security enthusiasts, the National Security Agency (NSA) has created and released a hardened version of Google's Android operating system called Security Enhanced (SE) Android. This open source project was undertaken to limit the damage that can be done to the phone by flawed or malicious apps. It is probably only a matter of time before we see this operating system installed and running on Android phones used by government agencies. The Defense Department has already distributed many of these phones. However, given the previous events surrounding the release of documents by Edward Snowden, we now know that the NSA has its fingers in many sources of electronic information, including encrypted data. We would be very wary of trusting any hardened version of Android at this time, especially one hardened by the NSA and recommend protecting data with methods that you, the user, control and configure.

For those users looking for a smartphone recommendation, we strongly recommend investing in Android phones. We officially made the jump three years ago to the Samsung Galaxy S3 and are not looking back. We have fallen in love with the Samsung Galaxy S5 device that has recently replaced our S3s. The Samsung Galaxy S5 is only available currently with 16 GB of internal memory. Our older Galaxy S3 was the 32 GB model and we were worried that 16 GB wouldn't be enough space. The operating system for the S5 appears to take less space since we have installed all of our applications and still have over 8 GB of memory available. Of course, we configured as many applications as possible to use the expansion micro SD card if the application allowed it.

There are many Android devices to choose from. It may help to first select your cellular provider and then see what options it has. We've been to many Sprint, Verizon, and AT&T stores—nowadays, they all pretty much have the same models in stock with many more options available online. For an Android, the Samsung Galaxy S5 is our current recommendation.

Over-the-air synchronization with Exchange Public Folders is a requested feature by many solo and small firm lawyers. You may require a third-party server implementation such as Goodlink to perform these functions. Good Technologies, Inc., makers of Good Mobile Messaging products, provides enterprise-level messaging and control for iPhone, Android, Windows Phone 7/8/8.1, Symbian, and PalmOS phones. Hosted versions of Good for Enterprise are no longer available through any major cell carriers. In fact, Good has priced the software so high that it is no longer an alternative for solo or small firm lawyers. Because of the licensing costs and minimum device requirements, a Good solution would cost several thousands of dollars (not counting the server cost) just to get started. Mobile Iron used to be another alternative to manage a small population of smartphones. Like Good, Mobile Iron has increased its licensing cost to a point that only makes sense for larger firms. Believe it or not, Black-Berry's Enterprise Service 10 Server Software may be the only cost-effective solution to manage solo and small firm smartphones. This free software can be downloaded from Blackberry's website at no cost and can be used to manage iOS and Android devices from a single console.

Another alternative may be to install special software on your computer to synchronize with the Public Folders. Your computer must be powered up and logged into Outlook for the over-the-air synchronization to occur. As you can imagine, this is a potential security vulnerability and must be carefully considered and engineered, and it requires a lot of administration by your IT provider.

On a side note, everyone is familiar with getting spam through e-mail, but how about on the phone? Spam text messages can be costly since most carriers will charge for both text messages sent and received unless you have an unlimited plan. There is no anti-SMS-spam software available to install on cell phones to prevent receiving these messages, but there is a way to block cellular spam, and it's quite simple. The vast majority of spam text messages originates on the Internet and do not come from other cell phones. Why? Because spammers don't have to pay anything when using the Internet to send the text messages. Most carriers, led by AT&T and Verizon Wireless, offer spam SMS-blocking features. To enable this feature, just log into your online account manager and the options should be available in your account profile. Most cellular providers allow you to block SMS messages only from certain phone numbers and addresses. What are you waiting for? We've signed up. Here are the websites you can use:

> AT&T (**mymessages.wireless.att.com**)
> Verizon Wireless (**www.verizonwireless.com**)
> Sprint (**www.sprint.com**)
> T-Mobile (**www.t-mobile.com**)

Make sure you pay attention to smartphone updates and security notices, as the number of malware threats targeting smartphones have skyrocketed over the past year. Currently, Android devices are the most frequently targeted by malware due to their popularity, open-source operating system, the relatively lawless Android Market, and the availability of apps from multiple sources.

For Android phones, we recommend a security product called Lookout Mobile Security (**www.lookout.com**). This product used to be free, but now is only free for personal use. The Enterprise version of this software provides many advanced features and an interface to manage all of your firm's devices from one console. This utility will scan all of your applications for malware and spyware and has a built-in "find my phone" feature, allowing you to locate your device using the GPS if it goes missing. This edition also includes a backup feature, which is helpful if you haven't integrated your Android phone with your Google account. Some of the other features include protecting your device from malware, blocking malicious websites, seeing which apps access your private information, and preventing encounters with phishing scams. Some of the advanced features in the Enterprise edition include the abilities to manage company data located on personal devices ("BYOD"), automate application approval, and investigate suspicious activity on mobile devices. Lookout also has a version for iOS devices, which alerts owners if their device may have been exposed to security vulnerabilities because of outdated software or if the device has been jailbroken. It also offers device location and backup functionality. Lookout now makes you contact its sales team for Enterprise Level pricing, which can be done from the website at **www.lookout.com**.

Even with the rising threat of malware, there are some basic steps you can take to protect yourself. First, make sure that when you're downloading an application, you do so only from Google Play or the App Store. When choosing an application to try or to purchase, be sure to carefully read through the reviews. Also, pay attention to the access permissions that an app requests when you install it, especially on an Android device. Finally, vendors of security software are now offering antivirus and antimalware products for smartphones. This is software that you should seriously consider purchasing to protect your mobile devices, especially if they contain confidential information.

Basic security measures for any smartphone should include strong passwords, passphrases or PINs, automatic logoff after a set time, encryption of the phone and storage cards, and remote wiping capability.

CHAPTER TWELVE

Productivity
Software

HAVING WORKED WITH SO many solos and small law firms through the years, we know that lawyers are constantly striving to be more productive and, therefore, increase their billable time. We see a few lawyers (fewer than the number of digits on one hand) who still prefer to use Corel WordPerfect over Microsoft Word, but that number is continuing to approach zero as Corel is becoming more and more of a non-factor in the productivity software market.

Microsoft Word is what the business world uses and will continue to use for the foreseeable future. There are alternatives, but they all come with some degree of pain and a large learning curve. There are adherents of WordPerfect who are religious in their fervor, and others who are evangelical in their admiration for open-source solutions. Whether you are a fan of Microsoft or not, the reality is that Word is the preferred application of the business world, and your clients will expect you to use it. They will not appreciate any conversion problems that may occur if you are using something else. In this section, we detail the latest and greatest releases of productivity software that can help lawyers be more productive.

Microsoft Office

Microsoft's latest version of Office, Office 2013, was released about two years ago and has been thoroughly vetted at this point. The software was redesigned to make the most of the Windows 8 operating system, work with mobile devices, and strongly push Microsoft's cloud services. It works and runs just fine on Microsoft Windows 7 and 8, and it is our choice and recommendation for a productivity suite.

To compete with Google's cloud storage options, Microsoft designed the new version of Office as a service in which applications and files are primarily stored in the cloud and not on your local computer system. This may come as a shock to most traditional Microsoft users, and lawyers should be aware that this type of service may pose ethical issues depending on how and where their information is actually being stored. However, users also have the ability to store documents on their local computer system.

Each of the three editions of Office 2013 includes Word, Excel, Power-Point and OneNote:

- ◆ Office Home & Student 2013, designed for families and consumers; retails for $139.99
- ◆ Office Home & Business 2013, designed for the small business market; provides e-mail, shared calendars, and web conferencing tools; retails for $219.99
- ◆ Office Professional 2013, designed for enterprise customers; provides advanced business and cloud deployment features; retails for $399.99

If your firm is using Microsoft Office 2007 or older, we would highly recommend that you upgrade to Office 2013 at this time. It is a closer call for Office 2010 users as there is little more Office 2013 has to offer unless you want to take advantage of the cloud capabilities.

Microsoft, like a lot of companies, is making a very strong push to get users to the cloud and away from local applications. To accomplish this goal, Microsoft has introduced a Software-as-a-Service (SaaS) called Office365, which gives users and companies the option to purchase a subscription (monthly or annual options) to use the Microsoft Office applications in the cloud, and in some instances, also includes the ability to install and use the stand-alone versions as well.

The subscription-based Office365 may not be for everyone, but for a solo or small firm, it at least presents another licensing option—rather than having to shovel out hundreds of dollars for the stand-alone versions of the Office 2013 suite. The Small Business subscription is entirely cloud-based, and costs $5.00 per user per month ($60.00/year), but doesn't include the ability to run Office on a mobile device, such as an iPad, or to install Office on your local computer. This requires you to be connected to the Internet in order to use Microsoft Office, which is a major downside. The Small Business Premium subscription costs $12.50 per month per user ($150.00/year), includes Office for tablets, and allows for the installation of Microsoft Office 2013 on up to five computer systems. For a small firm just starting up that is looking to be mobile, shelling out $12.50 per month for your employees to use Office may be easier to swallow than paying up to $400 per copy of Microsoft Office 2013. It's just another option to consider.

Editing Office documents on tablets (and other mobile devices) has long been a major headache, which could only be overcome by using third-party applications to perform the simplest tasks of opening, editing, and saving documents on the mobile device. Microsoft has finally released Office for mobile devices, including Office for iPad and Office Mobile for the iPhone, Windows Phone, and Android devices.

Office for iPad has been an app that the legal community has been anxiously awaiting, for the past few years. Now it is here. This app allows users to edit and create documents, including spreadsheets and presentations. Office for iPad requires a subscription to Office365; however, Office Mobile is free to download on your Android, iPhone, or Windows Phone. Just remember that an Office365 subscription is required if you want to edit Office files and not just view them.

Corel Suite

WordPerfect Office X7 is the latest version of Corel's Office Suite, and it is available in Standard, Professional, and Legal editions for the business user. WordPerfect Office X7, the successor to WordPerfect Office X6, was released in April 2014. New features of Corel WordPerfect Office X7 include a new PDF Form Feature, allowing users to create their own PDF forms, Macro Manager, and Roxio Secure Burn. The components of WordPerfect Office X7 Standard Edition include:

Main Applications
WordPerfect® word processor

Quattro Pro® spreadsheet program

Presentations™ slideshow creator

WordPerfect® Lightning™ digital notebook

Enhanced! eBook Publisher

Roxio Secure Burn disc burning software (new)

Also includes

900+ TrueType fonts

10,000+ clipart images

300+ templates

175+ digital photos

BrainStorm training videos*

The Pocket Oxford English Dictionary

WordPerfect® Address Book

Presentations™ Graphics—bitmap editor and drawing application

WordPerfect XML Project Designer

Batch Conversion Utility to convert Microsoft Word documents to WordPerfect documents

Corel X7 is offered in Standard, Professional, and Legal Editions, but the Standard Edition is best suited for serving solo or small firm needs. Unless a solo or small firm needs a database application, there is no reason for it to invest in the Professional Edition.

One of the touted advantages of WordPerfect over Microsoft Word is the Reveal Codes option, which allows users to manage document formatting with a fine-tooth comb. We are constantly amazed when lawyers mention the reveal code "excuse." Perhaps they are unaware that Word 2013 actually has a reveal code type display (and Office has since 2007), where the user can see formatting codes.

Even with the new features included with WordPerfect Office X7, we still prefer the more seamless, although imperfect, Microsoft Office 2013. Corel used to price the software suite at a much-reduced cost when compared to Microsoft Office, particularly for business-friendly packages, but that is no longer the case with the latest X7 version. Users who don't need the extensive features of WordPerfect or Microsoft Office might opt to use a product such as OpenOffice.org (described in the next section), which is free. Full license and upgrade costs for the three editions are below.

Edition	Full license cost	Upgrade cost
Standard Edition	$179.00	$129.99
Professionl Edition	399.00	259.99
Legal Edition	349.99	224.99

Table 11.1 Corel WordPerfect Office X7 Price Comparison

OpenOffice.org

Apache OpenOffice.org (formerly just OpenOffice) is a free open-source software office suite that is available for many different operating systems, including Linux, Windows, and Mac OS X. The latest release of OpenOffice.org (version 4.1) was in April 2014, and it contains many features and functions that are present in Microsoft Office and Corel WordPerfect Office. This suite was developed to reduce Microsoft Office's dominating market share by providing a free, open, and high-quality alternative. Some of the new features in the latest version 4.1 include comments on text ranges, support for IAccessible2, in-place editing of Input Fields, interactive cropping, and importing pictures from files.

OpenOffice.org can read and write most of the file formats found in Microsoft Office, including Office 2007/2010/2013 file formats, which is important if you are going to choose to use a free utility for your productivity software. It also natively supports the standard OpenDocument file formats (ODF) and has the capability to read WordPerfect Office, Rich Text Format (RTF), Lotus, and other common productivity file types.

The components of OpenOffice.org work together to provide the features expected from a modern office suite and include:

> Writer—word processor
>
> Calc—spreadsheet application
>
> Impress—presentation program
>
> Base—database program
>
> Draw—an editor used for drawing
>
> Math—allows for creating and editing mathematical formulas

All of the components of the OpenOffice.org suite look and feel like the corresponding components in Microsoft Office and Corel WordPerfect Office. Microsoft, seeing the need for and popularity of the open-source movement, has sponsored the development of a converter from Office Open XML to OpenDocument format and vice versa. Microsoft and Corel have included add-in support for the ODF file format into their office suite products to allow reading and writing to the format.

However much we all grimace at Microsoft's domination, we do not recommend that you use OpenOffice.org as your primary productivity suite. Because it is developed and maintained by freelance programmers and other companies that make contributions to the project, such as Apache, the software is not very well supported and may not contain all of the features provided by other productivity suites. In addition, most law office staff have never seen OpenOffice.org, so the learning curve would be pretty steep.

The current release of OpenOffice.org can be downloaded from the website free of charge at **www.openoffice.org**.

Adobe Acrobat

Adobe Acrobat, a family of application software developed by Adobe Systems, uses Portable Document Format (PDF) as its native file format. The PDF specification was originally a proprietary format but is now a published and approved ISO standard. The latest version of Adobe Acrobat (Acrobat XI) was released in October 2012, with version XII rumored to be released in October of 2014. Like its predecessor, Acrobat XI continues to provide the ability to store and share files online by using the Adobe Send (formerly SendNow) service. There is no trial for this newly revamped service, but it is relatively inexpensive. The Adobe Send service starts at $1.67 per month per user, or $19.99 for the year.

Acrobat XI is packaged differently from the prior versions. There are two retail offerings: Acrobat XI Standard and Acrobat XI Pro. The Acrobat XI family builds upon the features of the previous versions, and the feature comparisons can be viewed at **http://www.adobe.com/products/acrobat/product-comparison.html**. We would still recommend that you purchase the Pro version for the redaction and Bates numbering capabilities, which have come in handy on a number of occasions for us. The metadata removal feature is available in both versions.

The redaction and metadata removal tools can help mitigate the risk of unintended disclosure of information while submitting legal documents to clients, opposing counsel, or the courts. Bates numbering is a method of applying identifying labels to a set of related documents, where each page is assigned a sequential Bates number that uniquely identifies it while also establishing its relationship to other Bates-numbered pages.

Acrobat XI Pro contains some cool features that we're sure you'll take advantage of:

- PDF to Word
- PDF Portfolios

- Rich Media
- Action Wizard
- Version Comparison
- Extending Reader Functionality
- Streamlined Document Reviews
- Interactive PDF Forms
- Permanent Information Removal
- Standards Support (PDF/A, PDF/E & PDF/X)
- Online File Sharing

Adobe Acrobat XI allows you to combine multiple documents to create an Adobe PDF package while retaining the properties of the individual documents. With an Adobe PDF package, legal professionals can associate related project or client files, while individual files in the package can be encrypted, digitally signed, rearranged, removed, or added so that each recipient of the package can read or access only the relevant files that he or she has permission to view.

Security has been a big concern for Adobe. In an effort to minimize the impact to a user's system, Adobe has concentrated on reducing future vulnerabilities.

According to Adobe's website (**www.adobe.com**), "[t]he Acrobat XI Family of products delivers better application security on all platforms as a result of continuing code hardening work, additional administration capabilities that provide more granular control over the execution of JavaScript, tighter integration with the Microsoft® Windows® security architecture, and other best practices in secure software development, following the Adobe Secure Product Lifecycle (SPLC) methodology."

The Adobe Reader XI PDF viewer has a Protected Mode to limit the level of access to a user's system. Effectively, this is a "sandbox" type of environment, reducing the potential security threats on a client system from persistent malware. Adobe has also removed support for Windows 2000, a highly vulnerable operating system that should no longer be in use.

Some of the noteworthy features or enhancements in the latest version of Acrobat include:

- Improved PDF editing
- Conversion of PDF files to PowerPoint
- Creation of new PDF and web forms

♦ Improved options for electronic signatures

♦ Collection of form responses with FormsCentral

♦ Improved conversion of HTML pages to PDF

Even with some of the new features, Acrobat XI doesn't excite us as much as version 8 did. Here is our recommendation: If you currently are using Adobe Acrobat 7.0 or earlier, then the upgrade to Acrobat XI Pro is a must. The software contains added features for legal professionals that were not available in earlier versions of Acrobat, and those features alone are worth the purchase. If you are a user of Acrobat 9 or X Professional, stay with your current version unless you want to take advantage of some of the highlighted features mentioned above.

Adobe Acrobat XI Pro can be purchased online from Adobe's website (**www.adobe.com**) or from your local electronics store for $449 for the full version. The upgrade price is $199, which is a $40 increase from the previous upgrade pricing.

We have discovered a little trick for obtaining Adobe Acrobat XI Pro for a much lower price if you don't own any version of Acrobat (or own one prior to version 9). You should be able to buy a copy of Acrobat 9 Standard on the Internet for around $50. You then go to the Adobe site and purchase the Acrobat XI Pro upgrade for $199. This means you walk away with Acrobat XI for around $250 instead of the $449 retail price. That's a real bargain and would more than pay for this book! The audiences we speak to continue to report that this is one of their favorite tips.

Adobe, like other vendors, frequently releases security patches and updates for its products. By default, Adobe Acrobat XI products check for updates automatically. If you'd like to check for updates manually, you may do so from within the Help menu listing of your Adobe product.

Power PDF

We have to thank Bob Ambrogi, our friend and colleague, for suggesting an alternative to Adobe Acrobat. That product would be Power PDF Advanced by Nuance. It is certainly a worthy alternative and is only one-third of the retail cost of Acrobat Pro or 60 percent of the price using our upgrade tip previously mentioned. Power PDF Advanced has Bates stamping support to create custom profiles for stamping information into headers and footers. There's also an assistant function to convert legal pleadings into PDFs with stamp and line numbering options. Redaction ability is also included.

There are a lot of other features available with Power PDF Advanced. Suffice it to say that it has the majority of features present in Acrobat Pro that any attorney would find valuable. The cost is attractive as well. Make sure you take advantage of the thirty-day trial to determine if it will meet your needs.

OCR Software

Optical character recognition (OCR) software translates graphical images into editable text. This capability is used most commonly to edit a scanned document or image. It's widely used in law firms to convert scanned paper documents in a case file to searchable electronic files. OCR software will translate the image to text, such as a Microsoft Word document, which can be edited.

OmniPage Ultimate, by Nuance Communications, Inc., is an OCR software product enabling the conversion of paper documents and TIFF files to a text-based format for amending as needed with prominent business communications software. OmniPage Ultimate can convert scanned images to Microsoft Word, Excel, PowerPoint, Corel WordPerfect, e-mail, HTML, and even to the Amazon Kindle format. The program generates a formatted text document that preserves the layout and format, character, font, and style of the scanned image. This software boasts a 50 percent greater accuracy rate than its competitors when converting, and the updated recognition dictionaries for financial, legal, and medical specialties allow for legal-specific word recognition, which means that you will spend less time editing your legal documents. This software can also process, edit and recognize over 120 languages—a great feature for those firms with a global presence.

OmniPage supports data capture from a digital camera. The software can "read" a digital photograph, which may come in handy for lawyers who use photographs as exhibits. This software is the first OCR application designed for the multicore-processor computer, taking advantage of hyperthreading to increase the conversion speed of documents. It was also the first OCR software to support Microsoft Office 2007/2010 native formats. When converting legal documents, OmniPage now has a greater ability to recognize formatting such as line numbers, Bates stamps, signatures, and more.

Other new OmniPage Ultimate features worth mentioning include the ability to convert a scanned document into a readable format and send it to an Amazon Kindle, a "one click" toolbar in the Microsoft Office Suite that allows for document conversion with a simple click, and a faster load time than previous versions.

Also new in the latest version of OmniPage is the eDiscovery Assistant for searchable PDFs. eDiscovery Assistant provides the ability to safely convert a single PDF or batches of PDFs of all types into searchable documents without having to open PDF files one by one, giving the user greater flexibility when applying an OCR process to an entire group of documents.

As more and more firms look to use the features the Internet cloud provides, so do vendors. OmniPage includes the Nuance Cloud Connector application, which integrates with Evernote and Dropbox. The Cloud Connector also provides access to a number of cloud services, including Microsoft's OneDrive, GoogleDocs, Evermore, Dropbox, and more, allowing users to scan and/or save their documents to the cloud.

OmniPage Ultimate can be purchased and downloaded online directly from Nuance's website (**www.nuance.com**) for $499.99 for the full version and $199.99 for the upgrade version.

Adobe Acrobat includes an OCR engine, too, and the ability to batch OCR documents—and not just one at a time. We recommend purchasing Adobe Acrobat first to see if it meets your OCR needs before expending funds on another specialized product like OmniPage.

Voice Recognition Software

Arguably one of the biggest recent advances in productivity software is the continuing refinement of voice recognition software. Dragon Naturally Speaking 13 by Nuance (**www.nuance.com**) has made voice recognition software a respectable addition to your productivity arsenal. Many solo and small firm lawyers are now using Dragon as their primary composition tool. This is especially valuable for those who are not very accurate or fast typists. It takes only a short time to train Dragon to your voice, and its accuracy is astonishing. Nuance claims that the latest version is 15 percent more accurate than version 12, which is just incredible given how accurate the previous version of this product was.

Dragon can be used to compose e-mail messages, draft documents in your word processor, and even launch software applications without touching the keyboard or mouse. The software now allows users to search the Web and their computers through the use of voice shortcuts.

Along with new formatting and editing commands, the latest version also provides users with the ability to post to Facebook and Twitter by voice and even allows users to use their iPhone or iPad as a wireless microphone, untethering them from their computer.

Some of the new features in version 13 include:

- ◆ Accuracy is improved over the previous version—the new version continues to "learn" your voice and becomes more accurate the more you use the product.
- ◆ The software now learns words and phrases you use most.
- ◆ Multicore processors provide faster performance.
- ◆ Go hands free and headset free—the software now offers multiple microphone options, including those built into the latest laptops, so you can type even less and not have to use a headset.
- ◆ Dictate notes and ideas on the go and transcribe the audio files back at your computer.

This is a great tool and is used by many individuals with disabilities. But make no mistake—this is a mainstream product, and the able-bodied are moving to this technology in hordes!

Dragon Naturally Speaking comes in several versions. We recommend using the Legal or Professional version if you can afford it. The Legal version contains vocabulary specific to the legal profession and carries a price tag of $799.99. The Professional version is a higher-end package that allows for roaming user profiles and allows multiple custom dictionaries. The Professional version costs $599.99 and may be purchased from many webstores. The Premium package costs $199.99, and it may be a good, cost-effective alternative for some lawyers as it also supports digital recording devices, smart formatting, and text-to-speech, especially for those just wanting to get started with voice recognition software. Dragon Naturally Speaking 13 is licensed on a per-user basis. You can install and run it on multiple computers, but you need a license for each user's voice file.

The most important tip about using voice recognition software is to proof any output from Dragon. The speech-to-text is very good, and it "learns" and improves with time, but it's not perfect. Make sure you proofread your documents, especially those that may be submitted to a court.

If you use Dragon on multiple computers, make sure you know how to move your voice files among machines. This will save on the "retraining" time when you use several computers. The process is most appropriate for those lawyers who use a computer at home and one at the office. Moving the voice files between the machines allows you to take advantage of the aggregate training time instead of each machine "learning" on its own.

A key component to the success of voice recognition is the use of a good quality USB microphone headset. We have had great success using a Plantronics 510 headset/microphone system, but they are no longer manufactured. The Plantronics Blackwire 700 Series is available for $129.95 from the Plantronics website (**www.plantronics.com**) and should be an excellent replacement for the older 510 model. The lightweight headphones with noise-canceling microphone connect to your computer using a standard USB or Bluetooth connection. We would recommend the USB connection as Bluetooth wireless is more susceptible to audio errors. The wideband acoustic echo cancellation feature captures a broad range of voice signals for calls that are clearer and more natural sounding, perfect for use with Skype. The smart sensor technology lets you answer calls simply by putting on the headset, or pause mobile device media playback by taking it off.

CHAPTER THIRTEEN

Security Software

COMBINED WITH NETWORK FIREWALLS or IDS (Intrusion Detection System) devices, security software provides another line of protection in the defense-in-depth information security strategy against malware, including viruses, Trojan horses, worms, and other external forces. The defense-in-depth approach to securing your network is the best way to keep your systems safe from both internal and external threats. These threats can be extremely harmful to a law firm network and very costly to remove once an infection has occurred, assuming you've been able to identify that a breach or infection has taken place. Even in a solo or small firm network, your client data is of the utmost importance and securing your computers, servers, smartphones, and information should be taken very seriously. The top security protection suites providing antivirus, anti-spyware, and anti-spam protection for stand-alone computers, networks, and mobile devices are discussed below, with recommendations regarding the setup and configuration of the software.

Stand-Alone

The software selections described in the stand-alone section are primarily for the computers and laptops of solo practitioners.

We no longer recommend stand-alone products for targeted protection, such as antivirus protection. This type of software is not sufficient today to keep your systems protected. The Internet security suites are the only way to go, where you get much more functionality and protection and many more features for your computer at a much more affordable price.

Solos and small firms should definitely consider acquiring a single integrated product to deal with spam, viruses, and malware. Norton's security suite is a top seller for the single computer market, but we recommend avoiding the Norton Internet Security Suite software. We continue to find it, along with McAfee, to be a heavy load on computer processing, but not as bad as versions from several years ago.

For those users who want to avoid the problems that may be caused by Norton and McAfee, we recommend using Kaspersky Internet Security 2015, especially if you like your security suites to be hassle-free. This product contains firewall, antivirus, antispyware, rootkit detection, antispam protection, and much more. The antivirus engine that Kaspersky uses has been consistently highly ranked by independent testing labs.

The firewall included with this software provides two-way protection, scanning both incoming and outgoing network traffic, effectively blocking any hacker attacks against your system. The automatic exploit protection engine watches program behavior and aims to block zero-day vulnerabilities in the most commonly used software. The anti-phishing engine and URL advisor will keep you safe from drive-by-malware while browsing the Internet, and the anti-banner blocks annoying banners and other advertisements on web pages. With all the bonus features included in this protection suite, purchasing this product is a very good deal. Kaspersky is available directly from **www.kaspersky.com** and costs $59.95 for one-year protection on up to three computers. This is an excellent choice for the small firm environment, and it is Windows 8 compatible.

Enterprise Versions

Enterprise versions of integrated security solutions are designed for small, medium, and large computer networks, and the software administration is performed from the server rather than on each individual computer system. The client software is installed or pushed from the central server to the local workstations with little or no effort. The server supplies the clients with program and definition updates and provides an interface to centrally manage all clients from a single console. Of course, enterprise licenses are a little bit more costly than purchasing a single license, but not by much. Even with the slight increase in cost for an enterprise license, you'll more than make up for it on the money you will not have to pay your IT consultant to manage and support the product.

Integrated Security Solutions

Kaspersky Endpoint Security for Business protects Windows and Linux-based servers (including 64-bit versions), and even Mac computers from all types of malicious programs and threats. The product provides protection from threats such as viruses, Trojans, worms, keyloggers, malware, rootkits, bots, and so on. This is now the standard that we are seeing in the security product market. Former providers of antivirus software are providing protection from spyware and other malware, offering a more complete security solution to their business customers and all but eliminating the need for multiple applications to protect your systems from viruses and malware. This software provides real-time protection by scanning all files that are opened and quarantining infected files. The application can scan specified areas of the file system based on preconfigured, scheduled scans or on demand from the administrator. The scanning of critical system areas, such as running processes and startup objects, helps prevent malicious code from launching, and the ability to scan inside compound files provides an extra layer of protection.

Another great feature of this product is the inclusion of encryption. Administrators may select from full-disk or file-level encryption, protected through the implementation of the AES 256-bit encryption standard. This feature is even supported for removable devices.

Kaspersky Endpoint Security for Business is a scalable security solution, allowing administrators to define the number of instances of the program they would like to run simultaneously to accelerate the processing of server requests. The software offers flexible administration through centralized installation and control. The administration tool can be used centrally to install and manage client applications and, once they are downloaded and installed, to push updates to the clients for rapid deployment of critical security updates.

Endpoint Security for Business, similar to other integrated security solutions, scans not only for viruses but also for other threats and malicious programs, such as spyware and keyloggers. In most instances, this solution can serve multiple functions. We use a Kaspersky security solution on our network systems to provide us with complete malware protection. By using an integrated solution that is capable of handling both antivirus and antispyware protection, we have one less product to purchase and renew on a yearly basis. The product also allows for different configuration settings depending on the type of network to which the computer system is currently connected, similar to the way Microsoft Windows 7 and 8 handles the different firewall settings.

As the security of smartphones is brought to the public's attention, more vendors are integrating smartphone security with their products. Kaspersky is no different. Endpoint Security for Business protects smartphones from data leaks, malware, and viruses, and it also allows an administrator to remotely lock and wipe the device should it be misplaced, stolen, or lost. Some of the additional key features include GPS tracking, SIM card monitoring, privacy protection, and folder or device encryption. The antispam protection feature works to block both unwanted calls and text messages. For those firms that allow employees to bring their own devices (BYOD) and connect them to the firm's network and data, administrators can use this product to separate corporate and personal data on these devices. Through the creation of "containers," this software can store all of your firm's data within the encrypted work "container" fully separate and apart from your employee's personal information on the device. If a problem were to occur, such as a lost device or unexpected termination, you could wipe the firm's data off of the device without harming the personal information. Integrating security for mobile devices can save you money by not having to deploy a separate Mobile Device Management (MDM) solution, which could cost thousands of dollars.

Kaspersky Security for Mobile runs on Android, iPhones, Windows Mobile, Symbian OS, and Blackberry devices.

There is a ten-license minimum purchase for Kaspersky Business Space Security software. Cost for the product begins at $44.99 per license and includes technical support and upgrades for a year. Kaspersky is priced much lower per license than its competition and is an affordable, complete security solution that is rapidly taking over the market. This software product is offered for purchase with one-, two-, and three-year subscriptions. Licenses can be obtained directly from Kaspersky's website (**www.kaspersky.com**) or from any authorized reseller.

Besides Kaspersky, we also recommend the enterprise product Trend Micro Worry-Free Business Security. It is highly regarded and available in three editions: Advanced, Standard, and Services. We don't recommend the Services solution, as the entire configuration is set up and maintained by Trend Micro as a hosted solution.

All of the editions include antivirus and antispyware capabilities, as well as advanced security features such as the ability to limit or prohibit the insertion and usage of USB devices attached to company computer systems. The software will protect both servers and computers from malicious threats and will automatically change settings on laptops to protect employees when they are out of the office. The software will monitor active processes and applications to prevent unauthorized and harmful changes to your computers. Unlike the Standard Edition, the Advanced Edition includes antispam filtering for Microsoft Exchange Server as well as multilayered spam protection, and it offers protection for Mac clients and servers. Cost for the product starts at around $37 per license for the Standard Edition and $62 per license for the Advanced Edition, which includes technical support and upgrades for a year. This software product is offered in one-, two-, and three-year subscriptions, and licenses can be purchased directly from Trend Micro's website (**www.trendmicro.com**).

We see fewer and fewer installations of Symantec's enterprise products. There's a lot of "bad blood" out there since Symantec introduced their Endpoint Protection product. Independent testing has shown that Symantec is improving this product with each new version. It is getting better at detection, is less problematic with software conflicts, is more stable, and is not nearly the processor load that prior versions experienced. Even with these improvements, we are reluctant to suggest Symantec, especially since we've been burned in the past. We'll revisit this product next year.

Antispam Protection

For antispam protection in an enterprise environment, we use and recommend McAfee's SaaS Email Protection & Continuity service and love it. If you are not using enterprise products and have implemented a stand-alone solution, there is probably antispam capability contained within your stand-alone product.

McAfee's antispam solution provides a lower-cost alternative service for e-mail antispam and antivirus without any of the headaches that come with other products, including the products you actually need to install and run on your e-mail server. Note that your e-mail flow will be rerouted so that it goes through McAfee's servers before being delivered to your mail server or e-mail client. You can purchase the McAfee service directly from the vendor or through a reseller. McAfee's SaaS Email Protection & Continuity solution provides a web-based interface to manage the quarantine, where spam messages are held. Users receive a quarantine message in which they are provided with a summary of the e-mail messages quarantined throughout the day. From this message, a user can choose to release a quarantine message with just a simple click of the mouse.

That's all you need to do to release a captured "false-positive." As the administrator of the account, you can choose when and how frequently you'd like your quarantined summary delivered, whether at the close of business or sometime overnight and whether just once a day or a couple of times throughout the day. We recommend that you set the delivery of the quarantine summary for at least once near the end of the work day, so that any "false-positive" quarantined messages that need to be released can be released the same day without the need to wait overnight until you get back into the office the following morning.

McAfee also has a "mail bag" feature included with this recommended solution. This feature spools your e-mail in the event you lose your Internet connection or your e-mail server goes down. Once your connection or server comes back up, McAfee will feed you the e-mail that it held during the outage, which means you won't lose any e-mail even if your server goes down for a period of time. Even while your server is down, you can access your e-mail from the McAfee portal. In other words, you will not be without e-mail even when your server goes down. Some may think that is a curse rather than a benefit, so we'll let you choose.

McAfee has a very good reputation for quality service, and clients seem to be very happy with it. Since we started using this product two years ago, all of our clients have switched as well (now that Postini is defunct), and the feedback continues to be excellent. You may need to "tweak" the default rules a bit upon initial installation since McAfee is pretty aggressive in blocking messages. As an example, by default any message with the word webinar in it is blocked. That doesn't work for us since we attend (and give) a lot of webinars. Modifying the spam rules is easy, but your administrator should take on this task if needed.

McAfee provides 24/7 technical support; automatic maintenance and upgrades; and a monthly, annual, or multi-year subscription. This product can be purchased directly from McAfee's website (**www.mcafee.com**) and costs start at $23.71 per license for a one year subscription.

CHAPTER FOURTEEN

Case Management

IF YOU STILL LIVE in the paper world, you may not know that a case management application provides all of the functions that you are probably currently performing. You use a Rolodex or some other type of method to aggregate your contact information. We still see address books at the office supply store, but more and more contact information is collected in an electronic form and synchronized to mobile devices. You have a calendar to schedule events, which may be written in a Day Planner. You have a file for each client or each client matter. We hope you use a word processor—or at least your administrative assistant does—to generate documents. You track everything you do for each client matter or keep some sort of diary. You probably even generate some sort of status concerning each matter. These are all functions of a case management system.

Even in a world full of smartphones and wireless devices, it amazes us that most solo and small firm lawyers still don't use a computerized case management software application. We've been making that statement for at least the last ten years. Case management is a must-have for today's modern law office. You may have heard other terms that describe the same type of software. Vendors attempt to differentiate themselves by describing their products with different names. You may hear descriptions such as practice management, contact management, litigation management and so forth. Bottom line: They are all case management products, though they vary greatly in functionality. Arguably, the term practice management is more inclusive and encompasses what is termed "front office" (case/client information) and "back office" (accounting and billing).

There are several choices for case management, some of which we will cover here. The features vary by manufacturer, so make sure you understand what you're buying. Probably the feature we are asked about most is the integration of e-mail and contacts with case management. Make sure that the product will work with your e-mail system and that you understand how it needs to be configured. The synchronization is getting better, but most of our clients are less than impressed with many of the implementations of synchronization support. For example:

- How does the software deal with a common firm-wide Public Folder Calendar?

- Will the product synchronize with your iPad or smartphone?

- What if you don't have an Exchange server and use hosted Exchange services?

- What e-mail clients are supported?

- Can you synchronize data with your Google account?

- Will synchronization occur wirelessly, or do you have to connect a cable and manually sync your data?

- Can you sync everything in your personal mailbox, or are you limited to a subset, such as contacts and calendar only and not the tasks?

There are two mistakes that we consistently see when firms decide to implement a case management system. The first mistake is the failure to require everyone in the firm to use the system. You will not realize the full return on your investment if only a few employees use it. In fact, it tends to cause a whole new set of problems, because sometimes there is crossover between lawyers and cases, and some operate within the case management system and some don't. The second most common mistake is the failure to invest in training. Training will allow all employees to fully use the features of the case management system, thereby becoming more efficient and properly organizing all data for a client matter. Simply dumping a case management system into a firm is worse than useless. When you price the software, price the training as well.

As with other sections of this book, we cannot mention or address every case management package or every feature of every product. We mention the most popular and widely used case management packages that we see being used by solos and small firms.

Amicus Attorney

Amicus Attorney (**www.amicusattorney.com**) from Gavel & Gown Software is a good small firm package that provides a fairly simple approach to case management. The technical requirements are very reasonable and don't require a huge and expensive computer to run. There are essentially two desktop versions available, or you can choose to select the cloud version. The Amicus Attorney Small Firm Edition should work for most solo and small law firms. It is an on-premise solution that is limited to a maximum of ten users. The pricing has not changed in the last six years (highly unusual, but welcome) and remains at $499 for the first user license and $399 for each additional license.

The 2014 Premium Edition uses SQL Server to achieve unlimited user and unlimited data access. The good news is that the Premium Edition includes an embedded SQL Server Standard Edition Restricted Runtime for use with the Amicus Application Server, so you don't have to make a separate purchase unless you want a more robust environment.

For very large-scale installations, a separate SQL server is recommended. SQL Server 2012, 2008 R2, and 2008 (Standard or Enterprise) are supported. Certainly a consideration is the cost of the SQL Server software and the hardware to run it on, which can add a hefty price to the implementation costs. An improvement over prior years' versions is the support for 64-bit versions of the operating system and SQL server. This means that more memory can be supported if you implement the 64-bit versions.

The first user license for the Premium Edition costs $999 and each additional user is $699. The first user cost is the same as the last four years, but the additional user cost went up an additional $100 over last year's price.

Mobility is a real focus for the majority of vendors these days. Amicus is no exception. Amicus TimeTracker is used to connect your mobile phone to the features of Amicus Attorney. You can record your time, edit previous entries, see your list, and much more. Supported smartphones include iPhone 5/4, Android 4.4.x/4.3.x/4.2.x/4.1.x/4.0.x, and BlackBerry Z 10/Torch 9860 and 9850. Supported tablets include iPad with Retina Display/iPad/iPad 2/iPad Mini, Android 4.4.x/4.3.x/4.2.x/4.1.x/4.0.x/3.x, BlackBerry Playbook, and Windows RT Surface. Amicus TimeTracker is available for you during the evaluation period and will always be available if you run Amicus Attorney (Premium or Small Firm) that has a valid maintenance plan.

If you have the Premium Edition, you can synchronize contacts, tasks, and calendar entries by using Google or Outlook as a conduit without any additional purchase. If you need more than just contact and calendar synchronization, the Amicus Anywhere product is available to provide a secure remote connection to your Amicus Premium environment using a browser. Amicus Anywhere provides you with a remote access solution and keeps your data under your control on your server and not in the cloud. Amicus Anywhere also includes TimeTracker, which was mentioned above. Amicus Anywhere is only available for the Premium Edition and not the Small Firm version. There is no additional cost for Amicus Anywhere, but you will have to have a maintenance plan in place. In other words, as long as you pay for maintenance (a touchy subject among a lot of users) you'll be able to take advantage of Amicus Anywhere.

In addition to the on-premise solutions (Amicus Small Firm and Amicus Premium), there is now an option for a cloud-based implementation of Amicus. Amicus Cloud is a full-featured solution that includes matter management, calendaring, task management, global searching, billing, time entries, expense tracking, reporting, document management, and trust accounting. Amicus Cloud uses the cloud services of Microsoft Azure. It is accessible from any device using a modern browser. Supported browsers are Internet Explorer 9 or above, Firefox 9 or above, Safari 5 or above, and Chrome 16 or above. The cost for Amicus Cloud is $45.00 per user per month, or over $540 per user per year. These dollars are going to add up quickly, especially if you have more than one or two users. As with any other cloud service, make sure you understand the terms of service when placing client confidential data on a third-party server.

A trial version of Amicus Attorney (both on-premise and cloud) is available and highly recommended if you are considering purchase. Try the product first to make sure that it meets your needs and will work in your computing environment. Amicus Attorney is often mentioned in reviews as being the most user-friendly product, probably because of the graphic representation it uses as the interface.

Time Matters

LexisNexis has a couple of offerings suitable for the solo and small firm market. Time Matters (**www.timematters.com**) used to be the most popular case management package for solo and small firms (before being purchased by LexisNexis), but we have yet to do a single new installation in over ten years. Time Matters is a very powerful case management application, but it can also be fairly complicated for many small firm lawyers. It is an absolute necessity to purchase training if you are considering implementing Time Matters in your firm. The learning curve is steep but well worth it because Time Matters is truly a feature-rich program.

The current version is Time Matters 13, which includes a Mobility service to keep you connected via your smartphone. Time Matters requires the installation of a dedicated server, which can significantly increase implementation costs for the solo and small firm lawyer, but we agree that Time Matters needs a dedicated server for adequate performance of the application. Also, Time Matters is only supported in a local, directly connected environment. This means that the use of any wireless connections or WAN technologies for the application, which prevents most data center implementations, is not supported. The workstations and server need to be connected to the same local network. Peer-to-peer networks are not supported, hence the requirement for a dedicated server. Perhaps the installation requirements are why we haven't seen any new Time Matters installations for a long time.

New to version 13 is the Client Portal Online File-Sharing feature. This feature is designed to allow you to share your Time Matters documents with clients, experts, and other third parties. The capabilities include:

- Defining who can access the file—only the contact(s) associated with the matter, anyone with the same e-mail domain as the contact(s), or everyone
- Determining what recipients can do with the document—print, download, or view
- Preventing screen captures of the file by only displaying small portions at a time
- Defining the timeframe in which recipients can access the document
- Tracking the file's whereabouts at all times and maintaining an audit trail for compliance purposes
- Revoking access to files anytime

You must have an active maintenance contract to use the Client Portal Online File-Sharing service. Also, you only get 5 GB of data to share at a time, so it may not work for large document volume cases. You can also schedule automatic data backups with version 13. Finally, there are usability improvements to help you work more efficiently with the application.

Licensing for Time Matters is based on concurrent users. Time Matters 13 starts at $985 for the first user, which is the same price as last year and includes a maintenance plan for the first year. Additional users are $640 each. The ordering process for Time Matters has improved over last year, and you can complete the transaction online without contacting a sales representative as was required previously. We highly recommend that you register for the free thirty-day trial if you are considering purchase. Time Matters can be a very large investment for your firm, so you should try it before you buy it.

We have also heard that Time Matters customers are not impressed with the technical support quality and the pressure to purchase maintenance. Perhaps that's another reason to look at alternative case management products.

PracticeMaster

A highly rated case management application (and our personal favorite) is PracticeMaster by STI (**www.practicemaster.com**), which is the choice of most solo and small firms in our area. Version 17 is the current shipping version of PracticeMaster, and it comes in four versions: Basic, PracticeMaster, Platinum, and SQL. The first license for PracticeMaster Basic Edition is already included if you have the Tabs3 billing software. The Basic Edition is just that—basic. The regular version of PracticeMaster contains a number of useful features that most lawyers would desire. You can view a comparison chart for PracticeMaster at **http://practice master.com/products/practicemaster/pm_comparison.html**.

PracticeMaster introduced workflows with version 16. Workflows are essentially triggers that automate tasks within the software. In addition, PracticeMaster has one of the best e-mail integration schemes that we've seen. Smartphone support is excellent as well, especially with Tabs3 Connect.

PracticeMaster and Tabs3 licenses include the first twelve months of maintenance—the same as the distribution plan used by Time Matters. Perhaps it is a new trend to automatically include maintenance as a way to ensure that users pay for support. PracticeMaster Basic is no longer available as a separate purchase. The cost of the regular PracticeMaster version is $600 (including twelve months of maintenance) for the first active user license, and each additional license will set you back another $280. The pricing hasn't changed for the last two years.

In addition to the regular PracticeMaster version, STI offers PracticeMaster in a client server version, which scales to larger implementations. The Platinum version costs $1,320 (including 12 months of maintenance) for the first user license and $365 for each additional user. Don't forget to add the cost of the client server environment when calculating the total cost of the project. As an example, the Platinum Server Software is required for any client server implementation of Tabs3 or PracticeMaster. This Server Software could cost from $965 for 8 connections up to $7,475 for 1,024 server connections. An even more robust implementation would be using Platinum SQL Server Software. Cost for the SQL version is $1,320 for eight connections, and up to $39,340 for 1,024 server connections.

The good news is that STI has updated their website to calculate the software cost quickly. Just go to their price estimator page (**http://practice master.com/products/pricing_info.aspx**) and select which products you are interested in, the number of concurrent users and the number of billable entities if selecting any of the financial packages.

Version 17 of PracticeMaster is the current shipping version, and it includes several new features. QuickViews combines a filter, column layout, and default sort to quickly change the view on the records you see. Smart tabs allow an additional level of filtering by displaying a row of tabs at the bottom of the list. QuickViews can also be shared with other users. Another new feature is a search box at the top right corner of the List tab on every PracticeMaster file.

Mobile access requires the Platinum versions of PracticeMaster and Tabs3, and you must be enrolled in a maintenance plan. With Tabs3 Connect you have access to Tabs3 and PracticeMaster anywhere you can connect to the Internet. This means you can get to your data from your smartphone or other mobile device. You have access to your client and contact information, fee and cost entry, personal and firm-wide calendar, and more. The connection is secured using SSL, and the data resides in your Tabs3/ PracticeMaster environment in your office. Because you must have the Platinum Editions of Tabs3 and PracticeMaster to take advantage of Tabs3 Connect, however, the mobile access feature will be out of the reach of many solo and small firm lawyers, which is very unfortunate, especially since Tabs3 Connect is the best remote access solution to practice management data we have ever seen. After the original introduction of Tabs3 Connect, STI changed its offering, and you can now purchase a subscription instead of requiring all products to be on a maintenance plan. The subscription cost is $5 per user per month. You can learn more about Tabs3 Connect by visiting **http://www.tabs3.com/products/tabs3_ connect/tabs3_connect.html**.

Finally, it is highly recommended that you obtain the trial version of PracticeMaster. This will help you determine whether the product is right for your practice and your installed infrastructure. We don't think you can go wrong with this product. It is constantly being improved, and the support is among the best in the industry.

Clio

Clio (**www.goclio.com**) is a SaaS (Software as a Service) solution that is used by solo, small, and mid-sized firms. Access is via an Internet browser, which means it will work just fine on an Apple computer. The maker of Clio is Themis Solutions, which is headquartered in Vancouver, British Columbia. Themis Solutions has the excellent reputation of listening to its customers and constantly enhancing Clio based on user suggestions. The company also has remote offices in Toronto, Canada, and Dublin, Ireland.

Clio is a full-featured practice management platform. Features such as document management, time tracking, calendaring, tasks, billing, and so on, provide a complete solution. The billing component works well for hourly and flat-fee billing. Users have control over billing rates at the activity or matter level. Clio is highly customizable: Custom fields can be inserted into any matter file. These custom fields have many different formats, so lawyers can enter dates, dollar amounts, website addresses and even full text paragraphs.

Clio can also be configured to synchronize with Outlook and Gmail to provide bidirectional syncing of calendar, contact, and task entries. Clio integrates with many online service providers like Box, Dropbox, Google Drive, NetDocuments, PayPal, Law Pay and many others. Like many other practice management products, Clio is constantly being improved, as can be seen by the increased integration with third-party products.

Clio Connect is a feature that enables firm members to easily share resources and collaborate with clients, contacts, or co-counsels through a secure web-based portal. This grants clients, contacts, or co-counsels the latitude to review and contribute to relevant matter developments, and helps to mitigate associated inefficiencies related to time-consuming communications.

Clio's dedicated iOS application makes it easy to manage your law firm from your mobile Apple device. Clio also has a mobile web version of its service, making Clio accessible on Android and BlackBerry mobile phones as well as on iPads and other types of tablets.

Another key feature is the ability to use the Amazon S3 cloud for data storage, giving you complete control over your data. Your data is automatically backed up to Amazon S3 on a weekly basis. Once the data is replicated to the Amazon cloud, you have the option of downloading the data to your own computer. There is no additional cost to use this feature other than the cost from Amazon, which is pennies per gigabyte. Clio calls this the Data Escrow feature. Just search the help forum on the website for complete instructions on how to activate Data Escrow.

Lastly, Clio provides extensive support to customers free-of-charge. In-house telephone support is available seventeen hours a day. The same service is also available by e-mail and live online chat. Training webinars are available online, typically three days a week. Clio also offers a library of training articles and videos.

Take advantage of the free thirty-day trial to make sure Clio will work for you. The cost is $49 per month for each lawyer that uses Clio and $25 per month for each support staff user. Discounts are available as a member benefit from more than thirty state and municipal bar associations and the American Bar Association. Be sure to ask your bar association if a discount is available.

Clio is one of our favorite SaaS practice management systems, and we highly recommend it. Several of our clients have converted to Clio and never looked back.

Rocket Matter

Rocket Matter, around since 2007, is another SaaS practice management system, but it is web-based and designed specifically for the legal industry. It also contains a time and billing function, which provides almost all you need for your law practice. Rocket Matter is very popular among Macintosh users, as it is web-based. There really isn't any case management application that is geared toward the Apple user community, so Rocket Matter meets that need through web browser access. You can still use Rocket Matter if you are a Windows shop, since all you need is an Internet connection and a web browser.

Many practice management providers offer specific apps for the mobile market. Rocket Matter is no exception. There are specific apps for iOS and Android devices. As we become more and more mobile in our practice, we need mobile access to the firm's data. You can access Rocket Matter using the dedicated apps, but you can also use any mobile device capable of running a full browser. Rocket Matter has been optimized to work with the iPhone, Palm Pre, Windows Phone, Android, and modern BlackBerry phones.

Rocket Matter has released an app specifically designed for the iPad. As CEO Larry Port said, "This is not just a companion app to our Web version. It is a full-featured practice management platform." You have the full ability to edit and access contacts, tasks, matters, notes, etc. Probably one of the most valuable features is that you can operate the app with or without an Internet connection. This means that you can have your full practice management environment with you at the courthouse even if there is no WiFi access to the Internet, which many locations ban or prevent. Any information that you modify or add while you are offline will synchronize with your Rocket Matter environment once you re-connect to the Internet.

Last year, Rocket Matter introduced an offering called Portal 2.0, which allows users to create branded portals. You have the ability to share calendar information, documents, and invoices with clients or anybody else. The portal integrates with LawPay, allowing clients to pay their invoices online. Another feature is the integration with Copy2Contact to add new entries to your Rocket Matter contacts. Integration with Box and Skype is also available. Enter the Skype address for a contact and you can make a direct Skype call from Rocket Matter.

Rocket Matter has changed their pricing since the last edition of this book. Rocket Matter will cost you $65 per month for the first user and then $55 for each additional user. However, Rocket Matter does offer discounts if you make a longer commitment (more than month-to-month) and pay quarterly, annually, or for a two-year term. The discounts—10 percent for quarterly payment, 15 percent for annual payment, or 20 percent for the two-year term—apply to the initial user fee of $65 per month and the $55 per month for additional users. Larger discounts are available, but you have to contact Rocket Matter for details. These dollars can add up quickly when compared to an on-premise solution. As an example, your annual costs will be over $3,400 if you have five users paid on a monthly basis. You could get that cost down to around $2,700 a year for the five users if you commit to a two-year term. There is a thirty-day money-back guarantee, so you can try it out before making the financial commitment.

Rocket Matter is a SaaS implementation and carries the same issues as other providers. The data is held by a third party even though it is transmitted on an encrypted channel. Like Clio, Rocket Matter is always working on improvements to its product. For example, it now provides offline access to your data. You can download your billable time, matters, calendar, and contacts on demand. Those who have used Rocket Matter generally give it favorable reviews, and we recommend that solos and small firms who want a SaaS solution take a look at both Clio and Rocket Matter.

Firm Manager

LexisNexis has its version of a hosted case management system, which is called Firm Manager. It appears that Lexis has Rocket Matter and Clio squarely in its crosshairs as it competes in the SaaS market. Firm Manager is priced at $44.99 per month for the first user and $29.99 per month for each additional user, which is the same as last year. These costs put Firm Manager in a similar price band as the more robust Clio and make it quite a bit less costly than Rocket Matter. Some local bar associations may receive additional discounts. The Firm Manager pricing model is different from the others in that there is no contract commitment and billing is only done on a monthly basis. We hope the pricing holds by the time you read this book; however, Lexis has a disclaimer on its website stating that the pricing offer is only valid until December 31, 2014.

Firm Manager now has the ability to do basic billing and trust accounting for no additional cost. The billing function is new, but it should provide basic billable ability for the solo and small firm attorney.

We have yet to hear of any attorney using Firm Manager. Frankly, we don't think Firm Manager is going to get much traction as it is late to the SaaS game and faces stiff completion from Clio and Rocket Matter. If you are considering Firm Manager, be sure to take advantage of the thirty-day free trial to make sure it will meet your practice needs.

MyCase

We are seeing a lot of buzz surrounding another web-based case management product. MyCase is similar to the other products and provides similar functions, such as shared firm calendars and reminders, tasks, contact management, document organization, time and billing, and so on. It even has an iPhone app to facilitate mobile access. MyCase is also jumping into the lawyer marketing game by providing a MyCase website. Actually, the value of the website is working as a portal for clients to get information about their case, pay their invoices, and securely communicate with the firm. Besides the portal aspects, MyCase looks to be getting into the website provisioning business by building lawyer websites that integrate with MyCase (that's where the client portal feature comes in) and including a blog, social media integration, and basic Search Engine Optimization.

MyCase uses Amazon services to deliver its product to the end user. It runs on Amazon EC2 cloud servers and is backed up using Amazon S3 storage. Data is transferred using SSL encryption and encrypted before being written to disk. Originally, the client access portal differentiated MyCase from the other case management products, but today, the client portals of many of the others function similarly to MyCase.

MyCase costs $39 per month for each lawyer and $29 per month for each paralegal or staff member, at least according to the FAQs on the website. However, if you go to the pricing section of the website, you are immediately sent to the free trial signup page, without any indication of what the service will cost. There is a free thirty-day trial, which we recommend you take advantage of. In late 2012, MyCase was acquired by AppFolio, a provider of web-based software for vertical markets. Time will tell if MyCase will survive the acquisition or migrate more to a marketing application rather than dealing with the daily needs of the solo and small firm attorney. We still don't have any clients using MyCase, but the feedback on the listservs has been positive.

HoudiniEsq

New to this edition of the book is HoudiniEsq, interesting in that it offers an on-premise and a cloud-based version. The feature set is comparable to the other case management offerings. Document management, workflows, contacts, matters, invoicing, document automation, and much more are all functions contained within HoudiniEsq. It integrates with Outlook, Word, Excel, Quickbooks, Evernote, QuickBooks, and so on.

HoudiniEsq has no user software application; everything is accessed via a web browser. Even the on-premise solution uses a browser to run HoudiniEsq. The on-premise solution does require a dedicated computer to host HoudiniEsq, and the technical requirements suggest that you could get an inexpensive ($300–$400) computer from BestBuy to run HoudiniEsq. Sorry, but we certainly don't agree that a cheap consumer grade machine should be used to house your critical firm data and the core of your practice. Perhaps spending a couple hundred bucks is acceptable to run the trial and only for one user. The reality is that most firms (even solos) have at least one support person in addition to the attorney. Speaking of a trial, there isn't one. At least not in the traditional sense. The on-premise single user version is given away for free. It's a full-blown version of HoudiniEsq, but only supports one person.

Others

There are a few other on-premise options we want to mention. One offering is Practice, and it is for 2 to 50 users. You can purchase a one-time license fee of $1,280 per 10 seats or $192 per year per user. The other on-premise offering is Elite and is for 50 to 2,500 users. The cost of a one-time license is $7,992 per 50 seats or $192 per year per user. Finally, there is a SaaS cloud offering that costs $64 per user per month, which is at the high end of other cloud-based case management systems.

Additional products are available, but some of the vendors aren't public with the cost or system requirements. We are less than impressed with companies that aren't open about their pricing and technical requirements. Products like ProLaw (Thomson Elite) and AbacusLaw (Abacus Data Systems, Inc.) require you to fill out a contact form so that a representative can contact you about pricing. We are not fond of this practice and recommend a relationship with more open vendors, especially when you are entering this arena and want to make an apples-to-apples comparison.

CHAPTER FIFTEEN

Time and
Billing Software

$\mathbf{P}$ROBABLY THE SECOND MOST important function of your law practice is billing your clients for services rendered. Practicing law is clearly the most important, but getting paid is second, thereby ensuring the continued success and sustainability of your practice. Lawyers tend to hate the billing process and are not much fonder of the software that helps them generate invoices. A lot of solos and small firms still generate invoices manually. We'll look at both options and try to give you some guidance.

You have a lot of options for generating your bills, from a completely manual system to the fully automatic capture and assembly of invoices. Two components make up the items in your bills. One is time. This component is calculated by taking the hourly rate and applying it to the amount of time spent on a task. You can capture this time manually or automatically while the task is being accomplished. Flat fees are also considered time components, where the dollar amount is applied irrespective of the time spent. The second component is the fixed-cost items of the invoice. This would include such expenses as postage, copier costs, filing fees, courier charges, and any other fixed fees. As with the time components, you can track these expenses manually or automatically (to some level or another) through the use of technology.

We are seeing more and more firms adopting some sort of alternative fee arrangements (AFAs) for their practice. It may be flat fee only or a hybrid type of billing with a flat fee portion and an hourly portion. AFAs are more complicated to automate because of the various customized rules that may apply. The good news is that many of the software packages are sophisticated enough to handle customized rules and they are getting better and better as time goes by. You may have to deal with some manual override techniques if the billing software can't accommodate a particular AFA scenario.

As in other sections of this book, we'll try to cover a lot of the billing methods and applications that we see being used by the solo and small firm attorneys. This will not be an all-inclusive list, so if your favorite product isn't mentioned it probably means that we've never seen (or heard) of it being used by solo or small firms.

Manual Generation

Pencil and paper are the simplest way to capture time and expense. With manual generation, however, you must remember to log your time and the number of copies or whatever other chargeable component needs to be tracked. Make no mistake about it, studies have shown over and over again that this manual tracking results in a lot of lost time and expense. Because a lawyer's time equals money, many lawyers are shortchanging themselves by not moving to a technology-based solution.

Nevertheless, if this is what you do, on a periodic basis (daily, monthly, the end of the case, and so forth) you total the charges and generate the bill. Many solo practitioners start by using a word processing package to generate their bills to save some money. These bills are professional enough in appearance but still require manually adding up numbers and multiplying other numbers. In addition, another method is needed to keep track of payments made by the client and/or transfers of funds from other sources, such as the trust account. As the practice becomes more complicated, the billing process becomes more susceptible to mistakes.

If you must start with a manual method for generating your invoices, invest in billing software as soon as possible to improve your accuracy, maximize your income, and minimize your losses.

Accounting Software—QuickBooks

Some lawyers are actually using a financial accounting package to generate their bills. Certainly the most popular software application we see is QuickBooks by Intuit (**quickbooks.intuit.com**). Using QuickBooks to generate invoices allows the firm to have a total financial package, where all sorts of financial reports are available. However, productivity reports are not available. You won't be able to easily determine how many billable hours are attributed to a specific individual or how much money you lost due to write-offs. One advantage of using QuickBooks is the ability to generate payroll. This may not be a compelling reason for many lawyers, especially given the added cost, complexity, and reporting requirements. In general, it is more cost-effective to use a third-party service provider, such as ADP or Paychex, to handle solo and small firm payrolls. Quick-Books can also handle processing of credit card payments, thereby integrating another piece of the financials into a single product. We hear that most lawyers began using QuickBooks because their accountant told them to. Make sure your accountant sets up your chart of accounts in QuickBooks so you know where certain charges and fees should go. Your CPA should be familiar with financials for a law firm. If not, it's probably time to look for a new accountant.

QuickBooks comes in several different versions—even an online version that allows access from any computer and does not require installation of any software. We don't recommend using the online version, as it requires that your data be stored at Intuit. Your financial data is highly sensitive and we recommend that you control your own data and not risk compromise by holding it at a third-party site. Consider, too, the possibly severe consequences if the third party is "down" and you can't manage the financial part of your law practice. In the last quarter of 2010, Intuit announced that it was shutting down the Quicken Online service and users could only export their data in CSV (comma separated values) format. While Quicken is a consumer-based product, we certainly wouldn't want to be stuck in the same situation if Intuit decided to shut down QuickBooks Online.

Since QuickBooks is an accounting package, some knowledge of financial principles is helpful. You will need to set up a chart of accounts for your practice. We recommend consulting with your accountant before configuring QuickBooks so that your financial categories are consistent with the accountant's needs and your business needs. If you are new to Quick-Books, you may want to consider purchasing a support plan to help you learn the features of the software and get technical help. Many local community colleges also offer evening classes for QuickBooks, which would be a relatively inexpensive way to get some training in how to use the product.

The QuickBooks versions vary in cost from $249.95 up to $999.95 for a single user for the Enterprise version. The cost variance is due to the capabilities of the software and the number of concurrent user licenses that are needed. Most solo and small firms will find that QuickBooks Pro is more than sufficient for their needs. The cost is $249.95 for a single user. In previous years, Intuit offered a three-pack license at a reduced rate over the single user cost directly from the website. That discount is no longer available and three licenses will be three times the single user cost (actually it's slightly higher than three times). You can still get a "three pack" retail license version from traditional software sellers.

New this year is QuickBooks Pro 2014 Plus, which is an annual subscription product that includes support, data backups, and updates. The cost is $299.95 per user per year. Phone support is available on a 24/7 basis; up to 100 GB of data can be backed up, and recovered data is available up to forty-five days; and the updates and enhancements happen automatically. The $299.99 per year cost seems rather high to us, especially since you'll be spending money year after year. We would recommend purchasing the standard QuickBooks Pro software and upgrading the version every two or three years. That will save you several hundred dollars over the life of the software.

The QuickBooks Premier version contains additional features for specific industries and expanded reporting capabilities. As an example, you can track unbilled time and expenses for professional services, set different billing rates by employee, client, and service, and analyze profitability by matter. QuickBooks Premier 2014 is $399.95 per user. Like QuickBooks Pro, there is a QuickBooks Premier 2014 Plus version that includes support, backup, and updates. The cost of QuickBooks Premier 2014 Plus is $419.95 per user per year.

Besides the Windows version, a version for Macintosh computers is also available. Accountants love it when lawyers use QuickBooks as their billing software. They can take the QuickBooks data file at the end of the year and generate tax returns with relative ease.

However, we don't recommend using QuickBooks for billing for several reasons. First, the invoices are very sterile looking and can't be made to appear more professional. The data is there and clients can understand the information, but the invoice format lacks any capability for graphics, different fonts, custom text to identify different sections, or rearrangement of how the information appears on the page. Showing remaining balances properly is an issue too—a real problem if you want to show trust account balances and transfers, or automatically indicate how much of the evergreen retainer needs to be replenished. As previously mentioned, QuickBooks Pro won't provide you with any productivity reports either unless you purchase the Premier version. You're going to have to find a different way to determine how many write-down hours an associate had for a month or the amount of no-charge entries by client. In spite of these limitations, we still see a lot of lawyers using QuickBooks.

Billing Specific—Timeslips

Arguably the most popular and widely used billing software among solo and small firm lawyers is Timeslips by Sage (**www.timeslips.com**). Timeslips is a billing specific software package that generates bills, tracks receivables, and manages trust accounting. We see many Timeslips installations in solo and small firm offices, especially those that have no case management system. Even so, we are beginning to see firms implementing invoicing products that are included with the integrated solutions that we describe later on.

Probably one of the reasons for the popularity of Timeslips is that it can be configured specifically for the legal industry right out of the box and supports the LEDES billing format. When you first install Timeslips, you select the type of business. This configures Timeslips to use the types of tasks and expenses that are specific to the industry. As an example, when you select the legal profession, default tasks are automatically created that deal with those tasks that are performed in the law office. There will be tasks for consultations, document review, depositions, and so forth. The expense names are also automatically created and would include such costs as copier usage, courier fees, postage, and the like. Trust accounting is also built into Timeslips, which is another reason the software is very popular in solo and small firm offices. You can configure Timeslips to automatically deduct fees earned from the trust account or leave it as a manual transfer process. In addition, Timeslips can automatically create the dollar amount to place on the invoice to bring the retainer amount back to a set level. This is a very popular feature for those attorneys who have evergreen retainer arrangements.

Timeslips is licensed on a per-machine basis. Each computer that needs to access Timeslips will require the purchase of a license. In a small office, it is often the case that only one computer is used to process billing. The timekeepers (typically lawyers) may elect to manually track their time on paper and give the time sheets to the office manager or bookkeeper for entry into Timeslips. This arrangement keeps licensing costs down and allows for growth in the law firm. As the firm grows, additional licenses may be purchased and network access configured for the Timeslips database. Larger firms that may use a terminal server need licenses only for the number of concurrent users. With the expanded interest and implementation of virtual computers, this concurrent license model may be a way to control costs.

The current version is Timeslips 2015. Timeslips costs $519.99 for a single station, which is a slight increase ($20) over last year's cost. Additional network stations may be added up to a total of ten stations and can be purchased online. The cost per workstation keeps getting less and less as the number of workstations goes up. With ten workstations you will pay $318.39 per computer. If you only need five workstations, then your cost will be $340.79 per computer. You'll have to contact Sage if you need eleven or more licenses. Support options are also available for Timeslips. If you have never used Timeslips, we recommend that you purchase a support plan at least for the first year of operation. After the first year, we do not recommend that you prebuy any support unless you intend to use and implement features of the newer versions. Access to the free online knowledge base is usually sufficient to work through most issues that you are likely to experience.

There are two support plans available. The Billing Assurance Essential Plan is the recommended one if you are going to purchase support. It covers most incidents that you are likely to encounter. The Billing Assurance Premium Plan is more inclusive and includes database repair services. We don't feel that the Premium Plan is worth the additional cost. You should be backing up your database on a daily basis anyway. Timeslips was notorious for data corruption issues with past versions of the software. The recent versions of Timeslips databases are much more stable. Currently, we use Timeslips for billing and haven't experienced a data corruption issue for over seven years, but we do have our daily backups as well.

Timeslips can also link with QuickBooks. Setting up this integration is a manual process and can be complicated. You have to make sure that the Timeslips tasks and expenses have a corresponding QuickBooks account. Permissions (Timeslips and QuickBooks) also need to be considered. If you run a networked version of QuickBooks, multiuser versus single user could also cause some complications with the integration. A reader of a previous edition of this book advised us that Timeslips technical support will not help with any of the accounting aspects dealing with the QuickBooks link, as they feel it is giving financial advice and do not want the liability.

Perhaps this is one of the reasons why our clients who use Timeslips and QuickBooks don't bother with the integration and manually input data into QuickBooks.

Some of the providers for case management software have also built links to Timeslips. Case management product links are possible for Abacus Law, Amicus Attorney, Legal Files Software, and Time Matters. Contact the provider of the case management software if you are interested in how the link would work and what the limitations are.

Billing for a Mac

There are not that many legal specific software applications for Mac computers. Most Mac users will migrate toward web-based products for their firms. There are some native Mac applications, but like the Windows world, more and more users are moving toward the cloud.

Bill4Time

SaaS offerings are very popular in the Mac community. All you need is an Internet connection and a web browser. Bill4Time (**www.bill4time.com**) is one billing package we see used in law offices with Macs. It is a secure hosted environment that is available from any computer at any time. A free thirty-day trial will allow you to see if it fits your needs. Bill4Time now has a legal-specific version, which contains ABA Task Codes, LEDES export for invoices, Litigation Advisor export for invoices, Trust Accounting with Summaries and Reports, and Easily Check for Conflicts of Interest. Most attorneys will want to get the Legal Solo or Legal Pro version. All legal versions allow for unlimited clients and unlimited projects. The Legal Solo version limits data storage to 2 GB. The Legal Pro version has a 10 GB storage limit and the Legal Enterprise version has unlimited data storage. One convenient feature of Bill4Time is its mobile app. This means you can use your smartphone (Android or iPhone) to enter your time and expenses while out of the office. As we mentioned before, you need to keep track of all your billable activities—otherwise you are losing money. The mobile app feature is a great way to help maximize your revenue.

Before you commit to spending any money for Bill4Time, try their free plan. The free plan is limited to one user, three clients, five projects and 100 MB of storage. The limitations should be enough to see if the product can perform adequately in your firm. If so, then move to the actual paid solutions.

The Legal Solo version of Bill4Time is $19.99 per month and includes one user license. You can only add one additional user at a cost of $9.99 per month. This may be fine for the solo practitioner, but some small firms may need more than two users. The Legal Pro version is $39.99 per month and also includes one user license. However, you can add unlimited users at a cost of $9.99 per month for each user. Finally, the Legal Enterprise version is $99.99 per month and also includes one user license. Like the Pro version, unlimited users can be added for $9.99 per month per user. We think that $99.99 per month for unlimited storage and premium support is a bit much for a web-based billing package. At that rate, we would recommend investigating other billing alternatives to include on-premise solutions.

EasyTime

Many of the practice management implementations also include some sort of billing mechanism, so you may not need a separate software application. We'll mention a few of the billing packages that are available for the Mac, but we certainly can't mention them all. One such stand-alone package for the Mac is EasyTime. EasyTime, by Bright Light Software (**www.brightlightsoftware.com**), runs natively on Mac OS X and does not require any third-party database packages. The current version is 3.0.4, released June 24, 2014. It requires MacOS 10.7 or higher. The cost is $240 for a single user and $290 for a network version, which are significant increases over last year's cost.

Billings Pro

Another popular package is Billings Pro (**www.marketcircle.com/billingspro/**) by Marketcircle. The Billings Pro cost model is one that identifies how many invoices, statements, or estimates you can generate per month. The Freelance plan costs $5 per user per month and limits you to five invoices, five estimates, and five statements per month. This plan doesn't seem to be very practical unless you only have a couple of very large clients and don't invoice all that often. The Professional plan is $10 per user per month and gives you unlimited invoices, estimates, and statements per month. Since there is no contract commitment with Billings Pro, we would recommend starting with the Professional plan. If it looks like Billings Pro is something that works for your firm, then convert to the Professional Yearly plan, which costs $99 for a full year. Additional users are also $99 per user for the year.

A big concern with the Billings Pro cloud offering is that their datacenter is located in Canada. Your data is stored locally and gets synchronized to the servers in Canada. This means that you can continue to work if the network is unavailable or the servers are unreachable. Some attorneys may feel that storing billing information for their clients in another country is not a problem and accept potential cross border issues. Of course the Canadian attorneys welcome the fact that the servers are in their own country.

If you already have your own network and server, you can opt for hosting Billings Pro on your own equipment. The server-based version is called Self-Serve and is available for a one-time fee per user of $199.95. You will need a stationary Mac (iMac, Mac mini, or Mac Pro) as laptops are not recommended. As with most of the products mentioned, be sure to take advantage of the free thirty-day trial before purchase.

Integrated Packages

Many of the case management products now support integration with billing packages. This means that you enter your information into the case management system and the time or expense is automatically captured for the billing process. There are advantages to using the same vendor for your case management and billing needs. The products are designed to work together and share information in a very efficient manner. However, selecting these all-in-one packages may not give you the best features of each package. If you really want a "best of breed" implementation, then make sure you investigate how the case management and billing packages share the data. Many case management applications provide links to billing packages by other vendors. Be careful to understand how to configure these links, especially if it is a manual process. We've seen clients who added tasks to their case management software and forgot to define the linkage to their billing software. This means that you may not bill for the effort when you use these newly defined tasks.

PCLaw

LexisNexis has several billing options to address the needs of solo and small firm law offices. A very popular package is PCLaw Version 13 (**www.lexisnexis.com/law-firm-practice-management/pclaw/**), which includes a mobility function to keep your mobile devices synchronized with Outlook for access to calendar and contact information. PCLaw includes some features that you would expect from a case management system. You can keep track of contacts, calendar entries, phone calls, notes, tasks, and so on. This choice may be a good alternative for a solo practitioner to keep start-up costs down since it includes basic case management functions along with billing in a single package.

It seems like other vendors are adopting the Lexis model by including the first year of maintenance into the product cost. No more opting out of the annual maintenance for new purchases. You certainly have the option of not renewing your maintenance agreement, although you may not want to let it lapse. The Annual Maintenance Plan (AMP) bundles technical support, software upgrades, support, training, and access to PCLaw Mobility Service. Also, if you let your maintenance lapse, you will be charged a restart fee to get your AMP subscription back on track.

Transparency doesn't seem to be a hallmark of LexisNexis. If you want to know the cost of renewing your maintenance plan or add additional PCLaw users, you have to already own the product or contact a LexisNexis representative. The pricing is no longer available on the LexisNexis website for the public to view. As we've mentioned before, this is not a practice that we are fond of, and we recommend using products from vendors that are transparent with their pricing.

Juris is another billing software application offered by LexisNexis. It is typically used by larger law firms or in integrating with Time Matters. We have never seen Juris used in a solo or small firm setting. As with some of the other products mentioned, you have to contact Lexis to get pricing information. You can't even get a single license cost like you can with Time Matters or PCLaw.

Tabs3

Another popular billing package is Tabs3 by STI. Tabs3 is the companion product to PracticeMaster, which is STI's case management software. Tabs3 pricing is based on the number of billable entities. Like so many other vendors, the cost of the software includes the first year of maintenance. The solo and small firm pricing for a single-user is $415 for two timekeepers and increases to $675 for five timekeepers. You'll need to purchase the multiuser version if you need more than one person to access the data at the same time.

The regular multiuser version is available for 2, 5, 9 and 19 timekeepers. The cost is $675, $1,340, $1,915 and $3,065 respectively. The Platinum version of Tabs3 costs $950 for 2 timekeepers up to $15,940 for 100+ (maximum of 999) timekeepers. STI defines a timekeeper as someone whose time is tracked in the software.

See the Case Management chapter to learn about the new mobility features of Tabs3 Connect, which became available in version 16.2 Platinum Edition. Even though Tabs3 Connect is a killer application for mobile access to your data, we don't think many solo or small firms will spend the money to have both Platinum versions of Tabs3 and PracticeMaster along with the requisite maintenance plan to get the feature included for no cost.

Version 17 of Tabs3 is the currently shipping version. One of the new features is the ability to Undo Split Billing. This will let you reverse the split billing process for individual clients. Another new feature is Automatic Update Notifications, which will let you know when a critical update is available.

Unlike other billing packages, Tabs3 has separated out various financial functions and priced them as individual components. As an example, there are additional components, such as trust accounting, general ledger, and accounts payable. This means that you can expand Tabs3 from a pure billing package into a complete accounting package. You can find more information about Tabs3 at **www.tabs3.com**. We regard Tabs3 as highly as we do its case management counterpart, PracticeMaster. It also consistently receives high ratings from legal software experts.

Amicus Premium Billing

A less widely used billing option is provided by Amicus Attorney. A lot of solo and small firms use Amicus Attorney as a practice management package, but few use the billing option. There are two billing packages available, and the version of Amicus you are running determines which is appropriate. You would use the Amicus Premium Billing application if you are running Amicus Attorney Premium Edition. If you are running Amicus Attorney Small Firm Edition, then the Amicus Small Firm Accounting software is for you.

Amicus Premium Billing 2014 adds billing, collections, and trusts to your Amicus Attorney installation. Like most billing packages, it lets you capture time and expenses for hourly, flat fee, and contingent billing. Each license is priced at $249, which makes it one of the lowest-cost billing packages. This product will not run by itself; it is an add-on to the Amicus Attorney Premium Edition case management software. Maintenance and technical support plans are also available. You can purchase a maintenance plan that includes unlimited technical support, Mobility, and product updates. The first license will set you back $550 a year but also covers Amicus Attorney software maintenance. Each additional license is $495, so the dollars will add up quickly if you have more than a couple of users. You also have the option of purchasing a technical support plan only, without product updates. Unlimited technical support for a year is $295 for the first license (includes the required Amicus Attorney support) and $145 for each additional license.

Amicus Small Firm Accounting 2014 combines billing and accounting packages into a single software product. This is a completely standalone application and does not require the base case management software as in the Premium Edition. Although not a requirement, Amicus Small Firm Accounting 2014 will integrate with Amicus Small Firm to give you a total practice management solution for your firm. The initial license cost for Amicus Small Firm Accounting is $499 and each additional license is $399. Like the Premium package, the Small Firm version lets you purchase maintenance or technical-support-only plans. The maintenance plan, which includes product updates, Mobility, and unlimited technical support, is $385 and includes support for the base case management product. The maintenance cost would only be $85 per year if you are running only the Small Firm Accounting product by itself. Each additional license is $305 and includes the Small Firm maintenance. Each additional Small Firm Accounting maintenance charge is $85 per year. Unlimited technical support only is the same cost as the Premium version. The cost is $295 per year for the first license and $145 per year for each additional license.

Final Thoughts

One of the higher-level (expensive) billing alternatives is provided by ProLaw, which is a Thomson Elite product. ProLaw is an integrated package and the billing component is not available as a separate function. Very few solos and small law firms have chosen this route in our experience.

Most of our clients who use stand-alone applications have chosen QuickBooks or Timeslips for billing, and they are generally quite happy with what they have chosen—though everything has a learning curve. All of these vendors are happy to let you sample their product in one manner or another, so don't hesitate to try before you buy. Also, if you aren't keen on accounting, talk to your friends who are equally numbers-challenged and see what has worked for them. In many cases, the choice has been made by someone at the firm who is going to perform the accounting or bookkeeping functions, and that's fine. As long as you stay with one of the "majors," you won't be left scrambling to find someone who knows your obscure time and billing package if that person leaves.

CHAPTER SIXTEEN

Litigation Programs

SEVERAL PROGRAMS CAN AUTOMATE certain litigation support functions, and while they offer different features, they fall into two general categories: case organization programs and courtroom presentation programs. Case organization programs are databases that are set up to analyze and manage facts and evidence. The common ones include LexisNexis Concordance (**www.lexisnexis.com/en-us/litigation/ products/concordance.page**), LexisNexis CaseMap (**http://www .lexisnexis.com/en-us/litigation/products/casemap.page**), Thomson Reuters Case Notebook (**legalsolutions.thomsonreuters.com/law-products/solutions/case-notebook**), and Sanction Solutions Verdical (**www.verdictsystems.com/Software/Verdical**).

Summation is a case organization program now provided by Access Data. The litigation support products many of you have known, such as iBlaze, are still being offered by Access Data. Access Data is leveraging its forensic experience and merging e-discovery tools in an attempt to provide a total end-to-end solution. The Summation products are now integrated in the product offerings from Access Data. The newly named offerings are AD eDiscovery, AD Viewer, and Summation.

These programs help you organize and review the information for your case. You can accomplish various tasks such as tagging for privilege, creating privilege logs, identifying responsive documents, etc. They are typically installed on-premise on your own hardware, but some also offer cloud solutions. More and more companies are now offering cloud-based electronic discovery platforms, where you upload electronic files for review and ultimate production. Law firms are embracing these cloud solutions, which can be very cost effective and don't have the technical headaches of on-premise solutions.

CaseMap from LexisNexis is one of the most popular case organization packages for solo and small firm lawyers, given its lower cost and ease of use.

Trial presentation programs manage and display electronic evidence, including exhibits, video and text depositions, sound files, and more. They facilitate quick access during trials and hearings and include on-the-fly annotation, such as highlighting and call-outs. Trial presentation programs include Trial Director (**www.indatacorp.com/Products/Trial/trialDirector.aspx**) and Visionary (**www.visionarylegal.com/products/product.aspx?ProductsID=3**). Sanction (**http://www.lexisnexis.com/en-us/litigation/products/sanction.page**) is now a product of LexisNexis.

The above referenced products are full featured and can give a lot of whiz bang to the presentation of evidence at trial. The reality is that today's jurors want to see trials that seem like they are watching TV. They expect fancy effects, transitions, call outs, and quick access to exhibits. The day of the document camera is fading though by no means gone. Annotations similar to the "John Madden marker" are finding their way into courtrooms across the country.

More maturity is now evident in the trial presentation packages for the iPad. Products such as TrialPad (**www.trialpad.com**) turn the iPad into a presentation tool for litigators. Since we are seeing so many litigators equipped with an iPad, we would highly recommend starting with TrialPad for your trial presentation software. For $89.99 you can't go wrong by giving it a try. Trial Director for the iPad is a free download from the app store, but is a quite limited version of the flagship product for the PC. Free is a good price for the solo and small firm attorney, but reviews indicate that inData Corporation has a long way to go with its iPad application. Try it out, but we'll guess that you will end up using TrialPad instead. There are several other "competitors" to TrialPad such as Exhibit A and ExhibitView. We feel that TrialPad has maintained the beachhead for iPad trial presentation software. Unless you have a compelling, specific reason to use one of the other products, it appears that TrialPad is the product of choice for the majority of litigators.

Most of the above mentioned products have free downloads for a trial period or online demos. Although we do not review them in detail, they should be considered by lawyers with litigation practices. Be sure to read the iPad chapter by Tom Mighell and Paul Unger, which includes more detail about litigation products that are available for the iPad.

CHAPTER SEVENTEEN

Document
Management

DOCUMENT MANAGEMENT SOFTWARE SOLUTIONS can be relatively expensive for the solo or small firm operation, although there are some cost-effective alternatives. Several of the better-known document management products tend to be used more for enterprise-size companies because of their cost and complexity. As the industry matures, vendors are merging the functions of document management, content management, and knowledge management. This is especially true as electronic files are becoming a critical component of discovery. You may see applications described as document management systems, content management systems, knowledge management systems, or even enterprise content management systems. Just because a vendor chooses to describe its product using particular words doesn't mean there is anything unique or special about it. In general, all of the terms previously mentioned are used for applications that organize information.

The main purpose of a document management system is to organize information into a usable and searchable form. How many times have you looked for a file or document but couldn't remember the name or location? A document management system allows for fast and easy access to the data, whether in paper or electronic form. It also provides access control and enforceability of rules. As an example, perhaps one of your rules is that every document has a specific category (programmed ahead of time) tagged to it. This makes for consistency and removes the human error in typing or misspelling the category tag. In addition, security is another feature of document management systems. Typically, you can set security access to particular matters, specific types of files or even unique files themselves. One person could have full control over a document, whereas another might be able to view the content, but not modify it.

DocuShare

We will mention just a few of the products that are available, but understand that document management systems are not generally designed for small-scale operations. Xerox's DocuShare (**docushare.xerox.com**) has been around for many years. Pricing is available directly from Xerox or through partners. An entry-level version of DocuShare (DocuShare Express) is now available for small to mid-sized office installations, which starts at a couple thousand dollars for ten users. The current version (DocuShare 6.6) requires a 64-bit server, which would significantly increase costs if you don't have one available. DocuShare Express can run on 32-bit versions of Windows 2003 Server R2 or SP2 and Windows 2008 Server SP2. DocuShare may be a viable alternative, especially if you already have a Xerox copier that you could use for scanning documents. Be sure to take advantage of the free thirty-day trial if you are considering acquiring DocuShare.

WorkSite

It is really hard to stay current with a product that changes names and companies so many times over its life. Several years ago, we knew it as Interwoven. Then it was known as Autonomy iManage WorkSite. Today, Autonomy is an HP company and the product name is just WorkSite. As with DocuShare, expect to pay thousands of dollars for this system. It is a highly regarded document management environment (if you can remember the name) but is also geared more toward the intermediate to large-scale firms.

Worldox

The most popular and most used document management system for solo and small firm operations is Worldox (**www.worldox.com**). Worldox is licensed on a concurrent user basis and not per seat. There are now three versions of Worldox. GX3 Professional is the standard network client server installation that has been around for ages. It is the traditional desktop version. The next version is GX3 Enterprise, which is adapted for multi-office, remote access environments. It is typically hosted at a data center and has full communication with local applications, including Microsoft Office, Outlook, and third-party products such as case management. The final version is a SaaS hosted solution called GX3 Cloud. With the GX3 Cloud solution, your data is hosted on Worldox servers in its data center.

The cost for Worldox GX3 Professional is $425 per concurrent user, which makes it very affordable for solo and small firms, especially since there are no minimum seat purchase requirements. Annual maintenance is $91 per license and is mandatory for new orders. No separate server is required, and the indexer can be run on any workstation-class computer. The computer resource requirements for Worldox are very light when compared to other document management systems. The application is very robust and easy to use, hence its popularity within the legal community.

GX3 Enterprise is intended for multiple offices and remote access environments. It looks and acts just like the local desktop (GX3 Professional) version. You must contact Worldox to get pricing information at this time.

Worldox also offers a Web Mobile addition to the Worldox software. The mobile edition gives you access to your documents from multiple devices and locations. It currently supports a wide range of devices, including any web-browser notebook or desktop, iPads, BlackBerry smartphones, Android devices, iPhones, Treos, and Windows CE PDAs and smartphones. There are two pricing models for the mobile access. For $30 per user per month, you can implement the SaaS hosted solution, which installs the proxy software on your indexer. You can reduce the cost to $25 per user per month with a one year pre-payment. You can also install it on your own server, but the costs start to climb quickly. You will need a server license ($995), user licenses ($49 per named user), annual maintenance ($10 per user and $200 per server per year), a proxy server license ($600), and proxy server maintenance ($120). Doing the math, it will cost you $2,210 for five users in the first year. Years two and beyond would be $370 per year for the maintenance charges for the five-user system. Installing your own Worldox/Web Mobile server makes financial sense if you plan to use it for two or more years.

Worldox also includes a Legal Hold feature. The Legal Hold feature will be a great benefit for firms and companies as part of the litigation process. If you are in litigation or if litigation is reasonably anticipated, you have an ethical requirement not to destroy any potentially relevant evidence. Legal Hold will let you assign rights and restrictions to files. You can even create restricted-access security groups so that only authorized employees can access the designated files. In addition, each action is tracked to create an audit trail showing who did what to which file. The key feature for Legal Hold is the ability to "lock" a file so that it cannot be changed. The best news? The Legal Hold feature is free for all Worldox GX3 Professional users. You can't ask for anything better than that. Well, perhaps you can—it is also very simple to use. Do be forewarned that this is not complex "litigation hold software," which includes many more features. Worldox also has support for Mac computers, which includes many of the same functions as the Windows product. Worldox for Mac is not a stand-alone product. It requires an existing Worldox GX3 installation or the Worldox GX3 Cloud offering.

Last year, Worldox announced integration with Sony's Digital Paper device. Worldox will sync documents and notes with the Sony Digital Paper device using Worldox FileCloud. Worldox FileCloud works like Dropbox, but is hosted within the Worldox private cloud environment and does not require you to use the Worldox Document Management System. Think of it as walking around with a wireless tablet that has access to all of your documents. You can make notations and edits that will be saved with the document. Worldox FileCloud is available on a subscription basis for $120 a year. The subscription includes 5 GB of document storage.

Case management systems (see the Case Management chapter) are also used to provide a certain level of document management. Your electronic files are referenced to a client or client matter, making them easily accessible at the click of a mouse. A key point to remember about true document management applications is their stringent enforcement of the classification rules. The user must use the system within the configured rules, which sometimes frustrates people because of the rigid requirements. In contrast, applications that are not specifically document management software aren't restrictive or mandatory. The danger is that data may be lost or misfiled when the rules are not stringently enforced. Worldox is an excellent choice for document management, as it integrates with almost every case management system available. It consistently receives good reviews from legal software experts.

Matter Center

Microsoft is getting into the document management game. Matter Center for Office 365 was announced at the ILTA annual conference in Nashville during August of 2014. You can take advantage of Matter Center for an on-premise solution, but it requires SharePoint 2013, Exchange 2013, and Office 2013. That kind of infrastructure is an expensive proposition for the solo or small firm attorney. You can deploy it in a hybrid environment too, but we think that could also be a bit pricey. More realistically, the solo and small firm attorney would use Matter Center with Office 365, which includes the required components. According to the announcement, attorneys can have secure access to the information they need from virtually any devices with the following benefits:

Your briefcase in the cloud. Matter Center works with OneDrive for Business, providing 1 TB of individual storage and a personal briefcase, which automatically synchronizes your documents so you can access them online and offline from virtually any device.

Get more work done together. Share your files with others, both within and outside your firm. Work simultaneously on your documents with other attorneys, and easily track changes with automatic version control.

Robust matter and document search. Easily search and find matters and related documents directly within Outlook or Word. Track or pin frequently used or recent matters and documents.

Integrated and automated document management. Drag, drop, and save e-mails and attachments from Outlook into the right matter. Tagging and sharing each document separately is no longer necessary, as the matter documents are automatically saved with the right metadata, permissions, and version control.

Security-enhanced access and permission controls. Users can be granted or excluded access to a matter. All subsequent documents associated with the matter will inherit the same permissions, thereby reducing the worry about ethical walls and data leakage.

Reduce overhead and maximize time with clients. Matter Center helps you to reduce the amount of administrative resources needed to support a document management system, enabling you to spend more time working with clients.

The actual production release date is not known at this time since the product was just announced. The cost has not been set either, but we expect it to be priced at a reasonable level and possibly available by the time this book is in print.

Acrobat

Many solo and small firm offices are equipped with Adobe's Acrobat product. The latest versions of Acrobat provide the ability to manage documents. The collaboration components within Acrobat are used to organize and reference files in a manner similar to other document management systems.

Web-Based

Web-based document management systems are becoming very popular. The cost per user is typically more than purchasing a product for use within your firm, but you save on the hardware and internal support costs. The vendor provides the back-end hardware and software for the management of your documents. The nice part about web-based document management systems is that the information is accessible from any computer with an Internet connection. The bad part is that the vendor is holding your data and you are subject to the reliability of the Internet connection. If you elect to use one of the online document management systems, be aware of the security precautions for client data that is being held by a third party. At a minimum, make sure that the connection for accessing the documents is encrypted and that the data is stored in an encrypted form on the provider's equipment. You should also make sure that you have a copy of the data in your hands to avoid being "held hostage" by the third-party provider. And yes, we've seen that happen. More and more vendors now offer cloud solutions in addition to their traditional on-premise solutions.

NetDocuments

NetDocuments is a popular SaaS provider for document management. Many law firms, small to large, have had great experiences with NetDocuments. We have heard lawyers say that it was very easy to install and configure. In one case, a lawyer converted his firm (tens of thousands of documents) over to NetDocuments in a weekend all by himself. NetDocuments provides all of the features you would expect in a document management system, in addition to matter-centric workspaces, e-mail management, collaboration, and mobile access.

There are three versions of NetDocuments: Basic, Pro+, and Enterprise. The Basic version is $25 per user per month and has a two-user minimum. The Basic version is essentially a basic folder-based document storage system along with search capability, document versioning, the ability to set document permission and user access, as well as integration with Microsoft Office and Adobe. The Pro+ offering is intended for small to medium-sized firms and includes e-mail management. The cost is $40 per user per month with a two-user minimum. The third offering is the Enterprise solution, which is intended for firms with thirty or more users or complex implementation requirements. You will need to contact NetDocuments if you are interested in the Enterprise plan.

Previously, there were limits on the amount of storage you received with each plan as well as costs for various add-ons, but the website no longer references any additional costs or volume restrictions. We encourage you to take advantage of the thirty-day free trial before making any financial commitment.

Plain Folders

Finally, a very simple form of document management for solo and small firms is to follow a standard folder and file naming convention along with search software (see the Utilities chapter for search tools). Besides the potential cost for search software, this is a very low-cost solution. Some lawyers will use the search capabilities of Windows or Mac before even investing in supplemental search software. Typically, folders are named on a client or client-matter basis. Files are then given a very descriptive name, such as <client name>, followed by the file purpose and sometimes the date. As an example, "Rothburg request for admissions.doc" would be the file name for your request for admissions in the Rothburg matter. This is a very manageable method to organize data when your practice is small. As your practice grows, search software may be needed to assist in finding particular files pertaining to specific issues.

Searching

Search software such as dtSearch or X1 (see the Utilities chapter) can be used to index the files within your client folders so that you can quickly find the desired document. As an example you may be looking for the document pertaining to the request for electronic evidence or something concerning a partner's Motorola cell phone.

If you are considering the purchase of a document management system, Worldox is an excellent first choice. We have implemented this software many times and clients are always happy with it. No matter what product you are considering, see whether there is a trial version available, or at least participate in a demo of the product, to determine if it meets your firm's needs.

CHAPTER EIGHTEEN

Document Assembly

Essentially, DOCUMENT ASSEMBLY SOFTWARE automates the creation of legal documents that are used repeatedly. This would include such documents as wills, leases, contracts, and letters. You can think of document assembly as templates that can be used over and over. This shortens the time for document preparation and increases the efficiency of your practice. If you use flat fees, document assembly can be a godsend.

Document assembly software can be specialized for a particular industry or can be generic. As an example, specialized document assembly software is typically used in estate planning and tax preparation. In those situations, the user answers questions in a survey type of form and then the required documents are generated using the answers provided. If you have ever used one of the personal income tax programs (e.g., TurboTax, Tax-Cut), you've seen how document assembly works. You may see the term "document automation," but it means the same thing as document assembly for our discussion.

HotDocs

In law firms, the top three document assembly packages are HotDocs, ProDocs, and ProLaw according to the ABA's 2014 Legal Technology Survey Report. HotDocs (**www.hotdocs.com**) is the most popular document assembly software by a large margin. HotDocs is a very powerful solution and has significantly matured over the years. HotDocs is composed of many different products, such as those used for template creation, cloud-based access, desktop template distribution, and centralized server-based distribution to the users. HotDocs Developer 11 is one of the most power-ful platforms for document automation and allows you to convert word processing documents and PDF forms into document generation process applications, otherwise known as templates. You create a template and determine what text to include or exclude, depending on the answers entered by the user. This is the survey-type entry that was described earlier. The presentation walks you through the questions to gather the data needed to generate the document. The current version supports Microsoft Word 2003, 2007, 2010, 2013 and WordPerfect 12, X3, X4, X5, X6. (Wordperfect X3 SP2 and above are only supported for use on Windows Vista/Window 7). HotDocs User 11 is the other desktop product and it is used to generate finished documents. You cannot create or edit templates with HotDocs User 11.

As with other application software these days, HotDocs is available in a browser version too. The product, HotDocs Server 11, allows for docu-ment assembly using a standard web browser. This is particularly helpful for remote users and means you can deploy templates via the Internet. HotDocs Server 11 must be deployed in conjunction with a web applica-tion. It shouldn't surprise you that there are two additional software packages available (HotDocs Workspace and HotDocs Workspace for SharePoint).

HotDocs also has a SaaS offering, which extends the browser-based document generation to the small and mid-sized firm. The HotDocs Document Services are hosted in Microsoft's Azure Cloud. One of the features of Document Services enables you to e-mail links to your clients that process interviews directly. In other words, your clients can fill in the requisite data for the documents as part of an online interview process. Document Services is available at a monthly subscription rate, but you'll need to contact HotDocs to get a quote.

There is limited pricing information available without contacting HotDocs. The HotDocs Developer 11 is priced at $800 per license. The HotDocs User 11 is $330 per license. The other products (e.g. Server, Document Services) are customized, so you'll need to contact HotDocs for pricing.

Like many other software applications, HotDocs offers a thirty-day free trial. We always recommend the "try before you buy" process, especially if you are actually considering spending some money. Many of our friends on the lecture circuit regard HotDocs as *the* go-to document assembly software.

ProDoc

ProDoc (**www.prodoc.com**) is another document assembly application that is a legal resource from Thomson Reuters. One of the interesting features of ProDoc is how the licensing works. ProDoc is licensed on a subscription basis. The basic subscription license allows for usage on three computers or by three concurrent users. If you install ProDoc on a network, the licensing enforces the three-concurrent-user limit. You can only install ProDoc on three computers if they are stand-alone and not running in a network installation. The software is licensed for a single firm at one location. If you share office space with another firm, then each firm needs to purchase its own subscription to ProDoc. Pricing used to be transparent and easily determined from the ProDoc website. Not any longer. When you request pricing, the page is redirected to the West website and you are forced to fill out a form so that a Thomson Reuters representative can contact you. When a vendor goes from transparent pricing to "hiding the ball," it makes us wonder how many other things will be surprises.

The ProDoc forms are state specific and currently only available for California, Florida, Texas and Texas eFiling. Two years ago they also had Massachusetts and New York, but we're not sure what happened to them. There is also a national package available as a supplement library with links to parent BTS (Business Transactions Solution) forms on Westlaw. There are various document assembly systems available for the supported states. Be sure to check the website to see what modules are contained in each package and that your particular practice area is covered.

ProLaw

ProLaw by Elite (**www.elite.com/prolaw/**) is an integrated software product designed to automate the practice of law, complete with the business functions of billing, accounting, and other financial management. It is a complete package and combines case and matter management along with its document assembly features. ProLaw is targeted to mid-sized firms and no longer has an offering for the small-firm attorney. The document assembly component can create custom forms and templates with drag-and-drop fields. It can automatically convert documents to PDF and create templates that easily merge with the elements from the ProLaw database. ProLaw's document assembly capability also integrates with Adobe Acrobat and Microsoft Word. Pricing for the system must be obtained directly from Elite. This is not a cheap alternative and requires some pretty hefty hardware to run with acceptable performance. In fairness, ProLaw is much, much more than a stand-alone document assembly product such as HotDocs so the cost comparison isn't apples to apples.

Final Words

HotDocs is the clear recommendation for solo and small firm lawyers wanting to embark on document assembly. As a generic package, it is very well suited for any type of law practice. HotDocs integrates with many document management and practice management packages. There are many choices for technical support, including HotDocs Wiki, HotDocs Forum, HotDocs Resource Center, and HotDocs Documentation. HotDocs resellers are the primary method for consulting and product acquisition. Be sure to request the thirty-day trial and see if you can save some consulting expense by developing templates on your own.

CHAPTER NINETEEN

Cloud Computing

It SEEMS LIKE EVERYBODY is talking about the cloud, even more than last year—if that's possible The really scary part is that many users don't know what it means to use cloud computing and believe that the weather impacts the "cloud." That's not a joke—more than half of Americans believe that.

For our discussion purposes, the cloud is generally viewed as an external computing resource that is typically accessed via the Internet. You can participate in cloud computing by putting your own equipment in a secure data center and accessing your data (and perhaps applications) via the Internet. If you don't use your own equipment and software but elect to purchase applications through third parties, then you are using an SaaS (Software as a Service) solution. To make it easy to understand, imagine that you don't own a copy of Microsoft Office; you simply go to a site on the Internet where you are by subscription allowed to use Office. The resulting data is held by the provider, not you. This is exactly the environment that Microsoft is pushing with its Office 365 product.

News from the ABA Legal Technology Research Center's 2014 survey of ABA lawyers:

- ◆ A web-based software or solution was used by 30 percent (compared to 31 percent in 2013, 21 percent in 2012 and 16 percent in 2011).
- ◆ Solo practitioners were the most likely to respond affirmatively at 35 percent.
- ◆ Among those who had not used cloud computing, 42 percent said they did not intend to use the cloud in the future.

- Of those who had not used cloud computing, the top concerns they cited were:
    - 60%: confidentiality and security concerns
    - 48%: less control of data because it's hosted by the provider
    - 45%: unfamiliarity with the technology
    - 37%: losing access to and ownership of data
    - 23%: cost or effort of switching from their current solution

The traditional client/server model puts total control in the hands of the law firm. The data is held internally, and access is controlled by the firm. You can choose to encrypt the data locally, which we recommend, or leave it in plain text. Either way, it is within the technology walls of the law firm and not directly accessible by any third party.

In contrast, the SaaS model puts your data in the hands of a third party. This is not necessarily a bad thing, but do you really know if the information is safe? Your contract with the provider may specify that the data be stored in encrypted form, but what if a disgruntled employee has access to tools that allow him or her to decrypt the data and sell it to the other side in a major litigation? A new concern for lawyers, in light of the Edward Snowden revelations, is whether there is a government "back door" that allows it access to your data.

When you contract with an SaaS provider, you are required to accept the service as it is delivered to you. This means any upgrades or bug fixes will be implemented by the provider. Sound like a good thing? Just ask Ben Schorr, CEO of Roland Schorr, an information technology consulting firm with offices in Hawaii, Arizona, and Oregon and author of *The Lawyer's Guide to Microsoft Word 2010*, *Microsoft OneNote in One Hour for Lawyers* and *The Lawyer's Guide to Microsoft Outlook 2013*, all published by the American Bar Association:

> "One of my concerns about SaaS is the double-edged sword called 'upgrades.' A selling point of SaaS products is that the vendor just transparently updates it in the background, and you don't have to worry about it. Monday morning you log in and . . . "Oh, look, new features!" But what if you don't like those new features?
>
> "What if you're on a tight deadline and Google decides to do a massive upgrade to Google Docs? Do you have time to get yourself and your staff up to speed on how the new version works? With Microsoft Office, you upgrade when you're good and ready. We do quite a bit of work with

firms all over the country, in fact, helping them plan and approach that migration. Training their staff, preparing for the various consequences of the rollout, making sure their ancillary apps and add-ins are ready to support the new version. (Want some fun? Tell a managing partner that the new version of her e-mail app is NOT compatible with her case management system . . . the day AFTER she upgrades.)

"With SaaS, you don't generally get that. You may get no warning at all that features, user interface (UI), behaviors are about to change. You certainly aren't going to get a chance to use it before your staff does so that you can get up to speed on it and be ready to answer questions when the 9:15 messenger run is waiting to go and the documents still aren't printed (unless you want to sign into the SaaS app at 3 A.M., I guess).

"Hey, it's great that somebody else manages your upgrades and updates. That's usually a good thing. But it's not always a good thing. Unpredictability is not a quality I value in my mission-critical apps."

Enough said. Besides the data security and access concerns for the SaaS model, the financial stability of the provider may be a consideration, but it is becoming less of an issue as more and more vendors are providing cloud solutions. Even if you have adequate notice that the vendor will stop providing a contracted service, the cost to migrate your data to another provider or bring it back in-house can be significant. This brings us to the topic of exit strategy. At some point, you will likely want to bring the function back within your IT control or move to another provider. The contract should provide for specific costs and timetables to facilitate the move. It should also specify what file format you will get your data in. Will you get a copy of the complete SQL database along with the schema or just a comma delimited text file?

Another issue is the stability of the communications network. By design, you are dependent on the speed and quality of your Internet connection. Smart firms will have dual network connections to the Internet, although this will mean an increase in cost over what is normally installed at the firm. The Internet connection must be available at all times; otherwise, you will not have access to your data. There aren't many judges who are sympathetic to your problems if you miss a filing date because your Internet connection went down. And Internet connections, as we've all miserably learned, do sometimes go down—and always without notice.

To be fair, let's look at the upsides of using the cloud . . . and yes, there are some compelling upsides.

There can be some financial advantages to contracting service to a third-party provider. Your investment in hardware and software is minimized, since you are really only passing keyboard, mouse, and screen data over the communications link or accessing the application via a web browser. The actual processing occurs at the cloud provider. All configuration and data hosting are external to your firm's infrastructure. Costs for the SaaS model can be based on the number of users or the amount of data storage volume. Either way, it is fairly easy to identify and budget for the cost of the service, which is a big selling point for a lot of firms. However, to get these "stable" price points, the contract terms are typically three to five years. This means that the firm must make a pretty long commitment to using the SaaS model and the specific provider.

Another advantage to the SaaS model is the rapid reaction time to changes. It is very fast to add new users or increase the amount of space for data storage. By the same measure, it is very fast to decrease the number of users or amount of storage space. This means that you are more flexible in controlling your costs. If your firm is in contraction mode, you can reduce expenses, assuming that the contract doesn't tie you to a minimum amount. Many firms like the mobility aspect of the cloud model, since they can access the applications from any machine with an Internet browser. Typically, there isn't anything special that needs to be installed on the client computer. The user needs only a browser and perhaps some type of plug-in to access the application. This means that it is easy to gain access to the firm's data from the office, home, or an Internet café in the Bahamas.

Too often, all costs and all risks are not considered when analyzing a cloud solution. The cloud ballyhoo has drowned out all reasonable objections. We have moved slowly and carefully in moving clients to cloud solutions, but we do understand that some cloud services make sense for the solo and small firm attorney. More on that later. Client/server solutions can be clearly defined from implementation through the life of the solution. You control the implementation, configuration, and ongoing costs. While you can contractually specify some costs with a cloud provider, future upgrades, and exit conversions may tip the financial decision.

You may also hear of two other cloud solutions. Platform as a Service (PaaS) and Infrastructure as a Service (IaaS) are two additional cloud-computing services. With PaaS, the client creates software using features and capabilities as available from the provider. Most law firms will not entertain the PaaS model. With IaaS the necessary infrastructure is supplied by the solution provider. It owns and controls the equipment, operating system, network, and so on, and you load your applications onto the services. Think of it as having your data and applications running on "rented" hardware.

Contract Considerations

Now for a show of hands. How many readers have actually read the Terms of Service (ToS) or Terms and Conditions (ToC) for a cloud provider service? When we ask that question at CLEs, you could count the number of raised hands with the fingers on one hand. Shame, shame, shame. As lawyers you should be reading the contracts and the terms that you are agreeing to. Fear not. We'll point out some of the items and considerations you should be looking for in contracts with service providers.

Where will the data reside? Will it be in the United States or in some foreign country? Can you specify where the data will reside? Certainly, we would recommend that the data remain in the United States, which would avoid any cross-border issues and having to deal with international laws. And yes, even with the Snowden revelations, we don't want data in privacy-focused Europe where we don't know the laws and would potentially need a European lawyer to help in the event of a problem. "Better the devil you know," as we say ruefully.

- **Is the data encrypted in storage and in transmission?** Encryption will help protect the confidentiality of the information. The majority of cloud providers will encrypt the data in transit (e.g. SSL connections), but not necessarily at rest while it sits on their servers.

- **Who controls the encryption keys and is there a master decryption key?** Just because the data is encrypted doesn't mean it is accessible only to you. Services like Dropbox encrypt the data in transit and while it is stored on their servers; however, they hold a master decryption key and have the ability to decrypt your data. Services like Spider Oak allow you to define the encryption passphrase and they have no master decryption key.

- **Who can access your data?** This may not matter if you control the encryption, but it is worth knowing your exposure.

- **What is the exit strategy?** This was referenced above. Is there a cost? What form will the data be in? How long will it take to get your data? You certainly don't want to be held hostage by the vendor when trying to leave its service.

- **Who owns the data?** It seems like it should be a silly question, but is the data really yours or can the provider access it and redistribute it?

- **What about data breaches?** Make sure you understand who is responsible should there be a data breach. Who makes and pays for the data breach notifications? Will the cloud provider pay for any identity theft monitoring if required? Does the provider have adequate cyberinsurance protection?

- **Is your data stored on separate physical devices or are you co-mingled with other cloud customers?** Co-mingled storage puts you at risk should the authorities want to seize equipment for a cloud customer that you share storage with. Think of the Megaupload situation, in which many businesses went bankrupt when the authorities seized servers in a criminal investigation and their data was commingled with the company being investigated

Hybrid Solution

We think that moving your data and applications to a secure data center is a much better solution for most solo and small firm lawyers. Think of it as the best of both worlds. It's your data and software running on equipment that you own and control. If you don't like the data center, you can always move or bring it back in-house. The costs are even more predictable because you control any upgrades. We have purchased rack space at data centers over the last several years and moved our clients' equipment into the secured racks. Fairly recently, weather conditions in our area (massive snowfall and a drenching storm that had folks without power for weeks) made more firms cognizant of business continuity solutions. Data centers have redundant power (generators, too) and Internet connections. This means that weather conditions will not impact your ability to access your data and applications. Data centers generally guarantee 99.999 percent (called the five nines) uptime. Remember, though, that your own equipment could fail and you are still dependent on your local Internet connection. However, if your power in the office and at home is down, you can drive (as one of our clients did) to a Starbucks a few miles away and be back in business.

As you engineer the architecture to implement what we call a hybrid solution, be particularly aware of any software applications that contain databases such as your case management software. Database access using the Internet as the network is extremely risky and can corrupt the data. You may have to implement a Terminal Server type connection so that you run the client software from equipment at the data center instead of "dragging" all the data between your computer and the server over the Internet. Your IT consultant can help you determine the right connection scheme for each of your applications to achieve the greatest stability for your needs.

Bottom line: We have shifted our earlier opinion and are now actively moving clients to the cloud, though using the client's hardware rather than the cloud provider's. If you feel that you need to investigate and research SaaS vendors, we describe a few in this book. We just ask that you do it carefully and ask the right questions before making your decision.

We are listening to arguments that some cloud providers actually offer better security than law firms themselves. There's some truth in that, to be sure, and we are moving in the direction of recommending cloud solutions from proven providers with good track records for some clients. Finally, be sure to check with your bar, as a number of states now have ethics opinions regarding cloud computing. If you're wondering how states are dealing with the cloud from an ethical perspective, the general view is that it is acceptable to use the cloud as long as you investigate the provider, particularly making sure that confidential client data will be adequately protected. An excellent resource is provided (free of charge) by the Legal Technology Resource Center (LTRC) of the American Bar Association available at **http://www.americanbar.org/groups/departments_ offices/legal_technology_resources/resources/charts_fyis/cloud-ethics-chart.html**, where you will find a list of cloud ethics opinions for the various states. Remember that, ethically, you are outsourcing when you contract with a cloud provider, so the ethical rules relating to outsourcing also apply.

CHAPTER TWENTY

Collaboration

COLLABORATION MAY OR MAY not be at the top of your list, especially if you are a solo lawyer. However, we're sure you will have occasion to deal with other lawyers or even have a need to collaborate with your clients on a case. There are some great technology solutions to allow for collaboration—and solutions are multiplying week by week. These are just a few of the primary tools available for sharing information and working in a collaborative mode.

Social networking is a collaboration area that is gaining in popularity. Facebook has won the social networking war and is now being used extensively for business purposes. Twitter and LinkedIn are also very popular, with many lawyers preferring LinkedIn as a network for professionals. What about Google+? That's a darn good question. Google+ now has 540 million active users. This puts Google+ as the number two social network behind the "800 pound" Facebook. Move over Twitter and LinkedIn. So much for our previous predictions that Google+ would die a slow death. However, some experts are challenging how "active" Google+ is—even calling it a ghost town.

Some lawyers are getting business through social media sites, and others are raising their visibility with potential clients or colleagues who might provide referrals. Still others have obtained opportunities to write or speak on their area of expertise. See the social media chapter for more information on how lawyers are using these new applications.

Google Drive

Probably one of the most well known of the collaboration tools is Google Docs, which is now an offering within Google Drive. Most users know Google Docs as a web-based office suite that can create documents, spreadsheets, presentations, forms, and drawings. Not so fast. Google has repackaged its offering, and what used to be considered a suite is now separate applications known as Docs, Sheets, Forms, and Slides, all accessible within Google Drive. The popularity of this cloud product is no doubt due to the fact that it carries the favorite price tag of all lawyers—it is completely free. The applications allow you to work on a document, spreadsheet, form, drawing, or presentation with others and see the modifications in real time. You just use the web browser on your computer with your Internet connection. There are even enhanced features, which you may not be aware of.

You do need to have a Google ID to use Google Drive. Just go to **drive.google.com** and enter your login information. You can also create an account from the main entry page. Besides creating your files from scratch, the Google apps allow you to upload files you've already created on your computer. Documents can be downloaded to your computer as .docx, OpenDocument Format, RTF, PDF, TXT, or HTML (zipped). Spreadsheets can be downloaded as .xlsx, .csv, .tsv (tab separated value), and .ods formatted data, as well as PDF and HTML files. Presentations can be downloaded as .pptx, .pdf, and .txt formatted data or as Scalable Vector Graphic (.svg), .png or .jpg image files.

If you are used to the way Dropbox operates, you will not have any trouble with Google Drive. The easiest way to synchronize files and work on your spreadsheets, documents, etc. is to install the Google Drive application to your computer. Once it is installed, you will have a folder to drag and drop files into. They will then automatically get synchronized with your Google Drive storage. Google gives you 15 GB of free storage when you create your account. If you need more than that, you can get 100 GB or more space at a cost starting at $1.99 per month or 1 TB for $9.99 per month.

You can upload files to your Google Drive. The Google Drive viewer currently supports over 21 different file types:

- Image files (.JPEG, .PNG, .GIF, .TIFF, .BMP)
- Video files (WebM, .MPEG4, .3GPP, .MOV, .AVI, .MPEGPS, .WMV, .FLV, .ogg)

- Text files (.TXT)
- Markup/Code (.CSS, .HTML, .PHP, .C, .CPP, .H, .HPP, .JS)
- Microsoft Word (.DOC and .DOCX)
- Microsoft Excel (.XLS and .XLSX)
- Microsoft PowerPoint (.PPT and .PPTX)
- Adobe Portable Document Format (.PDF)
- Apple Pages (.PAGES)
- Adobe Illustrator (.AI)
- Adobe Photoshop (.PSD)
- Tagged Image File Format (.TIFF)
- Autodesk AutoCad (.DXF)
- Scalable Vector Graphics (.SVG)
- PostScript (.EPS, .PS)
- TrueType (.TTF)
- XML Paper Specification (.XPS)
- Archive file types (.ZIP, .RAR, tar, gzip)
- Audio formats (MP3, MPEG, WAV, .ogg)
- .MTS files
- Raw Image formats

By default, files are not shared until you make them shareable. This is certainly the preferred security policy and keeps your data private unless you make a conscious decision to share the information. Once you've created or uploaded a file to your Google Drive, you configure how the file is shared or, as Google puts it, define your "visibility options." Google's visibility options include "Private," "Specific people," "Anyone with the link" and "Public on the web." "Private" is just that: private. As mentioned, this is the default visibility setting. "Specific people" allow access to those you define. Those individuals must sign-in to a Google account in order to access the file. A document set to "Anyone with the link" is like an unlisted phone number. This means the data will not be visible unless you know the URL or are just plain lucky in guessing what it is. "Public on the web" means the document is available to anyone and may get indexed by search engines.

Besides the visibility, you can also change what a user can do with the data. The creator of the document is tagged as the owner and can obviously do anything. Once you share the file via a link, as Specific people or Public on the web, you can define what the user can do with the file. The choices for access are "Can edit," "Can comment," and "Can view." This gives you some level of granularity in the access and visibility options. The default access is "Can view."

As a practical point, multiple people can collaborate on a file and everyone doesn't need to have the same software or version. You can go online and create a file to start the process. Once completed, perhaps you download the file as a .docx file, since you use Word as your word processor. Another person downloads the .rtf version that he reads in an old version of WordPerfect and a third person downloads the .odt version because she uses OpenOffice. Each person downloads the same information but in a different file format to match what's used on each computer.

The current version of Google Drive now supports mobile access. As smartphones become the computing platform of choice, Google has developed additional methods for you to get to your information. Currently, Google Drive is accessible from an Android phone or tablet running Android 4.0 or higher. For an Apple device, you need to be running iOS 7.0 or above. The Google Drive app is what facilitates access to the Google files from your mobile device. You will need to install the Google Drive app to your Android or Apple mobile device. Just access the files from your Google Drive app and the changes are synchronized across all devices connected to your Google Drive.

The caution with Google Drive is that the data is being held by a third party. Obviously, you would not want to use it to work on highly proprietary information, such as a patent application. Even though you can control who has access to the files and what they can do, Google still holds the "keys" to all of the data. Google has had some highly publicized security issues over a period of years, so it is wise to consider what data you store there.

There have also been some recent stirrings over Google's privacy policy and what data Google accesses. We remind readers to review the terms of service and privacy policies for any third-party provided service, including Google. Apparently, there were a ton of folks that never read the terms and got all upset when they heard that Google scans the data you create and deposit on its servers. This is true for the free services that Google provides, such as Gmail and Google Drive. However, Google Business Apps ($50 per user per year) does not have the same terms of service. In fact, the terms of service for the Business Apps have specific confidentiality provisions, where Google will protect the data. They will also notify you if they are required by law to disclose confidential information so that you have an opportunity to challenge the disclosure.

Acrobat

Today, more and more lawyers have Acrobat (**www.adobe.com/products/ acrobat**), especially if they do e-filing of court documents. Acrobat allows for collaboration with PDF documents, so you can conduct shared document reviews that allow the participants to view one another's comments. Acrobat XI Standard and Pro allow for this type of collaboration. The free Acrobat Reader can annotate documents with the commenting tools, but cannot manage shared reviews or other advanced features that are included in the Standard and Pro versions.

Acrobat XI Standard is currently $299 and Pro is $449. Adobe now offers Acrobat XI Pro in two subscription plans. You can purchase a month-to-month subscription for $29.99 per month or an annual subscription for $19.99 per month. The subscription for the Standard version is $24.99 per month or $14.99 per month for the annual commitment. Adobe also offers a free trial download from its website. Like the other products we recommend, try the trial first if you are unsure of your purchase commitment.

Lawyers should opt for the Pro version, primarily for the enhanced security, Bates stamping, and redaction ability. Acrobat XI Pro allows you to create a document that your clients may find useful. It allows Adobe Reader (the free reader version) users to participate in reviews with complete commenting and markup tools, including sticky notes, highlighter, lines, shapes, and stamps. This means your clients (or other lawyers, for that matter) don't have to purchase Acrobat to collaborate with you.

This feature is not available with Acrobat XI Standard, hence the recommendation to purchase the Pro version. Consider purchasing Acrobat 9 Professional, especially if you can find it at a much reduced cost, since it is two versions back. Version XI is the current version, but there aren't any significant enhancements for the legal profession over those legal-specific functions that are included in Acrobat 9 Professional.

See the Acrobat section in chapter 12 to learn how to get the software for a lot less money.

Microsoft Word

Another collaboration tool is the Track Changes feature of Microsoft Word. With this tool, you can see the modifications made by each user who modifies the document. The caveat is that the software must be configured to properly identify the user. Some preloaded Office installations have the user configured as something generic, like "Owner" or "Satisfied Customer," and not the user's name. You can see how your Office (2003 and prior) installation is configured by going to Tools > Options and selecting the User Information tab. Word 2007 users would click the Office button in the upper left, select the Word Options button at the bottom, and see the user information in the Popular menu choice. Word 2010 and 2013 users select File and then the Options menu choice. Once this option is properly configured, the user information will show properly with the tracked changes. The user also has the ability to insert comments in addition to actually modifying the document contents. Do not strip the metadata (as you might normally do for confidentiality reasons) from the document if you are sending it to another party for collaboration. Removing the metadata also removes the tracked changes, so the recipient will not see the intended modifications. When you have the document ready and want to send it to a client, scrub the metadata at that point.

SharePoint

SharePoint is Microsoft's solution for collaboration. Basically, SharePoint is a web-based server environment that allows the end-user to collaborate on data that is managed through a SharePoint server. There is no special client software needed, as access is accomplished via a browser.

SharePoint 2013 is considered to be expensive for most solo and small firm operations, especially for new installations. Besides the cost of the server hardware, you will need the server software and Client Access Licenses (CALs). Microsoft has attempted to simplify the previously confusing licensing model for SharePoint. The on-premise solution is licensed using the server/CAL model. SharePoint Server 2013 is required for each running instance of the software and CALs are required for each person or device accessing a SharePoint Server. There is even an option for enterprise CALs if you need a very robust and flexible SharePoint environment to take advantage of Microsoft's Business Solutions or Business Intelligence for Everyone features not available with the standard CALs. Suffice it to say that it is all very complicated and can get rather expensive. If you need the services of a full-blown SharePoint server, you may want to consider some of the hosted solutions, which should be a lot more affordable for a solo or small firm office. Microsoft offers SharePoint Online, which is licensed on a per-user basis and starts at $3 per user per month. Another alternative is to investigate Microsoft's Small Business Server, which includes SharePoint in addition to Server, Exchange, and SQL.

Microsoft is continuing to push SharePoint in a major way. It keeps threatening to remove the Public Folders function of Exchange with each new release and force users to go with a SharePoint installation to get the same features you currently get with a base Exchange installation. We thought this was going to happen with the release of Exchange 2010 and then Exchange 2013, but we are happy to say that the Public Folders function is still there. Since Microsoft has been making this threat for many years, we have no reason to suspect that Public Folders will be removed from future Exchange versions.

We've written about SharePoint in the last several editions of this book. Microsoft continues to hype it, but we don't see much traction in the real world. Surveys show that 78 percent of the Fortune 500 companies are using SharePoint, but only one of our clients has it installed and we don't see that SharePoint is worth the expense, especially for an on-premise solution. Many solo and small firm practitioners use cloud solutions instead of investing in a complex SharePoint environment. We agree with that direction and don't think SharePoint is going to change the world, as Microsoft has often predicted.

Office 365

Microsoft has finally introduced a product that may give Google a run for its money. Office 365 is really a web-based productivity suite that also contains some collaboration capabilities. The solution is a subscription-based service, so the out-of-pocket cash flow is very reasonable. There are several subscription plans available, depending on the number of users and any advanced features that may be needed. Microsoft has changed the Office 365 offerings this year so our recommendation is different for this edition of the book. The company is trying to steer users toward a subscription model and away from the traditional retail software packages.

Solo and small firms will probably opt for Office 365 Business Premium, which is geared toward small businesses and can handle up to 300 users. The cost is $15.00 per month per user (billed monthly) or $12.50 per month per user (annual payment of $150.00), which is very affordable. It includes access to business class e-mail, shared calendars, 1 TB of OneDrive for Business storage space per user, the ability to use your own domain name, web conferencing, and document sharing. New is the ability to have Office on your desktop and on the go on up to 5 PCs or Macs. The Office applications include Word, PowerPoint, Excel, Outlook, OneNote, Access, Publisher, and Lync. With the desktop version you can work on your files while offline. Once you are connected to the Internet, all of your work will automatically sync. For you e-mail junkies, each user gets a 50 GB mailbox with the ability to send attachments of up to 25 MB in size. We would recommend starting with the month-to-month plan, which can be cancelled at any time without penalty.

Skype

Many users are familiar with the VoIP solution called Skype. Skype is now owned by Microsoft and things seem to be going along fairly well. Telephone calls are free between Skype users. You can opt for pay plans if you need to call mobile or landline numbers, and the cost is very reasonable.

Unlimited calling to United States and Canada landline and mobile phone numbers is only $2.99 per month. New features with Skype make it an excellent tool for collaboration. Video conferencing is now supported within Skype. You can create a low-cost or no-cost video conference call in just a few seconds. Many laptops now have a video camera built into the screen case, and there are Skype apps for mobile devices such as iPhones, iPads, Windows Phone, and Android smartphones. Finally, you can share files through Skype as well. File sharing, video conferencing, and free teleconference calls via the Internet make Skype a great low-cost collaboration tool.

Beware of security issues though. We learned in 2013 that Microsoft was now routing Skype calls through its servers, contrary to previous practice. Also, researchers have proven that Microsoft accesses users' content within Skype. Finally, documents revealed by Edward Snowden state that Microsoft has cooperated with the NSA and actually decrypted data at the behest of the NSA. We would not recommend using Skype for confidential conversations or file sharing.

Dropbox

Dropbox is not just for file synchronization between your computer and mobile devices. We have seen a tremendous increase in Dropbox being used to share files among multiple parties and even as a vehicle to deliver evidence for discovery. You can create a custom folder within Dropbox and share that folder with multiple people. Only those that you authorize can have access to the folder contents. This means you can collaborate with co-counsel, consultants, experts, and even opposing counsel.

Dropbox is free for the initial 2 GB of storage. You can purchase additional storage starting at $9.99/month for 1 TB (1,000 GB). Dropbox transmits the data in a secure fashion using SSL and also stores it in encrypted form on their servers. However, Dropbox holds the encryption key and can decrypt the data should it receive a valid court order or law enforcement request. Therefore, you should consider Dropbox to be an insecure service and not use it for transmitting any confidential or sensitive information. That doesn't mean you can't use Dropbox to share confidential information. Your data is safe if you encrypt it BEFORE you deposit it in Dropbox. That way you control the encryption key and not Dropbox.

Desktop Sharing

Several products enable you to share your desktop with other people, and sharing your desktop may be a good way to collaborate on a document or share pictures of an accident scene. Products like Webex, Teamviewer, join.me, and GoToMeeting allow for desktop sharing. If you elect to use desktop sharing products, be advised that you may not be able to determine if the remote party is recording the session. You may want to get agreement and confirmation from all parties that they are not recording the session, especially if you don't want it recorded or you want to be the only one with a record of the session. In addition, be wary if you give control over to a remote user as they may be able to transfer data from your computer without your knowledge. We would recommend that you "push" your desktop to the remote parties and not let them take control.

CHAPTER TWENTY-ONE

Remote Access

MOST LAWYERS ARE ROAD warriors today. If their entire office is not on a laptop or smartphone, a good chunk of it is—and the rest is accessible through remote access. Whether in court, on vacation, traveling, or in a meeting, lawyers need access to their e-mail, calendar, appointments, and files—and they need access fast.

Many lawyers have discarded workstations entirely, using only their laptop and a docking station at work and tablets and smartphones while on the move. Others have both a workstation and a laptop. The popularity of laptops and other mobile devices has zoomed in the last decade, to the point where the lawyer without a laptop or smartphone is a relative rarity. Our new mobile lawyers are now equipped with technologies that allow them to be as productive on the road as they are in the office, minimizing downtime and keeping those billable hours (or productivity hours, in the case of the alternative billers) up. Many clients and colleagues have a strong expectation that lawyers will be constantly accessible via e-mail—even, sadly, while on vacation. We privately joke (and lament) that vacations are times when our laptops and mobile devices get a nice view of the beach. Many clients will disregard your out-of-office message and will expect a quick response. So, how do we stay in touch with the office when on the road?

Virtual Private Networking

A virtual private network (VPN) connection is a secure communications network tunneled through another network, such as the Internet. The

VPN connection allows a user to connect to the office when working remotely. The communications tunnel encrypts the data traffic between the remote user and the office network, maintaining the security of the information as it is passed back and forth. This is extremely important for law firms whose lawyers work on client files while traveling or away from the office and have to download a local copy of a client file to work on. Best of all, the VPN service software is included with Microsoft's server operating systems, and the VPN client software is included with Microsoft operating systems, at no additional cost to the user.

The average lawyer is likely to be dumbfounded when confronted with setting up a VPN, especially if third-party software and a certificate are required, so this is best left to your IT consultant. However, it is not terribly expensive, and it offers terrific security for your data. The greatest advantage of VPNs is that they are multiuser, whereas other methods are one-on-one solutions.

GoToMyPC

GoToMyPC is a remote connection service that allows you to connect to your work computer when you are away from the office. This service is a great alternative if you're a solo practitioner or if your law firm does not have the ability to set up a VPN-type connection for remote users (for example, if you don't have a server). Like a VPN connection, data communications between the client and the host are encrypted and secured. To connect to your work computer, software must be installed and running on the host machine (the computer you wish to connect to), and both the client and the host computers must have Internet access. The GoToMyPC website maintains contact with the host computer so the IP address of the host is always known. This is critical: This solution works even if the host has a dynamic Internet connection (constantly changing IP address) instead of a static one, which remains constant. No modifications to the configuration of your firm firewall will need to be made to get GoToMyPC up and running.

Users can even connect to their work computers (Mac or Windows) from a tablet or smartphone. Apps are available for Android, iOS, and Kindle Fire devices.

GoToMyPC costs as little as $99 per year for one computer license and will need to be renewed yearly. There is a monthly plan, but the cost jumps to $9.95 a month. There is no limitation on how often you may connect to your host computer, and you are allowed to connect to your host computer from any device. The software requires little setup and configuration and can be purchased online from GoToMyPC's website at **www.gotomypc.com**. This software is more costly than its competitors, so be sure to check out all of your available options before selecting which remote access solution to purchase. GoToMyPC also has a thirty-day free trial, so take advantage as you experiment to find which remote access solution works best for you!

LogMeIn

LogMeIn Pro is a remote access solution that is very similar to GoToMyPC. The software works the exact same way, with the service provider maintaining the IP addresses of host computers. This is another good solution for those firms with dynamic (constantly changing) IP addresses. With this service and very little effort, you can gain seamless and total access to your office PC (Mac or Windows) from any computer with an Internet connection. To connect, a user logs into the LogMeIn website (or uses the app downloaded to their mobile device) and the connection to the host computer is made automatically. Some of the features include remote printing, the ability to transfer and share files between the connected computers, and the ability to map network drives to your local computer. Just like GoToMyPC, this service is extremely secure, using 128- to 256-bit SSL end-to-end encryption. When compared to GoToMyPC, this remote access solution is currently priced the same ($99 per year) but allows a user to access up to two different computers, instead of just one with GoToMyPC.

This service also supports connecting to your work computer from your iOS or Android device. We've used the iPad app, and it works as advertised—easy to use, great with the touch screen, and very convenient.

A LogMeIn Pro subscription costs $99 per year for two computer licenses and will need to be renewed annually. There is no longer a monthly plan to choose from. This service can be purchased online from LogMeIn's website at **www.logmein.com**. We strongly recommend the use of this product for remote accessibility because of its ease of use and ability to access two computers, instead of just one. Like GoToMyPC, LogMeIn offers a free trial, so we recommend taking the product for a test drive before purchasing it.

TeamViewer

TeamViewer Business Edition is a remote access solution on steroids. It contains a number of features that are not available with LogMeIn or GoToMyPC. Although it's a one-time purchase it comes with a hefty price. Just like the two remote access solutions described above, TeamViewer works flawlessly behind network firewalls and is a good solution for firms that use dynamic IP addresses. While TeamViewer is not difficult to install and run, the connecting computer will need to download, install, and run the client application, which, in our experience, may be a bit more confusing and cumbersome for lawyers to perform rather than just logging into the service with the web-browser. However, once the local application is installed, it's very easy to use.

Some of the additional features include:

- Multiplatform support, including Mac OS X, Windows 8, and Linux computers
- iOS, Android, and Windows Phone 8 support
- Communication tools that allow users to connect with each other through video chat or VoIP
- One-time charge for a lifetime license; no recurring yearly costs
- The ability to transfer files securely
- File box for common file sharing
- Microsoft Outlook calendar integration
- The ability to record meetings
- Space for up to fifteen meeting participants

Mobile device support is offered for iOS, Android, and Windows Phone 8, but users will need to purchase a separate add-on license for this feature, unlike the included mobile support offered in both of the LogMeIn and GoToMyPC alternatives to this product. TeamViewer can be purchased online from **www.teamviewer.com**, and a single lifetime business license for one computer costs $749. The cost to add additional computers to remotely control is $139 per system.

Mobility Tips

Besides providing remote access solutions for the legal road warrior, we wanted to include some useful tips to think about before heading out on the road:

—Pack a surge protector. It doesn't matter what brand. You never know when you will need more than two outlets to power all of your devices and to protect your electronic devices from power surges and dirty electricity.

—Purchase a lock for your laptop. Ninety-nine percent of laptops have a Kensington security slot, and it's prudent to use it. Kensington locks, such as the MicroSaver DS Notebook Lock, can be purchased online from Kensington's website (**www.kensington.com**) for around $50—a small price to pay to keep your laptop secure.

—If you use a wireless Bluetooth mouse, be sure to pack extra AA or AAA batteries.

—Pack a spare cell phone charger and tablet charger with an extra sync cable. You shouldn't travel without either one.

—Pack an AC extension cable. This will come in handy when you are far away from a power outlet.

—Keep an AC power adapter for your laptop in your bag. You never know when you might need one.

—If you're traveling internationally, be sure to pack multiple converters so that you can connect your devices. In the United States, we operate on a system that runs at 120 volts. Be sure to check the voltage of the country you're visiting before leaving and find out whether your power supplies will auto convert. You may not need voltage convertors if the power supplies auto adjust, but you will need the plug adapters to match the outlet connections.

—It is always a good idea to have a hard copy printout of your hotel reservation and itinerary, in the event your mobile device stops working or isn't accessible right when you need it. If you are using your mobile device to keep track of your itinerary, try using an app like TripIt, which can track all your travel arrangements, including your flights, hotel, and rental car information, and will eliminate the searching of your e-mail for your travel plans. How nice is it to have all of the information in a single place? Plus, another great feature is that this app allows you to share your itinerary with family and friends.

—Another tip for international travelers: Leave your cell phone at home. Roaming charges can be staggering and can be initiated even if you're not actively using your phone. Do you really trust putting your phone in airplane mode?

—Keep appropriate video adapters with your laptop in your laptop bag. You never know when you might need to connect your laptop or tablet to a TV or projector for a presentation.

—Pack headphones to keep the noise out. Have you ever tried to be productive on an airplane? It's hard when the person next to you can't stop talking. Just plug in your headphones and your problem is solved. You can even listen to relaxing music while you work. For those who want wireless Bluetooth headphones, check out the Jabra Revo Wireless, costing about $200, which can be found on Jabra's website at **www.jabra.com**; however, you may not be able to use these on an airplane because they are transmitting devices. For music aficionados, the Bose QuietComfort 25 Acoustic Noise Cancelling headphones offer top-of-the-line headphone technology and include the noise-canceling circuitry that you hear everyone talking about. The downside, though, is the price—very, very expensive at around $300. The authors are particularly fond of the Bose QuietComfort 20 earbuds. They are small, lightweight and have amazingly effective noise cancelling capability. However, they are also pricey at $300.

—Back up your data to an external hard drive or the network server. If your laptop crashes or is stolen, you will want a recent backup of your most important files.

—Encrypt your hard drive and data. There are many software tools available to do this, such as PGP, TrueCrypt (version 7.1a and not the compromised version 7.2), and PC Guardian. In the event your laptop is lost or stolen, your data is protected. Configure a power on or BIOS password on your computer, if available. Again, this adds another layer of data protection. One point to note, however, is that if you're traveling internationally, encryption is illegal in some countries, which could lead to the confiscation of your encrypted devices—so be prepared and know the local laws.

—If you have a tablet, be sure to password protect your device with a passphrase. PINs aren't as secure and can be easily cracked. On an iPad, a passphrase requirement on the Lock Screen will enable encryption of your data. On Android devices, you can encrypt your data as well through the configuration settings.

—If you have a smartphone with a data plan that allows device tethering or a mobile hot spot, take advantage of the data service you have already paid for and tether your laptop or tablet with your smartphone for Internet service. Avoid paying daily hotel fees for an Internet connection if it's not provided free during the course of your stay. However, data overage charges from your wireless carrier can be expensive, so it's best not to stream the movie at the top of your Netflix queue while tethered unless you truly have an unlimited data plan.

—Encrypt your USB flash drives and external hard drives.

—Disable your wireless auto-connection feature within the Windows operating system. Most laptops with wireless cards will automatically connect to any unencrypted, open wireless network when your default connection is unavailable. If by chance your device does connect to an open wireless network, never log into any e-mail or bank account when using an unsecure connection.

—Before leaving the office, make sure that your security software has the latest updates and definitions to protect your devices while you're away. The same applies to Windows updates.

—Download and install an app to track your club membership cards so that you don't have to carry all that plastic around with you. The one that we like the most for iOS and Android mobile devices is the Key Ring Rewards Cards app. Not only does it allow you to enter and store your club card or membership numbers, but it can also generate a bar code that can be scanned should one be required. You might as well get miles points and hotel rewards while on the go!

—Another great app to download and use on your mobile device is GateGuru. This app comes in handy when your flight has been canceled or delayed, and you're looking for a few hours to kill. This app provides maps of all major airport terminals, including restaurants and stores, along with reviews allowing you to find a bar or restaurant to relax and unwind until your flight.

These are just a few of the recommendations we have for the legal road warriors, all based on our own experiences traveling. We hope you find them useful.

CHAPTER TWENTY-TWO

Mobile Security

TECHNOLOGY ADVANCES IN THIS area have come at warp speed. Gone are the days when you carried around a 50-foot phone cord, looking for an analog phone jack that could be used with the modem in your laptop and America Online. Being übergeeks, we then carried along a splitter, coupler, and additional phone cords so we could work comfortably on the bed or desk while we traveled around the nation. No more. It's even difficult to purchase a modern-day laptop with a modem these days. We can't remember the last time we even saw a modem as an option when configuring a laptop purchase. Wireless, whether Wi-Fi or using a 3G/4G data connection with your cellular carrier, is the preferred method of connectivity in the modern age. More and more hotels, motels, conference centers, coffee shops, bookstores, cafés, and so on, are offering wireless access solutions, many without charge. The question is . . . should you use the free Wi-Fi?

Software

Before we jump into the boring details, let's cover some solutions that should be on your laptop no matter what other technology you use for remote connectivity. It goes without saying that you should have some sort of all-in-one security solution installed on your laptop. It should be configured to check for automatic updates and to perform a periodic full scan (we do weekly scans) to catch anything that may have "landed" before the signatures were updated. It would be just your luck to catch a virus or other malware on day one and be the first kid on the block to suffer the effects. Most of the current Internet Suites also analyze the computer operation and identify activity that could be virus-like or some process trying to access something it shouldn't. This type of real time monitoring provides added protection beyond mere signature files. Normally, the all-in-one security product will contain security features like antivirus, anti-malware, firewalls, spam control, and anti-phishing. Don't leave home without it. Software solutions for your smartphone and tablet are also available, but we'll discuss those later.

Encryption

Secure mobile computing must contain some method of encryption to protect valuable personal and client data. We prefer whole disk encryption. This means everything on the hard drive is encrypted and kept secure: we don't have to remember to put files into special folders or on the encrypted virtual drive. All too often, people are in a big hurry and may not save their data in the special protected encrypted areas, leaving the information vulnerable.

In addition, without whole disk encryption, it is possible that artifacts of the decryption passphrase would be present in various places (e.g., master file table [MFT], Page File, temp files, unallocated space). Forensics can extract these artifacts and make it probable that the passphrase can be determined. Many of the newer laptops have built-in whole disk encryption. To state the obvious, make sure you enable the encryption or your data won't be protected. Also, encryption may be used in conjunction with biometric access. As an example, our laptops require a fingerprint swipe when powered on. Failure at that point leaves the computer hard drive fully encrypted. A very comforting thought if laptop thieves, who constitute a large club these days, make off with your laptop.

If you think we are being too cautious, bear in mind that a laptop goes missing every 50 seconds in the United States. In 2011, **PCWorld.com** reported that about 12,000 laptops were lost or stolen at U.S. airports per week. Where does it happen most? In Chicago, fitting for a city whose history is so steeped in criminal lore. The fact that one of 10 corporate laptops will be lost or stolen over their 3-year life is enough reason to take steps to protect the data. We mean it when we say, "Be careful out there." Also, don't forget to encrypt your USB flash drives. Unfortunately for us good guys, these devices are easily lost and almost always contain our valuable data.

Wireless

What's next? We won't cover modem access in the traditional sense, since dial-up isn't desirable, effective, or even available these days for most travelers. Wireless is the norm for all the road warriors. There are two basic types of wireless access you'll encounter. The first type is generically termed a "wireless hot spot" and is what you find at your local Starbucks, fast food establishment, hotel, or airport. You may or may not have to pay for these wireless connection services. Many businesses are offering free wireless as a way to attract customers—heck, even McDonald's offers a free wireless hot spot. Most of these hot spots are unsecured and wide open. This means it is possible for your confidential data to be viewed by the customer at the next table or the one sitting on the park bench outside the café if you are not encrypting the traffic.

Does this mean you shouldn't use any of these wireless clouds? If you have a choice, we would say these clouds are best avoided by those who are technology averse and don't understand how to operate securely in an unsecured cloud. Read on, and determine whether you can safely be trusted to do what follows.

See if there is an option to have a secure connection to the cloud. This would be indicated if you use **https://** (note the *s*, denoting "secure") as part of the URL. Typically, website connections are unsecure and do not provide an encrypted session like the **https://** connections do. Be especially careful if you have to pay for the wireless connection. Be wary when you are at the screens that have you input your credit card and billing information. Do not enter any of this sensitive information without an **https://** connection. Once you've established a connection to the wireless cloud, be sure to use your VPN or other secure (**https://**) access to protect your transmissions. Also, when connecting to a secure website, if you're presented with an error message referencing a SSL certificate error or invalid certificate, proceed with extreme caution or better yet, don't proceed at all.

Some hotels may give you a wireless cloud that is already secured. Typically, these wireless implementations use WPA (Wi-Fi protected access) or WPA2 to secure your connection and data. The cloud will be visible to your computer, but you will be required to provide a password before your computer connects. Once connected, the data you transmit will be encrypted and secure.

One scheme we see all the time: You are in a hotel that requires you to pay for Internet access. But when you ask your computer to show "all available wireless networks," it will display something like "free public wireless" as a network name—or something else that sounds innocuous, usually using the word "free" to entice you. Beware—these are often data thieves offering up an insecure cloud for the sole purpose of making off with your data. You can get the "free Internet"—but at a terrible price. Never be tempted by these clouds.

AirCard

Another wireless connection method is commonly called an AirCard. These are cards that are used to connect to the high-speed wireless networks of cellular phone providers. We're pretty sure you've seen the cellular providers advertising their 3G/4G networks. You may see terms like EDGE or EV-DO to describe the older 3G networks and WiMAX or LTE to describe the latest 4G networks. Don't be swayed by the vendor claims for speed and availability. Make sure that you will be able to have service in those areas you travel to the most. Reliability is another consideration, as is whether you already have a cellular plan.

The AirCard itself is a hardware device that you can externally connect to your laptop or select as a built-in option when configuring a new computer system. External AirCards come in both USB and PC card formats. These cards can be used on any laptop with USB ports or PC card slots. Some laptops and netbooks have the electrical circuitry built in, so no additional hardware is required. The built-in capability means you have nothing to lose, but it is "married" to the laptop and can't be transferred between machines. Further, you would also be stuck with a single cellular vendor, as each vendor's radio is different. The external AirCards can cost several hundred dollars, but most providers offer significant discounts.

The service itself can be daily, weekly, monthly, or annually by subscription. The monthly plans typically measure the amount of data you transfer over the connection and charge you for any overage usage. Unlimited data plans appear to be a thing of the past with carriers limiting data usage, especially with the tremendous number of smartphones being purchased. The exceptions are Sprint and T-Mobile. They are offering unlimited text, talk, and data plans in an attempt to grab market share. We'll have to see how long their unlimited plans last. We are also seeing a move to offer shared data access, which means all devices on your account can share the amount of data to which you subscribe. In the present market, the data plans are all over the map. Some plans are as low as 1 GB per month and cap out at around 5 GB or 10 GB per month, unless you go with the unlimited plans. The cost will run between $50 and $90 per month, depending on the amount of data purchased. Be sure to read the fine print, especially on any unlimited plan. You may be surprised at the additional charges or restrictions that may be involved.

Obviously, you will want to purchase a monthly plan if you travel a lot or will use the service for more than a few days a month. The AirCard is the preferred wireless connection, as the data is secured from the very beginning. You don't have to worry about whether you have an **https://** session or not. The electronic circuitry itself and the cellular carrier provide a fully encrypted session immediately.

Also, it should be noted that if you have multiple devices that need Internet access, rather than purchasing a subscription for each device, which can be very costly, invest in something like the Verizon Ellipsis Jetpack or other mobile hot spot. These devices create a local wireless network that can provide Internet access (over the cellular network) to up to ten devices. Verizon offers the Ellipsis Jetpack for $0.99 with a two-year commitment.

Frankly, you should be using the "hot spot" capability that is built into your smartphone. That means you don't have to carry around or pay for another piece of equipment. Like the dedicated AirCards, the data connection is encrypted between the smartphone and the cellular carrier.

Public Computer Usage

A word of warning here. Be very careful about using a public computer, such as those in the library, an Internet café, or the business center of a hotel. Even if you are only accessing your web-based e-mail account, the data is temporarily written to the local hard disk. There is also the risk that some keystroke logging software is installed on the computer, thereby capturing everything that you do on the machine. Studies have shown an average of seven pieces of malware on these public computers.

Does that mean all public computers are off limits? Not at all. We are big fans of the IronKey hardware encrypted USB flash drive. Besides the drive encryption and secure management of passwords, the IronKey has portable applications intended for use with public computers. As an example, there is a specially modified version of the Firefox browser that doesn't write any data to the computer. All data stays on the IronKey, thereby making it secure and keeping it with you when you leave. Of course, this does mean that the computer has to accept the insertion of USB devices. Some business center machines are locked down and do not allow USB devices to be inserted, because it is a security risk to the business—USB devices can be used to introduce malware to the machine or network. Though we have tipped our hat to those who secure their computers this way (it's absolutely the right thing to do), it has prevented us from using our IronKey several times. Another reason to travel with your own equipment.

Smartphones

Want to know what the most secure smartphone on the market is? That really isn't the right question. The question should be . . . what smartphone can be made the most secure? The answer is an Android phone. Because of its design architecture, Android can be configured with enhanced security settings as well as installing security software to protect the OS. You can't do that with an iPhone. It's pretty clear that the iPhone was designed as a consumer phone first, with security just an afterthought. However, the latest versions of iOS on the newer iPhones have improved security to the point where it more closely approaches the other smartphones in protecting data. It still doesn't change the fact that the iPhone holds a tremendous amount of data, unbeknownst to the user, that is orders of magnitudes more than any other smartphone. In other words, the iPhone is very evidence rich.

At a minimum, everybody should have a PIN code programmed into their phone to prevent unauthorized access, along with a fairly short time-out period. It doesn't do much good to have an unlocking PIN and then have thirty minutes pass before the phone relocks. We know it's a pain to constantly punch in the unlock code, but that will keep your data from being accessed by prying eyes. Better yet, it will stop someone from installing spyware on your phone that can effectively trap all of your communications (voice calls, e-mail, text messages, etc.). For those devices that offer a passphrase alternative to the PIN, such as the iPad or iPhone, this would be the preferred choice to secure your device. Why, you might ask?

Because a passphrase can be longer than a PIN and can contain non-numeric values, vastly increasing the strength of the protection. In fact, we do not recommend that any iPhone or iPad be configured with the very weak four-digit PIN lock code. There are tools available to brute force a four-digit PIN on an iPhone or iPad in less than fifteen minutes, even if it is set to wipe the data after ten attempts.

Encrypt the phone! This is easier to do than you think. Enabling a lock code on the iPhone or iPad automatically encrypts the device. To encrypt a BlackBerry device, all you have to do is enable the "Content Protection." The last several versions of the Android operating system have built-in encryption. Just make the selection to encrypt the device within the Security settings. You may need a third-party application if you are running an older version of the Android OS.

Besides PIN protecting your phone, make sure you encrypt any memory cards or just don't store any sensitive data on them. We're talking about the SD, micro SD, etc. cards that you can insert into the smartphone to increase storage capacity. There are programs available for some models that allow you to encrypt the card contents if the feature is not already built into the phone. The point is, you don't want any confidential information to be accessible on the card if you lose your phone. The PIN will protect the phone access, but the "bad guy" will pop out the memory card and read it from his computer if it is not encrypted.

Finally, investigate the ability to remotely wipe the data from the smartphone if it is lost. You should have the phone configured to automatically wipe after a set number of invalid unlock attempts. This will clear the data even if you are not connected to a cellular network. Remotely wiping the device on demand requires that it be in communication with the cellular data network. Configure the "Find my iPhone" function within the iCloud settings on an iPhone or iPad. The remote wipe capability is built into the BlackBerry devices and can be invoked through the BES (BlackBerry Enterprise Server) console. Android devices can use the free Lookout application for the remote wipe function. Google has a new app called Android Device Manager that will help users locate or remotely wipe their phone. You must enable Android Device Manager from the Google settings on your phone and associate the phone with your Google account. Remember that the remote wipe feature is for the memory within the phone itself and may not wipe the memory cards we spoke about earlier.

Final Words

The options and requirements for mobile security have certainly changed quickly over the years. Talk to us next year and we're sure the world will have changed again. For now, make sure that you are aware of all the issues related to secure data transfer and that you are not relying on antiquated knowledge. You must assume that there is absolutely no protection of the communication stream between your laptop and your remote device. We've seen hotel networks that didn't have a firewall, so all traffic was allowed to flow through. We immediately saw probing attacks on our computers, which were stopped by the firewalls on our laptops. It's the wild, wild West out there, and you're the only marshal in town. Good luck, Wyatt.

CHAPTER TWENTY-THREE

More from Apple

APART FROM THE INFORMATION conveyed previously about Mac laptops and desktops, we want to offer you additional Apple recommendations in light of the continued interest lawyers have shown in potentially
switching to Mac computers. Many lawyers may have never used a Mac,
either in their personal life or for their job, but most have used one Apple
product or another. Most are only familiar with the iPod or the very popular iPhone and iPad. Many people argue that Macs are ready for "prime
time," to take on Windows-based PCs in the business setting. From a
hardware standpoint, Macs are just as good as, if not better than, PCs.
You can't really tell them apart since Macs made the switch to using
Intel-based processors. The major difference now is the operating system,
which is still the main obstacle for Macs gaining a greater piece of the pie
in the business marketplace.

Frankly, the problem lies with software compatibility with Macs. Most law
firms, no matter the size, use legal-specific software on a daily basis to do
their jobs. Whether you're looking at case management, billing, trial-
related or field-specific software, most vendors still do not make versions
for Macs. However, this argument is becoming more of a non-issue as
vendors move their applications to the cloud. But for lawyers who use a
computer just for word processing, Internet research, filing motions,
billing, and accounting, a Mac could suit these functions perfectly.

However, centralized management is much more difficult, if not impossible, in a Mac environment. Group policies and multiple third-party tools
enable a very cost-effective way to distribute updates and restrict abilities
in a Windows environment. The lack of centralized control and restrictions of Macs makes them less desirable (and much more costly) to deploy

in an enterprise setting. Macs are more expensive to maintain because you have to touch each individual Mac to make changes or install updates. The lack of centralized control is a large reason you see Macs in solo and small law firms and not uniformly implemented in larger firms. Below, we discuss some Mac-specific hardware and software solutions that may come in handy if you are or want to become a Mac user.

Hardware

Apple iPad

Just when you thought the fanfare for the iPad couldn't get any noisier, Apple has revamped the iPad line with the release of the iPad mini and iPad Air.

The arrival of very few technology devices have been met with as much excitement as the Apple iPad 2 received when it was released in March 2011—and since then, on a yearly basis, Apple has continued to update and refresh its line of iPads. While continually updating these devices, most of the new iPads since then certainly haven't received as much hype. There have been six versions of the iPad to date, including an iPad mini—which we find to be just ridiculous. The iPad mini is too similar in size to older iPhones to justify the purchase.

The most recent version of the iPad added the Apple A7 processor and the M7 coprocessor to measure motion from the device. The iPad runs the same iOS software as the iPhone and iPod Touch, and, like those devices, it can use iCloud for synchronization, removing the need for iTunes and a computer.

The iPad Air has a 9.7-inch diagonal Multi-Touch LED-backlit IPS screen glass display, with a resolution of 2048 × 1536 pixels (264 pixels per inch). The touch screen breaks away from the previous models—devices that required a user to press the screen with a stylus, as in the old days of Palm Pilots. An embedded three-axis accelerometer is used to determine the orientation of the device—portrait or landscape mode—and some apps and games take advantage of this feature.

The iPad Air comes with a built-in Wi-Fi network card with two antennas, enabling the device to connect to wireless networks, and the 4G model comes with a broadband AirCard (AT&T, Sprint, or Verizon) and GPS locator. The device also includes Bluetooth capability and a 32.4 watt-hour battery lasting up to ten hours, even when continually surfing the Internet. This version of the iPad is available with 16, 32, 64, or 128 GB of internal memory.

Some of the continuing criticisms of the iPad are the lack of Flash support, expansion capability, and alternate input/output sources. Many industry analysts say that the lack of Flash support significantly cripples Apple products since so many websites incorporate the technology. Even though the iPad comes with a fair amount of embedded memory, there are no options to add storage in the form of memory expansion cards (e.g., SD, micro SD). Finally, there are no USB ports available, which significantly limits what connections may be added. As an example, your only current printing option is to print via Bluetooth or wireless AirPrint printer, or to use a Bluetooth keyboard as an expansion device. USB printers and direct connected keyboards are not an option.

Before the release of iOS 4.2, users couldn't even print from these devices. It was in this iOS update that Apple provided support for wireless printing. The number of printers with AirPrint support continues to grow and includes a number of HP LaserJet and OfficeJet printer models. With the iOS 4.3 release, Apple added display mirroring, which replicates the iPad's display over the video out connection, rather than the video out feature working only with selected applications.

The latest version of the iPad has a number of features, including:

—Space Gray and Silver color options

—AT&T, Verizon, T-Mobile, and Sprint 4G models

—1.4 GHz dual-core Apple A7 processor with quad-core graphics

—5 megapixel iSight camera, dual microphones

—1 GB of processor memory

—Bluetooth 4.0 support

—1080P HD video recording

While we have been pleased with the upgrades that Apple included with this model, if you've purchased an iPad in the last year or two, we still wouldn't recommend upgrading at this time. However, the Retina display, increased processor speed, and amount of memory make this device even faster and more responsive, and to some, these features justify the desire to upgrade. The most current version of Apple's iOS software is version 8, which was released in September 2014.

Apple's iOS 8 is set to have an all new look and feel, including these new or improved features:

- All new Photos app, including powerful new editing tools
- Updated Messages app that allows you to add voice to any conversation, video clip, or location
- New way to respond to notifications
- Shortcuts to the people that you talk to most
- New, revised keyboard that makes typing easier by suggesting contextually appropriate words, and that can differentiate tone
- Family Sharing, which allows users in a household to easily share content from iTunes, iBooks, and the App Store
- iCloud Drive, an alternative to Dropbox. Apple will now store and make your files accessible right from iCloud, on whatever device you're using, Mac or PC
- New health app that gives you an easy-to-read dashboard of your health and fitness data and has the ability to track heart rate, calories burned, blood sugar, and cholesterol

In our opinion, the last revolutionary change to the iOS software was iOS 5, when Apple introduced its iCloud service. The iCloud service allows users to synchronize their music, photos, apps, documents, bookmarks, calendar, contacts, e-mail, and other data between multiple iOS devices. As a cloud service, Apple will actually store this data for you in an online account associated with your Apple ID. As with many Apple products, we have determined there are a number of security and privacy concerns with using this service. If you don't believe us, just read the Terms of Service—we did, and we will not use this service for anything business related. If you have enabled iCloud, be careful with what information you choose to synchronize with Apple. A lot of celebrities now understand that after the Celebgate debacle of 2014 when naked photos of them flooded the Internet. That's all we will say. We only have the Find My iPad feature configured in iCloud, so that we can locate the device if lost. Unfortunately, that also means Apple knows where our iPad is at all times.

Today, lawyers frequently use the iPad for court or meetings, rather than lugging around a laptop. Originally thought to compete against e-book devices such as the Kindle or Nook, the iPad has actually established a new class of devices that compete against smartphones, netbooks, smaller laptops, and ultrabooks. Lawyers are drawn to the functionality and portability of the device, and we believe their interest will only increase as future generations are released. The iPad can be purchased directly online from the Apple Store (**store.apple.com**) starting at $499 for the 16 GB Wi-Fi–only model.

Tom Mighell, lawyer and iPad expert, has three wonderful books available to assist lawyers who need help in understanding how to best use the iPad in their practice of law. The three books, *iPad in One Hour for Lawyers* (make sure you get the third edition), *iPad Apps in One Hour for Lawyers*, and *iPad in One Hour for Litigators*, can be purchased directly from the ABA's webstore and should be considered an invaluable resource for lawyers who are looking to test drive their iPads at work. You can get all three for less than $150, which is quite a deal!

Having given many lectures on the use of the iPad, we can tell you that this was the largest CLE magnet for the past two years. Though things have slowed a bit, it is clear that the iPad is the tablet of choice for most lawyers. As one of our attendees said while proudly brandishing his iPad, "This is a game-changer."

Apple Watch

Set to be released early in 2015, Apple has entered itself into the field of wearable technology with the pending release of the Apple Watch.

This device, available in three distinct flavors—Watch, Watch Sport, and Watch Edition—will suit everyone from young adults to working professionals. The watch will feature a Retina display, multifunctional input device that will let you zoom, scroll, and select without covering the screen through the use of the Digital Crown. The Digital Crown will allow you to zoom and scroll nimbly to the app of your choosing, or press the button to return to the Home screen. Users can even tap or deep press the display to access a range of contextually specific controls, such as an action menu in Messages. Incoming notifications will add a physical dimension to alerts and notifications, providing users with a gentle tap when you receive an incoming message. The device runs on an internal battery, which is charged using a combination of MagSafe technology with inductive charging. Like the iPhone, the Apple Watch is expected to be a battery killer. Several sources say that the watch must be plugged in each evening to stay operational as the battery will not last more than a day.

At the time of this writing, the price of the Apple Watch will start at $349 (ouch!) and will need to be paired with an iOS device (iPhone, iPad or iPod Touch) in order to function fully. At that price, John will keep his Citizen Eco-Drive dual time zone watch that is charged by solar energy and avoid searching for an outlet before going to bed. Why do we include a watch in this book? Because other smartwatches are starting to be used by lawyers to read and respond to texts and e-mails. How useful these watches will be to lawyers is as yet unknown, but wearable tech is a trend worth watching.

Touchfire Keyboard

Some have labeled this keyboard the accessory that turns the iPad into a true laptop killer. We won't go that far, but we are impressed with this piece of hardware.

This lightweight Bluetooth keyboard is actually a super thin keyboard overlay and not a separate external device like other Bluetooth keyboards. It attaches to the bottom half of your iPad with built-in magnets. This device provides tactile feedback when pressing the patented 3-D keys, enabling users to type much more quickly than on the flat keyboards often used with the iPad.

If you don't use a keyboard often, you can store it in the included carrying case; otherwise, you can keep it attached to your iPad. It is compatible with and fits into the Smart Case. The downside . . . it only works in landscape mode.

In terms of compatibility, this device works with all generations of the iPad. If you want to try out this device, you can purchase one from Touchfire's website (**www.touchfire.com**) for $40.

AirPort Extreme

Apple's AirPort Extreme is its wireless solution for home, school, and business. The wireless router plugs directly into your cable or DSL modem and connects you wirelessly to the Internet. This new version of router supports the 802.11a/b/g/n protocols, including the new 802.11ac standard, which provides data rates of up to 1.3 Gbps—triple the previous 802.11n standard. The wireless router supports NAT, DHCP, and VPN pass-through, allowing users the capability of connecting to their office network from home. The AirPort Extreme comes with built-in security features, such as a NAT firewall, Wi-Fi Protected Access, WPA/WPA2 and WEP encryption, and MAC address filtering. The router contains one GB Ethernet WAN port for connecting to a cable or DSL modem and three GB Ethernet LAN ports for connecting computers or networking devices.

The built-in USB port is provided to connect a printer or hard drive that is shared with other users on the local network. The AirPort Extreme is both Mac and Windows compatible, 64 percent smaller than its predecessor, only 6.6 inches from top to bottom, and comes bundled with software, power cord, and documentation. The AirPort Extreme can be purchased directly online from the Apple Store (**store.apple.com**) for $199.

AirPort Express

The AirPort Express is a portable wireless router, perfect for taking with you while on the road. However, this device has limited functionality in a business setting, allowing only fifty devices to connect to it at a time. The small wireless router is extremely portable, about the size of a postcard, and weighs less than 8.5 ounces. The router supports the 802.11a/b/g/n protocols and offers simultaneous dual-band 802.11n, transmitting at both the 2.4 GHz and 5 GHz frequencies at the same time. This provides 802.11n support no matter which band your wireless devices use. This wireless device is great for hotels, supplying your laptop with wireless Internet so you can surf from any location in the room.

The device has a built-in USB port for connecting a shared printer and an Ethernet port for connecting to your DSL and cable modem or your local network. The built-in wireless security supports WPA/WPA2, WEP, NAT, MAC address filtering, and time-based access control. The AirPort Express is both Mac and Windows compatible and comes bundled with the necessary software to get your computer connected to the wireless network. The AirPort Express can be purchased directly online from the Apple Store (**store.apple.com**) for $99.

AirPort Time Capsule

Looking for a solution to automatically back up your files? Time Capsule works seamlessly with Time Machine, backup software included with the Mac OS X operating system. Time Capsule is simply a wireless router with a built-in hard drive used for storing backups of your files. Using the Time Machine backup software, the application will back up your files and folders automatically, without user intervention. The data is backed up over the local wireless network to the Time Capsule hardware device.

Time Capsule can be purchased and used solely as a backup solution, or it can also provide wireless Internet connectivity to your local network. It has the same built-in features and functionality as AirPort Extreme. Time Capsule is offered in two models, with storage capacities of 2 and 3 TB. Time Capsule, like the AirPort Express, supports the new 802.11ac protocol, offering data rates of up to 1.3 Gbps. This device can be purchased directly online from the Apple Store (**store.apple.com**) starting at $299 for the 2 TB model.

Apple Thunderbolt Display

The Apple Thunderbolt Display is a high-definition (HD) flat-panel LCD monitor offering 27 inches of diagonal viewing area. Its wide-screen format makes this monitor a perfect display for legal professionals, providing enough real estate to display two or more documents side by side. The display is compatible with any Thunderbolt-enabled Mac notebook or desktop and supports resolutions up to 2560 × 1440 pixels.

The monitor has a 1,000:1 contrast ratio, 12-millisecond response time, and screen with an antiglare coating. The monitor has three USB 2.0 ports and can be purchased with an optional VESA wall mount. It also includes a built-in FaceTime HD camera with microphone and a 2.1 speaker system. The monitor even has an ambient light sensor that can automatically adjust the brightness of the LCD display. It also includes one GB Ethernet port, one Thunderbolt port, and one FireWire 800 port.

The Apple Thunderbolt Display comes with a one-year limited warranty and can be purchased directly online from the Apple Store (**store.apple.com**) for $999.

Apple Wireless Keyboard

The Apple wireless keyboard uses Bluetooth wireless technology, eliminating the need for obstructive and unfriendly wires to connect your keyboard to your computer. The wireless keyboard comes in a low-profile anodized aluminum frame that matches the Apple theme and takes up 24 percent less space on your desktop than full-size keyboards. The keyboard contains function keys for one-touch access to Mac features and has power management features to conserve the batteries when not in use. The Apple wireless keyboard requires Mac OS X version 10.6.8 or higher, takes two AA batteries, and can also be used with the iPad. It can be purchased directly online from the Apple Store (**store.apple.com**) for $69.

Apple Magic Mouse

Like the Apple wireless keyboard, the Magic Mouse uses Bluetooth wireless technology to connect the mouse to your computer. Laser tracking allows you to use the mouse on a number of surfaces while maintaining the precision and accuracy of tracking movement. The mouse uses multi-touch sensitive technology to detect both right and left clicks, and the innovative scrolling ball allows for 360-degree scrolling capabilities. The mouse is powered with two AA batteries and, when paired with the Apple wireless keyboard, allows you to work wire-free at your desk. This wireless device requires Mac OS X version 10.5.8 or later to operate. Sorry, folks, but there is no mouse support for the iPad, so this is limited to working with Apple computers only. The Apple Magic Mouse can be purchased directly online from the Apple Store (**store.apple.com**) for $69.

Apple iPod

Formerly Apple's most successful hardware device, the iPod has sold over 350 million units since its creation in 2001, and this number released by Apple hasn't been updated since 2012. It has only been supplanted by the iPhone in total sales within the past few years.

The portable digital-file-playing devices are the most popular hand-held multimedia devices in use today, and some models can be used to play and shoot video, take pictures, play podcasts, and even play games. All models are capable of playing music. The iPod is available in three models: Shuffle, Nano, and Touch. The iPod Shuffle is the smallest, with no display screen, and is available in a 2 GB size. The Shuffle allows you to shake the device in certain positions to change the song, play the songs in order, or shuffle the order. The newest version also includes a new VoiceOver function that will tell you the song or artist you're listening to. The iPod Shuffle costs $49 and is available in eight different colors.

The iPod Nano is one of Apple's more popular devices and has just recently had a makeover. The current version of the Nano includes a radio tuner with live pause functionality, VoiceOver, and even a pedometer. Some of the new features include a 2.5-inch multi-touch display, the ability to play video, Bluetooth 4.0, Nike+ support, and all-new EarPods. This device has been updated with Apple's new Lightning connector pin. The iPod Nano is offered in eight bright colors, and it is available only with 16 GB of storage capacity. The cost is just $149. Flash memory is used in the Nano, making it ideal for workouts at the gym.

The iPod Touch is probably the most versatile iPod, providing users with a way to listen to music, watch videos, and play games, as well as surf the Internet and check their e-mail. Like the Nano, the iPod Touch just went through its own refresh. The latest version is much thinner and lighter than the previous models weighing just 3.1 ounces. It comes with a 4-inch Retina display, upgraded iSight 5-megapixel camera, upgraded dual-core processor, and the all-new EarPods. The iPod Touch has a 4-inch diagonal color display and a touchscreen interface, and it is available in 16, 32, and 64 GB sizes. The iPod Touch even has a built-in Wi-Fi network adapter supporting 802.11b/g/n network connections. The device also includes Bluetooth 4.0 and Nike+ support. The iPod Touch costs anywhere from $199 to $299, depending on the model.

All of the iPod devices can be purchased online from the Apple Store or at your local electronics retailer. The devices are both Windows and Mac compatible, and they connect to your computer using a USB connection.

Software

Microsoft Office 2011 for Mac Home & Business

Microsoft Office for Mac 2011 is the latest version of Office for Macs and includes better compatibility across platforms, improved collaboration tools, and an improved user interface. The latest version also scraps Entourage and now includes Outlook, which will provide Mac users with the ability to import Microsoft Outlook PST files. Visual Basic support returns as well, which is a must-have for those running macro-based applications. Users can also store files online using their OneDrive folder, which affords secure access to edit or share your work, and 15 GB of free online storage is provided. Microsoft Office for Mac includes Word, PowerPoint, Excel, Outlook, OneNote, Office365 support, and free tech support for one year.

Like the Windows-based counterpart, users can opt to subscribe to Office365 instead of purchasing the stand-alone version of Office for Mac. Depending on the subscription level, users may be able to install Office for Mac on up to five computers.

The stand-alone version of Office for Mac 2011 requires Mac OS X v. 10.5.8 or later and is available only in a 32-bit version. A single license for this product can be purchased and downloaded online from Microsoft's web-site (**www.microsoft.com**) for $219.99.

Toast 12 Titanium by Roxio

Toast 12 Titanium is the latest version of Roxio's long-running disc-burning software for the Mac. With this software you can burn video or data to CDs or DVDs. This version gives users the ability to burn high-definition video to Blu-ray discs and record content directly from your screen with Live Screen Capture. Toast even allows a user to capture streaming audio from any website and then transfer the audio to an iPod or any other iOS-based device. The software has built-in basic features, such as the ability to compress, convert, and compile video in most for-mats, along with backup software that can be scheduled to back up your data. Features new to this version include the ability to extract clips from any DVD video and convert them to a format of your choice, to convert audiobook CDs for playback on iPod devices, and to build your MP3 library with the automatic capture and tagging of Internet audio. New to this version is the capability for users to convert video recorded on their TiVo DVRs, EyeTV tuners, and Flip Video camcorders to play on their iPad, iPhone, or video game consoles. Users can even share their video compilations directly to YouTube, Twitter, and Facebook.

The software can be purchased online from Roxio's website (**www.roxio.com**) for $99.99.

Norton Internet Security for Mac

Every Mac user needs to protect his or her computer from viruses and other threats. Using antivirus protection on a Mac is no longer an option; it's a necessity. Norton Internet Security has an edition specifically for Mac computers that offers protection from the latest viruses, spyware, rootkits, and other web-based attacks. Norton Internet Security version 5 is compatible with OS X v. 10.7 or higher.

The antivirus protection can automatically scan and clean downloaded e-mail files and attachments and provide real-time protection and removal of viruses and other threats.

Some users still believe there are no viruses or threats for a Mac. Not so. Just look at how many systems were infected with the MacDefender or Flashback Trojan over the past few years. These were such a problem that Apple released security patches just to address these specific threats. There are many other documented viruses and vulnerabilities that are specific to Macs and many more that are operating system–independent. The message here is to get and install an antivirus or security solution. You should never use a computer on your business or home network without the proper security protection, even if it's a Mac. Apple itself removed from its website (rather late, in 2012) language suggesting that it was impervious to malware. Norton Internet Security can be purchased online directly from Symantec's website (**www.symantec.com**) for $49.99 for a one-year subscription.

Kaspersky Internet Security for Mac

For users looking for an alternative to Norton Internet Security, Kaspersky has a great product called Kaspersky Internet Security for Mac. We use Kaspersky's security software on our networks and have tried this product on our Mac laptop, and it works as advertised. This software offers real-time protection against malware, phishing, and malicious websites, as well as antivirus protection and parental controls and is 80% of the cost of Norton. This product requires Mac OS X 10.7 or higher to run. The lower cost alone is a great selling point! This product can be purchased online from Kaspersky's website (**www.kaspersky.com**) for $39.95 for a one-year subscription.

Intuit Quicken 2015 for Mac

Intuit Quicken for Mac offers a complete personal financial management package, providing immediate access to your accounts from a single location. By using Quicken, you can better organize your financial information and easily track your finances. Quicken provides a simple way to track and enter expenses without launching the entire application through the QuickEntry Dashboard Widget. Some of the new features allow you to check your account balances and budget on the go using the free mobile app, which syncs the data between your phone and your computer. This product also allows you to see all of your accounts in one place. The software will run only on Intel-based Macs using 10.7.5 or higher.

Quicken users can export their basic tax information to TurboTax and other applications that can read a TXF or QXF file.

If you need to switch your data files from Quicken Windows to Quicken Mac, there is a walk-through guide on Intuit's website to help you out. You can find the instructions to complete this procedure at **https://quicken.intuit.com/support/help/what-quicken-data-can-be-converted-from-windows-to-mac-/GEN82214.html**.

Quicken 2015 for Mac is the latest version of the software from Intuit that is available for purchase and download on its website (**www.intuit.com**) for $74.99.

QuickBooks 2014 for Macs

QuickBooks, another financial and accounting package from Intuit, has an edition for Macs. QuickBooks 2014 for Macs can be used to organize your business finances. This software package will also track and manage your business expenses, invoicing, and payroll from a single financial application. QuickBooks for Macs can synchronize your contacts directly with the Mac OS X Address Book and set reminders in iCal. This software is compatible with Mac OS X v. 10.7 (Lion), or higher.

Some of the new features of QuickBooks 2014 for Macs include:

- ◆ Left hand toolbar lets users create shortcuts to their most used features.
- ◆ Enhanced, customizable Centers keep important customer, vendor, and transaction information in a central location.

♦ Income Tracker shows all your income-producing transactions in one spot.

♦ Reports can identify top sales performers.

♦ Quick adjustments for sales tax paid to your account, including sales tax paid from credit cards, are available.

QuickBooks 2014 for Macs can be purchased online from Intuit's QuickBooks website (**www.quickbooks.com**) for $249.95 for a new license. Two- through five-user versions are also available for purchase on the website.

Symantec Drive Encryption for Mac OS X

PGP Corporation (now owned by Symantec), a leading vendor of hard disk encryption software, has released an updated version of its hard disk encryption suite compatible with Mac computers (previously called Symantec Full Disk Encryption for Macs). Symantec Drive Encryption software provides comprehensive, nonstop disk encryption for Macs, securing data on desktops, laptops, and removable devices. A user name and passphrase are required to decrypt the contents of the hard disk, protecting the data from unauthorized access. Symantec Drive Encryption requires Mac OS X version 10.7 or higher and only runs on Intel-based Macs. Symantec Drive Encryption can be used to provide quick, cost-effective data protection for information on hard drives and removable media. Any lawyer using a Mac laptop should definitely have this software installed to protect sensitive and confidential information. An alternative is to enable File Vault or File Vault 2, which is included as part of the Mac operating system.

Symantec Drive Encryption software can be purchased online directly from Symantec's website (**www.symantec.com**) for $110 for a single license with one-year upgrade assurance.

Apple iTunes

If you've ever owned an iPod or older version of the iPhone or iPad, then you're certainly familiar with Apple iTunes. It is Apple Software's most popular product, mainly because it used to be necessary to manage your digital music library on your iPod, iPhone, iPad, or other Apple iOS device. The newest version of iTunes allows users to download more content with their purchased songs, such as the album cover, band pictures, and even song lyrics. Using the Home Sharing feature, users can share their digital libraries with up to five authorized computers in their home, allowing them to share purchased music files across multiple computer systems. Apple now allows you to follow your favorite artists and view what music your friends are downloading and listening to. A new feature called iTunes Match lets you store all of your music in iCloud—even songs you've imported from CDs—synchronizing your music across all of your iOS devices. iCloud provides users with the ability to access their music, TV shows, apps, and books from multiple devices without the need to manually synchronize files using iTunes across multiple iOS devices.

iTunes Radio, introduced by Apple in 2013 as a direct competitor to Pandora and Spotify, allows users to create radio stations based on the songs/artists that they like, all for free. It's about time—but is it too late? For now, we will continue to use Pandora—which doesn't require the installation of software to run.

Using the iTunes Store, users can download apps, music, videos, podcasts, and more and then synchronize them to their devices, such as an iPad or iPhone. Users can subscribe to podcasts, and, without any user input, the iTunes application can download the latest shows as they're made available. We use this feature a lot when it comes to managing the legal technology podcasts to which we subscribe and constantly monitor. Apple iTunes is available as a free download for Mac OS X and Windows 8 from Apple's website.

CHAPTER TWENTY-FOUR

iWin:
iPad for Litigators

by Tom Mighell, Esq., and Paul Unger, Esq.

Introduction and Tour of iPad

Since it was released in 2010, the iPad has quickly become a very useful tool for lawyers, and one of the biggest innovations in legal technology to come along in some time. The iPad's design is ingenious and handsome. Its functionality is equally as nice and continues to improve as legal software developers rush to create apps for lawyers. Indeed, the iPad remains the tablet of choice for legal app developers, far outpacing Android and Windows tablets in the number of legal apps available.

Tablets have integrated themselves into the workflow of lawyers, irrespective of firm size or practice area, and nowhere has that been more apparent than at trial. Whether you need to take notes, mark and handle exhibits, or manage deposition transcripts, these little computers can supercharge your litigation practice. But the iPad can make *any* lawyer more productive, regardless of practice; while we discuss how litigators can use tablet computers to enhance their day in court, we will also provide a general overview for anyone interested in using the iPad (see Figure 25.1) in your practice.

Figure 25.1 An iPad

Why Use an iPad in Your Practice?

We like to describe the iPad as an instant-on computer that you can control with your finger. There's no booting-up process, and no keyboard is needed. It provides instant access to information traditionally accessed from your desktop computer or laptop.

Although the iPad's initial purpose was thought to be as a consumption device—a tablet used primarily for reading and accessing information and very light typing—its ease of use and big screen is so addicting that it evolved into a tool that can do so much more, especially for lawyers.

If you carry around a legal pad and a lot of paper in a legal file or Redweld, the iPad can become your legal pad and digital folder. It is truly redefining the idea of the "paperless" law office. For courtroom work, the iPad can be used to access exhibits, pleadings, legal research, depositions, and just about any document you might need in hearings or at trial (see Figure 25.2).

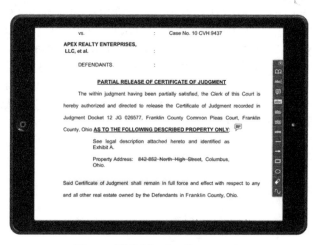

Figure 25.2 Viewing Documents

Trial presentation apps available for the iPad make it easy to display those exhibits on projectors or monitors (wired or wireless) in the courtroom.

Overview

iPad Air

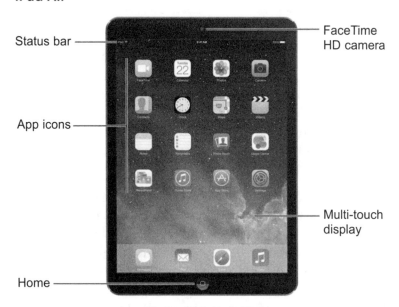

Figure 25.3 Front View

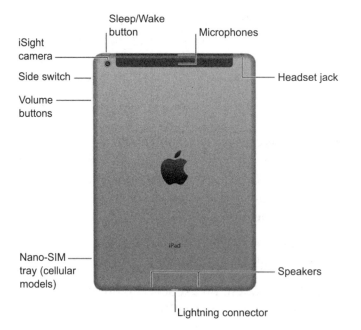

Figure 25.4 Back View

If you want to learn more about using the iPad, check out Tom's book *iPad in One Hour for Lawyers* (3rd edition), *iPad in One Hour for Litigators,* and *iPad Apps in One Hour for Lawyers*, all published by the ABA and available in the ABA webstore.

Why Use an iPad in the Courtroom?

Certainly, most of you have seen an iPad at this point (see Figures 25.3 and 25.4). The iPad has some drawbacks as a computing tool that make it unsuitable as a complete replacement for your desktop or laptop; however, we believe it is ideal for courtroom use because it is so light and easy to hold and operate. It is very easy to understand and use, with little training required. (In fact, if you already use an iPhone, you'll be able to start working with an iPad right away.)

Among the often-cited negatives of the iPad are (1) that it has no USB port for plugging the tablet into other devices and (2) that the battery is not removable or replaceable. One of the reasons that the lack of a USB port is not troubling is that the iPad comes with Bluetooth capability, so keyboards, printers, and other devices can be connected wirelessly to the device. Also, a number of cloud providers (Dropbox, Box, and SpiderOak, among others) make it easy for you to access all of your documents online, without needing to connect your iPad to anything.

The iPad Air has a 10.1-inch display, while the iPad Mini features the smaller 7-inch screen and has become very popular for its compact design and ease of use. Because lawyers need to work with documents during trial, however, we believe that the larger 10-inch display is far preferable and will make working with documents, legal research, and notes in court much easier.

In our opinion, it is this ease of use that explains why iPads are rapidly catching on with trial lawyers. A laptop, netbook, or even the traditional convertible tablet PCs, which are useful at counsel table, cannot be carried around the courtroom easily when the lawyer is standing at the podium or addressing the jury.

Essentially, the iPad is just a little heavier than a paper legal pad and not nearly as heavy as the lightest netbook or laptop.

When selecting a jury, it doesn't make sense to question a jury pool while keyboarding your responses into a traditional computer; there's probably no better way to get jurors to clam up and give them the impression that the lawyer is transcribing their personal information. (This is true even though the court reporter may be quietly transcribing it in many cases.) The iPad, however, is ideally configured to take notes on your jury panel, either within a jury selection app or your favorite note-taking application.

Let's take a look at some of the ways a litigator would benefit by using an iPad, from initial receipt of a lawsuit all the way through jury verdict.

iPad Apps for Lawyers

Deadline Calculators
Court Days Pro
($2.99, bit.ly/yT171w)

Court Days Pro is a rules-based legal calendaring app for the iPhone and iPad. It provides legal professionals with the ability to calculate dates and deadlines based on a customizable database of court rules and statutes. Once the rules are set up in the application, you can perform date calculations using a customizable list of court holidays. It comes with California's Superior Court rules pre-installed; however, if you do not live in California, you will need to add your own local court rules for the jurisdiction in which you practice. Unfortunately, Court Days Pro has not been updated in some time, which typically means the developers have lost interest in supporting it. We still believe it is a worthwhile app because it will allow you to input your own deadlines and reuse them over again, which is unique for a calendaring app.

Once you choose a triggering event (e.g., a motion hearing date or receipt of a complaint), the application will display a list of all events and corresponding dates and deadlines based on the triggering event (e.g., last day to file moving papers, opposition, reply briefs). Icons on the screen show the number of calendar days and court days from the current date for all resulting events (see Figure 25.5).

Date results can be added to the device's native calendar app, and all results can be e-mailed to your client or others straight from the application.

The app is preprogrammed with a list of all federal holidays but it is fully customizable to allow the addition or removal of any court holiday to the list.

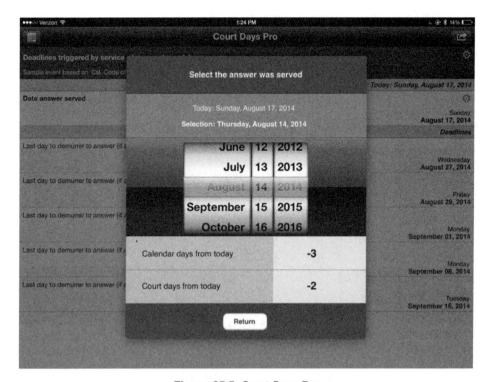

Figure 25.5 Court Days Pro

Other calendaring apps are DocketLaw (Free, **bit.ly/1NVjjUZ**) and Smart Dockets (Free, **bit.ly/1BHA666**). Both apps are free to download, but DocketLaw charges a subscription to access court deadlines. Like Court Days Pro, neither of these apps has been updated in some time—which suggests that there is not much demand for calendaring and docketing functionality on the iPad.

Lawyer's Professional Assistant ($4.99, bit.ly/x5j7Fq)

The Wolfram Lawyer's Professional Assistant (see Figure 25.6) is a reference tool that takes advantage of the company's Computational Knowledge Engine to help lawyers with calculations that may be relevant in their practice. Some of the features include:

- Calendar computations
- Legal dictionary
- Statutes of limitations for each U.S. state (see Figure 25.7)
- Visa types, including basic requirements, common issues, and extensions and limits

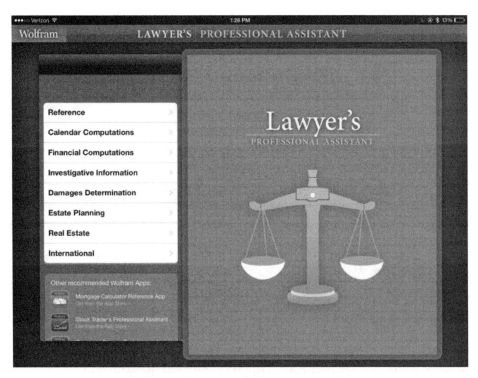

Figure 25.6 Lawyer's Professional Assistant

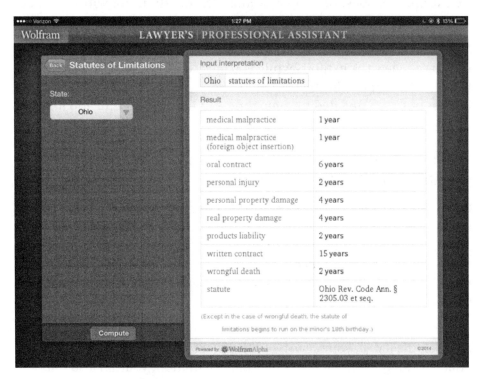

Figure 25.7 Statute of Limitations Screen

- Financial computations, including fee calculator, settlement calculator, current interest rates, historical value of money, and federal U.S. tax rates
- Crime rates and history for specific crimes, as well as state and national average comparisons
- Demographics of population and economy for a specific city
- Investigative information, including weather, company information, IP lookup, and blood-alcohol calculator
- Damages and estate planning computations for occupational salaries, cost of living, life expectancy, and present or future value

Depositions

The Deponent
($9.99, bit.ly/warTWI)

The Deponent is a deposition question and exhibit outline application for lawyers. It offers 150+ preprogrammed deposition questions by categories, but you can add your own questions as well. The app allows you to organize the order of questions and customize the questions for witnesses. Each question can be linked to an exhibit.

Exhibits can be loaded into the app from iTunes and Dropbox as PDF files, so you can view the exhibits while you are asking questions, or show them to the witness during the deposition (see Figure 25.8). The Deponent has not been updated in some time, but it is still a useful app for managing depositions.

TranscriptPad
($89.99, bit.ly/w7JGHt)

Once you have taken your depositions, you can load all of the transcripts into TranscriptPad to review them and create designations. The app only accepts text transcripts, so be sure to ask your court reporter for the deposition in TXT format. Once it's loaded, you can easily highlight testimony and code the designations with the issues you want to include (see Figure 25.9).

When you complete your designations, it's simple to e-mail them to co-counsel, the judge, your client, or others (see Figure 25.10). If you use TrialDirector or Sanction for evidence presentation, you can also import your designations directly into those tools from TranscriptPad.

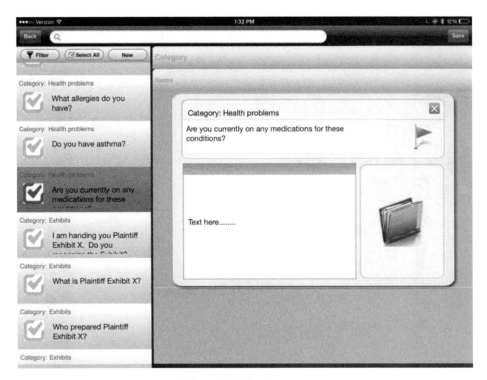

Figure 25.8 The Deponent

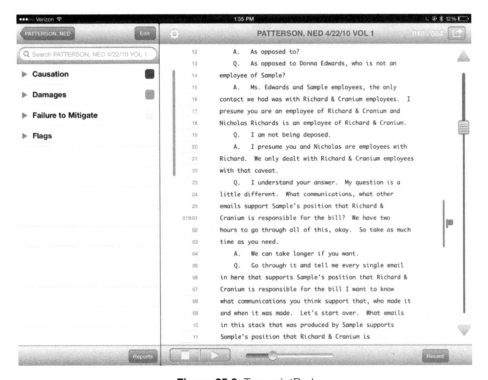

Figure 25.9 TranscriptPad

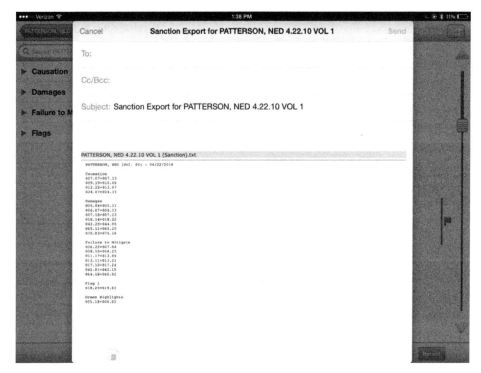

Figure 25.10 TranscriptPad e-mail

Jury Selection/Tracking

iJuror
($19.99, bit.ly/xJFIOT)

iJuror is an app developed to assist with jury selection (see Figure 25.11). Features include the ability to:

- Tap the seats to add juror information.
- Track patterns.
- E-mail the jury information to any e-mail address.
- Configure seating arrangements for up to ninety-six jurors.
- Get easy access to popular social networks to conduct quick research on potential jury members.
- Add notes as the trial goes along, and score jurors based on their answers to *voir dire* questions.
- Name view provides quick access to names and notes.

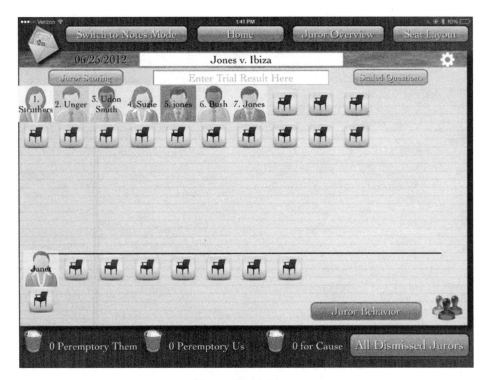

Figure 25.11 iJuror

- ♦ Drag and drop to choose jurors.
- ♦ Drag and drop to choose alternates.
- ♦ Drag and drop to dismiss jurors.

Honorable Mentions

- ♦ **JuryPad** ($24.99, **bit.ly/1tae75H**) Nicely designed, this app is not quite as intuitive as iJuror, but it has much of the same functionality.

- ♦ **JuryStar** ($39.99, **bit.ly/1qY0aSw**) Similar to iJuror and JuryPad, but it requires you to manually enter a lot more information.

- ♦ **iJury** ($14.99, **bit.ly/ZBL135**) This convenient jury selection tool has pre-populated questions and a system for ranking jurors based on their answers. However, you can only enter twelve people, which is not very helpful if you have a larger *voir dire* panel.

- ♦ **JuryTracker** ($4.99, **bit.ly/1taekWx**) This app goes to work after you have selected your jury; it works as your personal jury consultant to help track the reactions of jury members throughout the trial (see Figure 25.12).

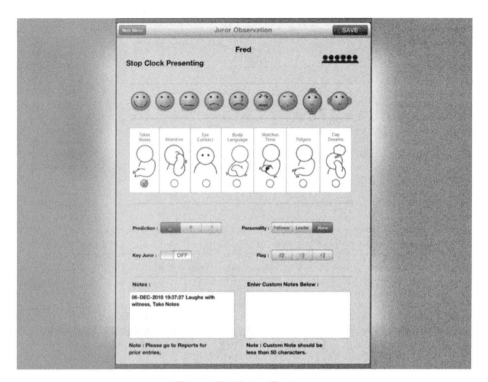

Figure 25.12 JuryTracker

Evidence Presentation

TrialPad
($89.99, bit.ly/ApMDjM)

TrialPad is a legal document and exhibit management and presentation tool originally developed for lawyers to use in the courtroom. Lawyers and other legal professionals also are finding other great ways to use the app, including client presentations and law school lectures. With TrialPad, you can organize, manage, annotate, and store your documents and video while leveraging the portability of your iPad. It is designed to work like full-featured tools such as Sanction or Trial Director; however, because the iPad is not as powerful as your laptop, TrialPad does not offer all the functionality of traditional trial presentation software. But for many types of trials and hearings, TrialPad is the ideal presentation tool.

TrialPad differs from programs like PowerPoint or Keynote in that the presenter can present documents, images, and video in any order. It's possible to jump around, zoom, magnify, or annotate an exhibit on the fly. TrialPad is not really a competitor to PowerPoint or Keynote because it was designed to handle different situations; PowerPoint and Keynote are designed for more rehearsed linear presentations (opening and closing), where TrialPad works in more spontaneous situations like witness examination. Unlike PDF readers, this app lets you create separate case folders, organize and sort important documents, and dynamically annotate and present documents via its flexible output options.

TrialPad cannot handle huge amounts of data as well as Sanction or Trial Director, and its video editing tool is not as powerful, but it works very well for hearings and most cases with manageable volumes of records. Features include the ability to:

- ♦ Organize and present evidence electronically (see Figure 25.13).
- ♦ Import via Dropbox, Box, WebDav server, e-mail, or iTunes. No Internet connection is needed once files are loaded.
- ♦ Present wirelessly with Apple TV or AirServer (requires iPad 2 and above).
- ♦ Highlight, annotate, redact, and zoom in on your documents (see Figure 25.14).
- ♦ Make multiple callouts from documents or depositions.

Figure 25.13 Presenting Evidence with TrialPad

Figure 25.14 TrialPad Photo

◆ View documents side by side, comparing pages.

◆ Edit video clips or take snapshots of frames of surveillance video.

◆ Create Key Docs with saved annotations, and then print or e-mail them with the annotations.

◆ Have your expert mark up an exhibit and save it as a Key Doc for closing.

◆ Use the whiteboard tool to draw freehand.

◆ Create separate case and witness folders.

◆ Support numerous file formats: Adobe Acrobat PDF, JPG, PNG, TIFF, multi-page TIFF, and TXT (Also imports DOC, DOCX, XLS, XLSX, PPT, PPTX, Keynote, Pages, and Numbers. *Please note:* Our best practices recommendation is to convert these files to Adobe Acrobat to maintain the formatting and look of the original document.)

◆ Support all video formats supported by iPad, such as .m4v, .mp4, and .mov

Honorable Mentions

◆ **ExhibitView** ($49.99, **bit.ly/zUwFnq**) This app is a worthy competitor to TrialPad. It offers a Witness View, where you can hand the witness your iPad to view an exhibit without showing any of your other case files.

♦ **Exhibit A** ($14.99, **https://itunes.apple.com/us/app/exhibit-a/ id392621180?mt=8**) Although this app is less full-featured than the other two apps, it performs basic document display and annotation. It's a good choice if you're looking for something less expensive.

Legal Research

When you go to court, how many rulebooks do you bring with you? During trial or a hearing, it's important to have access to the case law, codes, and rules that are applicable in your case. Tools like the iPad now make it easy to have access to your entire law library, no matter where you happen to be. Here are a few of the tools we like:

♦ **Fastcase** (Free, **bit.ly/ysOcTY**) It's the companion to the legal research service.

♦ **WestlawNext** (Free, but requires Westlaw subscription, **bit.ly/z5pKRs**) A great tool for the courtroom, it allows you to conduct legal research, annotate the results, and e-mail case law to the judge or others.

♦ **Lexis Advance HD** (Free, but requires Lexis subscription, **bit.ly/vo7wzp**) This Lexis version of WestlawNext provides the same features for accessing your Lexis account.

♦ **LawBox** (Free, **bit.ly/y36FeU**) This app provides free access to all federal law—rules, codes, and the Constitution. You can also purchase rules for certain jurisdictions at $4.99 each.

♦ **FedCtRecords** ($9.99, **bit.ly/yb7gav**) This is an iPhone app, but completely worth the purchase for your iPad. The app provides access to your PACER account, so you have anywhere access to records on just about any federal case.

♦ **ProView** (Free, but requires purchase of rulebooks, **bit.ly/wVrUZc**) If you practice in a jurisdiction that has rules published by Thomson Reuters, you can access the full version of those rulebooks on your iPad with this app.

♦ **My Legal Projects** ($1.99, **bit.ly/yVypHi**) Originally designed for summer associates or new lawyers, this app can be useful to anyone who likes to keep track of legal research. You can track research questions (issue, jurisdiction, deadlines, etc.) and connect to your WestlawNext account to do research on the particular project.

Courtroom Chatting

BT Chat HD
(Free, bit.ly/xE16tG)

If you have ever had the need to pass a note discreetly in the courtroom, you will completely understand the need for this app (see Figure 25.15). With BT Chat HD, you can chat with other iPad users via Bluetooth or Wi-Fi (Wi-Fi is better if you're sitting at a distance).

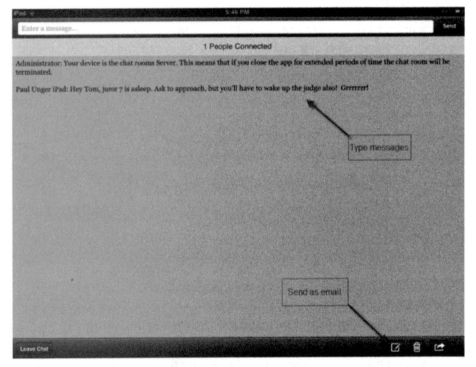

Figure 25.15 BT Chat HD

Other Must-Have iPad Apps

So many apps . . . which one is best? There are many incredible apps for the iPad. In fact, there are so many that you will probably be overwhelmed about which ones to select, especially if you are new to the iPad.

We have listed our picks below, and we also have some honorable mentions. Some of our honorable mentions may end up being your top picks. Don't let this overwhelm you. With so many fantastic apps out there, it is hard to go wrong. In deciding which apps are best for you, follow these guiding principles:

- Probably a dozen apps accomplish the same thing. Review legal app blogs, consumer reviews, and ask trusted people what they recommend.

- Your workplace may prefer one app over another. Consistency and uniformity at the office is typically a good thing.

- If your co-workers or friends use the app, they can provide you with a support network to better learn and use the app.

- If a new app is released from a competing software company, don't be too quick to switch! Your app will probably catch up pretty fast and may have features the other app doesn't have yet. Remember your time invested in the app you already own.

- Apps are cheap; if you are curious, just buy it. Most apps are less than $10. The most expensive app cited in these materials is $129.99.

- If you want more recommendations, check out Tom's book *iPad Apps in One Hour for Lawyers*—he lists more than two hundred of his choices for the best productivity, document creation and management, legal, travel, and leisure-time apps in the App Store. It's available from the ABA webstore.

1. Dropbox
(Free app, <u>bit.ly/z54Tpv</u>; Free Dropbox account up to 2 GB at <u>www.dropbox.com</u>)

Paul and Tom's Top Pick

If you have an iPad, Dropbox is almost mandatory. Setting aside debates about security, Dropbox has become the gold standard for storing files and getting them to the iPad. Most software developers build their apps to integrate with Dropbox because it has become so widely used.

Dropbox sets up a local folder on your computer that allows you to create any subfolder structure. These subfolders synchronize into the cloud and can be shared with other people (clients, co-counsel, co-workers, etc.), if desired. The iPad can also connect to your Dropbox account so it can see and access everything that you can see on your PC (see Figure 25.16).

If you can create a folder, copy and paste, and drag and drop, you can use Dropbox.

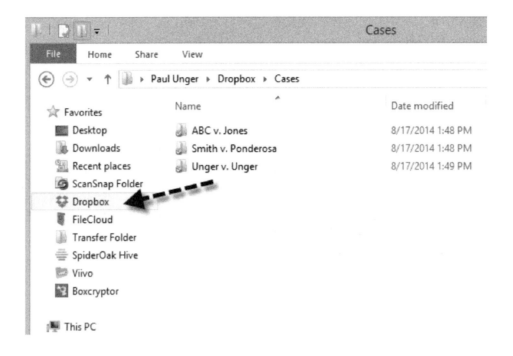

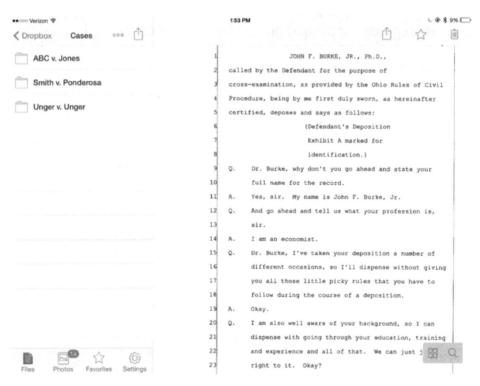

Figure 25.16 The iPad's View of a Dropbox Account

2. Dictate + Connect
($16.99, bit.ly/wuv1Mq)

Paul's Top Pick

Dictate + Connect is a dictation application for your iPhone or iPad (see Figure 25.17). Like a traditional digital recorder, it allows you to rewind, overwrite, and insert anywhere. Download recordings, send as e-mails, upload to Dropbox, iCloud, FTP, or WebDAV.

Figure 25.17 Dictate + Connect

3. GoodReader
($4.99, bit.ly/xb99kc)

Paul and Tom's Top Pick

Since documents are the lifeblood of the legal profession, it makes sense that one of the best uses of the iPad in a law practice is to read and annotate documents. GoodReader is best described as a universal document viewer, although it arguably works best with the PDF file format (see Figure 25.18).

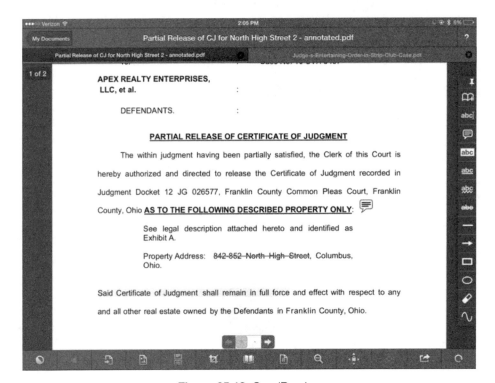

Figure 25.18 GoodReader

GoodReader provides excellent annotation tools for PDF files, including the ability to highlight text, insert text boxes, post "sticky notes" comments, compose freehand drawings, and add lines, arrows, rectangles, and so on (see Figure 25.19). These tools are extremely useful when you're reading a court opinion or law review article.

GoodReader also has a robust file manager and has the ability to sync directly with your accounts from Dropbox, Box.com, Google Drive, OneDrive or even your own web-connected server (see Figure 25.20).

Figure 25.19 GoodReader Annotations

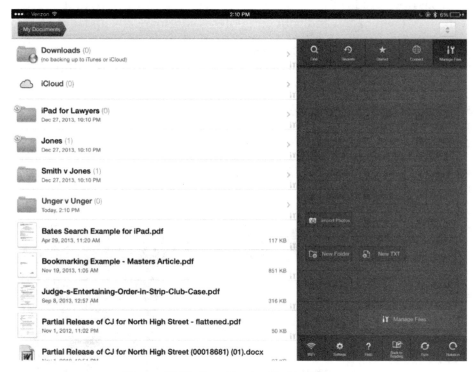

Figure 25.20 GoodReader File Management

4. Microsoft Office for iPad
(Free, Word: <u>bit.ly/1e17n4j</u>; Excel: <u>bit.ly/1g8csnl</u>; PowerPoint: <u>bit.ly/1jApmPu</u>)

Paul and Tom's Top Pick

Microsoft has finally brought its Office suite to the iPad, and for Office users, this is the recommended set of apps to use. Working in these apps is almost like working in the desktop versions of Word, Excel, and

PowerPoint, although Microsoft modified the layout to better accommodate the tablet interface. The experience using these apps is the closest you'll get on the iPad to working with the real thing.

There are two caveats to using these apps, however. First, while they are free to download, to use them to create and edit documents, you'll have to purchase a subscription to Microsoft's Office 365 product, which can range between $69 and $150 per year, depending on the version you purchase. This is actually a pretty good deal—for this price, you get five licenses to Microsoft Office. Further, there's no need to wait for the next version to come out and then use CDs to install it on your computer; the Office 365 model is download-only, so as Microsoft releases new versions of the software, it is downloaded and your computer is automatically updated.

The second caveat is that, at the time of writing, you can only save your documents to a OneDrive account. There are work-arounds to move documents out of OneDrive into another location, and you can also e-mail documents to another location, but neither of these options is particularly convenient.

Despite these qualifications, we still highly recommend the use of the apps on the iPad, especially if you plan to spend a lot of time on your tablet creating and revising documents, or presenting slideshows (see Figure 25.21).

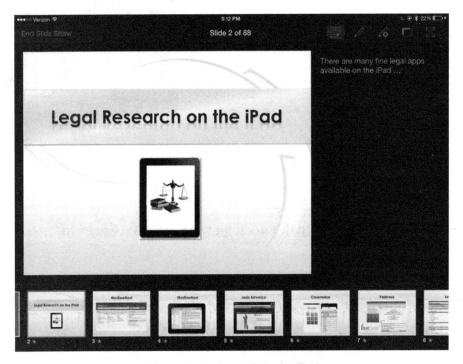

Figure 25.21 PowerPoint for iPad

Honorable Mention: Documents To Go Premium ($16.99, bit.ly/A5LPMq)

If you don't want to pay for Microsoft Office, Documents to Go is currently your best low-cost option. While it does not come close to the functionality of Microsoft Word or Excel for iPad, Documents to Go provides basic editing tools for Word, Excel, and PowerPoint documents. It also connects to most major cloud services for easy sharing and syncing.

5. Notability ($2.99, bit.ly/wZT4wD)

Paul and Tom's Top Pick

Very few note-taking apps perform *all* three functions of handwriting, typing, *and* audio. We have found that Notability provides a great writing experience. You can change the thickness of the pen and the width of lines and add lines and gridlines—all important to simulate an experience similar to writing on a piece of paper (see Figure 25.22).

You can use your finger to write notes on the iPad, but we recommend investing in a stylus so the writing experience is as similar as possible to writing on paper with a pen.

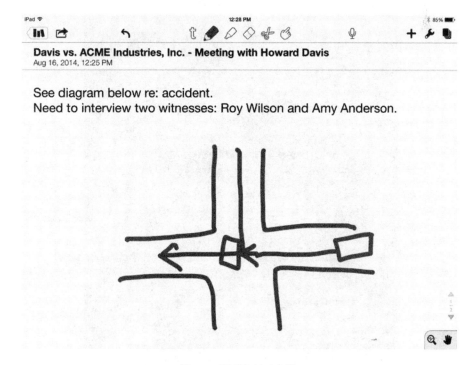

Figure 25.22 Notability

The audio feature not only records your meetings, conferences, or other gatherings but also synchronizes the recording to your notes so that you can simply tap a word or picture and hear what was being said at that moment.

Paul finds the ability to record a meeting, lecture, and so on, to be immensely helpful in certain situations. He absolutely loves this feature, as he does *not* want to have a separate notes program to do this (like Auditorium), a separate typing program, and a separate audio recorder. Notability provides all three functions.

6. Noteshelf
($5.99, bit.ly/y73OZd)

Tom's Top Pick

For pure handwritten note-taking, Noteshelf is one of the highest-ranking and most popular apps. You can create notebooks for your clients, cases, or projects and see them at a glance on your Noteshelf bookshelf (see Figure 25.23). You can e-mail notebooks to yourself or others, or

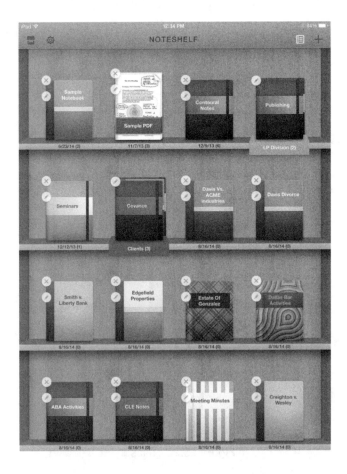

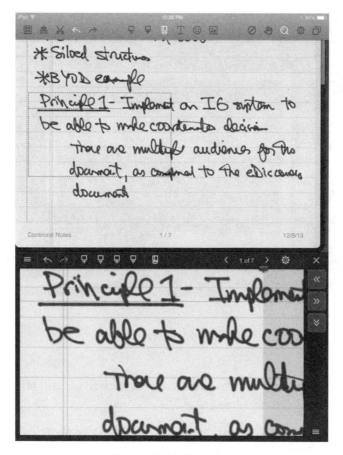

Figure 25.23 Noteshelf

they can be exported to a PDF file and saved in Dropbox or Evernote. Tom recommends this app because it has just enough features that lawyers need to take notes without being overwhelming. It just works, and works well.

7. Keynote for iOS
($9.99, bit.ly/z6C1R9)

Paul's Top Pick

Keynote for the iPad or Mac is the equivalent of PowerPoint in the PC world (see Figure 25.24). Keynote truly is an excellent presentation tool, and Apple has ported the software to the iPad iOS.

Keynote on the iPad can certainly be used to give presentations on a large screen with a projector. But many lawyers also use Keynote as a way to share a set of images and information with a small group, such as at a

Figure 25.24 Keynote for iOS

client meeting. Keynote is a beautiful app on the iPad, and you can easily manipulate the slides and images.

If you have an iPhone, you might want to enable the **Keynote Remote** feature, which turns your phone into a remote for the iPad's Keynote app. You can control your slides from the phone or another iOS device and even view any notes you might have included as part of the presentation.

8. Scanning Apps
Scanner Pro ($2.99, <u>bit.ly/1q9B3fT</u>) and PDFPen Scan+ ($6.99, <u>bit.ly/1vJyBEN</u>)

Paul and Tom's Top Picks

We believe that lawyers should be trying to reduce the amount of paper they create and use in their practice. To that end, these scanning apps are great for scanning paper files you receive from a client, opposing counsel, or in discovery into the PDF format. We like Scanner Pro because it is so simple to use, and does a great job of capturing and saving paper scans as PDF files. Just take a picture of the document, adjust the image to your preference, and e-mail the document or save the PDF to your Dropbox, Google Drive, or Evernote account (see Figure 25.25).

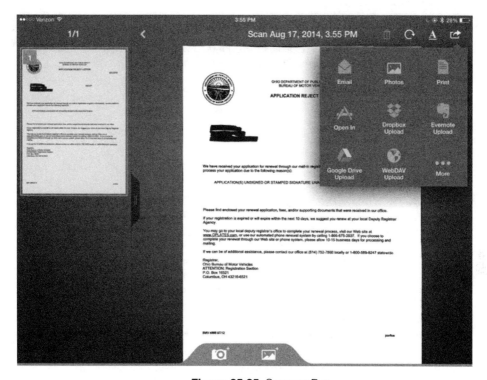

Figure 25.25 Scanner Pro

If you need to make your PDF files searchable, then you'll need an app that can perform Optical Character Recognition (OCR). That's where PDFPen Scan+ comes in handy. This app will scan your document and identify the text on a page—you can then save the file as a searchable PDF, or even copy the text from the PDF to paste it into an e-mail or another document.

9. PDF Expert
($9.99, http://bit.ly/1ra1wjz)

Paul and Tom's Top Pick

Many lawyers use PDF Expert because (1) clients can sign documents that can then be e-mailed back to the office and (2) form-fillable PDFs can now be "mobile" and filled out on the go (see Figure 25.26).

Similar to GoodReader, PDF Expert will let you read and annotate PDF files, and it has just the right amount of annotation tools a lawyer would need. But PDF Expert offers a few additional features that appeal to legal professionals and are hard to find in other apps.

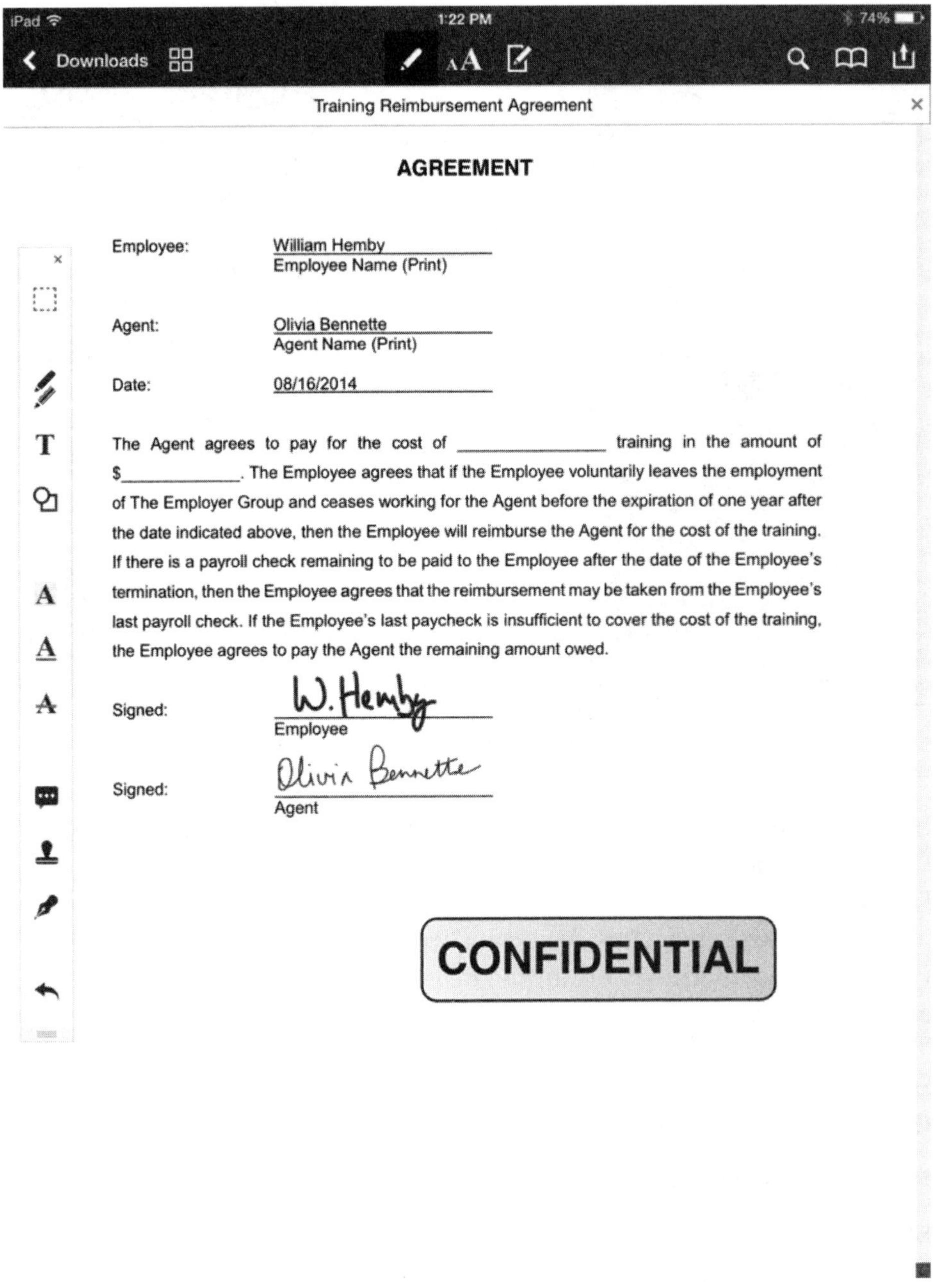

Figure 25.26 PDF Expert

PDF Expert supports PDF forms and allows you to fill them in using text fields, check boxes, radio buttons, and other form elements. You can create a PDF form on your computer and transfer it to your iPad when you need to complete the form away from the office.

10. LogMeIn/LogMeIn
(Free, bit.ly/ws9m3y)

Paul's Top Pick

As much as the iPad can do, a time will inevitably come when you need to work on your office computer or need to access a file that is only located on your home computer.

To access a computer from your iPad, you'll need to install the LogMeIn software client on the computer you want to access, and that computer will need to be running. When you need to access the computer from the iPad, you'll simply launch the LogMeIn app and put in your credentials (see Figure 25.27). Controlling and manipulating your computer from the iPad can be a little tricky due to the small(er) size of the iPad's screen. But when you need access to your office computer from the road, the LogMeIn app can be your saving grace.

To use LogMeIn on your computer, you'll need to purchase a subscription, which currently starts at $99 per year for two computers.

Figure 25.27 LogMeIn Ignition

11. Find My iPhone (for the iPad)
(Free, bit.ly/xbwDkm)

Paul and Tom's Top Pick

The Find My iPhone/Find My iPad service is part of the free iCloud service. Because so much personal information and confidential client data is stored on iOS devices today, we urge every legal professional with an iPad to sign up for a free iCloud account and enable the Find My iPad service. When you misplace or lose your iPad, you are able either to use the Find My iPhone app installed on another iPhone or iPad or to log on to any computer at **icloud.com/find** to geographically locate the iPad (see Figure 25.28). From there, you can lock your iPad, send a message to the person who might have it, or erase the data that's on it.

Since this service is free and the risk of losing so much information on an iPad is so high, many leading experts, like Brett Burney, argue that setting it up should be mandatory for any legal professional. See "Free Security for Your iPhone & iPad That Should Be Mandatory" at **www.macsinlaw.com/find-my-iphone-free-security/**.

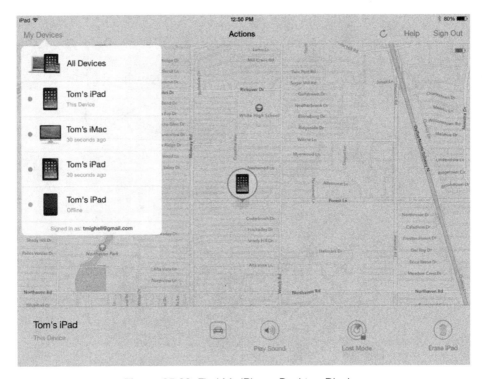

Figure 25.28 Find My iPhone Desktop Display

Library of Other Favorite Apps

We couldn't mention all of the apps we like in detail here, so we've listed the names of some of our favorite apps in several categories. To find out more about them, go to the App Store in iTunes or on your iPad or simply type "[app name] iPad app" into your favorite search engine.

Browsers—Alternatives to the iPad's Safari Browser
- Atomic Web
- Google Chrome
- Skyfire—allows you to view Flash-based content

Entertainment
- Fandango—great app for buying movie tickets
- HBO Go—subscribers can watch all HBO content for free
- Hulu+—for watching television shows
- IMDb
- Netflix
- YouTube

File Management
- Box.com
- Dropbox—probably the best-known cloud-based file management tool
- GoodReader
- Google Drive
- OneDrive
- SpiderOak
- SugarSync
- Transporter

Finance
- Bank of America
- Chase Mobile

Food
- Food Truck Fiesta
- OpenTable—make reservations online
- Yelp

Games

- Angry Birds
- Crosswords
- Plants vs. Zombies (1 and 2)
- QuizUp!
- Scrabble
- Words with Friends

Legal-Specific

- All Law
- Black's Law Dictionary
- CFR Live Lite—access to all CFR regulations
- Court Days Pro—deadline calculator
- Deponent—conduct an entire deposition from your iPad
- Fastcase
- FedCtRecords—Access your PACER account on your iPad
- iJuror
- iTimekeep—timekeeping app that works with most major time and billing software products
- JuryPad
- Jury Tracker
- LawBox
- TranscriptPad
- TrialPad

Meetings and Calendars

- Calvetica Calendar
- Fantastical
- Fuze Meeting
- GoToMeeting
- Join.me—easy-to-use screen-sharing app
- WebEx
- Zoom Group Messaging and Mobile Meetings

News

- AP News
- CNN

- LinkedIn Pulse
- News 360
- NPR
- USA Today

Photos

- Photogene—photo editor
- PhotoSync—transfer photos from iPhone to iPad
- Pro HDR—improved HDR photography

Productivity

- Documents To Go—document creation and editing
- DocuSign—sign documents on the iPad
- Dragon Dictation—fantastic voice recognition and transcription tool
- Elements—note-taking
- Evernote—a fantastic repository for notes
- iThoughts HD—mind-mapping app
- iType2Go Pro—text editor and camera viewer
- JotNot Scanner Pro—document scanner
- Keynote
- Microsoft Excel for iPad
- Microsoft PowerPoint for iPad
- Microsoft Word for iPad
- MindMeister—mind mapping
- Note Taker HD—note-taking
- Noted—note-taking
- Notes Plus—note-taking
- Office2 HD—document creation and editing
- Outliner—organize your thoughts
- Pages—document creation and editing
- PDF Expert—document editor
- Penultimate—note-taking
- PlainText—text editor
- Prezi—great alternative app for conducting presentations
- Prizmo—scanning and OCR

- SignMyPad—have clients sign documents on your iPad
- SmartNote—note-taking
- UPAD—note-taking
- WritePad—note-taking

Reading

- Feedly—probably the best news reader/RSS feed reader currently available
- Flipboard—creates magazine-style layout of Facebook/Twitter feeds
- GoodReader—best file reader, period
- iAnnotate PDF
- Instapaper—save articles to read later
- Kindle for iPad
- Mr. Reader—imports RSS feeds from just about anywhere
- NextIssue—"Netflix for Magazines"—for a low monthly price, subscribe to over 100 magazines
- Pocket—save articles to read later
- Reeder—another great choice for reading newsfeeds and RSS feeds
- Text'n Drive Pro—read text messages and e-mails
- Zinio—read magazines on your iPad
- Zite—creates magazine-style layout of latest news on many topics

Social Networking and Communications

- Facebook
- HootSuite—social media aggregator
- IM+—multi-platform instant messaging client—Skype, Google Talk, and so on
- Imo.im—another good multi-platform instant messaging client
- Skype—VoIP calls and video
- TextNow—send texts for free from your iPad
- Tweetbot—the best Twitter client for iOS
- TweetDeck—a Twitter client
- Twitter

Travel

+ FlightBoard
+ FlightTrack
+ GateGuru—airport information
+ Google Maps
+ Google Translate
+ Kayak—fantastic travel search engine
+ Orbitz
+ Taxi Magic
+ TripAdvisor
+ TripIt
+ xe Currency

Utilities

+ Air Display—create a second monitor with your iPad
+ Appzilla—over 100 utility-type apps
+ Citrix Receiver—remote access
+ Digits Calculator
+ Eye Glass—magnifying glass
+ Google Voice—phone service
+ GoToMyPC—remote access
+ IFTTT—Create "recipes" to make the services you use work better with each other
+ Jibbigo—voice translation
+ Text Expander—macro utility
+ Word Lens—translation

Navigation Tips & Settings

Add apps and folders to the iPad's dock. Out of the box, the iPad features four apps on the Dock, which is the always-visible bar at the bottom of the screen (see Figure 25.29). You can add up to six apps in the Dock, and you can also add folders containing multiple apps in the Dock.

Figure 25.29 iPad Dock

Launch apps from the Spotlight Search screen. While the Spotlight Search bar (accessed by swiping downwards on any screen) can be used to search Notes, E-mail, Calendar Appointments, and more, you can also search for an app and tap to launch it (see Figure 25.30).

Figure 25.30 Spotlight Search Screen

Double-tap space bar to add a period and a space. You can quickly add a period and a space to the end of a sentence by double-tapping the spacebar. You can turn this option off in the Settings menu if you prefer.

Use the side switch to lock rotation. The Side Switch on the right side of the iPad (above the volume rocker) can be used to either mute the sound on the iPad, or to lock the rotation of the screen. You can change this setting in the Settings menu of the iPad.

Turn on battery percentage indicator. While the iPad by default shows you a graphical representation of the battery level, you can also turn on the percentage indicator under **Settings** > **General** > **Usage** > **Battery Usage** (see Figure 25.31).

Undo typing. Many people aren't aware that there is an Undo option for the iPad. When you want to undo your most recent typing, you simply (and carefully!!) shake the iPad back and forth. A small window will appear, allowing you to undo your most recent typing.

Disable the clicking sound for typing and other sounds. You can turn off the clicking sound for typing by going to **Settings** > **Sounds**.

Take a screenshot. You can take a screenshot from your iPad by simply holding down the **Home** button (front-center of device) and **Wake/ Sleep** button (top of the device) at the same time. You'll see the screen flash once and the image will be saved in your iPad's Photos app.

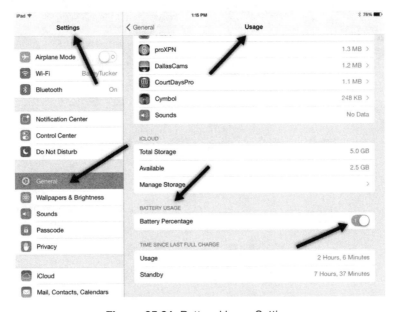

Figure 25.31 Battery Usage Settings

Use your iPad as a second monitor. You can use apps such as Air Display (Mac) and MaxiVista (Windows) to turn your iPad into a second monitor. This probably won't be your standard setup, but it can be helpful when you're traveling and need the convenience of a second monitor (see Figure 25.32).

Figure 25.32 iPad as Second Monitor

Save an image while browsing the Web. If you see a picture you want to save while browsing the Web on your iPad, simply tap and hold your finger on the image, and you'll be prompted to save the image into your iPad's Photo app (see Figure 25.33).

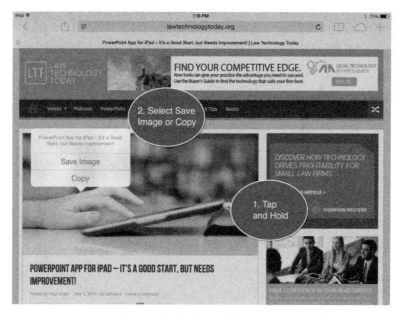

Figure 25.33 Save Web Image

Passcode Lock

It is very important to become familiar with the security settings of the iPad so that you can keep information stored on your tablet safe. You can access the security settings through **Settings** > **Passcode**.

At a minimum, lawyers and their agents should assign a passcode lock in conjunction with the auto-lock function. This will auto-lock your iPad after a set number of minutes and require a passcode to regain access to the iPad (see Figure 25.35).

The iPad defaults to a Simple Passcode, which is a four-digit number similar to your ATM PIN. We recommend that you turn Simple Passcode off and set a longer passcode—at least ten to twelve numbers, letters, and characters. You should also set a time for the iPad to be idle after which the iPad will then require the passcode. Lastly, you should enable the option that erases data after ten failed passcode attempts.

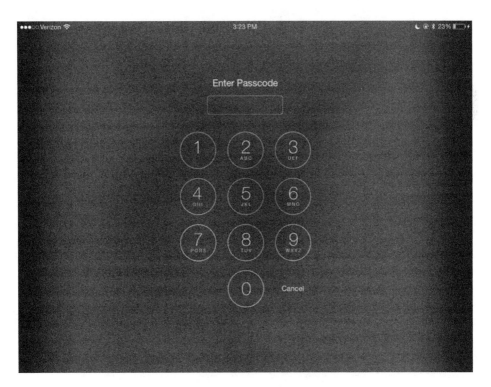

Figure 25.34 Passcode Lock

Resources

There are a number of good resources for lawyers using an iPad.

- *iPad 4 Lawyers* by Tom Mighell (**ipad4lawyers.squarespace.com**)
- *iPhone J.D.* by Jeff Richardson (**www.iphonejd.com**)
- *TabletLegal* by Josh Barrett (**tabletlegal.com**)
- *iPad Notebook* by Justin Kahn (**ipadnotebook.wordpress.com**)
- *Legal iPad* by Niki Black (**legal-ipad.tumblr.com**)
- *Walking Office* by Rob Dean (**www.walkingoffice.com**)
- *Macs in Law* by Brett Burney (**www.macsinlaw.com**)
- *The Mac Lawyer* by Ben Stevens (**www.themaclawyer.com**)

Another fantastic website to use for app recommendations and information is App Advice. It provides access to hundreds of articles and reviews of new iPad apps.

About the Authors

Tom Mighell, Esq.
Contoural, Inc.
tmighell@gmail.com

Tom Mighell is a Senior Consultant with Contoural, Inc., where he helps companies deal with their information governance, privacy, and litigation readiness issues. Before becoming a consultant, Tom was a litigator for eighteen years in Dallas, Texas. He is a frequent speaker and writer on the Internet and legal technology and is the author of several books: *iPad in One Hour for Lawyers* (third edition), *iPad Apps in One Hour forLawyers, iPad in One Hour for Litigators,* and *The Lawyers' Guide to Collaboration Tools and Technologies: Smart Ways to Work Together* (with Dennis Kennedy). He has published *Inter Alia* (**www.inter-alia.net**), a legal technology blog, since 2002. He and Dennis Kennedy are the co-hosts of *The Kennedy-Mighell Report*, a legal technology podcast. Tom is past chair of ABA TECHSHOW 2008, past chair of the ABA Law Practice Division and current chair of the Law Practice Division Publications Board.

Paul J. Unger, Esq.
Affinity Consulting Group
punger@affinityconsulting.com

Paul J. Unger is a national speaker, writer, and thought-leader in the legal technology industry. He is an attorney and founding principal of Affinity Consulting Group, a nationwide consulting company providing legal technology consulting, continuing legal education, and training.

He is the chair of the ABA Legal Technology Resource Center (2013–2014, 2014–2015) (**www.lawtechnology.org/**), former chair of ABA TECHSHOW (2011) (**www.techshow.com**), a member of the American Bar Association, Columbus Bar Association, Ohio State Bar Association, Ohio Association for Justice, and Central Ohio Association for Justice. He is also the author of *PowerPoint in One Hour for Lawyers*. He specializes in trial presentation and litigation technology, document and case management, paperless office strategies, and legal-specific software training for law firms and legal departments throughout the Midwest. Mr. Unger has provided trial presentation consultation for over four hundred cases. He is an Adjunct Professor for Capital University Law School's Paralegal Program. In his spare time, he likes to run and restore historic homes.

CHAPTER TWENTY-FIVE

Unified
Messaging and
Telecommunications

THE ABILITY TO MAKE and receive phone calls is an absolute necessity for a law firm. In addition, some sort of data access is critical to the success of a firm these days. We are a very connected society, and any potential client expects to be able to contact you with relative ease, whether via voice or data transmission such as e-mail. We'll cover some of your technology options for voice and data communications.

Unified Messaging

Unified messaging is the delivery of traditional voice communications into your e-mail box, including the delivery of facsimile transmissions. Unified messaging systems began to appear around 2001 and were fairly unsuccessful for the first couple of years, but now they are stable. As a result, you can now monitor your communications constantly from (potentially) one location—a blessing and a curse, but it is becoming a service that many clients expect you to have.

The simplest way to implement unified messaging is to have it integrated with your phone system. Some small firms may not even have a phone system, and we'll address that issue in a moment. Many of the newer PBX (private branch exchange) systems are incorporating a voicemail card directly into the telephone system chassis. Stand-alone voicemail systems are also an alternative for larger office environments.

You can even integrate unified messaging with your Exchange server or your VoIP implementation. The latest versions of Exchange Server (2007, 2010, and 2013) include unified messaging capability at no additional charge. Some outsourced providers of VoIP solutions will provide unified messaging capabilities too, which means you don't have to have any physical equipment to gain the benefits of integrating all your communication streams.

For budget purposes, plan on spending around $3,000 for a voicemail system with unified messaging. As is true for most technology solutions, your mileage may vary. Vendors implement unified messaging in many different ways. Some are better than others, and, frankly, some are nothing more than kludge workarounds to make their systems sound more robust than they really are. Our recommendation is to stick with well-known vendors of communication equipment. You really can't go wrong with suppliers such as Avaya, Cisco, NEC, Toshiba, and so on.

Some companies resell complete unified messaging solutions, thereby saving you the investment in hardware and software. These solutions are typically available for a monthly fee, and you may have to commit to a multi-year contract to obtain the service. Also, you are stuck with what-ever features and methods the vendor provides. As an example, you may not like the file format for a fax delivery into your inbox, but you'll have no choice but to accept what the vendor gives you. Another concern is that all of your communications may be going through a third party if it is not an on-premise solution. This means your phone calls actually route through the vendor's system before being delivered to your location. In that way, they can capture a voicemail message or fax and repackage it for delivery to your e-mail address. We are generally not fans of having client data move through third-party providers and would recommend that you first investigate systems you own and can control. While a price tag of $3,000 isn't cheap, the value is so great that a good number of solos and small firms have made the leap, and the numbers grow monthly. We are beginning to see on-premise solutions for the SMB market, which may reduce your cost and provide a more stable environment versus hosted solutions.

We'll attempt to cover some of the concerns and questions you should have when considering whether to implement a unified messaging solu-tion. These issues are related to equipment that is provided as part of your telephone communication system. The first issue is what communica-tions the system handles. Can it manage both voice messages and fax transmissions, or just one? Even though most systems will handle both voicemail and fax, generally firms use only the voice capability and route the faxes to a dedicated fax machine or printer rather than to a specific person's inbox.

How do you want the voice messages delivered? Most firms will elect to send only an e-mail notification that a voicemail message has been received. This configuration saves bandwidth because the message itself is not transmitted to the e-mail client. It stays on the voicemail server until you retrieve it—hardly convenient if you are traveling. In fact, as a security measure, some telephone systems are configured not to allow remote connections, even for voicemail retrieval. A lot of lawyers use some type of smartphone, and sending a notification-only message saves on their data usage, but what hoops do they have to jump through to actually listen to the message? The other alternative is to deliver the actual message to your inbox. Obviously, this method uses much more bandwidth, especially if you are delivering it to a cell phone that also receives your e-mail. If you elect this configuration you'd better have an unlimited data plan for your cell phone or a data plan that can cover your traffic load. Make sure your portable device can play back the file format for your voicemail if you elect to deliver the message to your inbox. As an example, the iPad doesn't natively play back WAV files, which is the format of our unified message system. This means you'll have to purchase an app just to play attached voicemail files.

Another question for your PBX provider is how it handles the message delivery itself. Is the message forwarded to your inbox and then deleted from the voicemail system? If so, there is only one copy of it and you'll never know you received a message if it gets trapped or trashed by your spam filter. If the original stays on the voicemail system and a copy gets delivered to your inbox, does the message light stay lit on your phone? You may not want this, but then again you may want a visual indication that a voice message was delivered.

How does the vendor identify the voice message in your inbox? Is the "From: address" something that is easily recognizable as the phone system, or does it come from you? What does the subject line contain? Showing the caller ID in the subject line is particularly helpful, but not all vendors package messages that way. How is the voice message delivered to your e-mail system? Do you have to have a user ID and password configured on your voicemail box that is consistent with your network credentials? If so, you have the issue of constantly synchronizing your logon credentials with the telephone system, assuming that your network passwords must be changed after a set number of days (shame on you if your password never expires). Many phone systems only accept numbers as a password, so you can't even use letters (forget capitals). This restriction may render your integration unacceptable.

Finally, how do you retrieve your messages? Are they delivered as standard audio attachments to an e-mail message? This is certainly preferred, since you don't need any special software to listen to the messages. Some of the lower cost (and kludge) solutions require that you install a software add-on to your e-mail client to listen to the voice message. This solution won't work if you are trying to deliver the voicemail to your cell phone. Another problem deals with specific software versions. You must make sure that any potential voicemail system is compatible with your firm's e-mail solution. If you have questions regarding what versions of Microsoft Exchange and Outlook the voicemail system is compatible with, make sure you ask your vendor before you make the investment. As you can see, having specialized software is not a recommended solution. Better to have the voice message packaged as a standard (not proprietary) audio file attachment. That way you can even retrieve your voicemail using a web browser from an Internet café while on vacation in Rio.

If all of this has given you a headache, don't worry. Make sure your IT consultant reads this chapter—he or she can answer all the questions for you. But make no mistake about it: No one who has successfully implemented unified messaging has ever discarded it. The value of unified messaging is phenomenal—being able to access your voicemail on your cell phone is a remarkable enhancement. You need never worry again about being out of touch. If you prefer not to give clients your home or cell phone number, you'll still get their messages. We cannot count the number of times that having voicemail sent to our cell phones has been worth its weight in diamonds.

Google Voice

For those lawyers constantly on the road, a free service you might find useful is Google Voice. If you'd rather not give your personal cell phone number to your pesky clients, who always have emergencies regardless of the time, then this service might be for you. Google Voice allows you to select a phone number local to your area that forwards inbound phone calls to your other personal phone numbers. This service allows you to provide your clients with a phone number (not your personal number), screen incoming phone calls, and receive voicemails left on the Google Voice phone number in your e-mail inbox. You can specify which e-mail address you would like the voicemails forwarded to. By default, the notification is sent to the address linked to your Google account, but you can add additional e-mail addresses. Google Voice will even transcribe your voicemails to text and provide them in the body of the e-mail, allowing users to read the content before they choose to listen to the messages. The voicemail itself can be downloaded and is delivered as an MP3 file, not a WAV file as most other voicemail systems. Google Voice also allows users to receive and record phone conversations (be mindful of the laws in your state if you do this), index and search voicemails, and set up conference calls.

If you are currently a Sprint customer, you can take advantage of the Google Voice features without changing your phone number. Be sure to review the Google Voice help section (**support.google.com/voice/**) to see exactly what features you get by integrating your Sprint account with Google Voice.

Voice over Internet Protocol (VoIP)

In its most basic definition, VoIP is a family of technologies for delivery of voice communications over Internet protocol networks, such as the Internet. VoIP systems are digital and can run voice and data systems over the same network, reducing investment in infrastructure. Corporate usage of VoIP phone systems has increased dramatically over the past decade, replacing the traditional copper-wire telephone systems that we all used in the past.

VoIP systems are primarily aimed at providing users with unified communications, delivering all services (voice, fax, voicemails, and e-mail) to a single location. VoIP systems are generally more flexible and less costly to implement than your standard copper-wire systems, and they can integrate easily with most existing data network infrastructures.

Security used to be a major concern for VoIP systems. That concern has been greatly reduced. It appears that vendors have finally overcome the performance hit associated with encrypting the voice traffic. You would be hard pressed to find a current vendor that sends voice traffic in an unencrypted stream. This means you'll sleep a little better knowing that your voice traffic travels in secure encrypted channels. That doesn't mean your VoIP traffic isn't subject to hacking. In fact, security guru Bruce Schneier has published several blog posts describing how to hack a VoIP data stream. His past post discusses how it is possible to even ". . . identify the phrases spoken within encrypted VoIP calls when the audio is encoded using variable bit rate codecs." Sound scary? Given the recent news of the capabilities and actions of the National Security Agency, VoIP systems carry just as much risk of interception as traditional phone networks.

Because the underlying IP network that a VoIP system uses is unreliable, it's not uncommon to experience latency or jitteriness when making a call using a VoIP phone system, especially to off-site destinations. Once your voice packet hits the already congested Internet, you are no longer in control of how fast your data gets to where it's going, and that's what causes the delays. Using a VoIP system on the same data network as your computer system might tremendously slow down how fast you can access your server and case management applications because of all the data traffic on your local network. Be sure your existing data network and Internet connection are capable of handling the increase in load before implementing a VoIP system. If you have to upgrade existing hardware or the speed of your Internet connection, those are hidden costs that you might not be aware of and that you will have to plan for.

Implementing an MPLS (Multiprotocol Label Switching) network gives you the option of configuring QoS (Quality of Service), where you can give the voice traffic a higher priority. MPLS networks are not cheap and tend to be used in larger firms with multiple office locations. Frankly, we think MPLS is overkill and too expensive for a solo or small firm considering VoIP. As an alternative, a large number of VoIP installations use the IP network on the local premises. They then route the external calls to the Internet and may even have some traditional phone circuits connected too. The reality is that the telephone carriers themselves are using VoIP between two IP gateways in order to reduce the long haul bandwidth.

Lastly, VoIP systems are susceptible to power failures and outages. Unlike analog phones that get their power directly from the copper phone lines, VoIP systems need electricity to operate, just like your computer system. You better have an analog phone line as a backup, or at least a cell phone. We're still hanging on to our traditional copper wire analog lines, despite the telcos trying to force fiber and VoIP down our throats.

VoIP phone systems have their pros and cons when compared to other digital phone systems. Be sure to ask your vendor the right questions to determine which type of system is right for you. And be wary of those vendors and definitely check their references. We have seen a lot of VoIP installations that caused major-league heartburn for the law firms that undertook them.

Not only have hidden costs pushed their budgets far beyond the original numbers, but vendors tend not to plan for redundancy or to warn of the potential downsides of VoIP. We have had both happy and unhappy VoIP clients, so we're not saying, "Don't do it," but be aware that VoIP may not be the right choice for everyone. As a side note, we have yet to hear of a client that wasn't happy with their Cisco VoIP installation. That has to tell you something about the quality and stability of Cisco products.

High-Speed Internet

None of our lawyers or other clients ever complain that their Internet connection is too fast. We have collectively almost forgotten how slow the Internet used to be and how patiently we had to wait for our screens to load. High-speed Internet is now a requirement for solos and small law firms. High-speed Internet has all but replaced dial-up Internet connections because of the low cost and fast connection speeds, although there are still some parts of the country where dial-up is the only option. Why continue to wait for web pages to load and attachments to open if you don't have to? Few creatures are more impatient than lawyers, so virtually all of them have jumped to high-speed Internet installations.

High-speed Internet connections are available from your local Internet service provider (ISP) and usually are provided over a cable, DSL, or fiber optic connection. These high-speed connections offer download speeds in excess of 25 Mbps (some can reach 75 Mbps) and varying upload speeds, depending on the provider and the service tier to which you've subscribed. If your firm hosts its own services, such as e-mail or a website, you can obtain static IP addresses from your local provider for these types of connections. The ISP may charge more to issue your business a static IP address than if you just require a dynamically leased IP address. High-speed Internet access connectivity generally will cost $75 to $200 per month.

If your firm requires a larger amount of bandwidth due to the number of users sharing the Internet connection or to run web-based applications, your local ISP may be able to provide a connection type that meets your requirements. Historically, the ISPs and telco providers classified upgraded service connections as T1 or fractional T1 connections. While they may call them upgrades, they are much slower than alternate technologies and will cost hundreds of dollars more per month. These types of connections also require longer service agreements and usually include a large setup cost. They do have the advantage of a service level agreement (SLA), which means the connection must be repaired within a particular time and must be available a high percentage of the time. DSL or cable modem connections do not carry an SLA, so repair times could be several days during an outage. T1 circuits are becoming less and less popular, even though they are very reliable and guarantee bandwidth. A full T1 provides only 1.544 Mbps up and down and typically will cost $300–$500 per month. Compare this to other broadband services (cable or DSL), where you can get 30 Mbps download and 5 Mbps upload for less than $200 a month. Do the math: 30 is a MUCH bigger number than 1.544.

If available in your area, a speedy alternative to a T1 is fiber optics. Fiber to the curb, such as Verizon FiOS, can offer business subscribers increasingly faster Internet connections at a much lower cost. Check with your local service providers to see if such a connection is currently available. In general, solos and small firms are well served by cable and DSL to meet their Internet connection needs.

Another option for Internet access is from your cellular provider. Mobile broadband Internet access has gained steam lately and is becoming a growing trend with mobile lawyers. Plus, it's a good way to avoid having to pay those outrageous prices for Internet access that hotels charge nowadays. You may have heard the terms 3G, 4G, and so on, used to identify mobile broadband. For about $60 per month, your cellular provider can provide you with Internet access when on the road. If you've purchased a laptop recently, you might already have a broadband card installed. For everyone else, most providers will throw in the broadband card for no cost when you sign up for their service. We have found that it is cheaper to activate the mobile hotspot feature on our smartphones instead of acquiring a separate mobile data plan. That way you use the data plan from your phone to create the WiFi "cloud" for other devices to share. You can then use the WiFi-only iPad (a lot cheaper) instead of one with the built-in 3G/4G capability.

CHAPTER TWENTY-SIX

Utilities

WHAT WE ALL NEED is Batman's belt, with a full repository of tricks that we can draw upon at any moment to perform the myriad tasks associated with the practice of law. Failing that, we must acknowledge that it is impossible to list all of the utilities that a solo or small firm might find useful. There are many great selections and just as many opinions as to what makes one utility more valuable than another.

The threshold question is, what constitutes a utility? For our purposes, we will consider a utility to be some software application that takes data and manipulates it for a specific purpose. That definition allows us a lot of latitude.

The challenge is to list utilities that offer a unique purpose for the solo and small firm lawyer. We have used many of these utilities ourselves and have had some great suggestions from our friends and colleagues. If you don't see your favorite utility here, just drop us a line and perhaps it will be listed in the next edition of the book.

X1

How often do you find yourself frantically searching your computer for a file only to discover that you have no clue where you saved it? It's happened to all of us, and the problem is compounded when you have copies of the same file saved in multiple locations. Which file is the right one? What a headache!

To relieve some of the stress, we recommend that lawyers use a X1 Search 8, which is a piece of software that enables users to search for and instantly find information, while keeping the resulting file in its native format. The product is marketed as a premium alternative to Windows Desktop and Outlook Search. No more messy conversions. X1 allows users to search for any file, whether located within their e-mail on the local computer, a network share, removable storage drive, or even within virtual desktops. This software currently supports more than 500 file types in their native format and layout, and it can even search for data within multiple Microsoft Outlook PST files and Lotus Notes without having to mount the files.

The X1 program displays the search results as you type, similar to the Google Instant Search, which allows users to modify their search query in real time. The advanced searching options allow users to search multiple e-mail metadata fields, such as From, To, and Subject,and then sort the resulting files by any of the file properties.

The X1 program is a powerful search tool that includes a number of advanced features, such as support for searching inside compressed ZIP files and RSS feeds, as well as a number of export options, such as exporting the search results to a folder or Microsoft Outlook PST file. The product is even administrator friendly, supporting integration with Active Directory and Group Policy, for ease of deployment and flexibility in its configuration.

Before installing, you will need to make sure that you have enough storage space for the search index this program will create, which is roughly 20 percent of the total volume of files indexed. X1 supports Microsoft Windows (32- or 64-bit) operating systems; Microsoft Outlook XP/2003/2007/2010 (32- or 64-bit); SharePoint 2007/2010/2013 and 365, as well as al IMAP-based e-mail accounts. Support for Lotus Notes, Eudora, and Thunderbird e-mail clients has been dropped in the latest version of X1 Search 8, and can only be found in prior versions of the X1 Search Professional Client.

The X1 Search 8 software costs $49.95 per license and can be purchased with varying levels of support. If you want to try before you buy, a fourteen-day trial is available as well. To view or purchase this product, visit **www.x1.com**.

dtSearch

dtSearch is another powerful search tool that has been used by lawyers for many years, dating back to the early MS-DOS days. This product has come a long way and remains one of our favorite and most popular searching tools—and honestly, it doesn't change much from year to year. That's how solid this product is. The dtSearch program is offered in a number of different versions, but solo and small firms should consider only the following versions:

+ Desktop with Spider
+ Network with Spider

The Desktop with Spider version is perfect for solo lawyers who need to be able to instantly search their client files on a single computer, although this version can also be configured to index network drives. The Network with Spider version allows multiple users to search the same search index, which is a must when working in a multiuser networking environment.

The dtSearch products include Unicode support, support for full-text searching, the ability to search a number of common metadata fields, and even the ability to search within nested ZIP files. The product highlights search hits in most web-based file formats, such as XML and HTML, while maintaining the format and layout of the page, including graphics and embedded hyperlinks. dtSearch also displays search hits in other popular file types, such as documents, spreadsheets, database files, and e-mails. The built-in spider can add website content to the searchable database, including secure password-protected websites. The ability to index and search website content is a great feature for those lawyers involved in cases or matters involving e-discovery.

Like other full-text search applications, dtSearch uses a large volume of disk space to store its search index, requiring approximately one-third of the total volume of files indexed. The software states that a single index file can handle more than a terabyte of indexed text, which is a lot of files. When creating the index, the default operation is to ignore "noise" words (e.g., *the, a, and,* etc.). If you need to search phrases that include those words, make sure you override the defaults and index the "noise" words too.

dtSearch supports Windows 8 operating systems (both 32- and 64-bit versions) and even has a version for Linux. dtSearch also supports the latest Microsoft Outlook/Exchange and Thunderbird formats. Also new in the latest version is the ability to highlight search hits within PDF files retrieved after a search using Adobe Reader X or XI. dtSearch Desktop with Spider can be purchased on dtSearch's website (**www.dtsearch.com**) for $199 per license. dtSearch Network with Spider can also be purchased at a cost of $160 per license for five to twenty-four users or $140 per license for twenty-five to ninety-nine users. Further discounts are offered for purchases of more than one hundred licenses.

Credenza

Are you looking for a way to enhance your ability to run and manage your law firm using just a single piece of software? It can be done, believe it or not, with Microsoft Outlook and a small add-in named Credenza. Surprisingly, many lawyers use Microsoft Outlook for their case management solution rather than purchasing a separate application for the job. While we don't recommend this, we have to bow to the inevitable and help those who choose to do this, even though Outlook is not a case management product. If you are one of those lawyers who uses Outlook for case management, you should consider Credenza.

Credenza is a legal-practice management tool that integrates with Microsoft Outlook and allows legal professionals to manage their firms more effectively. Credenza allows you to:

- Create and open a file for each client matter or case.
- Track time spent on individual e-mails (it even flags messages that may have been missed or forgotten).
- Keep and make notes regarding phone calls, voicemails, and other messages.
- View a complete chronology of a file.
- Check for conflicts, automate inbox controls, and share information with other users.

Previously, Credenza offered only a free trial version to its potential users. Now, it offers a Basic version of the program that is free to download and use. The Pro version can be purchased and downloaded from the Credenza Software website at **www.credenzasoft.com**. It costs $24.95 per user per month.

The Basic version includes all of the basic practice management features, while the Pro version is multiuser and includes collaboration tools, cloud integration, incorporated billing, and full text searching, along with many other more powerful features.

To determine which version of the software is right for you, you can view a comparison chart of the Basic and Pro version features at **http://www.credenzasoft.com/comparison.html**.

Outlook Send Assistant

Concerned about inadvertently sending an e-mail message to an unintended recipient? If so, we have the tool for you. This add-in warns or prevents accidental disclosure and sending of e-mails to unintended recipients. It is a must-have utility for every Microsoft Outlook user. Outlook Send Assistant (**http://www.thepaynegroup.com/products/outlooksend/**) is a small tool that packs a big punch.

Here are some of the features of this simple and elegant tool:

—Integrates with Microsoft Outlook 2013, 2010, and 2007

—Available in both 32- and 64-bit versions

—Supports HTML and Plain Text formats

—Alerts users when the Reply All button is selected

—Warns users that the message has a blank Subject line

—Prompts the user when external recipients are detected

—Confirms with e-mail senders if they'd like to continue sending the message

—Prompts when the e-mail is addressed to a Distribution List

—Alerts users when recipient(s) are detected in the BCC field

—Inserts BCC disclosure text into the recipients' message, thus notifying them of the BCC status

—Customizes warnings when specific recipient addresses are detected

—Automatically adds Marketing, Circular 230 Disclosure, SEC, SPAM warnings, and security disclaimers to e-mail messages

Outlook Send Assistant v3 can be purchased from Payne Consulting's website (**www.thepaynegroup.com**) at a cost of $45 per license.

GreenPrint

GreenPrint Technologies (**www.printgreener.com**) has a software product, GreenPrint, that eliminates unwanted pages from your printing jobs, saving you ink, toner, paper, money, and trees. The software intercepts your print jobs and highlights unnecessary pages, such as blanks, that can be removed. How many times have you printed a web page that prints on two pages of paper, with only a single line of text on the second page? Usually the second page contains only a URL, logo, or banner ad. No longer will these wasted pages need to be printed. The Enterprise Edition includes such additional features as the GreenPrint Advisor, a tool to help your firm select low-cost printers; GreenPrint Analytics, a powerful reporting tool documenting your firm's true savings; and GreenPrint preview+, an interactive preview of your print job that helps to eliminate print waste and reduce volume. If you don't already have Adobe Acrobat or another third-party PDF printer, you can also get a PDF printer from GreenPrint.

GreenPrint makes recommendations about pages that should be removed from the print job and prompts the user for approval before the job is sent to the printer. There is an edition for small business and home users and an Enterprise Edition for businesses. The Home Premium edition costs $19 per computer. A thirty-day free trial of the Home Premium software is available.

If you're firm is interested in the Enterprise Version, you have to contact the vendor at **sales@printgreener.com** to get pricing. The product works with Windows XP/Vista/7. Support for Windows 8 isn't currently listed on the website at the time of writing.

Winscribe for the Legal Profession

Winscribe, a leading developer of dictation software, has made a product specifically for the legal profession that allows dictations to be automatically transcribed, converting recorded words to text. Automating the process saves both time and money, increasing the efficiency of your employees. It marks the end of the "listen . . . type" era. Now your employees can spend their time doing something more productive and billable. Winscribe can even integrate with existing applications, such as your document management system, streamlining your workflow process. As the creator of the dictations, you can manage and monitor the status of your work, as well as retrieve jobs for review and editing.

Another innovative feature of this software is that it supports a wide range of input from recordings made on telephones, PCs and laptops, digital handheld devices, BlackBerrys, iPhones, and Androids. With the Winscribe Mobility Suite, the days of carrying around a digital recorder may be over. Now you can install mobile software on your smartphone to record dictations and transfer the files wirelessly to your firm's network. As always, client confidentiality is an extremely important issue. Winscribe protects dictations through the encryption of the files and through the implementation of a secure file transfer process. Winscribe has been vetted by the experts and found worthy. This product is available on Winscribe's website at **www.winscribe.com** and can be purchased as an in-house package or an on-demand Software as a Service (SaaS) over the Web.

Eyejot

What a slogan: "Video mail in a blink." Is video the future of e-mail? If so, Eyejot has got it right. Eyejot is a comprehensive, client-free, online video-messaging platform ideal for both personal and business communications. Eyejot is currently supported on Apple's iOS platform, with Android support expected soon—but it's not yet here. The vendor has been promising an Android app now for the past few years, and still hasn't released one. Maybe this upcoming year?

Users can sign up for the service by creating a free account, which allows an unlimited number of five-minute video e-mail messages and provides support for both RSS feeds and iTunes. If you can send an e-mail, then you can send an Eyejot.

The Free account keeps your video messages for up to one month, allows you to send a video message to any e-mail address (not just an Eyejot account), and, if needed, provides code for you to embed the Eyejot widget on your website. However, the free account is ad supported.

To send a video message, once an account has been created, a user must log into his or her account, upload the video, and then click the Send button. That's it, plain and simple. The software requires no client installation and works with all major web browsers. For those users who require more, there is a Pro account for $29.95 per year that allows you to upload videos, provides an enhanced mobile inbox, and is advertising-free—plus your messages never expire.

There is also a Pro+ account subscription for $99.95 per year that is advertising-free and allows you to attach other documents to your video messages as well as customize your own message templates. Users can purchase and create an Eyejot account online at **www.eyejot.com**.

Hightail (formerly YouSendIt)

What a wonderful resource to transmit large file attachments without charge. There are several service packages, one of which is free. The free offering, called Lite, can transmit an attachment that is up to 250 MB in size. The Lite package also provides a user with 2 GB of online storage space, mobile access, data encryption and a Desktop Sync application. Since many ISPs limit the size of attachments, Hightail is a great alternative to "push" the occasional large attachment. The service works by creating an account at **hightail.com** and actually uploading the file to the Hightail service. You provide the e-mail addresses for the recipient(s), and an e-mail message is sent with a hyperlink that allows for downloading the file from the Hightail website.

If you regularly need to transmit very large attachments, especially those larger than 250 MB, or need more than 2 GB of storage space, Hightail provides several pay services to accomplish this. These services provide enhancements such as e-mail support, longer availability for file downloads, reports, advanced security options, custom branding, and more bandwidth for downloads. The Professional plan costs $15.99 per month or $159.99 per year, while the Teams and Enterprise plans cost much more. We have found this resource to be invaluable for sending conference attendees copies of our PowerPoint presentations, which tend to be quite large because of the graphics. Don't forget to encrypt your data before uploading it to Hightail's servers if it is confidential. This terrific utility may be found at **www.hightail.com**.

Copy2Contact

Copy2Contact, formerly Anagram, is a piece of software that allows you to "sweep" text from an e-mail message and create a record within Outlook. You can sweep contact information that the sender has added in his or her message footer and instantly create an Outlook contact. The software is not limited just to creating of contacts. You can "grab" text and create calendar entries, to-do items, and even tasks. The text can originate anywhere. Copy2Contact will create the contact, calendar entry, task, and so on, in your personal folder area, which is fine for most solos. If you have a Microsoft Exchange Server with Public Folders, you will have to move the data from your personal folder if the intended destination is a Public Folder. Copy2Contact is currently available for Google Apps, Salesforce.com, Microsoft Outlook, Netsuite, iPhone, and BlackBerry. Copy2Contact is compatible with all Windows-based systems, including Windows 8. The program also has a version available for BlackBerry and iPhone devices.

The base Copy2Contact for Outlook product costs $34.95 for a single user. The Pro version is $49.95 and includes features like smart capitalization, formatting, address book selection, and extended hotkeys. There is a four-teen-day trial version to make sure that Copy2Contact will work on your computer and perform according to your expectations. Make sure you download and try the trial before you spend the money; however, we're sure (especially you solo lawyers) that you'll be typing in your credit card number shortly after your first use of Copy2Contact. This product can be purchased and downloaded from its website at **www.copy2contact.com**.

TwInbox

Are you a Twitter junkie? We've found a program that integrates with Microsoft Outlook that allows you to update your Twitter status directly from Outlook. TwInbox (**www.techhit.com/TwInbox/twitter_plugin_outlook.html**), a free add-on for Microsoft Outlook, allows you to receive your follower updates and archive, manage, group, and search your tweets in the same way that you manage your e-mail. Some of the additional features of this tiny program include allowing users to search and track keywords, group tweets by sender or topic, and upload and post picture files and Outlook e-mail attachments. A newly added feature also allows users to manage multiple Twitter accounts directly from within Microsoft Outlook. This product is free—why not give it a try?

TweetDeck

If you're a Twitter user and prefer not to tweet from within Microsoft Outlook or from the Twitter website, then this program might be for you. TweetDeck, another free utility, helps you organize Twitter and those you are following. You can group people so that you can concentrate on "special" individuals whose tweets are more important to you. This helps you reduce the noise level of Twitter and focuses attention on specific tweets. It also includes a URL shortener. TweetDeck used to require the installation of Adobe Air, which needs full administrative access to your hard disk, but since it was purchased by Twitter, the service is now offered as a web app within your Internet browser or as a desktop application that no longer requires Adobe Air. This is a wonderful dashboard for managing Twitter—we know because we use it. You can sign in to TweetDeck or download the desktop application at **tweetdeck.com**.

TinyURL

Have you ever wanted to give somebody a reference link only to discover that it is about 400 characters long and contains all kinds of goofy characters and non-word representations? Probably the biggest problem is the breaking up of the URL link, especially when the e-mail is viewed as text formatted. The last thing you want to do is have the recipient cut and paste the various parts of the URL back together. TinyURL stores the complete URL on its servers and provides a very small URL instead. The user selects the smaller TinyURL, which translates and redirects to the much larger one. This is a free service to make the posting of long URLs easier—especially handy for Twitter! If you're a frequent user of TinyURL, there's even a toolbar for your browser that you can install to make the service more accessible. It is available at **tinyurl.com**.

Security issues arise when dealing with any shortened URL. The "bad guys" are sending malware links disguised as shortened URLs in phishing e-mails appearing to come from someone you know. As the recipient of the shortened URL, you have no idea where the URL will actually send you unless you decode it first. If you want to use any URL shortening service, make sure you trust the originator of the URL or use a service to decode it first before you click on the link.

IrfanView

Do you have some graphic files for a construction case that you can't seem to view? Or a video or sound file for a wrongful termination case and don't know how to play it? IrfanView (**www.irfanview.com**) is a wonderful software application that can view a very large number of different graphic file formats and can play several audio and video formats. IrfanView is compatible with all Windows-based systems but not Mac or Linux. IrfanView is free only for home use, so you can't legally use it for your law practice unless you pay money. You will have to send an e-mail to **irfanview@gmx.net** to get the cost and payment method if you need to use IrfanView in a commercial setting.

Some of the common file types and formats that IrfanView supports include:

—JPG

—TIFF

—GIF

—MPG

—MP3

—AVI

—WMA

You can view all of the file formats displayed by IrfanView by visiting **www.irfanview.com/main_formats.htm**.

DBAN

Darik's Boot and Nuke (DBAN) is a free program that can be used to securely wipe the contents of your hard drive. DBAN is an open-source project that can be downloaded from **www.dban.org**. DBAN will automatically and permanently delete the contents of any hard disk it can detect. DBAN also allows the wiping of multiple hard disks at the same time. We all love "free," and this program is the perfect complement to any lawyer's software tool chest. You use DBAN to wipe the data contents from your hard drives and USB flash drives so that your confidential client information cannot be recovered. We have all read stories of customer data being found on hard drives purchased on eBay. Make sure that you wipe any media that may contain information you don't want someone else to recover. Could the National Security Agency recover something wiped with DBAN? Frankly, we think that's another urban legend, and we've never—ever—seen evidence of it, even with the documents released by Edward Snowden. However, we continue to monitor the capabilities of the federal government in particular. DBAN is free, it's safe, and it helps you comply with your ethical duty to keep your client data confidential. When you're getting ready to donate or ditch your old computers, this is an invaluable tool. DBAN is downloaded as an ISO file that can be burned to a CD or DVD, which would then be booted from to load the DBAN program.

Note one of this wiping program's limitations: DBAN does not detect or securely erase data from solid-state hard drives, which are becoming increasingly more common on new laptops. For those systems with a solid state hard drive, you can purchase a piece of software called Blancco (same company that now owns the DBAN product also has this tool) for $24.95 for a single license that will securely wipe data from solid state hard drives. This product can also be found on DBAN's website.

SimplyFile

Long ago, we realized how much time we were losing each day carefully dragging and dropping e-mail into the correct Outlook folder, often accidentally filing messages in a folder below or a folder above the intended destination. Maddening.

With the SimplyFile software, each e-mail will display the name of the folder SimplyFile believes it belongs in. After it initially indexes and "learns" your filing system, it is correct more than 90 percent of the time. If it has guessed wrong, there is a QuickPick feature. Open it, and you'll likely find that the correct folder is near the top of the list of possibilities presented. If not, you can just type in the first few letters of the folder and it will appear. Most of the time, you'll just be clicking "file" and it's done. It can also turn e-mail into a calendar or a task. Marvelous. Authors Nelson and Simek regarded this product as their "find of the year" from 2009 and don't know how they functioned without it. The current version is compatible with Outlook 2013 (32- and 64-bit versions) and Windows 8. This product does not work with Outlook Express.

The latest version, SimplyFile 3.1 may be purchased (or there's a thirty-day free trial) at **www.techhit.com/SimplyFile/**. The cost for a single license is $49.95.

Shred 2

PC Magazine has a free utility designed to wipe specific files or disk areas. Shred 2 "officially" runs under Windows 95, 98, 2000, ME, NT 4.0, and XP. Don't worry—we are successfully running it on Windows 7 systems, too. If you want to wipe the recycle bin, then you'll need an updated DLL file, which is discussed in the article about Shred 2 at **www.pcmag.com/article2/0,2817,13352,00.asp**, but current operating systems shouldn't need anything more than the Shred 2 program itself. The software can selectively wipe files or folders and can be configured to do multiple wipes of the same area if you are particularly paranoid. This utility is especially useful in removing data remnants of files and their associated file slack, which can be forensically recovered if wiping did not occur. The nice part about having a file/folder wiping utility is that data can be selectively eradicated from your computer without having to wipe the entire hard disk and having to reload the operating system and all of the applications. Remember, though, you cannot recover the file once it is wiped, so pay attention when you're clicking that mouse.

File Shredder

Another free file wiping utility is File Shredder, available at **http://www.fileshredder.org/**. The user interface is simple enough to understand, but the software author is a little lax with the consistency of the website. As an example, when you click the update menu option in the application, it sends you to a web page announcing a new version; however, the version being distributed is not the one announced. Even with the inconsistencies, though, the product works as advertised. You can select a file to "shred" or "wipe" by right clicking on the file name. You can also "drag and drop" files into the application interface. There are several wiping methods available from the simple single pass (good enough to prevent recovery) to the totally paranoid 35 pass overwrites. Even though the product is free, you should donate (via PayPal) to the software developer if you use the software and find value in its use.

SnagIt

No lawyer should be without a screen-capture program. SnagIt 12 is a screen-capture utility that can capture anything on your desktop. You can capture a specific window, a defined area, a specific object (e.g., the title bar), or a multitude of other things. There are more than 40 ways to capture the information you want to preserve. A screen-capture application is a great tool to "grab" images to place in a motion or brief that show exactly what is shown on the computer screen. This is particularly handy when you want only a specific area of the screen. SnagIt can output the "snagged" image to a multitude of formats as well. The latest version includes additional video capture options, new stamps, more zoom options, including features that make it easier to edit and resize captured images. SnagIt costs $49.95 for a single license version, with discounts for multiple copies. A thirty-day trial version is available, so you can see whether it fits your needs before purchase. It is available from **www.techsmith.com/download/snagit/default.asp** and now works on all Windows 32- and 64-bit operating systems, including Windows 8. A Mac version is available as well.

If you are using Windows 7 or Windows 8, you should try the Snipping Tool before deciding to purchase a third-party application for your screen-grabbing needs. The Snipping Tool, Microsoft's version of a screen-grabbing utility, is included by default and allows you to save the captured data to a file or copy it to the Clipboard, which is handy when creating PowerPoint slides. On a Mac, you should try the Grab app, which is Apple's equivalent screen-grabbing utility.

FavBackup 2.1.3

If you're like us, you probably have multiple browsers installed on your computer. If you're looking at upgrading your computer to Windows 7 or Windows 8, this tool provides an easy way to back up and restore your web browser settings and other data. FavBackup (**www.favbrowser.com/backup**) is a free utility and supports Internet Explorer 6 thru 8; Firefox 2 thru 8; Opera 9 thru 11.6; Safari 3 and 4; Google Chrome 1 thru 16; and Flock 2 thru 2.5. This is definitely a tool to keep in your tool chest.

If you are a Google Chrome user, you can use the Bookmark Sync feature, which makes it easy to keep the same set of bookmarks on multiple computers. When enabled, the bookmarks or favorites will be stored online in your Google Account and will be automatically synced with each computer you use where this feature is enabled. No need to back up or transfer them manually. Again, the only potential roadblock is that a Google Mail account is required.

QuickView Plus

If you're willing to spend a little money, you can get a utility that can view more than 300 file formats, including Microsoft Office 2013 and Corel WordPerfect Office X5. That's what you get when you purchase QuickView Plus 13 Standard. The file support comes without the need for the native application, potentially saving you the costs of having to purchase a license for a product just to view a file. QuickView Plus maintains the formatting of the files you view, so you can view and print files as they were originally created and meant to be seen. This is a great application to view file formats, especially from your electronic discovery cases. You can handle e-mail attachments and various obscure software packages that you've probably never heard of. QuickView Plus is compatible with Microsoft Windows computer systems, including Windows 8.

At $49 for a single download license of the standard edition, it is a perfect complement to IrfanView. QuickView Plus is available for purchase and download at **www.avantstar.com** and a fully functional evaluation copy of the product is offered for thirty days. The professional edition adds advanced viewing, searching, etc., and you must contact **sales@avantstar.com** for pricing for this version.

Sam Spade

The name of this utility, obviously, is meant to evoke Humphrey Bogart in *The Maltese Falcon*. Indeed, this utility can perform some gumshoe functions, such as troubleshooting and dealing with Internet communications. However, the most useful function of this free utility is the ability to decode e-mail headers so anyone can decipher the cryptic entries in a readable English form. Unfortunately, the original site for Sam Spade is down and no longer active. The good news is that there are several websites that have the latest version (1.14) available for download. Just do a Google search for "Sam Spade spam" and you will find several download locations on the first page of the results, including one from PCWorld. This product hasn't been updated since 2002 and most likely never will be again.

As we move forward into the world of electronic evidence, having the ability to decode e-mail headers is an invaluable asset to help ascertain where an e-mail really came from. Mind you, there are still ways for the world's miscreants to hide, but Sam Spade can provide you with a lot of helpful information. For instructions on how to use the application, the SANS Institute has a great white paper on the matter that can be downloaded here: **www.sans.org/reading_room/whitepapers/tools/sam-spade_934**.

Metadata Assistant

One of our favorite metadata analysis and removal tools is Metadata Assistant by Payne Group (**www.thepaynegroup.com/products/metadata/**). Metadata Assistant integrates with your Microsoft Office installation and is particularly valuable when sending file attachments. The product will display a dialog box asking if you want to clean the attachment or just send it as is. As we mentioned previously, don't clean the metadata if you are collaborating on a document with another person, as it will remove the tracked changes. Metadata Assistant can also convert the attachment to PDF on the fly. Some of the new features available in version 4, include both a 32- or 64-bit version, and the program now has support for OpenDocument, image, and some audio/video file types.

Metadata Assistant is extremely flexible and works with Word, Excel, and PowerPoint versions from 97 to 2013. It has e-mail integration with Outlook 2007 and higher, Office 2007 and higher, OpenText DM 5.2/5.3, Worldox GX/GX2/GX3, Autonomy iManage 8.5/9.0, and NetDocuments 14.1. This product is also compatible with Windows 8. Users may purchase this product directly from Payne Group for $98 per license. Discounts are available for Enterprise-level installations involving twenty or more licenses.

No lawyer should be without some sort of metadata scrubber to ensure removal of potentially confidential data. Some states are even addressing the removal of metadata in their ethics opinions. Whether you are required to scrub metadata or not, Metadata Assistant is a possible solution for your practice.

You can also remove metadata by converting the file to PDF. This does not remove all of the metadata, but it does remove a large portion of it and leaves only what are typically considered innocuous values. Microsoft also provides the ability to analyze and remove ("clean") a document's properties in Microsoft Office 2010 and 2013. However, some values that it leaves behind are still viewable by third-party products like Metadata Assistant.

Litera Metadact and Metadact-e

If you're looking for another possible solution for metadata analysis and scrubbing, we have become very fond of Litera's Metadact program. Metadact identifies and removes all of the commonly known types of metadata, such as author and creation date, as well as many of the hidden metadata fields that are behind the scenes. This product's features include:

—Profile management

—Clean and convert files

—Choose which types of metadata to clean

—View detailed reports

—Batch clean

—Clean metadata from within Microsoft Outlook

—Create custom policies and settings

—Specify safe e-mail domains

—Exclusion lists

—Seamless integration with Windows Explorer and document management systems

—Intelligent content clean, such as identifying and removing credit card/social security numbers from within Microsoft Word documents

—Risk assessment

This product integrates with Autonomy iManage, DM5, DocsOpen, PowerDocs, Worldox, NetDocuments, and Microsoft SharePoint.

The Metadact-e program, which is a server-based product, adds the ability to scrub metadata from documents in Outlook and Outlook Web Access on tablet, smartphone, and desktop-based documents. Whether it's a Microsoft Office, PDF, image, or ZIP file, this product will ensure that all metadata has been removed. We are not aware of any other product on the market that has the ability to enforce metadata policies on mobile devices such as smartphones. We are huge fans of Metadact-e.

Unlike stand-alone versions, this product is centrally managed and administered, and it's suggested that this application be installed on its own server, so your practice can enforce its metadata policies on employees without giving them the option to bypass your written policies and procedures. The benefits of a server-based solution include the ability to prevent the disclosure of client-confidential and other sensitive information, transparency for the users (no more waiting for a locally installed product to do the cleaning—you are immediately released to go to your next task while the server does the scrubbing), and compliance control through enforcing your practice's policies and procedures.

Metadact can be purchased from Litera's website at **www.litera.com** for $45 per license per user and must be renewed on a yearly basis. Users must contact Litera directly for Metadact-e pricing. Even though this product is licensed with an annual subscription model, we would highly recommend investigating purchase. It is a very cost-effective tool that is extremely flexible to meet the specific needs of your firm.

Livescribe Echo Smartpen

The Livescribe Echo Smartpen is a device that can record a user's written notes along with the accompanying audio. The Echo Smartpen can transmit the data to a computer via USB cable, allowing a user to view digitalized notes and hear recorded audio. The pen has an infrared camera that records seventy-five images per second to track the spatial movement of the device on the provided sheets of dot paper, the required use of which is one of the few downsides of the product. Users can now purchase their own dot paper, notebooks, and lined and unlined journals compatible with the Smartpen.

Using the bundled Livescribe Desktop software, users can manage written notes and recordings but cannot convert notes to text because the software lacks OCR capabilities. However, using the software's PDF export capabilities, you could always OCR the exported PDF files using Adobe Acrobat.

The Echo Smartpen, just like a computer, can be updated with new firmware and software and is currently offered with 2 GB of storage capacity. The Smartpen is compatible with Microsoft Windows XP SP3, Vista, and Windows 7/8, as well as Mac OS X 10.5.5 or newer.

Livescribe also has a Sky Smartpen, which features an embedded Wi-Fi adapter that sends recorded notes and audio directly to your Evernote account. The wireless connection removes the need for access to a computer or USB cable to transfer the data.

YouMail

Tired of the standard voicemail options provided by your cellular carrier? Looking for more advanced features? YouMail (**www.youmail.com**) is like Google Voice, without the extra phone number. YouMail provides your smartphone with a visual voicemail client that offers personalization of voicemail greetings based on the caller as well as voicemail sharing, caller blocking, and voicemail alerts by e-mail and text. You can even organize your voicemails into folders and download them to MP3 format. YouMail is compatible with iPhone and Android, but it has dropped support for new BlackBerry devices.

When a call doesn't get answered, the forwarded call is transferred to your YouMail voicemail box rather than to your cellular provider's voicemail box. The Personal Edition, which allows a user to store up to one hundred voicemail messages, is free but ad-supported. The Premium Edition, starting at $5 per month, allows a user to store up to five hundred voicemail messages and has no advertisements, and the Business Edition, starting at $10 per month, allows up to ten thousand voicemail messages and a host of other advanced features.

To view a comparison of these plans, visit YouMail's pricing page at **store.youmail.com**.

SmartDraw Business

SmartDraw Legal Edition has been merged with the VP version of the software, now called SmartDraw Business, which is a powerful software tool that allows lawyers to create sharp, professional-looking diagrams and trial exhibits with relative ease. It's a must-have for your software arsenal. The tool, more robust than Microsoft PowerPoint, can be used to create timelines, estate planning diagrams, accident reconstruction, crime scene layouts, and more. The look and feel of the software is similar to Microsoft Office, and creating diagrams from the provided templates is simple. The Business Edition provides specialized templates for the legal profession—more than one thousand—and if you can't find one to use, you can create your own. SmartDraw comes with more than twenty thousand symbols and shapes to choose from, giving you the power to dynamically re-create that crucial event in your case. SmartDraw provides a number of export options, allowing users to save their work in a variety of formats, such as PDF, DOC, XLS, WPD, or JPG. SmartDraw does a good job as an alternative product to Microsoft Visio or Project at a fraction of the cost.

The latest update to SmartDraw Business includes automatic formatting of charts and diagrams, more diagram templates, MS Office integration, automatic backup of your diagrams and presentations, and new features related to mobile access and viewing SmartDraw files on your iPhone or iPad.

SmartDraw Business can be purchased directly from the website (**www.smartdraw.com**) for $297 for a single-user license. A trial edition is also available for download for those users who wish to test-drive the software before purchasing.

CaseSoft TimeMap 5

Another great timeline-generating utility is CaseSoft's TimeMap, which was acquired by LexisNexis several years ago. TimeMap is a timeline-graphing tool that can be used to create polished timeline graphs for trial exhibits, presentations, and professional documents. TimeMap can be integrated with CaseMap or used on its own. Data can be directly imported into the application from Microsoft Excel, Summation, Concordance, Microsoft Access, or almost any other spreadsheet or database program, eliminating the need to manually enter data.

As data is entered into the program, TimeMap will automatically generate a proportional time scale and allow you to adjust it if necessary. Once your timeline graph has been generated, you can present the timeline using TimeMap's Presentation Mode, or you can embed the timeline directly into your PowerPoint or Sanction presentation. TimeMap 5 includes new features such as vertical timelines, additional timeline templates, a new PDF writer, and enhanced integration with presentation software. The latest version also includes a new Spreadsheet view, global find-and-replace option, expanded images, and improved date display tools. TimeMap 5 supports Microsoft Windows 2000/XP/Vista and Windows 7 and can be purchased directly from Casesoft's website at **www.casesoft.com**. Currently, Windows 8 support isn't listed on the products website.

Like the other LexisNexis products, you must register on the website before you can see product costs. This is a change from previous years, where the pricing was prominently displayed. A full-featured thirty-day trial edition is also available for download for those users who wish to give the software a test run before purchasing.

Evernote

Have trouble remembering everything? We sure do. That's why we use Evernote (**www.evernote.com**). This program makes it easy to remember things big and small, allowing you to capture everything you see when using your computer, cell phone, or mobile device. Using the program, you can clip a web page, snap a photo, or grab a screenshot and upload it to Evernote. Once uploaded, everything you capture is automatically processed, indexed, and made searchable. Of course, you can add your own tags and labels to your notes. Evernote will even scan handwritten notes and make the content searchable. There are a limitless number of ways to use this program, whether for play or work. Since all of the data you capture and tag is uploaded to your Evernote account, these files are accessible from all of your devices. Evernote is available for free, but the Premium ($5 per month) and Business ($10 per month per user) subscription levels offer the same features as Evernote Free, with the addition of enhanced search features and collaboration.

Evernote can integrate with your web browser, or you can install a small application on both Mac OS X and Windows-based computers or your iPhone, iPod Touch, iPad, BlackBerry, Android, Android tablet, or Windows Phone 7/8 smartphone. To sign up for a free account, visit Evernote's website at **www.evernote.com**.

WinRAR/7-ZIP

WinRAR is an application for compressing data. WinZip is a very popular program as well, but WinRAR has some distinct advantages. WinRAR is faster than WinZip and supports more archive file types. It can also create compressed archives that are much smaller than WinZip, so we see WinRAR used for transmitting large amounts of data. Data production as part of a discovery request would be one place to use WinRAR. This program supports all popular compression formats (RAR, ZIP, CAB, ARJ, LZH, ACE, TAR, GZip, UUE, ISO, BZIP2, Z, and 7-Zip). This is a valuable tool for sending data via the Web as well.

WinRAR is available in 32- and 64-bit versions. The cost is $29 per license, and it is available directly from the website at **www.win-rar.com**.

An alternative to WinRAR that we often use is 7-Zip (**www.7-zip.org**), which is an open-source archive utility program. You can use 7-Zip to create password-protected zip files in which the contents are encrypted to securely protect your data. We use this program almost daily and don't know how we'd get by without it.

Chrometa

Track your time and bill for it without any notes or timers. Chrometa is a piece of software that plugs into Outlook, Gmail, or into an app offered for your mobile device (Android and iOS) to help you keep track of time so that it can be billed to your clients. Think of it as a personal timekeeper, silently sitting in the background, recording how long you worked in a particular application, specifically noting what file or e-mail you were working on. You can have these entries categorized in a time sheet or use the keyword-based rules feature to automatically invoice clients.

There are several price plans available. The individual plans range from $12 per month for the Basic plan to $29 per month for the Plus plan.

The Plus plan holds twelve months worth of data, allows usage on up to three devices, creates invoices, and will export data to accounting packages or legal software such as Clio and QuickBooks. You may want to consider the Basic package ($19 per month), even though it only handles two devices and three months worth of data, especially if you are exporting data to Excel. Chrometa is an excellent add-on, especially if you are using a web-based practice management application like Clio or Rocket Matter, but you will need the Plus version for that. Chrometa also has mobile apps for Android and iOS devices.

eWallet

Do you have a hard time remembering all of your different passwords to your web-based accounts? We certainly do—especially since we should all be using a different password for each of our accounts. Whatever you do, do not use the same password over and over for your different accounts. This is basic security 101.

To help you remember your passwords without having to write them down, we recommend a product called eWallet. eWallet is an app that is available for iOS, Android, BlackBerry (OS 7 or OS 10.2.1 or higher), Windows Mobile 6.5, and both Windows-based (including Windows 7, 8, RT and 8.1) and Mac OS X 10.7 or higher. It keeps your passwords safe by remembering them so you don't have to. The app stores the passwords in a vault using 256-bit AES encryption and allows you to synchronize your data across all of your devices on which the application is installed. eWallet can store website passwords, frequent flyer numbers, credit card information, membership data and much more. This product can be purchased from your device's app store or eWallet's website at **www.iliumsoft.com**. The price varies, depending on the device for which you're purchasing the software, but runs between $9.99 and $19.99.

LastPass

Like eWallet, LastPass is another secure password management tool. LastPass allows you to save your passwords and form data in a secure database and access it when needed. You no longer have to remember another password, and filling out forms and password fields is as easy as a single click. This software works on Mac, Windows, and Linux-based computer systems, as well as all of the major smartphones.

There is a new security feature called LastPass Sentry, which will alert you if your logon credentials are compromised. LastPass checks the PwnedList database (database of compromised accounts) to see if your e-mail address is on the list. If so, you receive an e-mail notifying you that your ID has been compromised. The new feature is available for all versions of LastPass.

LastPass does offer a free version available for download, as well as a paid premium version that offers a few additional features. We recommend trying the free version to see if the software meets your needs before making any purchases. You can download and take this software for a test run from its website at **www.lastpass.com**.

WordRake for Microsoft Word

WordRake fundamentally consists of a set of rules designed to cut flabby verbiage from your writing. Even good authors (and we have a club ring!) clearly can use some editing. Even our editors missed most of what WordRake found. There is now also a version for Microsoft Outlook, which is sold separately from the Microsoft Word version.

To be sure, it's not perfect. The founders purposely do not include an "Accept All" button because they know we can never tame the infinite variety and positioning of words. You have to approve each edit. Because of that, we wouldn't use it for casual writing. But for articles or any other writing that is significant, we sure would.

WordRake's creator, Gary Kinder, is a lawyer himself, and he's taught over one thousand writing programs to firms like Sidley and Jones Day. He's also a *New York Times* best-selling author. He must use his own program!

WordRake is a Word add-on and inserts itself into Word's ribbon. It works with the 32-bit versions of Word 2007, 2010, and 2013 running on Windows XP, Vista, 7 and 8. Support for Word 64-bit versions includes 2010 and 2013. The program is licensed on a subscription basis. The one-year cost is $129, two years is $229, and three years will cost $259. All of them can be purchased from the website at **www.wordrake.com**. We recommend that you try the free thirty-day trial first before committing.

Users may opt to bundle the purchase of WordRake for Microsoft Word along with WordRake for Microsoft Outlook, saving you some money off of the two subscriptions should you be in the market for both products.

CHAPTER TWENTY-SEVEN

Social Media for Law Firms— An Overview

by Jennifer Ellis

SOCIAL MEDIA HAS BECOME a crucial part of the average American's life. As a result, whether they want to or not, attorneys must, at the very least, appreciate the impact of social media on their clients. Failure to understand how social media can impact clients' cases could lead to serious damage to a case which might result in a malpractice complaint. Further, wise attorneys will take advantage of social media to develop their practices through the networking and marketing opportunities provided by both their own websites and the various social media sites and applications.

The best way to appreciate how important social media has become in people's day-to-day lives is to look at some statistics for popular sites:

- ◆ Facebook: 1.3 billion users
- ◆ LinkedIn: 300 million users
- ◆ Pinterest: 70 million users
- ◆ YouTube: 4 billion views per day[1]
- ◆ Instagram: 200 million users[2]
- ◆ Google+: Almost 600 million active users[3]

---

[1] Facebook, LinkedIn, Pinterest and YouTube statistics taken from **expandedramblings.com/index .php/resource-how-many-people-use-the-top-social-media/** as of August, 2014.
[2] **http://instagram.com/press/**.
[3] Active Google+ users as of August 25, 2014, **www.internetlivestats.com/watch/google-plus-users/**.

♦ Tumblr: 200.5 million blogs[4]
♦ Twitter: 550 million users[5]

It is also important to know that the number of people accessing social media sites via mobile technology (smartphones and tablets) is increasing to the point where the majority of people (71 percent) use mobile devices to access social media.[6] This ease of access means people use social media on the go as a method to locate businesses they plan to hire. It also means people have a tendency to use social media to quickly share intimate details about their lives and activities. The former shows the value of social media as a marketing tool. The latter shows the amount of information people are sharing, which can be harmful to their cases.

Attorneys who seek to begin using social media should keep in mind that the ethical risks involved with social media, both in terms of evidence collection and marketing, are very real. Therefore a proper understanding of appropriate and ethical behavior is extremely important.

It is also important to understand that in certain areas of practice, it is now verging on malpractice—and the author would argue it *is* malpractice—to fail to communicate with clients about whether and how they use social media. Failing to warn the client to halt or at least limit social media use could result in that client posting materials that will harm his case. Failure to warn a client about evidence preservation could result in substantial sanctions for spoliation.[7] In addition, it is quite conceivable that the opposing party will post harmful information to his case, and failure on the part of the attorney to seek out possible harmful posts can result in loss of a substantially greater bargaining position, or even loss of a case that might have been won.

Specific Sites and Applications

Social media essentially includes sites and applications that enable people to share information, pictures, videos, and the like at a rapid rate, and, in return, allows other people to respond to the shared content. In some

---

[4] About Tumblr, **www.tumblr.com/about**.
[5] Jeff Bullas, 22 Social Media Facts and Statistics You Should Know in 2014 (2014) **www.jeffbullas .com/2014/01/17/20-social-media-facts-and-statistics-you-should-know-in-2014/**.
[6] Ray Pun, Adobe 2013 Mobile Consumer Survey: 71% of People Use Mobile to Access Social Media (July, 2013) **blogs.adobe.com/digitalmarketing/mobile/adobe-2013-mobile-consumer-survey-71-of-people-use-mobile-to-access-social-media/**.
[7] See *Lester v. Allied Concrete Co., et al.*; order dated September 1, 2011.

cases social media is referred to as Web 2.0. Web 1.0 refers to traditional websites and other sites that serve to provide one-way communication, much like a newsletter or a book.

Currently, the most popular social media sites and applications in the United States include Facebook, Twitter, LinkedIn, Google+, Pinterest, YouTube, and Instagram. Further, blogs are sometimes considered part of social media and so will be included in the discussion. At this point, there are over 150 million blogs on the web.

Marketing and Networking

It is not always easy to understand how social media can increase the potential for bringing in new clients. It is therefore important to think of social media as having uses for practice-building.

Advertising

Social media includes straightforward advertising. Sites such as Facebook, YouTube, LinkedIn and others provide the opportunity to purchase small ads that appear on the top or side of the page. These ads are controlled through various means: demographics, keywords, areas of interest, and so on. Generally, the cost of the ads is controlled through a bidding process known as pay-per-click. The site suggests a fee that its algorithm indicates will be successful. The purchaser identifies the amount he is willing to pay and competes against those who are seeking to advertise to the same individuals. Normally, the purchaser only pays when someone clicks on an ad.

Networking

Social media provides substantial opportunities for networking. It simply moves the networking from the bar association or educational program, to networking online. Providing information about interests, sharing day-to-day activities, responding to the posts of others—each of these behaviors is simply a way to connect with other people. Those people, in turn, may need an attorney or may need to refer someone else to an attorney just as in the offline world. Further, people tend to recommend individuals who they know, or feel they know, and social media allows the formation of that kind of relationship.

Content

Sharing useful content is a crucial part of social media for attorneys. Providing high-quality content that informs users about the areas of law in which an attorney practices is an excellent way to bring attention to that attorney. The content can be as simple as commenting on a case on Facebook, sharing a useful link on Twitter, or providing a detailed analysis of a certain specific issue on a blog. This content shows potential clients that the attorney is knowledgeable in her area(s) of practice. Further, well-written content provides a substantial boost to search engine optimization and online reputation.

Specific Sites

Different social media sites provide different tools. Further, some sites are better utilized by attorneys who tend to represent businesses, while others are better utilized by attorneys who represent individuals. It is important to target the correct site or mixture of sites for the best return on investment of time and money.

Content of Posts

When you post on social media, you need to consider whether you are causing any ethical problems for yourself. Given the open nature of social media, a number of issues can arise when lawyers post. Two important issues to focus on include: Is social media advertising and are you forming an attorney-client relationship by answering questions?

Is Social Media Advertising?

When choosing what to write on social media, it is important to determine whether your post is advertising under Model Rule 7.2 (or whatever rule applies in your jurisdiction). If your account is completely private and you share only with friends and family, chances are very good that your posts would not be considered advertising. However, the question becomes cloudier when you open up your account to a larger group. My position is that if you are not certain whether your post is advertising, assume it is and act accordingly as far as your jurisdiction's rules. Some jurisdictions define advertising very clearly. Others do not.

Twitter is a site that is problematic for states such as Florida, where any posting might be considered advertising. In its guidelines on social media, Florida's advertising standing committee states about Twitter that pages of individual lawyers on social networking sites that are used solely for social purposes, to maintain social contact with family and close friends, are not subject to the lawyer advertising rules. Pages appearing on networking sites that are used to promote the lawyer or law firm's practice are subject to the lawyer advertising rules. These Pages must therefore comply with all of the general regulations set forth in Rules 4-7.11 through 4-7.18

and 4-7.21."[8] This language means that many posts on Twitter would be considered advertising, simply because most people have their accounts entirely open and it is common for users to discuss a cross section of personal and work-related details of their lives.

Most problematic, given Twitter's 140-character limit, is that, in Florida, the Tweet must include geographic information as well as "the name of at least one lawyer in the firm." The attorney may use appropriate abbreviations for the geographic requirements, which helps to a degree. However, as soon as the poster puts both the full name of a lawyer and a geographic location, most of the allotted characters are used up, substantially limiting the value of any tweet. Florida is not the only jurisdiction with special Twitter requirements, so be certain to check your state's rules before you Tweet. That said, many jurisdictions have not placed onerous requirements on lawyer's abilities to use Twitter and a well-written tweet can be an excellent way to drive traffic to your website or share useful information.

California's Analysis[9]   In Opinion 2012-176, the State Bar of California provides an excellent analysis of how to determine whether a post is advertising. While California's determination of what constitutes advertising is likely to be different from other jurisdictions, many of its rules as to what is acceptable are commonly shared throughout the various jurisdictions.[10]

In California, a communication (i.e., advertising) is considered to be, "any message or offer made by or on behalf of a member concerning the availability for professional employment of a member or a law firm directed to any former, present or prospective client." Under the rules and articles of California, "[a]ny communication or solicitation shall not:

1. Contain any untrue statement; or
2. Contain any matter, or present or arrange any matter in a manner or format which is false, deceptive or which tends to confuse, deceive, or mislead the public; or

---

[8]The Florida Bar Standing Committee on Advertising Guidelines for Networking Sites (Revised April 16, 2013). **www.floridabar.org/TFB/TFBResources.nsf/Attachments/ 18BC39758BB54A5985257B590063EDA8/$FILE/Guidelines%20-%20Social%20 Networking%20Sites.pdf?OpenElement**.

[9]In the fall of 2014, the Pennsylvania Bar Association released *Formal Opinion 2014-300, Ethical Obligations for Attorneys Using Social Media*. The guidance opinion provides detailed analysis and recommendations surrounding numerous issues relating to legal ethics and social media use.

[10]California Rule 1-400 (Advertising and Solicitation,) California Article 9.5 (Legal Advertising).

3. Omit to state any fact necessary to make the statements made, in the light of circumstances under which they are made, nor misleading to the public; or

4. Fail to indicate clearly, expressly, or by context, that it is a communication or solicitation as the case may be; or

5. Be transmitted in any manner which involves intrusion, coercion, duress, compulsion, intimidation, threats or vexatious or harassing conduct."

The bar, using its Rule and Article as a basis for analysis, next examines several hypothetical posts. They are:

1. "Case finally over. Unanimous verdict! Celebrating tonight."

2. "Another great victory in court today! My client is delighted. Who wants to be next?"

3. "Won another personal injury case. Call me for a free consultation."

4. "Just published an article on wage and hour breaks. Let me know if you would like a copy."

In its analysis, the bar found posts 1 and 4 were not communications (i.e., advertising) but 2 and 3 did meet the requirements constituting a communication and therefore needed certain information that they lacked.

Post 1 was not considered a communication because it did not contain an offer concerning the availability for professional employment. Had the post used "Who wants to be next" as in hypothetical 2, the posting would have become advertising based on the attorney stating that he is seeking additional clients. Post 4 was not advertising because, again, it did not state that he was seeking clients, rather it was simply providing useful information.

Post 2 is a communication because it makes it clear that the lawyer is available for employment. Since the post is advertising, it now has several problems under California's rules. First, it does not contain a disclaimer. Second, it does not state it is an advertisement. Third, it offers a guarantee or prediction of winning. In order to make this particular post appropriate, a lawyer in California would need to add the required language. Such a post would become quite lengthy however, so a question would arise as to whether it would be worth it to share such information in the first place. It also would not be possible to share this particular post on Twitter in California. Post 3 is a communication/advertising for the same reason post 2 is. Asking for readers to call for a free consultation is clearly seeking employment from potential clients.

Remember, the rules in your jurisdiction(s) might be very different from California. However, the analysis in the bar opinion is one that you can apply to your posts. The first question is always going to be, *is it advertising?* The second question will be, *if it is advertising, does the post meet the ethical requirements?* Be certain to give your posts the appropriate consideration.

Is a Social Media Post Legal Advice?

The line for what is and what is not legal advice is a bit blurry. Given this, it is important that you stay on the right side of the line to make certain you are not inadvertently creating an attorney-client relationship. An attorney-client relationship is formed when a client has reason to believe that the attorney is handling his legal interests. The relationship can be formed expressly or it can be implied. The implied relationship is the one that can cause trouble online. The standard in determining whether an attorney-client relationship has been formed is based on the client's objectively reasonable belief. If you answer questions online, make certain there is an appropriate disclaimer, such as can be found on sites like Avvo and Quora. In addition, limit yourself to providing broad answers that are educational in nature as opposed to providing specific advice that directly answers the asker's question. At this point, there have been no lawsuits involving attempts to claim a lawyer has formed an attorney-client relationship through an ask-answer site. Keep in mind, not only could you inadvertently form an attorney-client relationship, but if you provide legal advice in a state in which you are not licensed, you could be engaging in the unauthorized practice of law.

Recommendations/Testimonials

The rules around recommendations and testimonials vary greatly across the United States. As a result, it is difficult to provide specific guidelines. Given this, it is crucial that you refer to the state(s) in which you are licensed to make certain you follow the rules. In most states, it is perfectly acceptable to ask for testimonials. However, those testimonials must follow all relevant rules. When clients write recommendations, those recommendations must not create false expectations, and they must be correct. If a client writes a recommendation that violates the rules, it is the attorney's obligation to correct it. In some cases, for example LinkedIn, the attorney will be able to control whether an improper testimonial is posted. In other cases, for example Google+, Avvo, and Facebook, the attorney is not able to approve the testimonial. In such cases the attorney must ask the client to remove the recommendation, or provide a correction in the comments.

Negative reviews are a serious problem on social media. A negative review can be very harmful to a law firm. That said, no matter how negative the review, it is crucial that lawyers respond appropriately if a past client attacks them online. Most importantly, attorneys may not share confidential information about the client in a response to a negative review. For example, a lawyer from Illinois responded to a negative review on Avvo by providing confidential information about her client. The Hearing board found that she engaged in misconduct which included:

1. [R]evealing information relating to the representation of a client without the client's informed consent, in violation of Rule 1.6(a) of the Illinois Rules of Professional Conduct (2010);

2. [U]sing means in representing a client that have no substantial purpose other than to embarrass, delay, or burden a third person, in violation of Rule 4.4 of the Illinois Rules of Professional Conduct (2010); and

3. [C]onduct which is prejudicial to the administration of justice or which tends to defeat the administration of justice or to bring the courts or the legal profession into disrepute.[10]

The complaint against the attorney also involved a bounced check. For both the check and the comment on Avvo, the disciplinary commission reprimanded the attorney.[11] The best way to deal with a negative review is to provide a polite response. If you are too angry to give a polite response, the best response is none at all.

Specific Rules

7.1. Honest Communication and 8.x Integrity   The first two rules for online behavior should be considered an umbrella under which all behavior is judged. First, attorneys should never be misleading in their communications in relation to their services. No communication should contain a material misrepresentation of either fact or law, nor should any statement omit facts necessary to make the statement appropriate under Rule 7.1. This concept flows throughout all communications by attorneys when discussing their services. The second set of rules, 8.x, involve maintaining the integrity of the profession; in other words, not holding the profession up to ridicule through one's behavior.

7.2. Advertising   The first rule of which attorneys need to be aware relates directly to advertising and it is Model Rule 7.2. One of the issues that can be a problem under Rule 7.2 is that various states require attor-

---

[10] *In the Matter of Betty Tsamis*, Commission No. 2013PR00095 (August 26, 2013.) **http://www.iardc .org/13PR0095CM.html**.

[11] **www.iardc.org/HB_RB_Disp_Html.asp?id=11221**.

neys to keep all ads for a certain period of time. In Pennsylvania, for example, attorneys must keep copies of ads for two years. Other states have longer requirements. It is also important to note that a specific attorney must take responsibility for the ad and its placement, so make certain that a specific attorney is responsible for every action, even if performed by a non-attorney. Fortunately, the various accounts are meant to stay intact, so it is easy to keep records. If a post needs to be deleted, grab a screenshot of it and store it where it will be easily located. Make certain to identify the attorney responsible for the item.

Various states have other requirements, so attorneys should check Rule 7.2 in every state in which they are licensed.

Rule 7.3. Solicitation of Clients   Also implicated by use of social media for communication with potential clients is Model Rule 7.3. Attorneys may not solicit potential clients through real-time communication. This aspect of the rule does not apply to family members, current clients, or other attorneys. Real-time communication includes telephone, in-person, and real-time electronic chat. There is disagreement as to whether attorneys may solicit new clients through large chat rooms in which a large number of people are present, versus instant messages, which are more personal and direct. Given this, it is safe to assume that starting a chat on Facebook is real-time communication and should be avoided. E-mail is considered written communication. To obey the rule, at a minimum, attorneys must label advertising as such and comply with Rule 7.1.

Attorneys may not solicit a client who has already made it clear he does not wish to be contacted, or if, "the solicitation involves coercion, duress or harassment." This means if someone has made it clear through social media that he desires not to be contacted, it would be a violation of the rule to contact him. The tone of writing matters as well. If the content is seen as inappropriate, it violates the rule.

Multi-State Practice—Rule 8.5   An area in which it is easy to get in trouble, due to the vast and multi-jurisdictional nature of the Internet, is multi-state practice. Attorneys must comply with their home states' rules in relation to:

- Where the office is located
- Where the attorneys are admitted
- How they are seeking clients
- How they engage in advertising
- All states' rules in which they market

Additional Ethical Issues

Aside from advertising, communication with potential clients, and inappropriate use of social media in discovery, there are other ways in which legal professionals have gotten themselves in trouble using social media.

Confidentiality and Honesty One potential area of trouble involves confidentiality, Rule 1.6. An attorney got herself in trouble by sharing confidential information about a case in such a way as to make it possible to identify her client. She also provided information that suggested that she knew her client had lied on the stand and did nothing about it. In addition to Rule 1.6, the attorney was accused of violating other rules involving honesty, fraud, and more.[12] In the end, the attorney lost her job of nineteen years[13] and was suspended for ninety days by two different jurisdictions.[14, 15]

Another serious consequence the attorney suffered is that when searching her name online; page after page of results show her disciplinary problems. Though she has since opened her own firm, it is difficult to find anything positive about her in a Google search.

While it is perfectly acceptable to discuss one's life, and even one's professional activities, it is important to obey the ethical rules while doing so. Discussing a case on a blog while it is going on, outside of appropriate PR, is a bad idea. Failing to protect a client's confidentiality is even worse. And, of course, failing to properly inform the court of inappropriate conduct by the client was a serious mistake. Judgment is a critical part of both practicing law and posting online.

Jokes and Satire Jokes can also be a serious problem online. It is impossible to see body language or hear the tone in a person's voice. Something one person might find amusing might not be so funny to another. As a result, joking through social media can be problematic, especially on a politically charged topic. An Indiana deputy attorney general learned this the hard way when he tweeted an unfortunate joke surrounding protests in Wisconsin in 2011. His tweet led to an argument

---

[12]*In the Matter of Kristine Ann Peshek*, Commission No. 09 CH 89, Illinois Attorney Registration and Disciplinary Commission (2009).

[13]Debra Cassens Weiss, Blogging Assistant PD Accused of Revealing Secrets of Little—Disguised Clients (2009). **www.abajournal.com/news/article/blogging_assistant_pd_accused_of_revealing_secrets_of_little-disguised_clie/**.

[14]Illinois Supreme Court disbars 12, suspends 26, **http://iln.isba.org/2010/05/18/illinois-supreme-court-disbars-12-suspends-26**.

[15]*Office of Lawyer Regulation v. Peshek*, 2011 WI 47 (2011).

with the editor of *Mother Jones Magazine*. In turn, the magazine researched the attorney and found similar comments on his blog. In the end, the price of the attorney's online behavior was his job.[16] The attorney general's office stated that it chose to fire the attorney after a "thorough and expeditious review;" noting that it respects First Amendment rights, but expects civility from its public servants.

Personal v. Private   Sometimes attorneys will develop both a private and public persona on the web, believing the two will remain separate. Unfortunately, this is simply not the case. It takes very little effort to perform research on the web and to connect the public and private behaviors of someone who has written something offensive or upsetting. In an infamous case, an assistant Michigan attorney general was fired due to his online (and perhaps offline) behavior surrounding the student body president of the University of Michigan. The attorney argued that his speech was political and also had nothing to do with his work as an assistant attorney general. But in the end, the public and private became much too intertwined, and the attorney general was left with no choice but to fire him. Recently the student won a verdict of $4.5 million for invasion of privacy, defamation, abuse of process, and intentional infliction of emotional distress.[17]

The attorney in this case did not hide who he was, but he did try to argue that his actions had nothing to do with his work. However, as a public servant and as an attorney, it was simply impossible to separate the public employee from the (not so) private behavior, and that cost him his job. He was fired for, "violat[ing] office policies, engag[ing] in borderline stalking behavior," and more. The attorney sometimes posted his online attacks while at work, and engaged in behavior that was, "not protected by the First Amendment. . . ."[18] Much of his behavior was offline, but it was his online behavior that brought an incredible amount of attention to what he was doing, so much so that he ended up on TV shows including *Anderson Cooper* on CNN.[19]

---

[16]Indiana state prosecutor fired over remarks about Wisconsin protests (2011). **www.cnn.com/2011/US/02/23/indiana.ammo.tweet/**.

[17]Kevin Dolak, Attorney Andrew Shirvell Ordered to Pay 4.5 Million for Attacks on Gay Student (2012). **abcnews.go.com/US/attorney-andrew-shirvell-ordered-pay-45-million-attacks/story?id=17028621**.

[18]David Jesse, Andrew Shirvell fired from job at Michigan Attorney General's Office (2010). **www.annarbor.com/news/andrew-shirvell-fired-from-job-at-attorney-generals-office/#.UFQIPVEQd60**.

[19]Anderson Cooper: Andrew Shirvell Responsible For His Firing Not 'Liberal Media,' **www.huffingtonpost.com/2010/11/09/anderson-cooper-andrew-sh_n_780874.html**.

It is unwise to believe that anyone can live two separate lives online. If one engages in controversial behavior, the result will be a magnifying glass of attention. In turn, it is virtually impossible for the individual to keep his private and public online lives from colliding.

Discovery of Social Media

Given the value of the information contained within social media accounts, it is no surprise that attorneys desire to obtain access to the information. It is not at all uncommon, for example, for an individual to say one thing in person to her attorney or a judge and to post completely contradictory information on Facebook. An individual might claim in court or interrogatories that she cannot leave her home due to emotional harm from an injury, but in turn post a video on Facebook showing her dancing at a party. In the past, it was necessary to hire a private investigator to prove someone was lying about his injury for a workers' compensation claim; now the plaintiff frequently posts a picture of himself chopping wood or carrying a heavy couch, the exact evidence the defense attorney needs to prove her case.

Privacy Settings Are Important

Privacy settings control what an individual shares on social media sites. However, many users never change their privacy settings, or simply find the settings too complicated to alter. Many social media sites barely have any privacy settings at all. Twitter, for example, is either open, limited, or private.[20] Facebook's settings are extremely complicated and confusing.[21] Blogs are meant to be open, and people frequently believe they are private when they are not.[22] Since many people do not change their settings, attorneys should and do look through the social media sites in an ethical

---

[20]**support.twitter.com/entries/14016#**.

[21]Approximately 13 million US users never change their Facebook privacy settings. Of those that do, the majority are unaware that their privacy settings can be compromised by allowing additional applications access to their accounts and do not take the steps necessary to further protect their data. Thirteen million US Facebook users don't change privacy settings, **www.zdnet.com/blog/facebook/13-million-us-facebook-users-dont-change-privacy-settings/12398**.

[22]Natalie Munroe was a teacher in Pennsylvania who blogged about her students. She believed her blog was only being read by a few people, apparently unaware that it could be widely read. **tinyurl.com/8hx95c6**. Munroe was suspended, brought back, and eventually fired. She claims she was fired due to the blog. The District claims she was fired for incompetence. Munroe has since brought a lawsuit against the district. Blogging Central Bucks Teacher is Fired, **www.philly.com/philly/blogs/bucksinq/160413996.html**.

manner and view and preserve the information they can find.[23] Keep in mind, if the attorney does the preservation, and authentication becomes an issue, the attorney could be forced to become a witness in her own case. It is best to have someone else in the firm do the preservation.

The Client's Social Media

The first step when a new client walks through the door is to ask if he uses any social media. The next step, in some cases, is to inform the client that he must stop posting immediately. Unfortunately, the addiction and use of social media can be so great that the client will be unwilling to stop. As a result, the attorney should also advise her client that if he does post, he should not post anything that deals with the case. The attorney must be clear about what "deals with the case" means, since many clients will simply think it means specifics about how the case is going, as opposed to comments about giving money to his mistress, lifting a heavy couch, attending a party, and so on. Make certain to ask the client not only about his own accounts, but his comments on blogs and websites that might be relevant to the case. Social media and other online surprises can be very harmful. It is also important to remind the client that he may not delete any content from his account, even if it is potentially harmful to his case.

The first meeting with a client is also the time to speak with him about changing his privacy settings to make certain that his account is secure. Providing instructions on how to change privacy settings in a written or video form can be very helpful. It is also a good idea to have the client sign a document making it clear that he was told not to delete any content. This will protect the attorney from accusations of spoliation later on. In some cases it might be wise to ask for access to the account(s). Asking to friend the client is not enough, the password is necessary for a complete review of the client's online conduct. You will have to make a decision as to whether connecting with the client and reviewing his account is wise. Remember, if you become aware of any content that shows the client is lying or will lie before the court, you will be in an ethical quandary.

Also, if the client has a personal relationship with the opposing party, ask about whether he is connected to the other side's social media, for example as a friend on Facebook. In addition, ask the client if any potential witnesses are using social media. Find out if the client is connected to those witnesses and therefore has access to private areas of the accounts.

---

[23]New York State Bar Association, Committee on Professional Ethics, Opinion 843, (September 10, 2010).

Last, it is important that attorneys speak with not only their clients, but other relevant individuals about their online conduct. In a recent case, the daughter of the plaintiff caused an $80,000 settlement to be overturned because she posted about the result on Facebook.[24] In the end, what matters is proper communication with the client in order to protect both the client's case and your ethical obligations.

Opposing Party and Witnesses

Immediately view the opposing party's accounts and witness accounts if they are freely accessible. It is permissible to view the accounts if the client has access. It is also permissible to ask witnesses to provide access to their accounts, though the attorney or other individual asking for access must be honest about her relationship to the case.

Also send a Notice of Preservation to opposing counsel. Fortunately, the amendments to the federal discovery rules from 2006 allow for discovery of electronic data to begin very early in the litigation process. Make it clear to opposing counsel that all data must be preserved. Do not just name specific social media sites, but be clear in the preservation that it means all sites and all accounts. Unfortunately, exactly what preservation is required is not yet clear. Does preservation mean keeping the privacy settings as is, so if an account was open it remains such? Does it simply mean that data may not be deleted? Be clear about expectations and do not be surprised if the matter ends up before a judge.[25]

Send out the Interrogatories relating to social media as quickly as possible and ask the right questions. Again, do not give the opposing client a chance to wiggle out by asking simply for Facebook when the client might have a Plaxo Account. Ask for everything. Ask for all e-mail addresses as well, because the opposing party might have several accounts under various e-mail addresses. Further, keep in mind that with strict privacy settings the opposing party can all but hide the existence of his account(s).

---

[24]Matthew Stucker, Girl costs father $80,000 with 'SUCK IT' Facebook post, March 2014. **www.cnn.com/2014/03/02/us/facebook-post-costs-father/**.

[25]In a recent opinion, the Philadelphia Bar Association made it clear that not only is it acceptable to change privacy settings, but to delete content, as long as that content is properly preserved prior to deletion. In addition, the lawyer must "make reasonable efforts to obtain a photograph, link or other content about which the lawyer is aware if the lawyer knows or reasonably believes it has not been produced by the client." The Philadelphia Bar Association Professional Guidance Committee, Opinion 2014-5, July 2014.

Trouble for Failure to Preserve

In the past, some have believed that it is acceptable to delete posts from social media accounts. A Virginia decision from 2011 puts the debate to rest. It is spoliation to delete relevant posts. In the case, the attorney instructed his client to "'clean up' his Facebook because we don't want blowups of this stuff at trial." The attorney further instructed the client to delete or deactivate the account, and then responded to discovery requests by informing opposing counsel that his client had no Facebook account. The client deactivated the account instead of deleting it. Upon reactivating the account, the client deleted 16 photographs, following his attorney's instructions. Based on the spoliation, the court held that sanctions should be granted against both the attorney and the client. The sanctions amounted to $722,000 in legal fees, over $500,000 of which was payable by the attorney. In addition, the judge in the case reported the attorney to the Virginia State Bar.[26] In the end, the attorney agreed to a five-year suspension of his license and ultimately left the practice of law.[27]

A recent New Jersey case shows the serious consequences of deleting content from Facebook. In that case the plaintiff claimed that he deactivated his Facebook account and did not restore it quickly enough, resulting in deletion of his account. Leaving aside that this is not how Facebook deactivations and deletions actually work,[28] the result was that the court found that deletion of the account was spoliation of evidence and granted an adverse inference against.[29] Given the cases and the trend, it seems to be straightforward that deleting posts, pictures, or videos is unacceptable and likely to lead to serious sanctions.

Ethical Pitfalls in Research, Discovery, and Communications

The New York City and State Bars,[30] the Philadelphia Bar[31] and the San Diego County Bar[32] Associations have provided a number of relevant

---

[26]See *Lester v. Allied Concrete Co., et al.*; order dated September 1, 2011.

[27]"On July 17, 2013, the Virginia State Bar Disciplinary Board suspended Matthew B. Murray's license to practice law for five years for violating professional rules that govern candor toward the tribunal, fairness to opposing party and counsel, and misconduct. This was an agreed disposition of misconduct charges." VSB Docket Nos. 11-070-088405, 11-070-0884222.

[28]In the author's experience, when a Facebook account is deactivated it is not deleted. When the owner logs into his account again, it is restored. In order for a Facebook account to be deleted, specific actions requesting deletion must be taken on the part of the account owner.

[29]*Gatto v. United Air Lines, Inc., et al.*, Case No. 10-cv-1090-ES-SCM (D.N.J. Mar. 25, 2013).

[30]New York State Bar Association Guidance Opinion 843 (2010).

[31]Philadelphia Bar Association Guidance Opinion 2009-02 (2009).

[32]SDCBA Ethics Opinion 2011-2 (May 24, 2011).

guidance opinions surrounding issues related to performing research using social media.

General Research

First, as already noted, it is perfectly acceptable to search and access social media sites that are freely accessible. The New York Guidance Opinion states, "[an attorney] may access the public pages of another party's social networking website (such as Facebook or MySpace) for the purpose of obtaining possible impeachment material for use in the litigation."[33] On the other hand, the 2009 Philadelphia Opinion makes it clear that an effort to obtain access to the account through deceptive or illegal means is unacceptable.[34]

Friending a Witness

In the 2009 Philadelphia opinion, the attorney asked whether it would be acceptable for the attorney to have a third party request a witness to "friend"[35] the opposing client. The third party did not intend to lie, but neither did he intend to reveal his relationship to the attorney.

The opinion noted that such behavior would violate several rules of ethical conduct. The lawyer would be "procuring conduct [and be] responsible for [that] conduct" in violation of Pennsylvania Rule 5.3 (Responsibilities Regarding Nonlawyer Assistants.) Also, the lawyer would be violating Rule 8.4 (Misconduct) by engaging in "deceptive" conduct. In addition, the attorney would be encouraging a third party to violate Rule 4.1 (Truthfulness in Statements to Others) by having the third party "omit a highly material fact."[36] Based upon the Philadelphia Bar Association's 2009 Guidance Opinion, it is very clear that having a third party (or the attorney herself) friend a witness without revealing her relationship to the case would be highly inappropriate.

A real world example of what can happen when an attorney lies to potential witnesses comes from a lawyer who is learning a hard lesson in negative publicity. This attorney, a prosecutor in Ohio, posed as the

---

[33]New York State Bar Association Guidance Opinion 843.

[34]Philadelphia Bar Association Guidance Opinion 2009-02.

[35]*Friend* is Facebook's term for two people who are connected to each other on the service. Different social media providers use different terms. For example, LinkedIn uses *contact* and *connection*. Friending someone requires the affirmative action of a request on the part of the individual seeking the connection and an affirmative action on the part of the individual accepting the connection. See Facebook, "How do I add a Friend?" **www.facebook.com/help/?faq=12062**.

[36]Philadelphia Bar Association Guidance Opinion 2009-02 (2009).

ex-girlfriend of a murder defendant on Facebook. The attorney's stated goal was to convince the two female alibi witnesses to change their stories. In the end, the prosecutor was fired and has seen numerous stories written about this conduct online.[37] The lesson from this case is that lawyers may not lie when communicating with anyone through social media, including witnesses.

Communicating with a Represented Party

The San Diego County Bar Association took on the issue of communicating with a represented party. In short, as is the case offline, it is inappropriate to communicate with a represented party online. In the instant case, the attorney did not identify himself as the attorney, which made the effort to communicate all the more grievous. An additional issue, of concern for those involved in employee cases, includes an analysis of whether the contacted employees were represented parties.[38]

In 2012, the issue of friending represented parties came up in New Jersey where two attorneys are likely to face sanctions due to their paralegal friending the opposing party in a case.[39] The issue came to light during a deposition when it became clear that the attorneys had access to the private areas of the plaintiff's Facebook account. The attorneys denied responsibility because they asked the paralegal simply to perform a general search of the web. The issue with this defense is that attorneys are responsible for the behavior of their staff. The attorneys are charged with violating New Jersey Rules 4.2 (communications with represented parties,) 5.3(a), (b), and (c) (failure to supervise a nonlawyer assistant,) 8.4(c) (conduct involving dishonesty and violation of ethics rules through someone else's actions or inducing those violations,) and 8.4(d) (conduct prejudicial to the administration of justice.) In addition, the more senior of the two attorneys is charged with RPC 5.1(b) and (c) (ethical obligation in relation to supervising another attorney.) These are all very serious charges, and regardless of the outcome, the publicity, which will spread rapidly through social media, will no doubt be very harmful to the two attorneys in question.

---

[37]Martha Neil, Prosecutor fired after posing as ex-girlfriend in Facebook chat with defendant's alibi witnesses (June 2013). **www.abajournal.com/news/article/prosecutor_is_fired_after_posing_as_woman_in_facebook_chat_with_murder_defe/**.

[38]SDCBA Ethics Opinion 2011-2, May 24, 2011.

[39]Eric Meyer, Ethics charges for two lawyers over Facebook friending a litigant (2012). **www.lexisnexis.com/community/labor-employment-law/blogs/labor-employment-commentary/archive/2012/09/13/ethics-charges-for-two-lawyers-over-facebook-friending-a-litigant.aspx**.

At this point it seems well settled that the action of friending someone or seeking to access their accounts through some form of communication is considered contact. Therefore, attorneys should never seek to friend or obtain access to the account of an opposing party through any form of communication with a represented party. If seeking to friend a witness, the attorney or individual assisting the attorney must make clear her relationship to the case.

How to Obtain Access

If an attorney believes useful information is contained in a social media account, she should seek to obtain access to the information in it. There are a number of ethical ways to do so, aside from just looking to see what is freely available.

See if the Client or a Friendly Witness has Access

In family law cases especially, the parties or witnesses might have access to each other's accounts. It is perfectly acceptable to view and use any information that is freely available through this method. Be cautious though if it looks like a witness might be sharing the information under duress. For example, in an employer-employee case, if another employee is friends with a plaintiff on Facebook, he might feel he has no choice but to share the information. If that employee complains later and says he was forced to share the access, it is uncertain how a court will look upon it.

Ask for Access to the Account

During the discovery process, unless there is a reason not to do so, ask for access to any and all social media accounts. In terms of Facebook, it is possible to download an entire account, so request that the opposing party do so and provide a copy.[40] Be sure to ask for continuing access as well. The opposing party will likely refuse this request, and wisely so. Social media postings can provide a plethora of private information, some of which may be harmful to a case. It is possible to simply ask the opposing party to adjust privacy settings so the account is viewable, but again, it is likely this request will be refused. It is always best to ask though because during the discovery process the judge will certainly ask if the request was made.

Send a Subpoena to the Site

Though generally the social media sites will not cooperate with a civil subpoena, from time to time they will be surprisingly helpful. As a result, it never hurts to send the subpoena. Even if the site won't provide con-

---

[40]Facebook's "Download your information" tool is located under Account Settings.

tent, citing the Stored Communications Act, it will normally provide assistance in connecting an account with an e-mail address. Knowing the address can be helpful if ownership of the account will be in issue. For example, in a criminal case the prosecution's verdict was overturned when it was shown that prosecution had failed to tie the account in question to the defendant's girlfriend.[41] Proof of ownership could have been shown with MySpace's assistance.

Compel Discovery

This is where things get tricky. Different judges tend to have different responses to the request to compel discovery of a social media account. The best approach, and the one that has shown the most results, is to capture what is already viewable (through appropriate ethical means) and to show it to the judge. If the judge can see that the account has relevant and contradictory information, she is likely to provide access to the account. If the judge has concerns about the privacy of those other than the account holder, request that the court review the data first to help resolve the issue. Some judges do not feel that there are any privacy rights in social media content.[42]

Case Law

There are a number of opinions related to discovery of social media when the account itself is not a part of the case, in other words when opposing counsel believes that she might find useful data in the account but the online behavior is not at the center of the dispute. At this point the trend in such cases is to provide access to social media accounts only when the opposing party can show that there is relevant and/or contradictory information contained in it. For example, in *McMillen v. Hummingbird Speedway, Inc.*[43] a review of the public areas of McMillen's Facebook page revealed information contradictory to what he was claiming in terms of his injuries. The judge provided access noting specifically that the Facebook information was not privileged.

Another case is simply the paragraph long *Piccolo v. Paterson.*[44] The judge denied access to the Facebook pages the defense desired. The judge noted

---

[41]Kashmir Hill, Bad MySpace Detective Work Results In Overturned Murder Conviction (2011). **blogs.forbes.com/kashmirhill/2011/05/10/bad-myspace-detective-work-results-in-overturned-murder-conviction**.

[42]*NY v. Harris*, 2012 NY Slip Op 22175, June 30, 2012.

[43]*McMillen v. Hummingbird Speedway, Inc.*, No. 113-2010 CD (C.P. Jefferson, Sept. 9, 2010).

[44]Gina Passerella, Facebook Postings Barred From Discovery in Accident Case (2013). **www.thelegalintelligencer.com/id=1202493920630/Facebook-Postings-Barred-From-Discovery-in-Accident-Case#ixzz3COUstMur**.

that the defense already had many pictures, and that no pictures or other data were freely available that showed contradictory information to what the plaintiff was claiming. It is interesting to note that the plaintiff actually changed her privacy settings early in the case, to preclude anyone other than a friend viewing her pictures.

In *Zimmerman v. Weis Markets Inc.,*[45] the judge granted discovery due to the public availability of pictures that contradicted the plaintiff's claim that he did not wear shorts due to his embarrassment about a scar. The plaintiff posted pictures on his MySpace profile that clearly showed him wearing shorts after his injury (the scar was visible.) Due to the public availability of this contradictory information the judge found that there was clearly relevant data to be found within the MySpace account and therefore access to the account was properly compelled.

Another important case comes from Judge R. Stanton Wettick. Judge Wettick is known as a discovery judge in Pennsylvania, so his view on the discovery of social media was quite welcome. Judge Wettick denied mutual requests for access to Facebook accounts in the case of *Trail v. Lesko* because he was not going to allow a fishing expedition when there was no evidence that contradictory or useful information could be found in either Facebook account.[46] Therefore Judge Wettick used the same reasoning as in many of the other cases on this issue.

In a Florida case, the judge partially granted the request by defense in a personal injury case for complete access to the plaintiff's social media network. He held that the plaintiff must provide copies of all pictures depicting herself since her injury, rather than provide access to the entire social media account in question. He further held that in requesting that the plaintiff provide every device on which she accessed her social media accounts, the defense had overreached.[47] In reaching his decision, the judge noted that social media sites are "neither privileged nor protected by any right of privacy." He also noted though that the discovery request must be properly tailored, and to support both assertions, he cited the decision in *Tompkins v. Detroit Metropolitan Airport.*

In *Tompkins*[48] the court found that while social media is discoverable, and "generally not privileged," the opposing party still may not, "have a generalized right to rummage through information that Plaintiff has limited

---

[45] *Zimmerman v. Weis Markets, Inc.*, No. CV-09-1535 (2011).

[46] *Trail v. Lesko,* No GD-10-017249.

[47] *Davenport v. State Farm Mutual Automobile Insurance Co.*, Case No. 3:110-cv-632-J-JBT, (M.D. FL, 2012).

[48] *Tompkins v. Detroit Metropolitan Airport,* Case No. 10-10413, 2012 WL 179320 (E.D. MI. 2012).

from public view." The court required a "threshold showing that the requested information is reasonably calculated to lead to the discovery of admissible evidence." As in the other cited cases, the court wanted to see some evidence that justified the defendant, "delving into the non-public section of [plaintiff's] account." The court noted specifically that if the public segment of plaintiff's account had "contained pictures of her playing golf or riding horseback," that the defendant would have had a better case to access the private portions of her account.

The conclusion to be drawn thus far about the majority of social media discovery decisions is that, while courts are willing to provide access to private sections of social media accounts, they are not willing to allow fishing expeditions simply based on the view that the accounts *might* have useful information. Some evidence that relevant information is in the account must be offered before discovery will be granted.

Won't the Social Media Provider Help?
Social media providers will not provide content from a social media account in civil cases. As recently as 2007 some providers did respond to civil subpoenas with content, but now the providers state unequivocally that due to the Stored Communications Act, 18 U.S.C. § 2701 *et seq*, they may not provide content.[49] The providers will respond to a subpoena only with information about who owns the account, perhaps dates and times of connections, IP addresses, and so on.[50] In other words, the only way to get the data is to have the owner of the account cooperate. In criminal cases, most social media providers will assist when provided with an appropriate subpoena or warrant. On occasion a social media site will be surprising, go against its stated rules, and provide the evidence. Therefore, it never hurts to ask with a subpoena in a civil case. Just be prepared for a no.

The various social media sites generally have details on the subpoena process, and what they will provide. Review each site to learn the appropriate steps.

What Happens if the Owner of the Account Deletes the Data?
Most social media providers claim that when a user deletes information from his account, it is gone forever. Facebook, for example, explains that its deletion system works much like a recycling bin. In essence, when a

---

[49]Facebook states, "Federal law prohibits Facebook from disclosing user content (such as messages, wall posts, photos, etc.) in response to a civil subpoena." **www.facebook.com/help/ ?faq=17158**.

[50]For Facebook this requires the e-mail address that the attorney desires to connect to the account. **www.facebook.com/help/?page=211462112226850**.

user deletes data, that data is stored on Facebook's server briefly until the system writes over it; this means, unfortunately, if someone is savvy and starts deleting harmful data, there is nothing that can be done to bring it back, once it is overwritten. Facebook does state, "[i]f a user cannot access content because he or she disables or deleted his or her account, Facebook will, to the extent possible, restore access to allow the user to collect and produce the account's content. Facebook preserves user content only in response to a valid law enforcement request."[51] Of course, if there is nothing to find because it has been deleted and destroyed, than the site cannot restore the data. And outside of criminal cases, it must be the account's owner who requests the data be restored.

Authentication

Authentication is another troubling issue when it comes to social media. Facebook states that the owner or someone familiar with the account can authenticate it. The issue however is that it is impossible to know whether the user deleted something in the account, leaving only helpful items. This is why it is extremely important to perform research early in the process, and to take screen shots of any evidence discovered immediately. Be certain to keep records as to how the evidence was preserved.

In terms of proving who owns the account, remember, it is very easy to create a fake social media account. Just because an account looks like it belongs to someone does not mean that it does. If there is any question about proving ownership of an account, at least subpoena the account-identifying information from the social media site.

The case law on authentication and admissibility of social media sites is contradictory. In *State v. Bell* the court found that the level of admissibility is low and accepted as good enough, testimony from a witness familiar with the MySpace account and e-mail address of the party the information was to be used against. Also the evidence showed that the defendant used certain code words and that those words were contained within the account. The court also noted that the witness agreed that the provided printouts seemed to be an accurate reflection of the MySpace account in question.[52]

On the other side, in *Griffin v. State*, the court was concerned about how easy it is to create a fake account and noted that information such as birthdate, picture, and residence were not enough to prove ownership.[53]

---

[51] See Information on a Civil Summons, **https://www.facebook.com/help/?page=211462112226850**.
[52] *State v. Bell*, 882 N.E.2e (2008).
[53] *Griffin v. State*, 2011 Md. LEXIS 226, 27-28 (Md. Apr. 28, 2011).

The Other Side–Responding to Social Media Requests

Being prepared to respond appropriately to requests for social media content is important. All businesses (including law firms) should have a social media policy that controls who may (and may not) speak on behalf of the company. The policy should also consider addressing whether supervisors may be connected to employees on the more social sites (as opposed to professional sites liked LinkedIn,) and remind employees about the fact that policies online are the same as policies off-line, specifically in relation to sexual harassment and other such issues. Employees should also be reminded not to discuss private information and/or litigation on their social media accounts. Employers should train employees on social media privacy settings to assist in security. As already explained, individuals should be warned not to post anything that can be harmful to their cases on social media.

Social media evidence needs to be preserved appropriately. For a business with a great deal of social media evidence to preserve, it is wise to involve a company that can help in the preservation process during litigation. An individual can simply print out the pages or download the account. If the account is large (and is not on Facebook where it can be downloaded) and if it is likely the history of the account will enter into the lawsuit, it might be wise to arrange for preservation of the account through a third party, to avoid any accusations of spoliation later on.

In the end, it is crucial for clients, indeed for everyone, to remember that any content posted on a social media site, even back in 2004 when Facebook was first created and the client might have been in college, could come up later during litigation. Therefore everyone needs to be careful to think before they post. This does not mean that people should go back and clean up their accounts just because some day they might, by chance, be sued. But it does mean they might want to give some thought to their online reputations due to their past and current postings.

Other Issues: Judges and Juries

Judges

Many judges enjoy having an online presence as well. This has led to questions about whether judges should be friends with attorneys, and what happens if a judge is a friend with a defendant.

In attempting to resolve the first issue, the Florida Supreme Court Judicial Ethics Advisory Committee determined that judges may not be friends on

Facebook with attorneys who appear before them.[54] In turn, a defendant sought to disqualify a judge based on his Facebook friendship with the prosecutor. The trial judge denied the request, but upon appeal the motion was granted. The court held that the Facebook friendship "conveys the impression that the lawyer is in a position to influence the judge."[55] Ohio came down on the other side, noting that it is acceptable for judges to friend lawyers who appear before them. However the judges must comport themselves properly, follow all ethical rules, and be careful to disqualify themselves should the online friendship cause a bias.[56]

Other states have seen issues arise when the judge learns he is Facebook friends with a defendant. Two cases occurred in Pennsylvania. In the first, the judge was asked to recuse himself, and eventually did so when it turned out he knew the defendant's father. He was, however, unaware of the Facebook friendship prior to being alerted to it. Like many people, the judge simply friended anyone who asked and thought nothing of it.[57] Another controversy arose when a judge suppressed evidence against a defendant resulting in dismissal of the case. After the fact the prosecution realized that the judge was Facebook friends with the defendant, though the defendant and the judge did not know each other. The prosecutor asked the judge to reverse the suppression and recuse himself. The judge decided not to recuse himself due to concern about setting a dangerous precedent.[58]

On February 21, 2013, the American Bar Association released Formal Opinion 462, Judge's Use of Electronic Social Networking Media. It offers a new acronym, ESM, meaning electronic social media. Judges are allowed to participate in ESM so long as they "comply with the relevant provisions of the Code of Judicial Conduct and avoid any conduct that would undermine the judge's independence, integrity or impartiality, or create an appearance of impropriety."

In the end, the best advice for judges is that they be careful who they friend, and also, be aware of who they friend. Friending everyone is not a good idea for a judge, since it is easy enough, as shown above, for the judge

[54]Florida Supreme Court Judicial Ethics Advisory Committee, Opinion Number 2009-20 (November 17, 2009).
[55]*Domville v. State*, No. 4D12-556 (Fla. 4th DCA 2012).
[56]Supreme Court of Ohio Disciplinary Board, Advisory Opinion: Judges May 'Friend' 'Tweet' if Proper Caution Exercised. (December 8, 2010).
[57]Sara Ganim, Cumberland County Judge Thomas A. Placey under fire for having too many Facebook friends (2011). **www.pennlive.com/midstate/index.ssf/2011/09/judges_facebook_friend_has_som.html**.
[58]Judge refuses to recuse himself from Parker DUI case, state plans an appeal (2011). **www.newsworks.org/index.php/neighborhoods/mt-airychestnut-hill-/item/30248-hayden-denial-story-**

to end up being friends with a defendant, and to be completely unaware of their online relationship. Judges who have many friends on social media sites might want to take a look at who those friends are, and determine whether they should remain friends. On the other hand, judges who prefer to have many friends online might find it wise to be certain they know who those friends are and at the least make both sides aware of the Facebook friendship prior to the trial beginning. If necessary, perhaps the judge could have a clerk make a quick check of his account to make certain that he is not friends with defendants who appear before him.

Jurors

These days it is extremely common to look over to the seats behind the prosecution, plaintiff, or defense, and see individuals hard at work on their computers during the *voir dire* process.[59] This is because jurors, like almost everyone else, provide an immense amount of information about themselves online. Some of this information might well disqualify an individual from serving on a jury, or simply show a particular side that it would be unwise to seat a potential juror.

While there are currently no conclusive decisions on the issue of research-ing jurors via social media, there is guidance on the subject.[60] A New York opinion, quite reasonably, makes it clear that it is acceptable to research jurors online, including viewing their social media accounts under several conditions. First, the accounts must be accessed appropriately, i.e. only looking at accounts and information that have been left freely accessible by the jurors. Also, it remains impermissible to communicate with the jurors in any fashion. That means no friending (or having a third party friend) a juror in order to obtain access to the private sections of an account.[61] However, the American Bar Association does not bar visiting the public portions of a site even if it makes the juror aware that an attorney looked at a profile. Such contact might include using LinkedIn to look at a juror's profile. Unless set properly, LinkedIn will show the name of a person who looks at a profile, under certain circumstances.

Of late, jurors have been engaging in social media or other Internet use that has caused serious trouble for the court system. Judges, prosecutors, and

---

[59]Michael Cary, Lawyers in Murray trial using Facebook, Twitter to screen jurors (2011). **articles.cnn.com/2011-09-20/tech/tech_social-media_social-media-jurors-murray_1_ prospective-jurors-potential-jurors-jury-selection?_s=PM:TECH**.
[60]NYCLA Committee on Professional Ethics, Formal Opinion 743 (May 18, 2011).
[61]The American Bar Association Standing Committee on Ethics and Professional Responsibility released an opinion, Lawyer Reviewing Jurors' Internet Presence, Formal Opinion 466, 2014, which agrees with previously stated guidelines from other states.

defense attorneys frequently find themselves throwing their hands up in the air due to the frustration caused by jurors who refuse to follow the instructions. While it might seem beyond belief that a juror would choose to engage in social media discussion or Internet research after being specifically told not to do so, the reality is that they do.[62] In response to juror behavior, many judges and court systems are developing instructions to provide to jurors to warn them away from social media use. For example, the Judicial Conference Committee on Court Administration and Case Management recently created, "Proposed Model Jury Instructions [on] The Use of Electronic Technology to Conduct Research on or Communicate about a Case."[63] Regardless of the language, it is crucial that judges warn the jury right at the outset of a case of the serious ramifications, and potential punishments, for violating court orders on use of social media during a trial.

Conclusion

Understanding how the public uses social media is important for attorneys, so they can appreciate the types of evidence they might find online to help their cases, and so they can appropriately warn their clients about social media use. Knowing the benefits and risks of social media in terms of networking and marketing can help an attorney grow her firm without harming her hard-earned reputation through improper online activities. Being aware of how judges and juries use social media and how that use might affect a case can help prepare attorneys to respond accordingly.

No doubt social media can be a serious minefield for day-to-day practice and ethical requirements. On the other hand, the substantial benefits available in terms of evidence, research, marketing, and networking cannot be overstated. With the number of people using social media increasing every day, social media will continue to impact the legal profession in every imaginable way, and perhaps some unimaginable ways, too. As a result, it is crucial for attorneys to embrace the technology and determine how they can use it both in their practice of law and in their efforts to grow their client base.

---

[62]Social Media's Clout Worries Legal System (2012). **www.digtriad.com/news/article/245301/ 175/Social-Medias-Clout-Worries-Legal-System**.

[63]Proposed Model Jury Instructions [on] The Use of Electronic Technology to Conduct Research or Communicate about a Case (2012). **www.uscourts.gov/uscourts/News/2012/jury-instructions.pdf**.

CHAPTER TWENTY-EIGHT

Taking Your Firm Paperless

by David J. Bilinsky, BSc, LLB, MBA

Introduction

Tame the wild paper beast and transition to paperless with ease." Well, *at least that is the plan.* However, this lofty and somewhat innocent statement calls to mind this saying: it is hard to remember that your objective was to drain the swamp when you are surrounded by snapping alligators . . . or at least lawyers waving around their paper files saying something about pulling them from their cold dead hands. . .

But the transition to paperless does not have to be a troubled and drama-filled exercise either. You can shift to paperless—indeed many law offices already have—with a minimum of fuss and disruption. With most technology projects—moving to paperless being no exception—the greatest hurdles are not technological at all. They are human-based: getting everyone on board, dealing with the passive-resistors, dealing with those who feel threatened by the introduction of new ways of doing things, *and the like.* As I say in my presentations, it is the carbon-based units that pose the greatest hurdles—not the silicone-based ones.

The hurdles that people present highlight several aspects to going paperless. Certainly part of the process is examining your technology and putting into place a well-thought out strategic technology plan that will ensure that all parts of the system are robust and can handle the load—and the lofty expectations—that will be placed on them.

So in this chapter we—you and I—will focus on how best to manage your shift to paperless and ensure you have considered all aspects of your new paperless office before making the jump. I think it is important to put as much time into planning as you can, as anticipating problems and knowing how to deal with them is much better than having them land on your desk unexpectedly in the midst of the change.

We will also discuss the various procedures you will want to introduce, such as scanning, OCR (optical character recognition), document management, and the emerging mobile and cloud-based practice of law. Security and having good off-site backups are essential. Before you start, you need to evaluate your hardware and software and determine what needs upgrading. Then you need to make all necessary hardware and software upgrades and test the systems before starting to go paperless.

Then . . . taking that first deep breath . . . begin with your most receptive lawyer and legal assistant and have them pilot the system. Having done all your homework, planning, upgrading, and piloting, you will soon see that flying paperless is not half the challenge you thought it might be . . . and soon the whole office will be there.

So let's take that first step towards your future. . .

Transitioning to Paperless: It Isn't (All) about the Technology (Really!)

I have spoken and consulted with many lawyers and law firms who have called about taking their law firm paperless. Certainly lawyers are very anxious about giving up paper and practicing in a paper-*less* world, however, there will probably never be a situation where we fully abandon paper. Yet lawyers and staff express many misapprehensions in going paperless, part of which is rooted in a concern that *somewhere* the regulations of practice *require* firms to keep paper files. There is, of course, no such specific requirement. Information is information, and the medium that it is stored on is largely irrelevant so long as you can meet the requirements of practice (there are exceptions such as original wills and such but even these are changing as new enabling legislation comes into effect).

The typical concerns that I hear can be summed up as follows:

- There is no paper trail.
- Computers can go down.
- No backup exists.
- You can be hacked.
- Data obsolescence is a factor.
- Media degradation is a factor.
- You can lose an e-document.
- There is no structure to the documents on the system.
- Documents can be sent outside the office easily.
- Changes are required to policies, procedures, and work routines.
- Time costs will increase, including costs of running dual systems.
- Jobs may be eliminated or reassigned.
- A lack of training in how to work the new system could lead to a loss of face.
- The firm would face increased costs of transferring a file.
- What about all the transition issues?
- How do we go from here to there?
- What about increased hardware and software costs?
- What do we do with the original documents?

The requirement in any paperless office would be that the office could produce a full and complete record of the client's file (and render this to paper, CD-ROM, DVD, flash drive, or upload it to a cloud service if required). So long as you have a *complete* record of the file (which is organized in a manner that the whole file could be reviewed and produced if necessary), which would necessarily include documenting all transactions and related client instructions, it should not matter on what type of *media* that file is stored. (Indeed, ethics rulings have been consistent in holding that transferring a file electronically is acceptable in many jurisdictions and, in fact, may offer greater utility than printing up and transferring a paper file). The important consideration is that the file is well organized: it is in a common format that if necessary, someone could review, and it reflects the level of documentation expected in a well-run law office. If this is met, I submit that it should not matter on what media—paper or electronic—the file is stored on or transferred from.

Of course, there are also many benefits of going paperless:

♦ You can search the entire network—and file—easily and quickly, particularly compared to paper files.

♦ You can reuse documents easily—and thereby craft a precedent library and build on the knowledge transfer in the firm.

♦ Document management software imposes greater organization compared to a paper-based office, where documents can be left in piles on desks, cabinets, and floors.

♦ The cost of electronic storage is *much* less compared to paper storage.

♦ Paperless offices enable remote access and telecommuting for full- and part-time lawyers and staff.

♦ Paperless offices are greener.

♦ Paperless systems can integrate and share data thereby saving time and money.

♦ Handling files can be faster, cheaper, and easier.

♦ Offices are neater.

♦ The ability to meet new client needs (via SharePoint and other extranet portals for example) increases. At a recent Corporate Counsel meeting, counsel stated that they *preferred* electronic war and closing rooms or portals over e-mailing documents around. You can control access, distribution, and versioning. More importantly, these documents do not travel on unsecured e-mail systems.

♦ Photocopying and printing costs usually decrease.

♦ Courts, land title offices, and other organizations and tribunals are increasingly accepting paperless filings in many jurisdictions.

♦ Forging or altering a properly secured electronic document is more difficult. Moreover, metadata associated with an e-document records a great deal of information about who created it, when it was modified and by whom, and so on, that is not typically accessible in a paper file.

♦ Your clients' systems are electronic, and they expect their lawyers to be able to accept and use e-discovery documents electronically.

♦ Having a paperless office requires the firm to at least consider a file retention and destruction policy that is consistently applied in accordance with The Sedona (Canada or USA) Principles to avoid any suggestion that files were destroyed to eliminate evidence.

♦ The Courts are calling on lawyers to be paperless in court (see Justices Turnball's and Granger's posts to this effect at **www.slaw.ca**).

Of course there are many other reasons for and against going paperless. However, there is no denying that the world is moving in a paperless direction: Barker, Cobb and Karcher, back in a 2008 publication entitled "The Legal Implications of Electronic Document Retention: Changing the Rules", stated that 99 percent of business documents are currently being produced electronically. Now, going against the tide is pointless; lawyers need to adjust to the new reality and embrace the possibilities, examine the risks and benefits in moving to a paperless world. We are headed for a new horizon.

Assessing Your Office Procedures and People: How Suited Are They to Going Paperless?

Moving to paperless means having to examine the workflows in the office and how they should be changed to maximize the investment that you are making in the paperless world. Your handling of paper must change, as must the ways you save, store, find, and archive documents. Furthermore, you need to increase your attention to security, backup procedures, and the like. You definitely want to avoid carrying the costs of dual systems because it provides you with no advantages and only additional costs.

Here are some of the considerations for office policies and procedures.

Document Naming and Filing

A software document management system (DMS), such as Worldox, NetDocuments, or even PCLaw which has a document manager built-in, should ensure that no document is saved to the network without being "profiled," which means the author has told the system the metadata (such as author, client, lawyers, file, date created, version, etc.). The metadata allows the DMS to find a document when anyone in the office searches for it.

However not all firms elect to acquire DMS software, so they have to implement a file- and folder-naming convention that, if followed, will allow the document to be stored in the correct location. And here is the rub: if you have people or even one person who doesn't follow the convention, the system will fall apart. It is this one factor alone that drives firms to a DMS: they need a "traffic cop" who ensures that everyone acts appropriately and doesn't break the rules. The DMS becomes their traffic cop.

Common naming and folder conventions use some variation of date (usually year, month, date in the format of 2014 08 21 for August 21,

2014), nature of the document (LTR for letter, PLD for pleading, etc.) and description of the document (2014 08 21 LTR to john smith on offer to settle, for example). A common folder structure is used for files that separate electronic documents into subfolders in the same way that a "bucket" folder is separated into pleadings, correspondence, research, and so on. Combining a good folder structure with a good file naming convention can go a long way toward electronic file organization provided, of course, that everyone plays by the rules.

Converting Paper Documents to PDF

Paper is not going to go away any time soon. Accordingly, all paperless firms need a policy on how paper documents are to be converted into electronic files and in what format. The most common format is Adobe Acrobat's PDF (or PDF/A for archive) formats. I know that many firms like the PDF/A format as it is an ISO standard, essentially ensuring that the files can be opened and read years into the future. However, I dislike how PDF/A removes data from the document such as images and the like. Personally I prefer to use PDF and keep all the data in the document and hope for the best when it comes to being able to open and read documents into the foreseeable future.

Typically firms go one of two routes when handling paper in a paperless firm. Either they have tasked specific people with the job of taking all incoming paper and scanning it (centralized scanning on a large networked scanner/printer), or it is left to each person in the firm (distributed scanning on smaller scanners). There are advantages and disadvantages to both methods.

Centralized scanning ensures that documents are handled in a business-like and consistent manner, and it provides a degree of quality control that the scans were done correctly. For example, scans should always be dual layer, incorporating the image of the document along with OCR or of the text in the image, which allows the computer to search the words in the document. Distributed scanning means that you have smaller scanners scattered across the office and that everyone is responsible for ensuring that the scans were done correctly.

Document Retention

You will also need a policy for how long to keep the original documents before shredding. In one firm that went paperless, a legal secretary confessed to the principal of the firm that she had taken home and stored every single document for the last three years, as she was convinced the system would fail and she would have to recreate all the files. Her basement became stuffed with documents and the originals were never needed. Typically three to six months should be sufficient time to catch any scanning errors before the documents are shredded.

Of course you will need a storage policy for documents that should never be shredded such as original wills, government documents, and so on. These can be scanned (of course!), but the originals need to be retained for other purposes.

Backups and Archives

If you put all your eggs in one electronic basket, there is a consequential rule that you should watch that basket very, very carefully. Accordingly, it is prudent to make copies of your electronic data and ensure that this data is stored in at least two locations: one on a hardened hard drive (such as the ioSafe line of hard drives that are designed to withstand fire, flood, temperatures, immersion, and so on, for extended periods of time) and the other on a cloud storage system.

One firm that the writer has spoken to was hit with the Cyberlocker malware. This application encrypts everything it can find on your network and demands a ransom to be paid. Otherwise it disappears, taking the decryption algorithm with it and leaving your data useless. Fortunately their cloud backup, which only backed up on a schedule and not continually, was left untouched by the malware and the firm was able restore the data without paying the ransom.

It is important that you have a multiple-layer, redundant backup system. Don't depend on a sole backup. If that backup fails, you are left totally vulnerable. And test your backup system to ensure that it is operating properly in the event you need it so you can restore your data.

The benefit of having a local hardened hard drive is that you can restore your data quickly in the event of a loss. Cloud backups, while wonderful for preserving your data in a safe location, will take considerable time to restore onto your network.

File Retention and Destruction

You should check with your local bar association and insurer to see what requirements and recommendations they have for retention and eventual destruction of closed files. Certainly follow their guidelines when setting up your retention and destruction policies. You should also ensure that you follow these policies to be able to demonstrate that you destroyed data pursuant to a written office policy that was consistently and clearly followed to avoid any allegations of spoliation of data.

Knowledge Management

The ability to start developing a consistent set of precedents, library of research memos, and other resources is one of the benefits of a paperless office. Give some thought to how you can take documents from files and convert them to office precedents by removing names and other identifying information. Once you start along this path you will quickly see how you can add articles, books, and other resources to create your own library that supports your area(s) of practice.

Begin with the End in Mind: Defining the Goals

Stephen Covey, the esteemed author of *The 7 Habits of Highly Effective People* has stated that you should "begin with the end in mind." So how do you build your plan to take yourself paperless? What are the goals of the move to paperless? Here are some of the components to consider:

1. Decide on what your paperless office will look and feel like. Will you aim to eliminate paper as much as possible? Will everyone be working on workstations with dual monitors and using a central document repository (with a document management system) that has remote access capability and client portals? By creating as many written goals as possible, you can make the transition "real" and decide how to stage the transition to paperless over time.

2. Commit to going paperless. Call your staff to a meeting and explain the advantages for each of them individually and for the group. Fully involve them in the process and invite them to raise any concerns now while you are at a planning stage. Ask for their support and commitment to a successful transition.

3. Involve your IT support as early as possible. They will have to check your existing computer hardware including your server, backup and RAID systems to make sure they can handle the increased load from all paperless applications (hardware and software requirements). They will have to ensure that your backup system is reliable and includes storage off-site). They will need to make sure the software and hardware will run quickly and effectively, a process that requires checking such aspects as whether your security is sufficient and whether the bandwidth from your Internet connection is adequate. You don't want people to become frustrated waiting to get online.

4. Analyze your current and future needs. Think about what you're likely to need in the future as your business grows as well as what you need now. Think about which documents need to be accessed often or quickly, which may need extra security or encryption, and which could be weeded out after a certain time. After all, you don't want to be storing all documents **forever** but you do have requirements for document storage and retention times from your ethics regulator or insurer (or both).

5. Develop a paperless transition plan and a timetable. The timetable should be tight enough to keep everyone in line but not so tight so that it doesn't allow for reasonable adjustments and setbacks. Plan to be flexible! Writing down the plan allows for everyone to read, think about, and provide feedback on the process, the goals, and the methods. You wish to make this as painless as possible for everyone. Listening to their feedback will make everyone feel part of the process and like they have a part in the plan.

6. Start small. Use a single lawyer and legal assistant to start. Learn from the pilot project so you can address any problems before broadening your scope. It is easy to correct small things at the pilot stage before they become much bigger things in a firm-wide rollout.

7. Research. Thoroughly investigate the available tools to help you—document management systems, electronic faxing, scanners, data backup systems, security systems, document conversion companies, process consultants, storage formats, storage devices, remote access devices, and so on. Knowledgeable consultants can provide more help than you might imagine.

8. Budget. No exceptions! Select your needs in advance—hardware, software, training and installation, consultants—and arrange to incorporate these into your budget and into your business plans. You may have to spread things out a bit to accommodate everything in the budget. For software, consider what will fit with your needs, including ease of use and implementation, cost, and integration with your existing systems. And by all means, don't neglect backup needs.

9. Do a small test project. Make any needed changes and then move to the transition into the rest of the practice, using your early adopters as change agents.

10. Develop a plan for ongoing practice-wide use. Include a document storage plan with specific guidelines for employees or clients with specific needs.

11. Do a celebration followed by a post-mortem. Learn from the experience!

A Bit about the Hardware That You Will Need

When there was no alternative to paper, the costs of building and maintaining a paper-based filing system were simply taken for granted. Rows of filing cabinets along with physical storage, photocopiers, and fax machines all had to be purchased and maintained and took up (expensive) rented floor space. Associated filing clerks also had to be hired. The environmental effects of having to manufacture all that paper had a cost as well, from deforestation to consumption of fossil fuels and electricity to taking up space in landfills for unwanted documents.

Today according to IBM (**www.ibm.com**), as of 2012, every day 2.5 exabytes (2.5×10^{18}) of data are created. One exabyte is 1 billion gigabytes. To put this in perspective, according to Wikipedia: "Earlier studies from the University of California, Berkeley, estimated that by the end of 1999, the sum of human-produced information (including all audio, video recordings, and text/books) was about 12 exabytes of data.[1]

With that volume of information being created electronically, it is apparent that new ways of storing, searching, sharing, annotating, signing, retrieving, and eventually destroying information had to be found. In the context of a law office, we will be increasingly under pressure to deal with all kinds of electronic records, such as for litigation discovery requirements.

So with this as background, what software and hardware do we need to implement a paperless office?

Hardware

While it is always fortunate when you discover that an office's hardware infrastructure is sufficient to implement a paperless plan, in most cases that is not the case. If you host your own servers and network switches,

---

[1](Juan Enriquez. "The Data That Defines Us." *CIO Magazine*, Fall–Winter 2003. Retrieved 2006-07-19).

chances are that they will require an upgrade to handle the increased load that a paperless office will place on them. If you have implemented a hosted office, where you use remote file servers that are on a third-party's platform, you may need to increase your storage and Internet bandwidth capacity to handle the load.

Servers

You will need, at a minimum, a dedicated server running up-to-date server software (such as a Windows Server operating system or a Mac server if you are in an Apple environment). With a dedicated server, all your files can be kept and indexed in one place, and all your documents can be organized efficiently. A server can be configured to manage which users can access what resources. It can handle your document management system as well as host your website, e-mail, print server software, databases, and accounting software, as well as allow remote access and more.

According to *PCMagazine*, these were the top-rated servers as of April 2014:

- HP ProLiant MicroServer Gen8
- HP Proliant DL380p Gen8 Server
- Dell PowerEdge R420
- Dell PowerEdge T620
- Dell PowerEdge T110 II
- Dell PowerEdge R515
- Lenovo ThinkServer TS200v
- Apple Mac mini with Snow Leopard Server
- Asus Server TS500-E6/P4
- HP Proliant ML330 G6
- Apple Xserve
- HP ProLiant DL380 G5
- Silex SecurePrint
- DiskSites FilePort DS-100, DiskSites FileController DS-100
- Aberdeen Stonehaven A261S

What should you look for when purchasing a server?

- **Scalability/Price:** Needless to say, you get what you pay for. A lower-end server may be fine for current needs, but if your needs grow because you add additional people or your volume of information grows, then you may exceed the storage capacity of the server, which is supposed to store all documents on your system. Accordingly, look for a server that can have additional drives installed, and these drives should have fault-tolerance built in. (As a reminder, RAID, or redundant array of independent disks is the measure of fault tolerance. If one drive fails, the other drives have copies of the data on the failed drive and can take over handling the load until you replace the failed drive.) If possible, choose a server that has at least a RAID 5, or even better, a RAID 6, which has tolerance for up to two failed drives.

♦ **Degree of Use:** Servers typically come in different configurations. Try to anticipate the volume of transactions that you will process in any day and purchase a server that can easily handle that volume so you avoid delays in waiting for information. Your IT person should be able to assist you with deciding which configuration would be best for you.

♦ **Scalability:** Look for the ability to add memory upgrades and hard drives. You also want a server with a processor that can handle an increased load.

♦ **Virtualization:** Many organizations have moved to running virtual machines housed in one physical server. This approach has many advantages, not the least of which are energy savings, smaller data centers, almost instant capacity increases, increased up-time, improved disaster recovery, isolated applications, the ability to run legacy applications, and perhaps most important, to prepare your office to move data and applications into the Cloud.

♦ **IT Support:** If you have an experienced IT person to manage your network, great. But if you largely have to go it alone, then at least get a server that is easy to administer.

♦ **Match the Server to Your Environment:** If you run Windows machines, then acquire a Windows server and software. Similarly with Macs. Make life easy for yourself.

♦ **Form Factor:** If at all possible, look for an expandable, rack-mounted server with a large number of drive bays. Consider airflow, temperature, noise level, and fan quality (overheating is a common factor in crashes).

♦ **Memory:** Again, the ability to add memory (RAM) is important as needs increase.

♦ **Network Speed:** You will need multiple ports on the server as well as a GigE network switch. The slower your network, the more time spent waiting. Accordingly, have a network switch that supports GigE speeds connect all your devices.

+ **Operating System:** Is it included in the price of the server? Is it a standard server system? Look for an up-to-date Windows or Mac operating system.

+ **Power:** You will need an uninterruptable power supply (UPS) that will allow for the orderly shut-down of your system in the event of a power failure to avoid data loss and corruption.

+ **Drives:** Your server should have a drive—CD, DVD, Blu-ray—to allow you to install software.

Hard Drive Storage

Today you can have solid-state storage or traditional hard-drives. Traditional hard drives have higher capacity, but solid-state drives are typically much faster. Whichever media you choose, buy as much as you can afford; you will not regret having large storage capacity!

Scanners

There are two camps when it comes to scanners. One or more scanners are necessary to take paper documents and transform them into electronic documents that can be brought into MS Word or converted to PDF formats (preferably both). On one hand, some firms that have one large networked printer-scanner with a good sheet feeder than can handle large print and scan jobs. Other firms have gone to small individual scanners such as the Fujitsu Scansnap iX1500s or the older S1500s that are scattered around the office. Which route you go depends on the size of your office, the volume of paper that you will need to scan, whether you will have dedicated staff for scanning, how your office is laid out (Will it be easy to find a scanner or will it involve a trek?). The latest iX1500s can work with both Macs and PCs and have some significant improvements, such as WIFi scanning, over prior versions. They also come bundled with software, such as Adobe X Standard for PCs, that makes them very cost effective. Here are the features to look for:

+ **Reliability** (The Fujitsu's reputation is awesome).

+ **Sheet feeder v. flatbed** Flatbed scanners can be slower but can take various-sized documents.

+ **Size of originals** (Legal-sized documents as well as business cards).

+ **Output** Ideally you want to directly select OCR'd PDF format (described previously).

- **TWAIN compliance** With this feature you can open a scanned document in any software application that supports TWAIN. If the scanner is not TWAIN compliant, you may have to save the document separately before opening it in your application of choice (Personally I have never really found this to be a barrier, but some feel otherwise).

- **Resolution** Low resolution may mean you can't OCR the document, or it could result in increased OCR errors. I would use a minimum of 300 dots (black and white) per inch.

- **Black-and-White and Color** In most cases black and white is fine, but you may want to scan some documents in color to preserve the ability to differentiate data that may be in different color inks that would be lost in black and white.

- **Wireless Connectivity** (very convenient).

- **Full duplex scanning** (both sides at the same time).

- **Size**

- **Weight**

- **Ethernet port** (for connecting it to the network).

Backup Systems

For anyone who has faced the "blue screen of death" or, in haiku, you know that

A crash reduces
your expensive computer
to a simple stone.

You know the angst and frustration caused by data loss. Moreover, the effects can be far-reaching: many businesses that have been hit by environmental calamities, fires, and even terrorist activities have failed if they could not resurrect their lost data.

Accordingly it is important that you match your expensive computer system with a good and robust backup system that will preserve your data and allow you to be up and running as quickly as possible. Fortunately electronic data can be backed up and stored in multiple locations easily once the system is configured and set up. Contrast that with an office with paper files in a single location: if it is hit by fire or flood, the files would be destroyed with no backups.

I recommend that you backup your system to a rugged external hard drive that is resistant to fire and flood (such as the ioSafe SoloPro or for larger firms, their NAS storage devices) as well as to a cloud-based back up service. Your rugged hard drive can be used to restore your network quickly, provided that the hard drive survives (which there is a good chance that it will). However, if the calamity is such that your entire office is destroyed, then the cloud-based backup will be your fail-safe method of preserving your data: cheap insurance vs. going out of business or even facing a malpractice claim.

Monitors

Like scanners, there are two camps when it comes to monitors in a paperless office. The benefits of having two (or even more) monitors on your desk are easily demonstrated. You can have your reference information on one screen (or on one half of a very large screen) while you craft documents on another. Personally I always prefer to work on two large monitors as I find the time saved in not having to repeatedly open windows adds up quickly.

Consulting with an ergonomic consultant can help you position your monitors and in general design workspaces that are comfortable as well as functional (the writer has done this and I can say it was well worth it!). Improper monitor placement can lead to neck, shoulder, and back issues.

Flat panel displays are now the current state of the art. Other features to look for in a good monitor:

- **Definition:** While most people think that higher resolution is a good thing, it may not be depending on the age of your eyes since increasing the resolution, while it makes thing sharper, also makes things smaller. Most flat panel displays have a recommended resolution. In Windows, click on **Start** > **Control Panel** > **Appearance and Personalization** > **Adjust Screen Resolution**, and the recommended display resolution should be shown. On a Mac, click **System Preferences** > **Displays** and select **Resolution: Best for Display**. Microsoft has a listing of recommended resolution based on monitor size at: **http://windows.microsoft.com/en-ca/windows/getting-best-display-monitor#getting-best-display-monitor=windows-7**.

- **Dot Pitch:** This is the spacing between different pixels on the monitor. It can range from .30mm to .15mm. Generally speaking the smaller the distance, the better.

- **Brightness and Contrast:** Most monitors have their own controls to set the contrast and brightness of the displays. Windows has a feature called Adaptive Brightness that will adjust the monitor display if your computer has a light sensor installed and enabled. Check for this by going to **Power Options** in **System and Security Settings** and enabling **Adaptive Brightness**. Apple computers have a setting under **Displays** in **System Preferences** that allows the automatic adjustment of brightness. You can adjust contrast on external displays if you find that helps. Windows has a feature called ClearType that makes fonts easier to read and this should be turned on and adjusted to your monitor to ease your eyes.

♦ **Size:** Monitors now come in sizes up to 82 inches (NEC LCD8205 for $49,999.00)! Accordingly you should be able to find a monitor to match your space and size requirements.

♦ **Ports:** Look for multiple ports to match those on your computer. Common formats are VGA, DVI and HDMI. You don't want to end up with a monitor that will only accept a DVI cable when your computer only has a VGA port.

♦ **Warranty and reviews:** Check both the applicable warranty that comes with the display (two to three years is good) as well as online reviews from actual users. Common problems to watch for are the backlight failing as well as multiple pixel defects. Is there a restocking fee if you return the unit?

A Bit about the Software That You Will Need

Document Management Considerations

There is much discussion about e-document formats (the archival format Adobe Acrobat PDF/A, in particular), the media on which the electronic documents are to be stored (Is it local, backed up onto a remote device, or on the cloud?), scanners, remote access, and the like. Some firms choose to use only electronic storage for their closed files, eliminating the expensive cost of storing paper files for years, while others prefer to have all open and closed files in electronic form. Still other firms are concerned about cultural issues around going paperless and the change management process that would entail.

But lost in this discussion is a much more basic issue—an issue fundamental to taking a law firm paperless and an issue that is often overlooked. In the paper world, there are file folders and filing cabinets, both of which help keep the documents organized. The file folder has its brads (places to attach correspondence, pleadings, and so on, in date order), and the filing cabinet keeps the file folders organized.

When a law firm goes paperless, however, there typically isn't the appreciation for the electronic equivalent of the file folder and filing cabinet. Records, which could be pleadings, correspondence, e-mails, and so on, are usually found in numerous different places on the network. E-mails may be stored in Outlook folders, while documents, such as pleadings, research memos, and correspondence, may be saved in various Windows folders. Worse yet, Outlook stores sent e-mails in "Sent Items" while incoming e-mails are typically filed in other folders.

Unfortunately, each software application an office uses stores its data in different folders, and they are scattered across the network. As the number of electronic files grows, the ability to gather all these disparate bits of information together into a "client file" gets harder and harder. With paper files, the firm would typically print out all this information and store it in the file folder. In that situation, the way in which each application and user names and stores the records on the network and hard drives is largely irrelevant. But as the firm moves to a paperless office, the disorganized nature of electronic record-keeping starts to become a problem. It is now harder to reproduce "the file" and the collection of folders that would otherwise be found in the steel filing cabinet.

Some firms use indexing and desktop search engines, such as Windows Search, X1, or Copernic, to find documents on the network, but this is not a workable equivalent to a good document management application. Other firms claim that their "standardized file-naming and storage convention" is good enough. Unfortunately, this convention only works as long as everyone, at all times, complies. Once someone decides "just this time" to not follow the convention, the system starts to break down. (The second law of thermodynamics basically says that any system, over time, goes from an organized to a disorganized state without the continual addition of energy to keep it organized—otherwise known as *entropy*.)

So what should a firm do? The solution is document management software. This software is the equivalent of the steel filing cabinet, organizing all "records"—be they documents, e-mails, pleadings, or whatever—into the electronic equivalent of the paper folder. Document management software keeps each folder distinct from the others, offering the organizational ability of the filing cabinet.

With document management software, a document must be "profiled" before it can be saved on the network. Profiling entails keying in some information called metadata about the document: nature, author, form (pleading, e-mail, etc.), client, matter, and more. Metadata allows the document management software to know how to categorize the document properly. E-mails, pleadings, correspondence, memos, and so on, are all organized by client, matter, lawyer, and date created.

Document management software also allows searching (including Boolean searches) by keyword, type of document, client name, and other criteria. It offers version control, tracking and audit (who created what version), and other activities around document creation, modification, and the like. Best of all, it offers the ability to draw together in one place on the network all the disparate records that would otherwise be affixed to the brad of a paper file. Remote access is enabled, and most programs allow "briefcasing" or mirroring the documents on a laptop with synchronization once you reconnect to the network.

Entropy is avoided since the user must profile the document *before* it can be saved. This is how the document management software achieves its goal: it imposes order on chaos.

By making a document management system the foundation of your paperless office, you can achieve the degree of rigor, organization, and systemization that will allow you to develop your business even as people change and clients come and go. Otherwise, finding a document on the network is like looking for a needle in a haystack. Here's what to look for in a good DMS system:

♦ First, determine if the application will work well with your existing software and hardware. Particularly with a DMS you will want to ensure that it works easily with your existing scanners, e-mail system, server, and any other software that you use in the office.

♦ Second, it should be easy to use. A DMS that is complicated with a search feature that is difficult to understand will not be well-liked in the office.

♦ Third, it should be able to work with PDF files easily.

♦ Fourth, it should facilitate mobile devices, such as iPads, smartphones and laptops, so you can have staff work outside of the office easily.

♦ Fifth, it is important that it supports a client extranet. E-mail is dying and insecure. A secure client portal or extranet allows the firm and the client to exchange documents securely and privately without the need to use e-mail.

Think about the Role of Cloud-Based Services

Several tools for helping you consider cloud-based services are available. The Law Society of British Columbia released a report and a checklist on cloud computing for lawyers. The cloud-computing due diligence guidelines are at **www.lawsociety.bc.ca/docs/practice/resources/guidelines-cloud.pdf**, and the cloud computing checklist is at **www.lawsociety.bc.ca/docs/practice/resources/checklist-cloud.pdf**. Ethical decisions and guidance from the ABA and numerous bar associations can be found at **www.americanbar.org/groups/departments_offices/legal_technology_resources/resources/charts_fyis/cloud-ethics-chart.html**. Before you move to the cloud, research what may be published in your jurisdiction and what steps you have to take before you jump into the cloud.

The cloud offers many benefits, but they have to be balanced against possible privacy, security, ethical, and client concerns. There is no right answer; rather each firm has to determine the appropriate protections and such (for example, using encryption with cloud applications like Dropbox) to meet their and their client's needs.

Think about Mobile Computing, Remote Access, and Apps

Mobile computing and apps are dealt with in a different chapter in this book. However, it is worth noting that the mobile practice of law does go hand-in-glove with the paperless practice of law since all your office files are already in digital form. You need to consider how to grant access to your staff and whether access is through smart phones, laptops, tablets, or other devices. Consider the policies that you should you put into place (such as using only secure connections and not insecure public Wi-Fi hotspots) and how you will enforce them.

There are any number of applications for the iPhone, Android, and BlackBerry smartphones (such as DocsToGo) that allow you to read, annotate, and in some cases, work on documents on the road. With Microsoft Office now available for the iPad along with Office 365 for virtually any device that hosts a browser, the ability to work remotely has never been better. The ability to work remotely on virtually any device wherever you can access an Internet connection is definitely one of the strongest reasons for fully implementing the paperless office.

Setting New Business Processes to Align with Your Goals

There is an expression tossed around in IT circles about "paving the cow paths." AgileConnection's web site states:

> *In the IT world, "paving cow paths" means automating a business process as is, without thinking too much about whether or not that process is effective or efficient. Often business process automation initiatives require figuring out entirely new ways of doing business processes—impossible prior to automation (for example, work flow automation and digital image processing)—defining more effective and efficient process highways.*

If you are making the transition to paperless, you need to give some thought to how you can rework your business processes to make them more efficient and effective. For example, consider centralized conversion of paper documents to PDF. If you have a small group involved in conversions, you ensure that all documents are converted to PDF quickly and consistently. You are not waiting for some people to take the piles of papers on their desks and bring them into the DMS system, and you avoid the tensions and delays as people wonder when the laggards in the office are going to "get with the program."

Don't just pave your cowpaths. Think about how you can make your systems better and faster by eliminating outdated ways of working so you can take advantage of the new technologies in the office.

How Will You Transition to Paperless?

There are two recognized ways of bringing the existing paper files into the paperless system. One could be called the brute force method; the other could be called the accretion method. Which one you adopt depends on the size of your office and the willingness of your staff to pitch in and do the conversion all at once.

The brute force method typically involves a long weekend and as many scanners as possible. On Friday the office closes; from that point onward everyone's sole task is to take every open file and scan and OCR the contents and bring them into the DMS system. You can see that you need a dedicated team to throw all their effort at the conversion of the files, so when you open again on Monday morning, every file is in paper-less form.

With the accretion method, the first time you need to touch a file on or after the stated conversion date, you stop everything and scan and OCR the contents to bring it into the DMS. In this approach, the most active files are brought in first—with the least active files being last. The disadvantage is that the time to convert files is much longer.

Which approach you take all depends on the culture of the firm, the commitment of your staff to take a long weekend for work purposes and the ability of everyone to pitch in.

Getting Buy-In from Your Team Members: Leading the Change

Let's discuss the change management aspects of going paperless.

Awareness about the Nature of Change

Before you start, think about and come to an understanding of the scope or magnitude of this change to paperless. How many people, structures, systems, and so on will be impacted by the introduction of change? Will people in the firm regard this change as a voluntary one or not? How do you deal with people who feel that this change is being thrust upon them rather than change being led from within? Notice that in most cases, law firms deal with change from outside the organization—now, however, you are being a catalyst of change from within, and you need to make your staff and lawyers appreciate that this will result in a better and more efficient and effective organization once the change is implemented.

The Three Levels of Change

There are three levels of change that you will deal with: procedural, structural, and cultural. What are the implications of each in your change to paperless? Procedural change refers to the rules or policies around handling, storing, searching, and retrieving documents. Structural change means that the office will no longer look or feel the same; paper will disappear, documents will be scanned and stored, and files will be only electronic. With cultural change, people will have to adapt to living and working in a paper-less world, and new entrants will have to learn and become part of the new system.

Management of Change

The old expression states that you never get a second chance to make a first impression. Therefore, it is vitally important to give considerable thought to the plans for introducing the change and for exposing people and organizations to the new system. Identify the roadblocks and strategies to cope with them well ahead of time. Develop tactics to deal with issues before they appear. Bring people into the process early on and let them shape the eventual systems, policies, and procedures. Listen to their concerns and respond accordingly.

Focus on Who Matters Most

There will always be three groupings of people and organizations when change is involved:

- ◆ Enthusiasts, who recognize the benefits of the new system and line up to help spread and support the new system
- ◆ Backbones, the great majority of people and organizations who are solid performers and who will support the change
- ◆ Resisters, those who oppose change either due to a perceived loss of power, status, money, or other attribute or who simply do not wish to expend the energy to change

Obviously you need as many people in the first two camps and as few in the last one as possible. You may have some hard decisions to make; if someone who stands in the way of the change consistently opposes you, you may have to decide if their future may lie outside of the firm.

Celebrate the Successes

Every project has its milestones, setbacks, and successes. By positively communicating your successes, you help keep the momentum going and the change process positive. You also need to have strategies in place to deal with the setbacks in order to avoid having your project derailed by the naysayers.

Learning from Your Experience and Continuing to Improve Your Systems

A learning organization is one that has adopted a culture of continually evaluating and learning from their change processes. Adopting the paperless practice of law is a perfect time to implement learning concepts into the firm. As each step is achieved in a change process, ask your teams: "What went right? What went wrong? How can we do this better?" Keep a record of what you have learned and draw on that each time you need to implement a change in the firm.

When you recognize that leading, dealing with, and managing change is one of the most important skills that any person or organization can develop, then you have taken the first step towards implementing a learning—or change management—culture in your organization. Seek to build on this and instill it into the culture of your firm. You and your law firm will be stronger, more adept, and have a greater capacity to absorb the changes that are thrust upon it as a result.

Conclusion

OK, you have now read all the advice that I can give you on going paperless. As you stare over the abyss, recall that anticipation is almost always worse than reality. The process can be managed through properly planning, anticipating, executing, adjusting, and learning. Don't forget involving everyone in the project at the start—and celebrating with them at the end! The firms that have gone paperless all say the same thing: it is cost-effective, it enables remote work and greater work-life balance, it allows you to carry your documents with you and access them on multiple remote devices wherever you may be. You can take your case to court and present it with ease. Moving to e-filing in government registries and tribunals is eased. It is easier—and cheaper—to store documents electronically than on paper.

So take a deep breath . . . and take that first step.

CHAPTER TWENTY-NINE

Tomorrow in Legal Tech

Technology is supposed to make our lives easier, allowing us to do things more quickly and efficiently. But too often it seems to make things harder, leaving us with fifty-button remote controls, digital cameras with hundreds of mysterious features and book-length manuals, and cars with dashboard systems worthy of the space shuttle.

—James Surowiecki, columnist for The New Yorker

The first rule of any technology used in a business is that automation applied to an efficient operation will magnify the efficiency. The second is that automation applied to an inefficient operation will magnify the inefficiency.

—Bill Gates

Introduction

Each year, I remind readers that this chapter belongs to me (Sharon). I have no gift for the technological details that Mike and John excel at. But my eyes are always fixed intently on the horizon of legal tech—as in the real world, it isn't possible to see more than about three miles out. Even on the one-hundred-foot tower of imagination, we can see no further than approximately twelve miles. Yes, I looked all that up online. And your eyes can go bleary staring at a horizon that is ever shifting.

As Mr. Surowiecki notes, the number of possibilities we have is so huge that we are capable of using only a few. We are overwhelmed by our technology—certainly lawyers say this constantly. This book is in part a testament to how confusing and crowded the legal tech world has become. Beset on all sides by vendors hawking their wares, lawyers are often bemused and perplexed. There are too many possibilities, too many services and products to choose from. And that is why you will not find every technology in this book—not even close. You'll just see what we have found to be best of breed and affordable for what is delivered.

As for the second quote, thank you, Mr. Gates. You have articulated beautifully what we see so often. Some firms are using all kinds of technology, but in an anarchic way. Not everyone has to participate in case management systems. Partners get non-standard technology (and everything else they demand). Let's not even talk about the Bring Your Own Device (BYOD) madness that has infiltrated so many firms. It is a disease in and of itself to think that bringing your own devices or your own networks is a good idea. *Buy* them whatever mobile device you want them to use, have the firm own and control it, and ban the use of unauthorized devices on the network. We are seeing this policy more and more, and we predict that it will continue as cybersecurity concerns continue to dominate the headlines and the thoughts of managing partners.

But so far, the BYOD folks have been prevailing. Hence our name for BYOD—Bring Your Own Disaster.

Legal Technology Audits (LTAs)
What big firm does not have lots of technology? And yet, junior associates, who you would expect to have some technology experience just by virtue of their age, failed the legal technology audit devised by KIA Motor's counsel, Casey Flaherty. The audit involved four mock assignments that a law firm associate had to complete using standard software (e.g., Word, Excel, and Acrobat). Done efficiently, the first assignment should have taken less than twenty minutes. Done inefficiently (not using the software correctly), it would take more than five hours to complete.

Not a single tested associate came anywhere close to the twenty-minute mark on the first assignment. They approached the assignment inefficiently, in ways that required five to fifteen times longer than necessary. At $200 to $400 per associate hour, that's one heck of a price to pay for inefficiency.

The tested associates came from different firms. Some were auditioning for work and failed to get it. Others were long-time outside counsel, and their firms agreed to rate reductions (5 percent) after their associates failed the audit with a proviso that the rate would be restored if they subsequently passed an audit.

So what can't associates do? They can't use Excel's Sort and Filter features; instead they needed to go line by line to take a provided spreadsheet and generate discrete lists of exhibits associated with witnesses on specific topics. They cannot manipulate PDFs. They cannot batch search PDFs.

We have even seen associates, confronted with a Word document and told to PDF it, send it to a printer and then scan the document manually—apparently completely unaware of the Save as PDF option.

I mentioned last year that Mr. Flaherty was working with the Suffolk University School of Law's Professor Andy Perlman to automate the audit so it can be done online rather than in person as KIA's original audit was. So now I am happy to say that the audit was "open for business" in the fall of 2014.

Law firms and similar service providers are charged $250 per user for a one-year subscription. The LTA Tutorial is an additional $150 per user. In-house counsel and government entities are charged $25 per test taker for a one-year subscription to the LTA, but the LTA is free for the judiciary.

Score requests are free. But it looks to me as though anyone who registers you to take the test can then see your score. This could be a real knuckle-biter for those lawyers who are inept with technology.

I can't see most senior partners lining up to take the audit or many general counsels that would have the *cojones* to ask them to. But for the younger generation, LTA may become a bridge that must be crossed to obtain professional advancement, especially in larger firms and corporations. In the next year, it will be interesting to see how widely used the audit is, what improvements in law firm efficiency are achieved, and the consequences of failing the audit. Stay tuned.

Giving CLE Credit to Law Practice Topics

Everyone is getting on the bandwagon when it comes to encouraging lawyers to learn more about law practice issues, specifically technology. On August 12, 2014, the ABA House of Delegates adopted the following Resolution:

> "RESOLVED, *That the American Bar Association urges all state and territorial continuing legal education accrediting agencies to approve law practice skills programs and training, including the use of technology, law practice management and client relations for mandatory continuing legal education requirements and to not restrict the maximum number of credit hours that can be earned for such programs and training.*

> FURTHER RESOLVED, *That the American Bar Association encourages all state and territorial continuing legal education accrediting agencies to partner with law schools, bar associations and law student and young lawyer organizations to offer law practice skills programs and training to students and recent graduates.*

FURTHER RESOLVED, *That the Standing Committee on Continuing Legal Education is encouraged to consider amendments to the ABA Model Rule for Continuing Legal Education to effectuate the purposes of this Resolution, including provisions for distance learning through technology, and such other issues as deemed appropriate by the Committee."*

Needless to say, I was delighted to see this resolution pass and hope that state bars will take it to heart. We have struggled for two decades to get state bars to understand the importance of offering law practice education—and giving it full credit, including ethics credit where warranted. It took years to get our own state of Virginia to give ethics credit to cybersecurity sessions whose focus is to teach lawyers how to comply with Rule 1.1 (Competence) and Rule 1.6 (Confidentiality of Information).

Kudos to the House of Delegates for passing the Resolution, and here's hoping that everyone will spread the gospel to the state bars. I do predict resistance—largely based on the "we've always handled it this way" argument.

Disruptive Innovation

As regular readers know, I have long preached that lawyers must embrace technology. I know many attorneys who have retired or will retire shortly because they cannot bridge the gap beyond law as it was once practiced and as it is practiced today. The raw choice is that lawyers must choose between adaption and extinction. They will no doubt choose the former en masse, but reluctantly. The slower lawyers are to adapt to the digital age, the harder it may be for them to survive as events overtake them.

Not everyone agrees with your oracle. In fact, an interesting article was written in 2014 by Neil Squilante, founder and publisher of *TechnoLawyer*, expressing the belief that lawyers have nothing to fear from disruptive innovation.

Neil talks about three types of disruption: low end, new market, and professional services. He believes that none of them are a threat to lawyers. I don't entirely agree with Neil, but then the fun is in having the conversation. One of the problems with disruptive innovation is that it is happening faster and faster, and much of it involves technology. As I mentioned before, I know many lawyers who have retired or left the practice of law to avoid the impact of the digital era.

Over a companionable glass of wine, I would argue with Neil about the impact of companies like LegalZoom. What LegalZoom offers is precisely the sort of work offered by solo and small firm lawyers—not all of it to be sure—but a considerable amount. And I should know. I have been a solo practitioner for more than thirty-five years. These days, no matter how much clients like their lawyers, they are intent on saving money. Legal-Zoom and its brethren are an attractive alternative to most lawyers' legal fees for garden-variety legal matters.

Neil talks about protective regulations such as rules against non-lawyer ownership of law firms and the unauthorized practice of law (UPL). I think most people would argue that non-lawyer ownership of law firms has a limited life—even Virginia is now studying this issue—and we certainly are not alone. As for UPL, most states have given up the battle against people who are now doing work once reserved for lawyers, including LegalZoom, accountants, and so on. They are more concerned with notario fraud (people who are holding themselves out to be lawyers when they are not), disbarred lawyers who continue to practice, and so on.

Even with respect to things like predictive coding, I see a continuing loss of jobs. Some lawyers, especially just out of law school, are eking out a meager living by doing document review without any job security or benefits. To my shock, as I was writing this chapter, I read about an ad spotted in South Carolina advertising for a contract document reviewer at $8 per hour. The document reviewer who had read the ad was, to say the least, disheartened.

While predictive coding will not take out the higher-end lawyers, I think it will cut a broad swath through the ranks of those doing contract document review. As the machines become smarter, fewer humans will be required. The machines, in the end, will be cheaper and more accurate. For the sake of the humans, it pains me to say that, but it is true.

The young lawyers are pretty well scared without any of the scaremongering that Neil references in his article. In my year as the Virginia State Bar President, I visited a number of law schools, asking students what field of law they wanted to practice in. All I heard in return, with more than a touch of desperation, was "I just want a job."

At the 2014 House of Delegates meeting we were shown a "Be the Change" video, which you can view here: **http://www.americanbar.org/groups/ leadership/office of the president/legal access jobs corps.html/**. Fifty years ago, we had 294,372 lawyers. Now we have 1,268,001 lawyers, a 431% increase. In the same period, the population increased by only 74 percent. It is telling that in 2012, only 56 percet of law graduates found long-term legal jobs after graduation.

Law schools are cutting back enrollment and letting faculty members go. It's not a pretty picture out there. If law schools will shift to having third-year law students in clinics where they serve the poor, and other attorneys work to help the underserved, we will narrow but not close the gap. And, though it sounds harsh, one reason law schools have attracted students is because they hope to make a very good living by practicing law. The "Golden Age of Law" has run its course. Having too many lawyers is part of the problem, and the rise of the machines is another. Long term, we need to graduate fewer lawyers to accommodate a changing job market.

Passwords—Not Dead Yet

There was some surprising news about passwords in 2014. While I reported in last year's edition on the imminent death of passwords, the truth is that the death does not entirely appear to be "imminent."

While two-factor authentication, hardware-based tokens, biometrics, and other security measures are certainly the roadmap for the future, the truth is that passwords are entrenched and they won't go away soon. So I was not just surprised, but somewhat amazed, to see that cybersecurity god Bruce Schneier recommended writing down passwords and being very darn careful where you store them.

Still, I get it. If you can't have easy access to your many, many passwords, the temptation to reuse passwords everywhere is just too great. And I belong to the school of thought that believes "If Bruce Schneier says it's ok, it must *be* ok."

As an alternative, we are often asked about having a spreadsheet of passwords on your computer. That's not as crazy as it sounds either. But for heaven's sake, don't name the file "Passwords" and make sure you encrypt the document.

Can you store passwords in the cloud? Lots of people do. But cloud providers go down—and then you are toast until they are back up—unless you have a local copy. And the same rules apply, don't name the file "Passwords" and make sure it is encrypted.

Our favorite solution remains the software eWallet by iLium Software. It synchronizes across multiple platforms and devices but never goes to the cloud. The data is held in an encrypted vault. Consider it a digital wallet that can hold passwords, medical data, hotel rewards numbers, frequent flyer numbers, passport data, membership data, and pretty much anything else you can think of. eWallet is available for both Windows and Mac OS X computers, as well as most mobile devices (iOS, Android, BlackBerry, Windows Mobile, Windows 8).

More advice for the coming year? Make your password at least fourteen characters, upper case and lowercase letters, numbers, and special characters.

Hopefully, this is enough to get you through several more years as new technology advances. We are particularly looking forward to tokens, which we think might be wearable tech (the catch phrase of 2014) like fitness bands, watches, ID badges, smartphones, USB fobs or digital tokens such as the SecureID card. I will undoubtedly revisit this subject every year for the foreseeable future.

Wearable Tech

I don't think I ever heard the phrase "wearable tech" in 2013. But it was everywhere in 2014. Lots of hype and lots of anticipation. After all, it is much easier to look at an e-mail or text on your watch while driving than it is to fumble to get your phone out of your pocket. And even with some negative reviews, there was a lot of buzz about the G Watch from LG and Gear Live, both on the Android platform. There is a downside to wearable tech of course. All too often, wearable tech is part of what we are now calling "The Internet of Things." Some devices send medical information to our relatives or doctors via the Internet, others sync data about what we eat and how much we weigh, and still others record our physical activity—and worse—our exact location. Worse yet, all these Internet-connected devices are susceptible to hackers—including some of the nursery monitors we've seen. And it isn't just scaremongering. People driving by have been known to view babies in their cribs—even to talk to them. Terrifying.

All these Internet-connected devices are built for ease of use, not for security. Your thermostats, webcams, video surveillance systems, kitchen appliances, home entertainments systems, exercise equipment—all can be potentially compromised.

The day will come when your smartphone tells your house that you're on your way home and turns on lights, kicks up the heat, and puts on your favorite news program. You will be able to unlock your door when the maid comes rather than giving him or her a key. Fanciful? Not at all.

Can self-driving cars (Internet-connected of course) be far behind?

And you know what all these intelligent gadgets create? Evidence. People like the three authors of this book will glean digital forensics information from your devices (which will have memory to allow them to be "smart") and from the places on the Internet where synched data resides. Just imagine the evidence one can obtain in divorce cases from Google Glass wearers who use the app Glance (to experience sex as seen from their partner's vantage point). My, oh my.

Privacy? What's that? There will come a time when a future generation will ask that. Indeed, some young people ask it now.

Cybersecurity

There were more developments on cybersecurity in 2014 that will bear watching in the future. On August 12, 2014, the ABA House of Delegates passed, without opposition, a new cybersecurity resolution, Resolution 109, which reads as follows:

> RESOLVED, *That the American Bar Association encourages private and public sector organizations to develop, implement, and maintain an appropriate cybersecurity program that complies with applicable ethical and legal obligations, and is tailored to the nature and scope of the organization, and the data and systems to be protected.*

You might be forgiven for thinking as you read the resolution, "Wow, that really says a whole bunch of nothing." And you'd be right. It is really a cautionary resolution intended to raise awareness.

There is a back story to the resolution, which was, in its original format, much longer. The original resolution appeared to command all law firms, large and small, to come up with a cybersecurity program that met national and international standards.

This met with fierce opposition from a number of ABA entities, including our own Law Practice Division. The resolution was submitted by the ABA Cybersecurity Legal Task Force and the Section of Science & Technology Law.

In answer to the controversy, the language of the Resolution (which stands on its own and is not governed by the accompanying Report) was watered down to the tepid version above. At the behest of other entities, language in the Report was also changed to make it clear that the Resolution was not attempting to make a change in lawyers' ethical duties and to add language recognizing that smaller firms could not be expected to adopt a program that made no sense considering their size and budget constraints.

Clearly, for small firms, the international and national standards cited in the Report appeared fearsome. There are standards for smaller firms.

The report states: "Small organizations, including small law firms and solo practitioners, can prioritize key cybersecurity activities and tailor them to address the specific needs that have been identified." For help with this, you might check out NIST Interagency Report 7621: *Small Business Information Security: The Fundamentals*." Written in 2009, it's a bit dated, but many fundamentals remain the same.

Remember that the Resolution governs—not the Report. So if you hear a vendor quoting from the Report to get you to buy something, don't think the Report operates to set standards you must meet. I was one of the folks shaking my head as I read the Report, which is a marked improvement over the original version, but still dangerous in the wrong (and self-interested) hands. We'll see what happens in 2015.

2014 was the year of ransomware. We saw many law firms get hit, including one of our own clients, before there were security "signatures" to prevent it. As soon as there was protection against Cryptolocker (the original "we've encrypted your data and you have to pay to get it back" malware) variants emerged against which there was no protection. You can rest assured that ransomware will continue onward until law firms recognize the important of having backups that are not connected to the network as a drive letter! As one pundit put it, 2014 was year that "extortion went mainstream."

Information Governance

2014 was also the year the Information Governance Initiative was created. A hat tip to our friend Jason Baron for introducing me to the initiative. As the home page for the organization says, we manage our voluminous information as though we were in the Stone Age. Electronic data, which is now priceless to all of us, is no good if it is broken, lost, or stolen.

You will start seeing CLEs on Information Governance everywhere, if you haven't already. Want a definition? Information governance is the activities and technologies that organizations employ to maximize the value of their information while minimizing associated risks and costs. This goes way beyond the old "Records Management" days. You can learn more about the initiative at **http://www.iginitiative.com/**

Tablets Becoming True Laptop Replacements

If I had to make a single prediction about 2015, it would be that we will finally see the rise of tablets that are true laptop replacements.

Much as lawyers love their iPads—and they are great for surfing, e-mailing, and presenting evidence in court—they are not true laptop replacements when it comes to business productivity. This is the next true war: consumer tablets have reached a saturation point, and consumers are not replacing them as fast as manufacturers had hoped.

Always in search of profits, the major manufacturers have finally come to recognize that the enterprise tablet market is hot, hot, hot for any company that can get the technology and the security right.

While we attended the ABA Annual Meeting in Boston in August 2014, John and I had a chance to visit a Microsoft store and test drive the Microsoft Surface Pro 3. To put it mildly, we were both impressed and left the store discussing when we would buy them and with what configurations.

The only thing that irritates us is that the keyboard is "optional" (not if you want to work) and carries an additional charge of $129.99.

I bought the Surface Pro 3 in November—and yes, the high end version can and does replace my laptop!

Business-grade tablets, those that can truly replace a laptop, are quickly becoming the next big thing in solo and small firm technology as well as in the general marketplace. We are being bombarded with questions on this topic at our CLEs. Everyone is looking for a laptop replacement. Happily, you can now leave your 4.5-pound laptop and clunky travel bag at home when you need to hit the road.

Read the chapter on computers for the technical specifications and recommended model. And as I've written this, I have decided that our corporate budget can afford the purchase of two Surface Pro 3 tablets so John can leave his laptop at home too. As the posters and greeting cards say, "It is good to be the Queen."

Office 365

Lawyers flocked to Office 365 in 2014, happy that the subscription (monthly, from $4 to $24 per mailbox, which tends to map closely to the number of users) gives them the standard Office Apps (Word, Excel, and PowerPoint) on multiple machines. The lawyers have especially appreciated the increase in functionality when Office 365 is on their iPads. It is still a bit of a kluge to move documents in and out of the apps on your iPad, but still, it has greatly enhanced the iPad's ability to do real work.

If you want to understand Microsoft Office 365 (as an owner or a prospective buyer) you definitely need to purchase *Microsoft Office 365 for Lawyers* by Ben Schorr. Ben manages to be both informative and witty; he is very easy to read. Ben helpfully guides you on the right path to choosing the plan you need and runs through all the Office 365 essentials. At $49.95, you can't beat it. You can purchase the book through the ABA webstore.

Though Office 365 was launched in June of 2011, it is notable how much it has recently soared in popularity. You use a browser to access it like Google Docs. However, you also have an option (except for the basic plan) to install it by streaming it from the Net and it will reach back to Microsoft periodically to get updates, which is great because you don't have to worry about installing them.

Stats Tell Us Where Legal Tech is Heading

As the need for mobility increases, these were the stats for ILTA's Technology Purchasing Survey. Amazingly, 28 percent of the respondents reported purchasing BlackBerrys (really?), and 63 percent purchased iPhone (down 9 percent from 2013).

In the tablet market, 44 percent bought iPads (down 15 percent from 2013, which I thought was telling; they want laptop replacements these days). Seventeen percent purchased Microsoft Surface and 10 percent chose Android devices. Remember the ILTA Survey tends to reflect purchases at mid to large size firms.

Given the numbers above, it is clear that many lawyers next year will be buying the iPhone 6 and the new "Lollipop" Android phones.

The stats also tell us that we are moving to toward taking cybersecurity seriously. According to a 2014 LexisNexis survey, here's what lawyers are doing with respect to e-mail:

- 77% include a confidentiality statement
- 22% encrypt e-mails
- 22% include a confidentiality statement in the subject line
- 17% require the clients' consent for transmission
- 14% password protect documents
- 13% share links to documents on a secure site

Are we getting there with painful slowness? Yes, but we are getting there finally.

The ABA 2014 Legal Technology Survey is always a wealth of information.

Fees: 72 percent of legal fees are still hourly, which will astound some people; 15 percent are fixed and 9 percent are contingent.

Tablets: 40 percent of lawyers are using tablets to do legal work with 84 percent of them using iPads. Look for that to change as manufacturers rush to produce enterprise tablets probably making inroads on the iPad's dominance.

Smartphones: 77 percent of lawyers reported using smartphones to do law-related work; personally, I would have thought that number would be higher because it would include e-mail.

Time and Billing Software: The top four packages were TimeSlips, Quickbooks, TABS3, and PCLaw.

Case Management Software: 49 percent of law firms have some sort of case management software. Like everyone else on the lecture circuit, we keep advocating the adoption of case management, so that figure should continue to rise. However, note that only 31 percent of survey respondents indicated that they actually *used* the software. The really amusing footnote was the type of case management software respondents cited: Microsoft Outlook (51 percent), CaseMap and Time Matters (11 percent each), and PCLaw (8 percent). Microsoft Outlook is definitely *not* a case management system, but it is remarkable how many lawyers believe that it is.

A surprising stat to me is that only 30 percent of the lawyers indicated that they use conflict-checking software. Hopefully, that number will rise over time.

Fifty percent of lawyers report the availability of encryption software at their firm, but fewer than a third actually use it. This is where I pound my head on my desk and cry, "What is wrong with you people?" No doubt lawyers will resist encryption, no matter how essential it is, until an ethics opinion or a client makes the use of encryption mandatory.

Thirty percent indicated that they used some sort of cloud-based software or service, with Dropbox, Google Docs, iCloud, Evernote, Clio, Box, and Rocket Matter leading the pack. Interesting to me that the number is so low.

Cloud Computing: Lawyers are Still Resistant

As we saw above, and have seen in many other surveys, lawyers are slow to move to the cloud. Those who do cite the consistency and ease of access, low cost of entry, predictable costs for budgeting, a reduction in IT needs, and so on. The doubters cite security concerns, the loss of control over firm data, distrust of vendors, a lack of ethical guidance, clients' desire that a law firm not store data in the cloud, and a number of other factors.

Fifty-six percent of those who don't use cloud computing flatly say no, they have no plans to use it in the future. They do not lack certainty on that point!

Every state that has looked at cloud computing for lawyers has said it is ok, though some impose more conditions than others. You can find a terrific infographic with links to all the state ethics opinions on cloud computing at the ABA Legal Technology Resources Center: **http://www .americanbar.org/groups/departments_offices/legal_technology_ resources/resources/charts_fyis/cloud-ethics-chart.html**.

While the cloud is a tad worrisome in that someone else controls your security (and who knows which clouds cooperate with the NSA?), it is hard to beat the "five 9s," 99.999 percent guarantee of power and Internet connectivity. We like the hybrid solution, where your own equipment resides in the cloud and your data is not commingled with that of others. If your data is stored encrypted, only your IT provider (presumably trusted) will have access—not the datacenter which hosts your data— except in an emergency, which you can contractually require the data-center to document immediately.

Can you negotiate with the big cloud providers? Probably not, but the smaller ones want your business and are pretty good about negotiating a win-win deal.

Windows 8 and 9

Windows 8 definitely flopped, even after some tinkering. Only about 15 percent of lawyers adopted it with about 54 percent preferring (wisely) to stay with Windows 7. About 14 percent remain on XP, which is now unsupported. Come on folks—you can't be compliant with your ethical obligations to protect client data when you aren't getting security updates! And with all the popularity of Macs, the Mac OS was in use only about 6 percent of the time.

Windows 10 is coming but we don't have a date as of this writing. What the reliable rumor mills, if there are such things, are saying is that Windows 10 will be a step backwards to many of the things lawyers liked about Windows 7 and away from all the things they hated in Windows 8. I sure hope so.

Final thoughts

As always, I have jumped hither and yon, selected the topics that were hot during 2014 and bound to have an impact on the practice of law in the coming year. There is always a hodgepodge of subjects that piqued my interest as well, for one reason or another.

Next year? I think it's safe to say that cybersecurity will remain a major concern and that we'll see a rapid rise in the use of enterprise tablets. But from one hundred-foot tower of imagination, it's only possible to see so far. One comment from a lawyer friend was right on point: He said, "The technology we buy becomes obsolete with increasing speed." Ain't it the truth?

Glossary*

Active Directory (AD) is an implementation of Local Automatic Data Processing (LADP) directory services by Microsoft for use primarily in Windows environments. Its main purpose is to provide central authentication and authorization services for Windows-based computers. Active Directory also allows administrators to assign policies, deploy software, and apply critical updates to an organization. It stores information and settings in a central database. Active Directory networks can vary from a small installation with a few hundred objects to a large installation with millions of objects.

ActiveSync is a synchronization program developed by Microsoft. It allows a mobile device to be synchronized with either a desktop PC or a server running Microsoft Exchange Server, PostPath Email and Collaboration Server, Kerio MailServer, or Z-Push.

Adware is any software package that automatically plays, displays, or downloads advertising material to a computer after the software is installed on it or while the application is being used. Some types of adware are also spyware and can be classified as privacy-invasive software.

AppleCare Protection Plan is Apple's warranty with a new product. It includes ninety days' complimentary telephone support and a one-year hardware guarantee. Both can be extended to a three-year (for computers) or two-year (for iPods and iPhones) warranty and telephone support (inclusive of the initial support) through the AppleCare Protection Plan packs, which can be purchased separately within the initial one-year warranty or simultaneously with new Apple products, mainly Macs, iPods, and iPhones.

---

*This glossary was compiled from definitions available online at Wikipedia (**www.wikipedia.org**).

Advanced technology attachment (ATA) is a standard interface for connecting storage devices such as hard disks and CD-ROM drives inside personal computers. The standard is maintained by X3/INCITS committee T13. Many synonyms and near-synonyms for ATA exist, including abbreviations such as IDE and ATAPI.

Auto document feeder (ADF) is a feature in single-function and multi-function (all-in-one) printers, fax machines, photocopiers, and scanners that allows several pages to be loaded and fed one at a time into the scanner, allowing the user to scan (and thereby copy, print, or fax) multiple-page documents without having to replace each page manually.

Boot Camp is a utility included with Apple's Mac OS X v10.5 Leopard and higher operating systems that assists users in installing Microsoft Windows XP or Windows Vista on Intel-based Macintosh computers. Boot Camp guides users through nondestructive repartitioning (including resizing of an existing HFS+ partition, if necessary) of their hard disk drive and using the Mac OS X Leopard disc to install Windows drivers. In addition to device drivers for the hardware, the disc includes a control panel applet for selecting the boot operating system while in Windows.

Byte is a unit of measurement of information storage, most often consisting of eight bits. In many computer architectures, it is a unit of memory addressing.

Category 5e cable (Cat5e) is an enhanced version of Cat5 that adds specifications for far-end crosstalk. It was formally defined in 2001 in the TIA/EIA-568-B standard, which no longer recognizes the original Cat5 specification. Although 1000BASE-T was designed for use with Cat5 cable, the tighter specifications associated with Cat5e cable and connectors make it an excellent choice for use with 1000BASE-T. Despite the stricter performance specifications, Cat5e cable does not enable longer cable distances for Ethernet networks: cables are still limited to a maximum of 328 ft. (100 m) in length (normal practice is to limit fixed ["horizontal"] cables to 90 m to allow for up to 5 m of patch cable at each end). Cat5e cable performance characteristics and test methods are defined in TIA/EIA-568-B.2-2001.

Category 6 cable (Cat6), commonly referred to as Cat6, is a cable standard for gigabit Ethernet and other network protocols and is backward compatible with the category 5/5e and category 3 cable standards. Cat6 features more stringent specifications for crosstalk and system noise. The cable standard provides performance of up to 250 MHz and is suitable for

10BASE-T/100BASE-TX and 1000BASE-T (gigabit Ethernet). It is expected to suit the 10GBASE-T (10 gigabit Ethernet) standard, although with limitations on length if unshielded Cat6 cable is used.

Cathode ray tube (CRT) is an evacuated glass envelope containing an electron gun (a source of electrons) and a fluorescent screen, usually with internal or external means to accelerate and deflect the electrons. When electrons strike the fluorescent screen, light is emitted.

CD-ROM is a compact disc that contains data accessible by a computer. While the CD format was originally designed for music storage and playback, the format was later adapted to hold any form of binary data. CD-ROMs are popularly used to distribute computer software, including games and multimedia applications, though any data can be stored (up to the capacity limit of a disc).

Central processing unit (CPU), or sometimes just "processor," is a certain class of logic machines that can execute computer programs. This broad definition can easily be applied to many early computers that existed long before the term ever came into widespread usage. However, the term and its acronym CPU have been in use in the computer industry since at least the early 1960s. The form, design, and implementation of CPUs have changed dramatically since the earliest examples, but their fundamental operation has remained much the same.

Client Access License (CAL) is a kind of software license distributed by Microsoft to allow clients to connect to its server software programs.

Code division multiple access (CDMA) employs spread-spectrum technology and a special coding scheme where each transmitter is assigned a code. In communications technology, there are only three domains that can allow multiplexing to be implemented for more efficient use of the available channel bandwidth, and these domains are known as time, frequency, and space. CDMA divides the access in signal space.

Computer monitor is a piece of electrical equipment that displays viewable images generated by a computer without producing a permanent record. The word *monitor* is used in other contexts, in particular in television broadcasting, where a television picture is displayed to a high standard. A computer display device is usually either a cathode ray tube or some form of flat panel, such as a thin film transistor liquid crystal display (TFT-LCD). The monitor comprises the display device, circuitry to generate a picture from electronic signals sent by the computer, and an enclosure or case. Within the computer, either as an integral part or a plugged-in interface, there is circuitry to convert internal data to a format compatible with a monitor.

Computer virus is a computer program that can copy itself and infect a computer without permission or knowledge of the user. However, the term virus is commonly used, albeit erroneously, to refer to many different types of malware programs. The original virus may modify the copies, or the copies may modify themselves, as occurs in a metamorphic virus. A virus can only spread from one computer to another when its host is taken to the uninfected computer—for instance, by a user sending it over a network or the Internet, or by carrying it on a removable medium, such as a CD or USB drive. Additionally, viruses can spread to other computers by infecting files on a network file system or a file system that is accessed by another computer.

Contrast ratio is a measure of a display system, defined as the ratio of the luminosity of the brightest color (white) to that of the darkest color (black) that the system is capable of producing. A high contrast ratio is a desired aspect of any display, but with the various methods of measuring a system or its part, remarkably different values can sometimes produce similar results.

DAT72 backup tapes store up to 36 GB uncompressed (72 GB compressed) on a 170-meter cartridge. The Digital Audio Tape (DAT) 72 standard was developed by HP and Certance. It has the same form-factor and is backward compatible with DDS-3 and -4.

Database application is a structured collection of records or data that is stored in a computer system. A database usually contains software so that a person or program can use it to answer queries or extract desired information. The term *database* refers to the collection of related records, and the software should be referred to as the database management system.

DDR2 SDRAM, double-data-rate two synchronous dynamic random-access memory, is a random access memory technology used for high-speed storage of the working data of a computer or other digital electronic device.

Digital copier is a copier that effectively consists of an integrated scanner and laser printer. This design has several advantages, such as automatic image quality enhancement and the ability to "build jobs," or scan page images independently of the process of printing them.

Some digital copiers can function as high-speed scanners; such models typically have the ability to send documents via e-mail or make them available on a local area network. In recent years, all new photocopiers have adopted digital technology, replacing the older analog technology.

Digital subscriber line (DSL) is a family of technologies that provides digital data transmission over the wires of a local telephone network.

Digital visual interface (DVI) is a video interface standard designed to maximize the visual quality of digital display devices such as flat-panel LCD computer displays and digital projectors. It was developed by an industry consortium, the Digital Display Working Group (DDWG). It is designed for carrying uncompressed digital video data to a display.

Display resolution of a digital television or computer monitor typically refers to the number of distinct pixels in each dimension that can be displayed. It can be an ambiguous term, especially since the displayed resolution is controlled by different factors in CRT and flat-panel or projection displays using fixed picture-element (pixel) arrays.

Domain controller (DC) on Windows Server systems is the server that responds to security authentication requests (logging in, checking permissions, etc.) within the Windows Server domain.

Dots per inch (dpi) is a measure of printing resolution, in particular the number of individual dots of ink a printer or toner can produce within a linear one-inch (2.54 cm) space.

DVD (also known as digital versatile disc or digital video disc) is a popular optical disk storage media format. Its main uses are video and data storage. Most DVDs are of the same dimensions as compact discs (CDs) but store more than six times the data.

E-mail spam is unwanted e-mail messages, frequently with commercial content, sent in large quantities to an indiscriminate set of recipients.

Encryption/decryption is the process of transforming information (referred to as plaintext) using an algorithm (called cipher) to make it unreadable to anyone except those possessing special knowledge, usually referred to as a key. The result of the process is encrypted information (in cryptography, referred to as ciphertext). In many contexts, the word encryption also implicitly refers to the reverse process, decryption (e.g., "software for encryption" can typically also perform decryption), to make the encrypted information readable again (i.e., to make it unencrypted).

Enhanced- or Extended-definition Television (EDTV) is a Consumer Electronics Association (CEA) marketing shorthand term for certain digital television (DTV) formats and devices. EDTV generally refers to video with picture quality beyond what can be broadcast in NTSC or PAL but not sharp enough to be considered high-definition television (HDTV). A DVD player with progressive output is considered the lower end of this class when playing a progressively encoded disc. (The maximum EDTV frame rate of 60 per second is not possible from a DVD.) The common implementations of EDTV are 480- or 576-line signals in progressive scan, as opposed to 50 to 60 interlaced fields per second (see NTSC or PAL and SECAM). These are commonly referred to as "480p" and "576p," respectively. In comparison, a standard-definition television (SDTV) signal is broadcast with interlaced frames and is commonly referred to as "480i" or "576i." EDTV can also refer to a display device that has a maximum resolution of 480p or 576p.

Extensible markup language (XML) is a general-purpose markup language. It is classified as an extensible language because it allows its users to define their own elements. Its primary purpose is to facilitate the sharing of structured data across different information systems, particularly via the Internet. It is used to encode documents and serialize data.

FireWire is Apple's brand name for the IEEE 1394 interface (although the 1394 standard also defines a backplane interface). It is also known as i.LINK (Sony's name). It is a serial bus interface standard for high-speed communications and isochronous real-time data transfer, frequently used in a personal computer and digital audio/digital video.

FireWire 400 can transfer data between devices at 100, 200, or 400 Mbit/s data rates.

FireWire 800 (Apple's name for the nine-pin "S800 bilingual" version of the IEEE 1394b standard) was introduced commercially by Apple in 2003. This newer 1394 specification (1394b) and corresponding products allow a transfer rate of 786.432 Mbit/s via a new encoding scheme termed beta mode. It is backward compatible to the slower rates and six-pin connectors of FireWire 400. However, while the IEEE 1394a and IEEE 1394b standards are compatible, FireWire 800's connector is different from FireWire 400's connector, making the legacy cables incompatible. A bilingual cable allows the connection of older devices to the newer port.

Gigabyte (derived from the SI prefix *giga-*) is a unit of information or computer storage equal to either exactly 1 billion bytes or approximately1.07 billion bytes, depending on context. It is commonly abbreviated as Gbyte or GB.

Global System for Mobile Communications (GSM) is the most popular standard for mobile phones in the world. Its promoter, the GSM Association, estimates that 82 percent of the global mobile market uses the standard. GSM is used by over 2 billion people across more than 212 countries and territories. Its ubiquity makes international roaming very common between mobile phone operators, enabling subscribers to use their phones in many parts of the world. GSM differs from its predecessors in that both signaling and speech channels are digital call quality, and so it is considered a second-generation (2G) mobile phone system. Data communications were built into the system using the 3rd Generation Partnership Project (3GPP).

Hard disk drive, commonly referred to as a hard drive, hard disk, or fixed disk drive, is a nonvolatile storage device that stores digitally encoded data on rapidly rotating platters with magnetic surfaces. Strictly speaking, drive refers to a device distinct from its medium, such as a tape drive and its tape or a floppy disk drive and its floppy disk.

Hash function is a reproducible method of turning some kind of data into a (relatively) small number that may serve as a digital "fingerprint" of the data. The algorithm "chops and mixes" (i.e., substitutes or transposes) the data to create such fingerprints. The fingerprints are called hash sums, hash values, hash codes, or simply hashes.

High-definition multimedia interface (HDMI) is a licensable compact audio/video connector interface for transmitting uncompressed digital streams.

High-definition TV (HDTV) is a digital television broadcasting system with greater resolution than traditional television systems (NTSC, SECAM, PAL). HDTV is digitally broadcast because digital television (DTV) requires less bandwidth if sufficient video compression is used.

Hub is a device for connecting multiple twisted pairs or fiber optic Ethernet devices, making them act as a single network segment. Hubs work at the physical layer (layer 1) of the OSI model, and the term *layer 1 switch* is often used interchangeably with *hub*. The device is thus a form of multi-port repeater. Network hubs are also responsible for forwarding a jam signal to all ports if they detect a collision.

Institute of Electrical and Electronics Engineers (IEEE; read: *i triple e*) is an international nonprofit professional organization for the advancement of technology related to electricity. It has the most members of any technical professional organization in the world, with more than 360,000 members in around 175 countries.

Intel Core 2 Duo Processor The Core 2 brand refers to a range of Intel's consumer 64-bit dual-core and quad-core CPUs with the x86-64 instruction set and based on the Intel Core microarchitecture, which derived from the 32-bit dual-core Yonah laptop processor.

Intel Corporation (Intel) is the world's largest semiconductor company and the inventor of the x86 series of microprocessors, which are found in most personal computers.

Internet Information Services (IIS) is a set of Internet-based services for servers using Microsoft Windows. It is the world's second most popular web server in terms of overall websites, behind Apache HTTP Server.

Internet protocol (IP) address is a unique address that certain electronic devices currently used to identify and communicate with each other on a computer network utilizing the Internet protocol standard—in simpler terms, a computer address. Any participating network device—including routers, switches, computers, infrastructure servers (e.g., NTP, DNS, DHCP, SNMP), printers, Internet fax machines, and some telephones—can have its own address that is unique within the scope of the specific network. Some IP addresses are intended to be unique within the scope of the global Internet, while others need to be unique only within the scope of an enterprise.

Intrusion detection system (IDS) is a piece of hardware that detects unwanted manipulations of computer systems, mainly through the Internet. The manipulations may take the form of attacks by hackers. An IDS is used to detect several types of malicious behaviors that can compromise the security and trust of a computer system. These include network attacks against vulnerable services; data-driven attacks on applications; host-based attacks such as privilege escalation, unauthorized logins, and access to sensitive files; and malware (viruses, Trojan horses, and worms).

IPsec (IP security) is a suite of protocols for securing Internet protocol (IP) communications by authenticating and/or encrypting each IP packet in a data stream.

iSight camera is a webcam developed and marketed by Apple. The iSight is sold in retail outlets as an external unit that connects to a computer via FireWire cable and comes with a set of mounts to place it atop any current Apple display, laptop computer, or all-in-one desktop computer. The term is also used to refer to the camera built into Apple's iMac, MacBook, and MacBook Pro computers.

Keyboard is a peripheral in computing, partially modeled after the type-writer keyboard. Physically, a keyboard is an arrangement of rectangular buttons, or keys. A keyboard typically has characters engraved or printed on the keys; in most cases, each press of a key corresponds to a single written symbol. However, to produce some symbols requires pressing and holding several keys simultaneously or in sequence; other keys do not produce any symbol but instead affect the operation of the computer or the keyboard itself.

Laser printer is a common type of computer printer that rapidly produces high-quality text and graphics on plain paper. Like photo-copiers, laser printers employ a xerographic printing process but differ from analog photocopiers in that the image is produced by the direct scanning of a laser beam across the printer's photoreceptor.

Light-emitting diode (LED) is a semiconductor diode that emits incoherent, narrow-spectrum light when electrically biased in the forward direction of the p-n junction, as in the common LED circuit. This effect is a form of electroluminescence.

Linear tape-open (LTO or LTO2) is a magnetic tape data storage technology developed as an open alternative to the proprietary digital linear tape (DLT). The technology was developed and initiated by Seagate, Hewlett Packard, and IBM. The standard form-factor of LTO technology goes by the name Ultrium.

Liquid crystal display (LCD) is a thin, flat display device made up of any number of color or monochrome pixels arrayed in front of a light source or reflector. It is often used in battery-powered electronic devices because it uses very small amounts of electric power.

Macintosh AirPort is a local area wireless networking brand from Apple based on the IEEE 802.11b standard (also known as Wi-Fi) and certified as compatible with other 802.11b devices. A later family of products based on the IEEE 802.11g specification is known as AirPort Extreme. The latest family of products is based on the draft-IEEE 802.11n specification and carries the same name.

Macintosh/Mac is a brand name that covers several lines of personal computers designed, developed, and marketed by Apple, Inc. The original Macintosh was released on January 24, 1984; it was the first commercially successful personal computer to feature a mouse and a graphical user interface (GUI) rather than a command-line interface. (Newer models are referred to as Macs.) Apple consolidated multiple consumer-level desktop models into the 1998 iMac, which sold extremely well. Current Mac systems are mainly targeted at the home, education, and creative professional markets. They are the aforementioned (though upgraded) iMac and the entry-level Mac mini desktop models; the workstation-level Mac Pro tower; the MacBook, MacBook Air, and MacBook Pro laptops; and the Xserve server.

The MagSafe power adapter is a power connector introduced in conjunction with the MacBook Pro at the Macworld Expo in San Francisco on January 10, 2006. The MagSafe connector is held in place magnetically. As a result, if it is tugged on—for instance, by someone tripping over the cord—it comes out of the socket safely, without damage to it or the computer or pulling the computer off its table or desk.

Media access control (MAC) address is a quasi-unique identifier attached to most network adapters. It is a number that acts like a name for a particular network adapter, so, for example, the network interface cards (NICs, or built-in network adapters) in two different computers will have different names, or MAC addresses, as would an Ethernet adapter and a wireless adapter in the same computer and as would multiple network cards in a router.

Megabyte (MB) is a unit of information or computer storage equal to approximately 1,000,000 bytes, depending on context.

Message-digest algorithm 5 (MD5) is a widely used cryptographic hash function with a 128-bit hash value. As an Internet standard (RFC 1321), MD5 has been employed in a wide variety of security applications and is also commonly used to check the integrity of files. An MD5 hash is typically expressed as a 32-character hexadecimal number.

Microsoft Exchange Server is a messaging and collaborative software product developed by Microsoft. It is part of the Microsoft Servers line of server products and is widely used by enterprises using Microsoft infrastructure solutions. Exchange's major features consist of electronic mail, calendars, contacts, and tasks and support for the mobile and web-based access to information. The software also supports data storage.

Microsoft SQL Server is a relational database-management system (RDBMS) produced by Microsoft. Its primary query language is Transact-SQL, an implementation of the ANSI/ISO standard Structured Query Language (SQL) used by both Microsoft and Sybase.

Microsoft Windows is the name of several families of software operating systems by Microsoft. Microsoft first introduced an operating environment named Windows in November 1985 as an add-on to MS-DOS in response to the growing interest in graphical user interfaces (GUIs). Microsoft Windows eventually came to dominate the world's personal computer market, overtaking Mac OS, which had been introduced previously. At the 2004 IDC Directions conference, IDC vice president Avneesh Saxena stated that Windows had approximately 90 percent of the client operating system market. The most recent client version of Windows is Windows 8.

Modem (from modulator-demodulator) is a device that modulates an analog carrier signal to encode digital information and also demodulates such a carrier signal to decode the transmitted information. The goal is to produce a signal that can be transmitted easily and decoded to reproduce the original digital data.

Mouse (plural, mice or mouses) in computing functions as a pointing device by detecting two-dimensional motion relative to its supporting surface. Physically, a mouse consists of a small case, held under one of the user's hands. It has one or more buttons and sometimes has other elements, such as wheels, which allow the user to perform various system-dependent operations, or extra buttons or features that can add more control or dimensional input. The mouse's motion typically translates into the motion of a pointer on a display.

MPEG-1 audio layer 3 (MP3) is a digital audio encoding format. This encoding format is used to create an MP3 file, a way to store a single segment of audio, commonly a song, so that it can be organized or easily transferred between computers and other devices, such as MP3 players.

Network address translation (NAT) is a technique of transceiving network traffic through a router that involves rewriting the source and/or destination IP addresses and usually also the TCP/UDP port numbers of IP packets as they pass through.

Network card/adapter, LAN adapter, or NIC (network interface card) is a piece of computer hardware designed to allow computers to communicate over a computer network.

Optical character recognition, usually abbreviated OCR, is the mechanical or electronic translation of images of handwritten, typewritten, or printed text (usually captured by a scanner) into machine-editable text.

Peripheral devices In computer hardware, a peripheral device is any device attached to a computer to expand its functionality. Some of the more common peripheral devices are printers, scanners, disk drives, tape drives, microphones, speakers, and cameras.

Portable document format (PDF) is the file format created by Adobe Systems in 1993 for document exchange. PDF is a fixed-layout document format used for representing two-dimensional documents in a manner independent of the application software, hardware, and operating system.

Private branch exchange (PBX) is a telephone exchange that serves a particular business or office, as opposed to one that a common carrier or telephone company operates for many businesses or for the general public.

Radio-frequency identification (RFID) is an automatic identification method that relies on storing and remotely retrieving data using devices called RFID tags or transponders. An RFID tag is an object that can be applied to or incorporated into a product, animal, or person for the purpose of identification using radio waves. Some tags can be read from several meters away and beyond the line of sight of the reader.

RAID (redundant array of independent disks) 5 uses block-level striping with parity data distributed across all member disks. RAID 5 has achieved popularity due to its low cost of redundancy. Generally, RAID 5 is implemented with hardware support for parity calculations. A minimum of three disks is generally required for a complete RAID 5 configuration.

Random access memory (usually known by its acronym, RAM) is a type of computer data storage. Today it takes the form of integrated circuits that allow the stored data to be accessed in any order—i.e., at random. The word *random* thus refers to the fact that any piece of data can be returned in a constant time, regardless of its physical location and whether or not it is related to the previous piece of data.

Redundant arrays of independent disks (RAID) is the most common definition of RAID. Other definitions of RAID include "redundant arrays of independent drives" and "redundant arrays of inexpensive drives." RAID is an umbrella term for computer data storage schemes that divide and replicate data among multiple hard disk drives. RAID's various designs balance or accentuate two key design goals: increased data reliability and increased I/O (input/output) performance.

Remote desktop protocol (RDP) is a multichannel protocol that allows a user to connect to a computer running Microsoft Terminal Services. Clients exist for most versions of Windows (including handheld versions) and other operating systems such as Linux, FreeBSD, Solaris, and Mac OS X. The server listens by default on TCP port 3389. Microsoft refers to its official RDP client software as either Remote Desktop Connection (RDC) or Terminal Services Client (TSC).

Revolutions per minute (rpm, RPM, r/min) is a unit of frequency: the number of full rotations completed in one minute around a fixed axis. It is most commonly used as a measure of rotational speed or angular velocity of some mechanical component.

Rootkit is a program (or a combination of several programs) designed to take fundamental control (in Unix terms, "root" access; in Windows terms, "administrator" access) of a computer system without authorization by the system's owners and legitimate managers. Access to the hardware (i.e., the reset switch) is rarely required, as a rootkit is intended to seize control of the operating system running on the hardware. Typically, rootkits act to obscure their presence on the system through subversion or evasion of standard operating system security mechanisms. Often they are Trojans as well, thus fooling users into believing they are safe to run on their systems. Techniques used to accomplish this can include concealing running processes from monitoring programs or hiding files or system data from the operating system.

Router is a piece of hardware that connects two or more different networks (e.g., LAN to WAN) to route data between them.

Scanning resolution describes the detail of the scanned image. The term applies equally to digital images, film images, and other types of images. Higher resolution means more image detail.

Secure Sockets Layer (SSL) is a cryptographic protocol that provides secure communications on the Internet for such things as web browsing, e-mail, Internet faxing, instant messaging, and other data transfers.

Serial advanced technology attachment (SATA) is a computer bus primarily designed for transfer of data between a computer and storage devices (like hard disk drives or optical drives). The main benefits are faster transfers, the ability to remove or add devices while operating (hot-swapping), thinner cables that let air cooling work more efficiently, and more reliable operation with tighter data integrity checks than the older Parallel ATA interface.

Serial-attached SCSI (SAS) is a computer bus technology primarily designed for transfer of data to and from computer data storage devices such as hard drives, CD-ROMs, DVD tape drives, and similar devices. SAS is a serial communication protocol for direct attached storage (DAS) devices. It is designed for the corporate and enterprise market as a replacement for parallel SCSI, allowing for much higher-speed data transfers than previously available and is backward compatible with SATA drives.

Server is an application or device that performs services for connected clients as part of a client-server architecture. A server application, as defined by RFC 2616 (HTTP/1.1), is "an application program that accepts connections in order to service requests by sending back responses." Server computers are devices designed to run such an application or applications, often for extended periods of time, with minimal human direction. Examples of d-class servers include web servers, e-mail servers, and file servers.

Service set identifier (SSID) is a name used to identify the particular 802.11 wireless LANs to which a user wants to attach. A client device will receive broadcast messages from all access points within range that advertise their SSIDs and can choose one to connect to based on preconfiguration or by displaying a list of SSIDs in range and asking the user to select one.

SHA hash functions are five cryptographic hash functions designed by the National Security Agency (NSA) and published by the NIST as a U.S. Federal Information Processing Standard. SHA stands for secure hash algorithm. Hash algorithms compute a fixed-length digital representation (known as a message digest) of an input data sequence (the message) of any length. The five algorithms are denoted SHA-1, SHA-224, SHA-256, SHA-384, and SHA-512. The latter four variants are sometimes collectively referred to as SHA-2. SHA-1 produces a message digest that is 160 bits long; the number in the other four algorithms' names denotes the bit length of the digest they produce.

Shadow Copy (also called Volume Snapshot Service, or VSS) is a feature introduced with Windows Server 2003 and available in all releases of Microsoft Windows thereafter that allows taking manual or automatic backup copies or snapshots of a file or folder on a specific volume at a specific point in time. It is used by NTBackup and the Volume Shadow Copy service to back up files. In Windows Vista, it is used by Windows Vista's backup utility, System Restore, and the Previous Versions feature.

Small computer system interface (SCSI) is a set of standards for physically connecting and transferring data between computers and peripheral devices. The SCSI standards define commands, protocols, and electrical and optical interfaces. SCSI is most commonly used for hard disks and tape drives, but it can connect a wide range of other devices, including scanners and CD drives. The SCSI standard defines command sets for specific peripheral device types; the presence of "unknown" as one of these types means that in theory it can be used as an interface to almost any device, but the standard is highly pragmatic and addressed toward commercial requirements.

Smartphone is a mobile phone offering advanced capabilities beyond a typical mobile phone, often with PC-like functionality.

Spyware is computer software that is installed surreptitiously on a personal computer to intercept or take partial control over the user's interaction with the computer without the user's informed consent. While the term spyware suggests software that secretly monitors the user's behavior, the functions of spyware extend well beyond simple monitoring. Spyware programs can collect various types of personal information but can also interfere with user control of the computer in other ways, such as installing additional software, redirecting web browser activity, accessing websites blindly that will cause more harmful viruses, or diverting advertising revenue to a third party. Spyware can even change computer settings, resulting in slow connection speeds, different home pages, and loss of Internet or other programs.

SuperDrive is a term that has been used by Apple for two different storage drives: from 1988 to 1999, to refer to a high-density floppy disk drive capable of reading all major 3.5-inch disk formats, and from 2001 onward to refer to a combined CD/DVD reader/writer. Once use of floppy disks started declining, Apple reused the term to refer to the (originally Pioneer-built) DVD writers built into its Macintosh models, which can read and write both DVDs and CDs. As of December 2006, SuperDrives are combination DVD ±R/±RW and CD-R/RW writer drives offering speeds of 4x to 36x and supporting the DVD-R, DVD+R, DVD+R DL, DVD±RW, DVD-9, CD-R, and CD-RW formats along with all normal read-only media.

Switch is a computer-networking device that connects network segments. Low-end network switches appear nearly identical to network hubs, but a switch contains more "intelligence" (and comes with a correspondingly slightly higher price tag) than a network hub. Network switches are capable of inspecting data packets as they are received, determining the source and destination device of the packets, and forwarding them appropriately. By delivering each message only to the connected device it was intended for, a network switch conserves network bandwidth and offers generally better performance than a hub.

Tagged Image File Format (TIFF) is a container format for storing images, including photographs and line art. Originally created by the company Aldus for use with what was then called desktop publishing, it is now under the control of Adobe. The TIFF format is widely supported by image-manipulation applications; publishing and page layout applications; and scanning, faxing, word processing, OCR, and other applications.

Tape drive is a data storage device that reads and writes data stored on a magnetic tape. It is typically used for archival storage of data on hard drives. Tape generally has a favorable unit cost and long archival stability.

Terminal Services is a component of Microsoft Windows (both server and client versions) that allows a user to access applications and data on a remote computer over any type of network, although normally best used when dealing with either a wide area network (WAN) or local area network (LAN). Ease and compatibility with other types of networks may vary. Terminal Services is Microsoft's implementation of thin-client terminal server computing, where Windows applications, or even the entire desktop of the computer running Terminal Services, is made accessible from a remote client machine.

Time Machine is a backup utility developed by Apple that is included with Mac OS X.

Universal serial bus (USB) is a serial bus standard to interface devices. USB was designed to allow peripherals to be connected using a single standardized interface socket and to improve plug-and-play capabilities by allowing devices to be connected and disconnected without rebooting the computer (hot-swapping). Other convenient features include providing power to low-consumption devices without the need for an external power supply and allowing many devices to be used without requiring manufacturer-specific individual device drivers to be installed.

Unix is a computer operating system originally developed in 1969 by a group of AT&T employees, including Ken Thompson, Dennis Ritchie, and Douglas McIlroy, at Bell Labs. Today's Unix systems are split into various branches developed over time by AT&T as well as various commercial vendors and nonprofit organizations.

USB thumb (flash) drives are NAND-type flash memory data storage devices integrated with a USB connector. They are typically small, lightweight, removable, and rewritable.

Video card/graphics adapter, also referred to as a graphics accelerator card, display adapter, graphics card, and numerous other terms, is an item of personal computer hardware whose function is to generate and output images to a display.

Video graphics array (VGA) refers either to an analog computer display standard (the 15-pin D-subminiature VGA connector, first marketed in 1988 by IBM) or the 640 × 480 resolution itself. While this resolution has been superseded in the computer market, it is becoming a popular resolution on mobile devices.

Virtual private network (VPN) is a communications network tunneled through another network and dedicated for a specific network. One common application is secure communications through the public Internet, but a VPN need not have explicit security features, such as authentication or content encryption. VPNs, for example, can be used to separate the traffic of different user communities over an underlying network with strong security features.

Web 2.0 is a trend in web design and development and can refer to a perceived second generation of web-based communities and hosted services—such as social networking sites, wikis, and folksonomies—which aim to facilitate creativity, collaboration, and sharing between users. The term gained currency following the first O'Reilly Media Web 2.0 conference in 2004. Although the term suggests a new version of the World Wide Web, it does not refer to an update to any technical specifications, but to changes in the ways software developers and end users use webs.

Wi-Fi is a wireless technology brand owned by the Wi-Fi Alliance and intended to improve the interoperability of wireless local area network products based on the IEEE 802.11 standards. Common applications for Wi-Fi include Internet and VoIP phone access, gaming, and network connectivity for consumer electronics, such as televisions, DVD players, and digital cameras.

Wi-Fi protected access (WPA) is a class of systems to secure wireless (Wi-Fi) computer networks. It was created in response to several serious weaknesses researchers had found in the previous system, wired equivalent privacy (WEP). WPA implements the majority of the IEEE 802.11i standard and was intended as an intermediate measure to take the place of WEP while 802.11i was prepared.

Windows Recycle Bin is temporary storage for files that have been deleted in a file manager by the user but not yet permanently erased from the physical medium. Typically, a recycle bin is presented as a special file directory to the user (whether or not it is actually a single directory depends on the implementation), allowing the user to browse deleted files, undelete those that were deleted by mistake, or delete them permanently (either one by one, or by the Empty Trash function).

Windows SharePoint Services, or Windows SharePoint, is the basic part of SharePoint, offering collaboration and document management functionality via web portals by providing a centralized repository for shared documents, as well as browser-based management and administration. It allows creation of document libraries, which are collections of files that can be shared for collaborative editing. SharePoint provides access control and revision control for documents in a library.

Wired equivalent privacy (WEP) is a deprecated algorithm to secure IEEE 802.11 wireless networks. Wireless networks broadcast messages using radio, so they are more susceptible to eavesdropping than wired networks. When introduced in 1999, WEP was intended to provide confidentiality comparable to that of a traditional wired network.

Index

AbacusLaw case management system, 123
Accounting software. *See also* Billing
    software
    QuickBooks, 126–129
    Timeslips, 129–131, 137
Acrobat XI, 98–100
Active Directory (AD), 339
ActiveSync, 339
AD (Active Directory), 339
ADF (auto document feeder), 340
Adobe Acrobat, 98–100, 146
    Acrobat XI Pro, 98–100
    Acrobat XI Standard, 98
    Acrobat XII, 98
    collaboration software, 165
    OCR engine, 102
    PDF package, 99
    Reader XI PDF viewer, 99
Advanced technology attachment (ATA),
    340
Advertising, social media and, 277
    California's analysis of, 279–281
Adware, 339
AFAs (alternative fee arrangements),
    125–126
AirCard, 182–183
Airport Extreme Wi-Fi adapter (Apple),
    11–12
Alternative fee arrangements (AFAs),
    125–126
Ambrogi, Bob, 100
American Power Conversion (APC)
    Back-UPS 350, 80
    NetShelter SX rack, 73
    Smart-UPS 1500VA, 81
Amicus Attorney, 113–114

Amicus Cloud, 114
Amicus Premium Billing, 135–136
Apache OpenOffice.org, 97–98
APC. *See* American Power Conversion
    (APC)
Apple
    AirPort Express, 193
    AirPort Extreme, 192–193
    Airport Extreme Wi-Fi adapter, 11–12
    AirPort Time Capsule, 193
    iPad. *See* iPad, Apple
    iPhone, 85–88
    iPod, 195–196
    iTunes, 199–200
    Magic Mouse, 194–195
    Thunderbolt Display, 194
    touchfire keyboard, 192
    Watch, 191–192
    wireless keyboard, 194
AppleCare Protection Plan, 339
Apple computers (Macs), 5–8
    billing software for, 131–132
    Intuit Quicken 2015, 198
    Kaspersky Internet Security for Mac,
        197–198
    laptops, 11–12
    MacBook Air ultrabooks, 13
    MacBook Pro laptops, 11–12
    Microsoft Office for Mac 2011, 196
    Norton Internet Security, 197
    Quickbooks 2014, 198–199
    Symantec Drive Encryption software,
        199
    Toast 12 Titanium, 196–197
Apps, paperless firms and, 319
Archives, 307

ATA (advanced technology attachment), 340
Authentication, social media and, 296
Auto document feeder (ADF), 340

Backups, 307
Backup solutions, 83–84
Backup systems, for paperless firms, 314–315
Bates stamping, 100–101
Battery backup devices, 80–82
Billing software. *See also* Accounting software
  about, 125–126
  Amicus Premium Billing, 135–136
  Billings Pro, 132–133
  Bill4Time, 131–132
  EasyTime, 132
  integrated packages, 133
  for Macs, 131–132
  manual generation, 126
  PCLaw, 133–134
  Tabs3, 134–135
  Timeslips, 129–131
Billings Pro billing software, 132–133
Bill4Time, 131–132
Boot Camp, 7, 340
BoxCryptor, 88
Brother IntelliFax-2940, 82–83
BT Chat HD app, 216
Byte, 340

Cabling, 74–75
CAL (Client Access License), 341
Case management systems
  AbacusLaw, 123
  about, 111–112
  Amicus Attorney, 113–114
  Clio, 118–119
  Firm Manager, 119–121
  HoudiniEsq, 122–123
  MyCase, 121–122
  Practice, 123
  PracticeMaster, 116–118
  ProLaw, 123
  Rocket Matter, 119–121
  Time Matters, 114–116
CaseSoft TimeMap 5, 269–270
Category 6 cable (Cat6), 74–75, 340–341
Category 7 cable (Cat7), 74–75
Category 5e cable (Cat5e), 74–75, 340
Cathode ray tube (CRT), 341

CDMA (code division multiple access), 341
CD-ROM, 341
Central processing unit (CPU), 341
Change, managing, and paperless firms, 321–322
Chatsworth, 73
Chrometa, 271–272
Cisco
  ASA 5500-X Series Adaptive-Security Appliance, 72
  Small Business RV Series routers, 70
Client Access License (CAL), 341
Clients, social media of, 287–288
Clio case management system, 118–119
Cloud computing, 153–157, 337
  contract considerations, 157–158
  hybrid solutions, 158–159
  paperless firms and, 319
Code division multiple access (CDMA), 341
Collaboration software
  about, 161
  Adobe Acrobat, 165
  desktop sharing, 169
  Dropbox, 169
  Google Drive, 162–165
  Microsoft Office365, 167–168
  Microsoft Word Track Changes feature, 166
  SharePoint, 166–167
  Skype, 168
Color network printers, 37–38
CompleteCare Accidental Damage Protection Plan (Dell), 10
Computer usage, public, mobile security and, 183–184
Content, social media and, 277–278
Contrast ratio, 342
Copy2Contact, 258–259
Corel Office Suite, 95–96
Court Days Pro, 205–206
Courtroom chatting apps, 216
Covey, Stephen, 308
CPU (central processing unit), 341
Credenza, 254
Cybersecurity, 332–333

Database application, 342
DAT72 backup tapes, 342
DBAN (Darik's Boot and Nuke), 261
DDR2SDRAM, 342

Deadline calculator apps, iPad, 205–208
    Court Days Pro, 205–206
    DocketLaw, 206
    Lawyer's Professional Assistant, 206–208
    Smart Dockets, 206
Decryption/encryption, 343
Dell
    Latitude E6430, 10
    Latitude E6440 laptop, 9–10
    Latitude laptops, 8–10
    OptiPlex, 1–5
    PowerEdge T320 server, 46–47
    PowerEdge T620 server, 47–50
    P2214H monitor, 22
The Deponent, 208, 209
Deposition apps
    The Deponent, 208, 209
    TranscriptPad, 208–210
Destruction, of files, 307
Dictate + Connect iPad app, 219
Digital copiers, 342–343
Digital subscriber line (DSL), 343
Digital visual interface (DVI), 343
Discovery, compelling, 293
Display resolution, 343
Disruptive innovation, 328–330
DocketLaw, 206
Document assembly software
    HotDocs, 149–150, 152
    ProDoc, 150
    ProLaw, 151–152
Document management software
    about, 141
    Acrobat, 146
    DocuShare, 142
    Matter Center, 144–145
    NetDocuments, 146–147
    plain folders and, 147
    web-based, 146
    WorkSite, 142
    Worldox, 142–144
Document management systems (DMSs), 305–306
Documents To Go Premium iPad app, 223
DocuShare, 142
Domain controller (DC), 343
Dots per inch (dpi), 343
Dragon Naturally Speaking 13, 102–104
Dropbox, 88, 169
    for iPad, 217–218
dtSearch, 147–148, 252–254
DVD, 343

EasyTime billing software, 132
eDiscovery Assistant, 102
802.11 standard, 76–77
85W MagSafe 2 power adapter, 12
E-mail spam, 343
Encryption/decryption, 343
Encrytpion, 88–89, 176, 177, 180
Enhanced- or Extended-definition Television (EDTV), 344
Enterprise Service 10 Server Software (BlackBerry), 90
Evernote, 270–271
Evidence presentation apps
    Exhibit A, 215
    ExhibitView, 214–215
    TrialPad, 212–214
eWallet, 272
Exchange Public Folders, 90, 91
Exhibit A app, 215
ExhibitView app, 214–215
Extensible markup language (XML), 344
External storage devices, 26–30
    flash drives, 28–30
    hard drives, 27–28
Eyejot, 257

Fast case app, 215
FavBackup, 264
Fax machines, 82–83
FedCtRecords app, 215
File Shredder, 263
Find My iPhone/Find my iPad service, 230
Fire safes, 79–80
Firewalls, 71–72
FireWire, 344
FireWire 400, 344
FireWire 800, 344
Firm Manager case management sysstem, 119–121
Flaherty, Casey, 326, 327
Flashback virus, 6
Flash drives (thumb drives), 28–30
Flat panel monitors, 21–22
Friending, a witness, 290–291
Fujitsu fi-5530C2, 43
Fujitsu ScanSnap iX500 Desktop Scanner, 42, 313

GateGuru app, 177
Gigabyte, 344
Global System for Mobile Communications (GSM), 345

Goodlink, 90
Good Mobile Messaging products, 90
GoodReader iPad app, 220–221
Good Technologies, Inc., 90
Google Lollipop operating system, 89
Google Voice, 246–247
GoToMeeting, 169
GoToMyPC, 172–173
GreenPrint, 255–256
Griffin v. State, 296

Hard disk drive, 345
Hard drives, external, 27–28
Hard drive storage, for paperless firms, 313
Hardware, for paperless firms, 310–311
Hash function, 345
Headphones, 30–31
    Plantronics 510 headset/microphone system, 104
    Platronics Blackwire 700 series, 104
Hewlett Packard (HP)
    Color LaserJet CP4025dn printer, 37–38
    LaserJet Enterprise M4555h Multi-function Printers, 36–37
    LaserJet Pro P1606dn laser printer, 34
    LaserJet Pro 400 Printer M401dw, 36
    Smart Web Printing, 35
High-definition multimedia interface (HDMI), 345
High-definition TV (HDTV), 345
High-speed Internet, 249–250
Hightail, 257–258
High-volume network printers, 36–37
High-volume scanners, 43
HotDocs, 149–150, 152
Houdini Esq, 122–123
Hub, 345
Hyper-V virtualization system, 52–53

iCloud service, 88
iJuror, 210–211
iJury, 211
Information governance, 333
Infrastructure as a Service (Iaas), 156–157
Ink-jet printers, 34–35
Institute of Electrical and Electronics Engineers (IEEE), 345
Intel Core 2 Duo Processor, 346
Intel Corporation (Intel), 346
Internet Information Services (IIS), 346

Internet protocol (IP) address, 346
Intrusion detection systems (IDSs), 70, 346
Intrusion Prevention Systems (IPSs), 71
Intuit Quicken 2015 for Macs, 198
iPad, Apple, 188–191
    Air, 188–189
    courtroom chatting apps, 216
    criticisms of, 189
    deadline calculator apps, 205–208
    deposition apps, 208–210
    evidence presentation apps, 212–215
    introduction, 201
    iOS 8 features, 190
    jury selection/tracking apps, 210–212
    keyboard, 192
    legal research apps, 215
    library of favorite apps, 231–235
    must-have apps, 216–230
    navigation tips and settings, 235–238
    passcode lock, 239
    reasons for using, in courtrooms, 204–205
    reasons for using, in practices, 202–204
    resources for lawyers using, 191, 240
iPhone, Apple, 85–88
IPsec (IP security), 346
IrfanView, 260–261
IronKey hardware encrypted USB flash drive, 183–184
IronKey Secure Drive, 29–30
iSight camera, 346

Jabra Revo Wireless headphones, 31
join.me, 169
Jokes, social media and, 284–285
Judges, social media and, 297–299
JuryPad, 211
Jury selection/tracking apps
    iJuror, 210–211
    iJury, 211
    JuryPad, 211
    JuryStar, 211
    JuryTracker, 211–212
JuryStar, 211
JuryTracker, 211–212

Kaspersky Endpoint Security for Business, 107–108
Kaspersky Internet Security 2015, 106
Kaspersky Internet Security for Mac, 197–198

Keyboards, 25, 347
    wireless desktops, 25–26
Keynote for iOS iPad app, 224–225
Kinder, Gary, 273
Konica Minolta Bizhub C224e MFP, 39

Laptops, 8–12
    Apple computers (Macs), 11–12
    Apple MacBook Pro, 11–12
    Dell, 8–10
    personal computers (PCs), 8–10
    tablets becoming replacements for, 334
Laser printers, 34–35, 347
LastPass, 272–273
LawBox app, 215
Lawyer's Professional Assistant, 206–208
Legal research apps
    Fastcase, 215
    FedCtRecords, 215
    LawBox, 215
    Lexis Advanced HD, 215
    My Legal Projects, 215
    ProView, 215
    WestlawNext, 215
Legal technology, statistics for, 335–336
Legal technology audits (LTAs), 326–327
LegalZoom, 328–329
Lexis Advanced HD app, 215
LexisNexis CaseMap, 139
LexisNexis Concordance, 139
Light-emitting diode (LED), 347
Linear tape-open (LTO or LTO2), 347
Linksys, 76
    Smart Wi-Fi Router EA3500, 76–77
Linux-based operating systems, 65
Liquid crystal display (LCD), 347
Litera Metadact/Metadact-e, 266–267
Litigation programs, 139–140
Livescribe Echo Smartpen, 268
Logitech
    LS21 speakers, 31
    Wireless Wave Combo MK550, 26
LogMein iPad app, 229
LogMein Pro, 173
Lollipop operating system, 87, 89
Lookout Mobile Security, 91–92
Low-volume network printers, 35–36
Low-volume scanners, 42

MacBook Air (ultrabook), 13
MacBook Pro laptop, 11–12
Macintosh AirPort, 347

Macintosh/Mac, 347–348
Mac OS X Server 10.7 (Lion), 63
Mac OS X Server 10.9 (Mavericks), 64
Mac OS X Server 10.8 (Mountain Lion), 7,
    63–64
Mac OS X Server 10.10 (Yosemite), 64–65
Macs (Apple computers). *See* Apple com-
    puters (Macs)
The MagSafe power adapter, 348
Matter Center, 144–145
McAfee, 106
McAfee SasS Email Protection &
    Continuity service, 109–110
McMillen v. Hummingbird Speedway, Inc.,
    293
Media access control (MAC), 348
Megabyte (MB), 348
Message-digest algorithm 5 (MD5), 348
Metadata Assistant, 265–266
Microsoft
    Comfort Mouse 4500, 24
    Exchange Server, 348
    Hyper-V virtualization system, 52–53
    Natural Ergonomic Keyboard 4000, 25
    Office 365, 94–95, 167–168, 334–335
    Office 2013, 93–96
    Office for iPad, 221–222
    Office for Mac 2011, 196
    Server 2008 Enterprise Edition, 60
    Server 2008 Standard Edition, 60
    Small Business Server 2011, 47
    Small Business Server 2011 Standard
        and Essentials, 60–61
    SQL server, 348
    Surface Pro 3, 13–14
    Windows, 349
    Windows 10, 338
    Windows Server 2003, 57
    Windows Server 2012, 61–62
    Windows Server 2008 R2, 57–59
    Windows Server 2012 R2, 62
    Windows 7, 16–17
    Windows Small Business Server (SBS)
        2008 Standard and Premium
        Editions, 59
    Windows 8, 18, 337
    Windows Vista, 15–16
    Windows XP, 15, 337
    Wireless Mobile Mouse 4000, 24
Mobile computing, paperless firms and,
    319
Mobile Iron, 90

Mobile security
  AirCard, 182–183
  encryption, 180
  public computer usage and, 183–184
  smartphones and, 184–185
  software, 179–180
  wireless, 181–182
Modem, 349
Monitors, 21–22, 341–342
Monitors, for paperless firms, 315–316
Mouse, 23–24, 349
MPEG-1 audio layer (MP3), 349
MSHOME, 54
Multifunctional printers (MFPs), 38–39
Must-have iPad apps, 216–230
  Dictate + Connect, 219
  Documents To Go Premium, 223
  Dropbox, 217–218
  Find My iPhone/Find my iPad, 230
  GoodReader, 220–221
  Keynote for iOS, 225–226
  LogMein, 229
  Microsoft Office, 221–222
  Notability, 223–224
  Noteshelf, 224–225
  PDF Expert, 227–228
  Scanner Pro, 226–227
MyCase case management system, 121–122
My Legal Projects app, 215

Netbooks, 12–13
NetDocuments, 146–147
NETGEAR switches
  ProSAFE Fast Ethernet Unmanaged, 68
  ProSafe Gigabit Smart, 68–69
Network address translation (NAT), 349
Networked printers
  color, 37–38
  high-volume, 36–37
  low-volume, 35–36
Networking, social media and, 277
Networking hardware
  cabling, 74–75
  firewalls, 71–72
  IDS/IPS devices, 71–72
  intrusion detection systems (IDSs), 71
  intrusion prevention devices (IPSs), 71
  racks, 73–74
  routers, 69–70
  switches, 67–69
  wireless, 75–77

Norton Internet Security for Mac, 197
Norton Internet Security Suite software, 106
Notability iPad app, 223
Noteshelf iPad app, 224–225
Nuance Communications, Inc., 101, 102–104

OmniPage Ultimate, 101–102
OpenOffice.org, 97–98
Operating systems. *See also* Server operating systems
  Mac OS X version 10.7 (Lion), 18–19
  Mac OS X version 10.9 (Mavericks), 19–20
  Mac OS X version 10.8 (Mountain Lion), 19
  Mac OS X version 10.10 (Yosemite), 20
  Microsoft Windows 7, 16–17
  Microsoft Windows 8, 18
  Microsoft Windows Vista, 15–16
  Microsoft Windows XP, 15
Optical character recognition (OCR) software, 101–102, 349
Outlook Send Assistant, 254

Paper, converting, to PDFs, 306
Paperless firms
  about, 301–302
  apps and, 319
  assessing office procedures and people, 305–308
  benefits of going, 304–305
  change management aspects of, 321–322
  cloud computing, 319
  concerns for, 303
  defining goals, 308–310
  hardware required for, 310–316
  learning from experience and, 322–323
  mobile computing and, 319
  remote access and, 319
  setting new business processes and, 320
  software required for, 316–318
  transitioning to, 320–321
Passwords, 330–331
PCLaw billing software, 133–134
PDF Expert iPad app, 227–228
PDFs, converting paper to, 306
Peer-to-peer servers, 54–55

Peripheral devices, 350
Personal computers (PCs)
    Apple (Macs), 5–8
    Dell OptiPlex, 1–5
    laptops, 8–12
    netbooks/ultrabooks, 12–13
    tablets, 13–14
Piccolo v. Paterson, 293–294
Plantronics 510 headset/microphone
    system, 104
Platform as a Service (PaaS), 156–157
Platronics Blackwire 700 series, 104
Portable document format (PDF), 350
Power PDF Advanced, 100–101
Practice case management system, 123
PracticeMaster, 116–118
Printers
    multifunctional, 38–39
    networked, 35–38
    stand-alone, 33–35
Privacy settings, social media and, 286–287
Private branch exchange (PBX), 350
ProDoc, 150
Productivity software
    Adobe Acrobat, 98–100
    Apache OpenOffice.org, 97–98
    Microsoft Office365, 94–95
    Microsoft Office 2013, 93–96
    optical character recognition (OCR)
        software, 101–102
    Power PDF Advanced, 100–101
    voice recognition software, 102–104
    WordPerfect Office X7, 95–96
ProLaw, 136, 151–152
ProLaw case management system, 123
ProView app, 215
Public computer usage, mobile security
    and, 183–184

Quickbooks, 126–129, 137
Quickbooks 2014 for Macs, 198–199
QuickView Plus, 264–265

Racks, 73–74
Radio-frequency identification (RFID),
    350
RAID (redundant array of independent
    disks) 5, 350
Random access memory (RAM), 350
Recommendations, social media and,
    281–282

Redundant arrays of independent disks
    (RAID), 350
Remote access, 171
    GoToMyPC, 172–173
    LogMein Pro, 173
    mobility tips, 174–177
    paperless firms and, 319
    Team Viewer, 174
    virtual private networking (VPN),
        171–172
Remote desktop protocol (RDP), 351
Retention
    document, 306–307
    file, 307
Revolutions per minute (rpm, RPM,
    r/min), 351
Rocket Matter case management system,
    119–121
Rootkit, 351
Routers, 69–70, 351
    Linksys Smart Wi-Fi Router EA3500,
        76–77

Sam Spade, 265
Samsung Galaxy S3 smartphone, 90
Samsung Galaxy S5 smartphone, 90
Sanction, 140
Sanction Solutions Verdical, 139
Satire, social media and, 284–285
SBS. *See* Microsoft Windows Small
    Business Server (SBS) 2008 Standard
    and Premium Editions
ScanDisk Ultra USB 3.0 flash drive, 28
Scanner Pro iPad app, 226–227
Scanners, 41
    high-volume, 43
    low-volume, 42
Scanners, for paperless firms, 313–314
Scanning apps, iPad, 226–227
Scanning resolution, 351
Schorr, Ben, 154–155
Seagate Backup Plus Desktop Drive, 27
Searching software, 147–148
Secure Sockets Layer (SSL), 351
Security Enhanced (SE) Android, 89–90
    antispam protection, 109–110
Security software
    enterprise versions, 106–110
    stand-alone, 105–106
Serial advanced technology attachment
    (SATA), 351
Serial-attached SCSI (SAS), 352

Server operating systems
  Linux-based, 65
  Mac OS X Server 10.7 (Lion), 63
  Mac OS X Server 10.9 (Mavericks), 64
  Mac OS X Server 10.8 (Mountain Lion),
    63–64
  Mac OS X Server 10.10 (Yosemite),
    64–65
  Microsoft Server 2008 Enterprise
    Edition, 60
  Microsoft Server 2012 R2, 62
  Microsoft Server 2008 Standard
    Edition, 60
  Microsoft Small Business Server 2011
    Standard and Essentials, 60–61
  Microsoft Windows Server 2003, 57
  Microsoft Windows Server 2008 R2,
    57–59
  Microsoft Windows Server 2012, 61–62
  Microsoft Windows Small Business
    Server (SBS) 2008 Standard and
    Premium Editions, 59
  X64, 62–63
Servers, 352
  peer-to-peer, 54–55
  for small firms, 47–50
  for solo firms, 45–47
  virtual, 50–54
Servers, for paperless firms, 311–313
Service set identifier (SSID), 352
The 7 Habits of Highly Effective People
    (Covey), 308
Shadow Copy, 352
SHA hash function, 352
Sharepoint, 166–167
Shred 2, 262–263
SimplyFile, 262
Skype, 168
Small computer system interface (SCSI),
    353
Smart Dockets, 206
SmartDraw Business, 269
Smartphones, 85–92, 353
  mobile security and, 184–185
SnagIt, 263–264
Social media
  about, 275–276
  advertising and, 277, 278–281
  applications, 276–277
  authentication and, 296
  case law related to discovery of, 293–295
  of clients, 287–288

content, 277–278
deletion of data and, 295–296
discovery of, 286
ethical pitfalls in research, discovery,
    and communications and, 289–292
failure to preserve and, 289
jokes/satire and, 284–285
judges and, 297–299
jurors and, 299–300
networking, 277
obtaining access, 292–29296
opposing party and witnesses and, 288
personal v. private, 285–286
as post legal advice, 281
privacy settings and, 286–287
recommendations/testimonials and,
    281–282
responding to requests for content, 297
sites, 276–277, 278
specific rules for, 282–286
subpoenas and, 295
Social networking, 161
Spam, 91
Speakers, 30–31
Spyware, 353
Stand-alone printers, 33–35
Stand-alone security software, 105–106
State v. Bell, 296
Storage devices, external, 26–30
  flash, 28–30
  hard drives, 27–28
Summation case organization program,
    139
SuperDrive, 353
Switches, 67–69, 353–354
Symantec, 109
Symantec Drive Encryption software, 199

Tablets, 13–14, 334
Tabs3 billing software, 134–135
Tagged Image File Format (TIFF), 354
Tape drives, 354
Team Viewer, 174
Teamviewer, 169
Technology, 325–326
Terminal Services, 354
Testimonials, social media and, 281–282
TGrial Director, 140
Thomson Reuters Case Notebook, 139
Thumb drives (flash drives), 28–30
Time Machine, 354
TimeMap, 269–270

Time Matters, 114–116
Timeslips billing software, 129–131, 137
TinyURL, 260
Toast 12 Titanium, 196–197
Tompkins v. Detroit Metropolitan Airport,
    294–295
Trail v. Lesko, 294
Trend Micro Worry-Free Security, 108–109
TrialPad, 140
TrialPad app, 212–214
Trial presentation programs, 140
Trojan viruses, 6
TweetDeck, 259
TwInBox, 259

Ultrabooks, 12–13
Unified messaging, 243–246
Universal serial bus (USB), 354
Unix, 354
USB thumb (flash) drives, 355
Utilities
    CaseSoft TimeMap 5, 269–270
    Chrometa, 271–272
    Copy2Contact, 258–259
    Credenza, 254
    DBAN (Darik's Boot and Nuke), 261
    dtSearch, 252–254
    Evernote, 270–271
    eWallet, 272
    FavBackup, 264
    File Shredder, 263
    GreenPrint, 255–256
    Hightail, 257–258
    IrfanView, 260–261
    LastPass, 272–273
    Litera Metadact/Metadact-e, 266–267
    Livescribe Echo Smartpen, 268
    Metadata Assistant, 265–266
    Outlook Send Assistant, 254
    QuickView Plus, 264–265
    Sam Spade, 265
    Shred 2, 262–263
    SimplyFile, 262
    SmartDraw Business, 269
    SnagIt, 263–264
    TinyURL, 260
    TweetDeck, 259
    TwInBox, 259
    WinRAR/7-Zip, 271
    Winscribe, 256–257

WordRake, 273
X1, 251–252
YouMail, 268–269

Video card/graphics adapter, 355
Video graphics array (VGA), 355
Virtualization, defined, 50–51
Virtual private networking (VPN), 171–172
Virtual private networks (VPNs), 355
Virtual servers, 50–54
Viruses, 342
Visionary, 140
VMware vSphere Hypervisor, 53–54
Voice over Internet Protocol (VoIP)
    systems, 247–249
Voice recognition software, 102–104

Wearable tech, 331–332
Web 2.0, 355
Web-based document management
    software, 146
Webex, 169
Websites. *See specific product or company*
Western Digital My Book, 82–83
WestlawNext app, 215
Wettick, R. Stanton, 294
Wi-Fi, 355
Wi-Fi protected access (WPA), 355
Windows
    Recycle Bin, 356
    SharePoint Services, 356
WinRAR/7-Zip, 271
Winscribe, 256–257
    Eyejot, 257
Wired equivalent privacy (WEP), 75–76,
    356
Wireless networking devices, 75–77
Witnesses, friending, 290–291
WordPerfect Office X7, 95–96
WordRake, 273
WORKGROUP, 54
WorkSite, 142
Worldox, 142–144

X1, 147–148, 251–252
X64 operating systems, 62–63

YouMail, 268–269

Zimmerman v. Weis Markets Inc., 294

The Lawyer's Guide to Microsoft® Outlook 2013
By Ben M. Schorr

Product Code: 5110752 • LP Price: $41.95 • Regular Price: $69.95

Take control of your e-mail, calendar, to-do list, and more with The Lawyer's Guide to Microsoft® Outlook 2013. This essential guide summarizes the most important new features in the newest version of Microsoft® Outlook and provides practical tips that will promote organization and productivity in your law practice. Written specifically for lawyers by a twenty-year veteran of law office technology and ABA member, this book is a must-have.

The Lawyer's Guide to Microsoft® Word 2013
By Ben M. Schorr

Product Code: 5110757 • LP Price: $41.95 • Regular Price: $69.95

Maximize your use of Microsoft® Word with this essential guide. Fully updated to reflect the 2012 version of the software, this handy reference includes clear explanations, legal-specific descriptions, and time-saving tips for getting the most out of Microsoft® Word—and customizing it for the needs of today's legal professional.

LinkedIn in One Hour for Lawyers, Second Edition
By Dennis Kennedy and Allison C. Shields

Product Code: 5110773 • LP Price: $39.95 • Regular Price: $49.95

Since the first edition of LinkedIn in One Hour for Lawyers was published, LinkedIn has added almost 100 million users, and more and more lawyers are using the platform on a regular basis. Now, this bestselling ABA book has been fully revised and updated to reflect significant changes to LinkedIn's layout and functionality made through 2013. LinkedIn in One Hour for Lawyers, Second Edition, will help lawyers make the most of their online professional networking. In just one hour, you will learn to:

- Set up a LinkedIn® account
- Create a robust, dynamic profile--and take advantage of new multimedia options
- Build your connections
- Get up to speed on new features such as Endorsements, Influencers, Contacts, and Channels
- Enhance your Company Page with new functionality
- Use search tools to enhance your network
- Monitor your network with ease
- Optimize your settings for privacy concerns
- Use LinkedIn® effectively in the hiring process
- Develop a LinkedIn strategy to grow your legal network

Facebook® in One Hour for Lawyers
By Dennis Kennedy and Allison C. Shields

Product Code: 5110745 • LP Price: $24.95 • Regular Price: $39.95

With a few simple steps, lawyers can use Facebook® to market their services, grow their practices, and expand their legal network—all by using the same methods they already use to communicate with friends and family. *Facebook® in One Hour for Lawyers* will show any attorney—from Facebook® novices to advanced users—how to use this powerful tool for both professional and personal purposes.

Blogging in One Hour for Lawyers
By Ernie Svenson

Product Code: 5110744 • LP Price: $24.95 • Regular Price: $39.95

Until a few years ago, only the largest firms could afford to engage an audience of millions. Now, lawyers in any size firm can reach a global audience at little to no cost—all because of blogs. An effective blog can help you promote your practice, become more "findable" online, and take charge of how you are perceived by clients, journalists and anyone who uses the Internet. Blogging in One Hour for Lawyers will show you how to create, maintain, and improve a legal blog—and gain new business opportunities along the way. In just one hour, you will learn to:

- Set up a blog quickly and easily
- Write blog posts that will attract clients
- Choose from various hosting options like Blogger, TypePad, and WordPress
- Make your blog friendly to search engines, increasing your ranking
- Tweak the design of your blog by adding customized banners and colors
- Easily send notice of your blog posts to Facebook and Twitter
- Monitor your blog's traffic with Google Analytics and other tools
- Avoid ethics problems that may result from having a legal blog

The Electronic Evidence and Discovery Handbook: Forms, Checklists, and Guidelines
By Sharon D. Nelson, Bruce A. Olson, and John W. Simek

Product Code: 5110569 • LP Price: $99.95 • Regular Price: $129.95

The use of electronic evidence has increased dramatically over the past few years, but many lawyers still struggle with the complexities of electronic discovery. This substantial book provides lawyers with the templates they need to frame their discovery requests and provides helpful advice on what they can subpoena. In addition to the ready-made forms, the authors also supply explanations to bring you up to speed on the electronic discovery field. The accompanying CD-ROM features over 70 forms, including, Motions for Protective Orders, Preservation and Spoliation Documents, Motions to Compel, Electronic Evidence Protocol Agreements, Requests for Production, Internet Services Agreements, and more. Also included is a full electronic evidence case digest with over 300 cases detailed!

Android Apps in One Hour for Lawyers
By Daniel J. Siegel

Product Code: 5110754 • LP Price: $19.95 • Regular Price: $34.95

Lawyers are already using Android devices to make phone calls, check e-mail, and send text messages. After the addition of several key apps, Android smartphones or tablets can also help run a law practice. From the more than 800,000 apps currently available, Android Apps in One Hour for Lawyers highlights the "best of the best" apps that will allow you to practice law from your mobile device. In just one hour, this book will describe how to buy, install, and update Android apps, and help you:

- Store documents and files in the cloud
- Use security apps to safeguard client data on your phone
- Be organized and productive with apps for to-do lists, calendar, and contacts
- Communicate effectively with calling, text, and e-mail apps
- Create, edit, and organize your documents
- Learn on the go with news, reading, and reference apps
- Download utilities to keep your device running smoothly
- Hit the road with apps for travel
- Have fun with games and social media apps

Twitter in One Hour for Lawyers
By Jared Correia

Product Code: 5110746 • **LP Price:** $24.95 • **Regular Price:** $39.95

More lawyers than ever before are using Twitter to network with colleagues, attract clients, market their law firms, and even read the news. But to the uninitiated, Twitter's short messages, or tweets, can seem like they are written in a foreign language. Twitter in One Hour for Lawyers will demystify one of the most important social-media platforms of our time and teach you to tweet like an expert. In just one hour, you will learn to:

- Create a Twitter account and set up your profile
- Read tweets and understand Twitter jargon
- Write tweets—and send them at the appropriate time
- Gain an audience—follow and be followed
- Engage with other Twitters users
- Integrate Twitter into your firm's marketing plan
- Cross-post your tweets with other social media platforms like Facebook and LinkedIn
- Understand the relevant ethics, privacy, and security concerns
- Get the greatest possible return on your Twitter investment
- And much more!

Virtual Law Practice:
How to Deliver Legal Services Online
By Stephanie L. Kimbro

Product Code: 5110707 • **LP Price:** $47.95 • **Regular Price:** $79.95

The legal market has recently experienced a dramatic shift as lawyers seek out alternative methods of practicing law and providing more affordable legal services. Virtual law practice is revolutionizing the way the public receives legal services and how legal professionals work with clients. If you are interested in this form of practicing law, *Virtual Law Practice* will help you:

- Responsibly deliver legal services online to your clients
- Successfully set up and operate a virtual law office
- Establish a virtual law practice online through a secure, client-specific portal
- Manage and market your virtual law practice
- Understand state ethics and advisory opinions
- Find more flexibility and work/life balance in the legal profession

Social Media for Lawyers: The Next Frontier
By Carolyn Elefant and Nicole Black

Product Code: 5110710 • **LP Price:** $47.95 • **Regular Price:** $79.95

The world of legal marketing has changed with the rise of social media sites such as Linkedin, Twitter, and Facebook. Law firms are seeking their companies attention with tweets, videos, blog posts, pictures, and online content. Social media is fast and delivers news at record pace. This book provides you with a practical, goal-centric approach to using social media in your law practice that will enable you to identify social media platforms and tools that fit your practice and implement them easily, efficiently, and ethically.

iPad Apps in One Hour for Lawyers
By Tom Mighell

Product Code: 5110739 • **LP Price:** $19.95 • **Regular Price:** $34.95

At last count, there were more than 80,000 apps available for the iPad. Finding the best apps often can be an overwhelming, confusing, and frustrating process. iPad Apps in One Hour for Lawyers provides the "best of the best" apps that are essential for any law practice. In just one hour, you will learn about the apps most worthy of your time and attention. This book will describe how to buy, install, and update iPad apps, and help you:

- Find apps to get organized and improve your productivity
- Create, manage, and store documents on your iPad
- Choose the best apps for your law office, including litigation and billing apps
- Find the best news, reading, and reference apps
- Take your iPad on the road with apps for travelers
- Maximize your social networking power
- Have some fun with game and entertainment apps during your relaxation time

The Lawyer's Essential Guide to Writing
By Marie Buckley

Product Code: 5110726 • **LP Price:** $47.95 • **Regular Price:** $79.95

This is a readable, concrete guide to contemporary legal writing. Based on Marie Buckley's years of experience coaching lawyers, this book provides a systematic approach to all forms of written communication, from memoranda and briefs to e-mail and blogs. The book sets forth three principles for powerful writing and shows how to apply those principles to develop a clean and confident style.

iPad in One Hour for Lawyers, Third Edition
By Tom Mighell

Product Code: 5110779 • **LP Price:** $39.95 • **Regular Price:** $49.95

Whether you are a new or a more advanced iPad user, *iPad in One Hour for Lawyers* takes a great deal of the mystery and confusion out of using your iPad. Ideal for lawyers who want to get up to speed swiftly, this book presents the essentials so you don't get bogged down in technical jargon and extraneous features and apps. In just six, short lessons, you'll learn how to:

- Quickly Navigate and Use the iPad User Interface
- Set Up Mail, Calendar, and Contacts
- Create and Use Folders to Multitask and Manage Apps
- Add Files to Your iPad, and Sync Them
- View and Manage Pleadings, Case Law, Contracts, and other Legal Documents
- Use Your iPad to Take Notes and Create Documents
- Use Legal-Specific Apps at Trial or in Doing Research